Cultural Studies

Theorizing Politics, Politicizing Theory

VOLUME 18 NUMBER 2/3 MARCH/MAY 2004

Special Issue
Rethinking Everyday Life: And Then Nothing Turns Itself Inside Out

Edited by
Michael E. Gardiner and Gregory J. Seigworth

Editorial Statement

Cultural Studies continues to expand and flourish, in large part because the field keeps changing. Cultural studies scholars are addressing new questions and discourses, continuing to debate long-standing issues, and reinventing critical traditions. More and more universities have some formal cultural studies presence; the number of books and journals in the field is rapidly increasing. *Cultural Studies* welcomes these developments. We understand the expansion, reflexivity and internal critique of cultural studies to be both signs of its vitality and signature components of its status as a field. At the same time, cultural studies has been – and will no doubt continue to be – the subject of numerous attacks, launched from various perspectives and sites. These have to be taken seriously and answered, intellectually, institutionally and publicly. *Cultural Studies* hopes to provide a forum for response and strategic discussion.

    Cultural Studies assumes that the knowledge formations that make up the field are as historically and geographically contingent as are the determinations of any cultural practice or configuration and that the work produced within or at its permeable boundaries will be diverse. We hope not only to represent but to enhance this diversity. Consequently, we encourage submissions from various disciplinary, theoretical and geographical perspectives, and hope to reflect the wide-ranging articulations, both global and local, among historical, political, economic, cultural and everyday discourses. At the heart of these articulations are questions of community, identity, agency and change.

    We expect to publish work that is politically and strategically driven, empirically grounded, theoretically sophisticated, contextually defined and reflexive about its status, however critical, within the range of cultural studies. *Cultural Studies* is about theorizing politics and politicizing theory. How this is to be accomplished in any context remains, however, open to rigorous enquiry. As we look towards the future of the field and the journal, it is this enquiry that we especially hope to support.

Lawrence Grossberg
Della Pollock

January 1998

Contributions should be sent to Professors Lawrence Grossberg and Della Pollock, Dept. of Communication Studies, CB #3285, 113 Bingham Hall, The University of North Carolina at Chapel Hill, Chapel Hill, NC 27599-3285, USA. They should be in triplicate and should conform to the reference system set out in the Notes for Contributors. An abstract of up to 300 words (including 6 keywords) should be included for purposes of review. Submissions undergo blind peer review. Therefore, the author's name, address and e-mail should appear *only* on a detachable cover page and not anywhere else on the manuscript. Every effort will be made to complete the review process within six months of submission. A disk version of the manuscript must be provided in the appropriate software format upon acceptance for publication.

Reviews, and books for review, should be sent to:

Stuart Price
School of Arts
de Montfort University
The Gateway
Leicester LE1 9BH
UK
poumista@hotmail.com

Gil Rodman
Department of Communication
University of South Florida
4202 East Fowler Avenue, CIS1040
Tampa
FL 33620 7800
USA
grodman@chuma.cas.usf.edu

Alvaro Pina
Rua Jose P. Chaves
6-3 Dto
1500-377 Lisboa
Portugal
alvaro.pina@mail.telepac.pt

Ien Ang
Institute for Cultural Research
University of Western Sydney
Parramatta Campus
BCRI Building L2
Locked Bag 1797
Penrith South DC NSW1797
Australia
I.Ang@uws.edu.au

Contents

VOLUME 18   NUMBER 2/3   MARCH/MAY 2004

Articles

Gregory J. Seigworth &
Michael E. Gardiner

RETHINKING EVERYDAY LIFE
And then nothing turns itself inside out

The contingencies and permeabilities and rhythms of everyday life make it notoriously difficult to pin down in any determinant way. Hence, everyday life places unique demands upon critical practice and conceptualization. In following one potential angle of approach, this essay looks at the influence that philosopher Gottfried Leibniz played in the thinking of sociologist and everyday life philosopher Henri Lefebvre. Lefebvre's theory of moments and his conceptions of 'the everyday' draw upon often overlooked (and controversial) elements from Leibniz's monadology and other later writings. This essay concludes by considering how substituting 'everyday life' for the 'culture' of cultural studies requires, among other things, a closer consideration of the immanently biopolitical implications that Lefebvre teased out of Leibniz. As the introductory essay for this special issue of Cultural Studies, *we also set up, in the final section here, an overview of our contributors' own unique angles of approach to the study of everyday life at the dawn of the 21st century.*

Keywords articulation; biopolitical; everyday; Lefebvre; Leibniz; rhythmanalysis

The *unrecognized*, that is, the everyday, still has some surprises in store for us. Indeed, as I was first rethinking the everyday . . .

(Lefebvre 1988, p. 78)

It was a moment, and it passed. I already see the furniture around me, the old designs on the wallpaper, the sun through the dirty windows. I saw the truth for a moment . . . Not knowing oneself is living. Knowing oneself badly is thinking. Knowing about oneself suddenly, as in this glowing moment, is suddenly to have the notion of the intimate monad, the magic word of the soul.

(Pessoa 1998, p. 146)

What is there under your wallpaper?

(Perec 1997, p. 211)

Cultural Studies Vol. 18, No. 2/3 March/May 2004, pp. 139–159
ISSN 0950-2386 print/ISSN 1466-4348 online   © 2004 Taylor & Francis Ltd
http://www.tandf.co.uk/journals   DOI: 10.1080/0950238042000201455

Routledge
Taylor & Francis Group

To be determined, interminably

We begin knowing this: there is nothing to know of everyday life. That is, everyday life does not easily or readily submit itself to either questions or answers from the knowing (and variously disciplined) subject/s of epistemology. Of course, ask almost any classroom full of students and they will immediately tell you as much: 'What?! Everyday life? You're wasting your time' – and, by extension, theirs. Between the always already and ever-not-quite-yet, the everyday transpires, suspended, as the infinitely strung-out process of perpetually leaving too soon and arriving too late. Or is it arriving too soon and leaving too late? Either way, you will somehow have missed it because the everyday passes by, passes through. It sails past, sails over. It goes around, goes under. Under the wallpaper. Under the rocks and stone (there is water underground). Under the cobblestones, the beach. Nothing (clearly) happens but something (obscurely) is and has been afoot. Under foot: the ground is shifting – have you felt it too? – as a growing dissatisfaction gnaws along the hinges and through the very hearts of different academic disciplines in the humanities causing these fields, each in their own way, to simultaneously (if not also paradoxically) draw back into themselves, sub-divide, and inter-blur. Yes, it is cultural studies that is regularly held up to alternate honour or horror in such instances.

One of the more interesting recent instances comes from the journal *Critical Inquiry*'s symposium on the 'end of theory' (even while we set aside the comparatively few digs and ducats explicitly tossed in the direction of cultural studies therein). Our favourite response, among the *Critical Inquiry* contributors and editors, to the 'end of theory' (post-9/11) question comes from Lauren Berlant. Carrying forward de Lauretis' own observations on this matter – that '[t]hinking . . . originates in an embodied subjectivity, at once overdetermined and permeable to contingent events' – Berlant wonders about what might turn out to be a coming 'sensualist turn' in the realm of theory (2003, p. 1). She writes:

> There is much more to be said on this topic of theory and embodied histories of the present. How else to make sense of this shift in tracking change, thinking system, and constructing objects or scenes that require explanations? Who is embodied, and how, and what is served by the sensual turn? Can we think about the relation of critical optimism to our vertiginous awareness of escalating violence in ways that continue to challenge our professional contexts? Or is it the case, as the *New York Times* opined recently, that this is a time of resistance without a critical imaginary? One could dilate infinitely on these questions.
>
> (2003, p. 1)

Between de Lauretis and Berlant, our argument here is neatly previewed: to unfold a contemporary philosophy of the everyday that both highlights and aids in the critical emergence of an infinitely dilating, embodied subjectivity (as a return to the human and to collectivity without passing through or resurrecting, as Berlant also notes, the old metaphysically transcendent subject) that is ever-and-again rendered affectively overdetermined and permeable to contingent events. Alternatively, as Hoboken rhythm-and-drone rock band Yo La Tengo (2000) has phrased it from a slightly different though complementary angle: 'trying to embrace the nothing of the everyday' (repeat to fade-out). Among the whole host of things that might come through the currently frayed and bare-wire ends of theory, why not an even more pressing necessity for critically embracing the polyrhythmical fluctuations of the everyday's contingent eventfulness and overdetermined uneventfulness (especially in those in-between moments when we feel it change track, re-route, and call for new ways to 'think system')? Hence, we will dilate on this notion further in what follows . . . though maybe not infinitely (after all, we are working under a word-limit).

Perhaps, then, we will be forgiven for wondering if, in such times as these, everyday life might serve as good and as unbound a place as any other (maybe even better?) to gather-round and remind ourselves of all the disciplinary ways that we can still agree to disagree. As Highmore has remarked, following Lefebvre: 'If . . . the everyday lies both outside all the different fields of knowl-edge, while at the same time lying across them, then the everyday isn't a field at all, more like a para-field, or a meta-field' (2002, p. 4). Multiply singular in its totality, the everyday is the groundless ground of lived/living concatenation, conglomeration and visceral cross-reference – even if one must immediately hasten to add that any mention of the 'lived/living' should not be understood to somehow exclude the unlived, inorganic, incorporeal and non-human in whatever form such matters might take: such is the impetus that fully saturates, through and through, the notion of *life* in the couplet 'everyday life'. Indeed, it's hard to fathom what might actually fall outside everyday life since eminently tangible remainderings and immanently fleeting ambiences (and everything in-between) provide its building blocks, its cobblestones (and what flows beneath), and the designs on its wallpaper (and what extends beyond).

Thinking along similar lines and like the Leibnizian urban-dweller that he was, Lefebvre notes that 'everything is in everything and everything is total – and yet nothing that is, is in anything other than itself. Within oneness, there are differences and disjunctions; both actively and potentially, there is multi-plicity' (1961/2002, p. 273).[1] Even the most seemingly intimate monad, as Leibniz maintained, never bears less than the rest of a world along with itself, from one fluctuating moment to the next. Monads persist by constantly shuf-fling, dilating and contracting their regions of clarity and opaqueness, reconfig-uring by often barely perceptible rhythms. Hence, this provides one of the reasons why Lefebvre's 'theory of moments' calls up, by necessity, his pro-cedure of 'rhythmanalysis' – a connection that Lefebvre makes, forthrightly, in a footnote to the 'Theory of Moments' chapter from his *Critique of Everyday Life:*

Volume II, where he states: 'Philosophically, the "theory of moments" is linked to an interpretation of Leibniz. The "substantial link" (*vinculum substantiale*) between monads is itself a monad' (1961/2002, p. 370). More pointedly, what Lefebvre alludes to here is the crucial importance of thinking everyday life as a whole, but a whole of a highly particular (even peculiar) sort: not that fairly commonplace conceptualization of a whole which comes to be perpetually ensnaring or encircling (based around the relational character of identity and contradiction) and, thus, sucks up and seals off all that occurs (or has occurred or will occur) into its own endlessly assimilative totality. Rather, the everyday is a whole that reconstitutes itself in each moment as that which subsists (insists) (persists) (ex-sists) as – more modestly? – one additional part alongside any and all of the other parts: the everyday as a whole moving alongside all of the other moments of the day-to-day. This is an everydayness that does not close-off but, instead, perpetually opens up: an open totality arising with every moment, a beach beneath every cobblestone.[2]

Thus, each moment – in such a theory of moments – is wholly extended across the open infinity of moments, but forever in the next moment (of the whole's eternal return) ranges across all of them in infinitely varying dispersion, with different emphases and diminuations: a different(ial) whole at each moment. Everything is in everything while nothing is in any thing other than itself. Take, for example, the human being. As Lefebvre continues: 'Every human "being" is physical, biological, economic, social or sociological, but unevenly, according to the aspects and the moments, sometimes this one more than that one, sometimes that one more than this one, but without ever losing unity completely' (1961/2002, p. 273). Almost like music, certainly like rhythm, the event-full (and always more-than-human) movement from moment to moment undulates (as the substantial link between monads is itself a monad) – like the infinity of water particles that gets re-cast from one wave to the next, or like the smallest dancing specks of dust, caught in a certain angle of light, rising, falling, and hovering against a dark backdrop. 'The spectre of undulatory movements (with or without trajectories) extends', writes Lefebvre, 'indefinitely, even infinitely, from the macro to the micro, from corpuscular movements to the movements of metagalaxies' (1985/1999, p. 12). As we will see, this undulation (of moments, of movements), with or without trajectories (seemingly either shimmy and comet-trail or shimmer and blink), is no mere wavering and half-hazy thought-image for everyday life philosophizing.

In some ways, catching hold of this conveyance continues to pose one of the greatest difficulties for contemporary approaches to everyday life (and, without a doubt by this point, that aforementioned classroom full of students has begun to manifest a shimmy and blink of their own): how to give thought-image to something that has, more often than not, neither thought nor image? How to imagine something that phases-out at very nearly the same time as it phases-in, as each and every daily moment passes by – passes through – pulsating along that faintly lingering string of unevenly lit instants where 'ordinary' and 'remarkable' gather themselves up again along the gradual shade-off cast by the other's cross-light? In short, how to bring into critical conceptualization and practice some thing that is, in fact, not strictly a thought, an image or a thing at all?

It is hardly a secret (indeed, over time, it has come to feel more like a riddle): how does one present everyday life critique – in its movements and moments, processes and rhythms – without reducing it to a 'some thing', without present-ing it as a 'some thing' to be known, or, that is, a clearly demarcated object of knowledge (as if it ever could be)? Perhaps better to begin with 'no thing in particular' (a 'whatever'): to leap, as Lefebvre (and a few others) understood, into the very midst of the differential itself and, thus, follow the Leibnizian swoon from universal to singular as folded and flected in the (momentarily eternal and intimately exterior) monad. It is a move that sets one on the decidedly less-travelled terrain of that which circulates in the beyond-thing-ish realm of the 'processual', of the transitional, of the affectual, of relations of force, of the in-between (of that which precedes and is outside its own terms). Signs, even structures, have long been erected to prevent such an unhesitant (that is, non-deferred) leap into the differential – they read simply 'a void.' Numerous bodies have danced along the edge of this void, while consciousness has regularly rumbled across it, hearing itself by times, circling and seemingly lost in its own echo (by default or by design) at other times. Labelled 'a void', since it means then having to bring into account those quite potentially messy non-things that are above (and below and between and vaguely 'about') all else: a-signifying, real but incorporeal (i.e. virtual), pre-individual and non-conscious, inorganic, more-than-human, a-human. None of these, and needless to say there are more, are anti- (say 'human') or un- (say 'conscious') or otherwise negating or starkly oppositional. These (wave)particles and long durations of existence bear a prox-imal, unlocalizable – indeed, circulatory – otherness without falling into absolute difference or contradiction. The immanence of their void – the seem-ingly treacherous sink into the collective whirl of the variously unaccountable – serves as that indiscernible area toward which everyday life critique regularly gestures (usually late in the day and off to one side of its main path), but has only rarely been pursued as full (and, from certain vantage points, potentially fool-hardy) immersion.

However, Lefebvre's everyday life approach is seldom averse to such immer-sion and, as a result, what methodologically sometimes appears as rather scatter-shot and soft-focus comes into sharper view when his penchant for entering in among the differential movements of this (teeming) void is better understood.[3] Neglecting such movements (and moments) in Lefebvre's own analytic leaves one rather doomed to dissective stillness, insurmountable alienation and the bare repetition of fetish-objects (whether devolved from bureaucratic-capitalist imperatives or theoretical ones): fated to partake in an interpretative practice that can always uncover a conveniently determined end-product (in a reductive present) but endlessly miss its producibility (in its undetermined futurity). As Lefebvre maintains:

> Beneath an apparent immobility, analysis discovers a hidden mobility. Beneath this superficial mobility, it discovers stabilities, self-regulations, structures, and factors of balance. Beneath the overall unity, it uncovers diversities, and beneath the multiplicity of appearances it finds a totality. Analysis must maintain these two sociological aspects (incessant change, the disappearance of elements, nascent conjunctures – the structuring of the whole, relative stability) and grasp them in the wholeness of a single history.
>
> (1961/2002, p. 238)

The wholeness of a single history arriving in each moment. Exhausting without extinguishing, gathering itself up to go on into the next moment in order to reconstitute itself anew: the continual variation of everyday life and its analytic procedures, interwoven.

Pessoa's insomniac (and quasi-autobiographic) bookkeeper Bernardo Soares describes this intertwined process vividly as it overtakes him during his cross-town commute through Lisbon of the early 1930s: so vividly, that it is worth quoting his diary-entry at length.

> I'm in a trolley, and, as is my habit, I'm slowly taking notice of the people sitting around me. For me details are things, words, sentences. I take apart the dress worn by the girl in front of me: I turn it into the fabric that makes it up, the work that went into making it – but I still see it as a dress and not cloth – and the light embroidery and the work involved in it. And immedi-ately, as in a primer on political economy, the factories and the labor unfold before me – the factory where the cloth was made, the factory where the twist of silk, darker in tone than the dress, was made, which went into making the twisted little things in the border now in their place next to the neck; and I see the components of the factories, the machines, the workers, the seamstresses, my eyes turned inward penetrate into the offices, I see the managers trying to be calm, I follow, in the books, the accounts involved in it all; but it isn't only that: I see, beyond that, the domestic lives of those who live their social lives in those factories and those offices . . . All of them pass before my eyes merely because I have before me, below a dark neck, which on its other side has I don't know what sort of face, a common, irregular green edge on a light green dress.
>
> The entire life of society lies before my eyes.
>
> Beyond all that I sense the loves, the secret life, the souls of all those who worked so that this woman seated in front of me in the trolley can wear around her neck the sinuous banality of a band of dark green silk on less dark green cloth.

> I become stupefied. The seats on the trolley, made of a tightly woven strong straw, carry me to distant regions and into multiple industries, workers, workers' houses, lives, realities, all.
>
> I leave the trolley exhausted and sleepwalking. I just lived an entire life.
>
> (Pessoa 1998, p. 115)

Exhausted not so much from a newly heightened awareness (as might be invoked through models of consciousness-raising) but, even more, in the passing of sensation into depthless processes, their interconnections, the wholeness of their single histories, and the sinuous banality of their surfaces and colours. 'Let your eyes transgress their own limits,' say Lefebvre and Regulier (1985/1999, p. 11): as eyes turn inward (seeking after a modality beyond the visually perceptual register) to penetrate offices, moving on to jittery managers, accounting books, multiple industries, secret lives, all. Motility. Of multiplicity. Immersed, of a circulating void. Singularly every day: once again, for the first time.

So exhausted is Soares/Pessoa that, in fact, the next diary-entry does not follow until apparently months later, wherein Soares/Pessoa asks himself if it might be possible to create a '[p]hilosophy without thought?' as something unmediatedly 'felt. . . . carnal, direct' (1998, p. 116). How to create an everyday philosophy that would venture into life through the outside of knowing: just as Leibniz' monad is famously without windows, interior though not privative, or, as Fenves puts it: 'The windowless condition of the monad is . . . the positive condition of not being "influenced" by anything in the world and yet corresponding with everything worldly nevertheless' (2001, pp. 9–10). No 'influence' (which has been set in quotation marks by Fenves because this manner of influence will never knowingly register as such), or, that is, a short circuit of consciousness (because unmediatedly felt, carnal, direct). This is not an argument for the omission of consciousness or for otherwise blocking it off but, instead, the admission of the impinging, circumambient influx of everything, everything that consciousness – at least as historically conceived in the West – has been typically bent upon shunting aside. In his essay 'The ambivalence of disenchantment', Virno concurs:

> Along the parabola of modern philosophy that stretches from Descartes to Hegel, only Leibniz valorizes an experience that depends on what falls outside of the self-reflective subject: 'There are hundreds of indications leading us to conclude that at every moment there is in us an infinity of perceptions, unaccompanied by awareness or reflection.' For Leibniz, it is these 'little perceptions,' the opaque side of the spirit, that connect each individual to the complete life of the universe. But this is an exception.
>
> (1996, p. 30)

However, perhaps, this is an exception that proves the rule: by positing a banal/ neutral a-consciousness, endlessly differential of-itself, because infinitely, impersonally and permeably indifferent to everything (including itself). In corre-spondence with the world.[4] In correspondence with everything.[5] Catch a wave (or catch a Lisbon bus). Take notice of the dispersive patternings in the dust. Get rhythm.

Rhythms of mattering

Certainly, this kind of talk can get you into trouble: speaking of philosophy without thought, and of a body (human or non-human) as a purely affective surface that registers everything without parsing or hieracharizing difference on its exterior, but by making itself the living interior of difference.[6] A philosophy without thought – or at least without thought always and only at its head (literally) – necessitates a continuously adjacent non-philosophy of life on its outside. Nothing ruled out, most especially nothing's penchant for turning itself inside out.

Adorno describes how his friend Walter Benjamin believed that 'everything habitually excluded by the norms of experience ought to become part of experience to the extent that it adheres to its own concreteness instead of dissipating this, its immortal aspect, by subordinating it to the schema of the abstract universal' (1955/1988a, p. 4). Thinking like this got Benjamin into all kinds of seemingly intractable trouble (the persistent danger of an everyday monadology turning acephalic was, as Benjamin knew, its grimmest inside joke). Still, the procedure remains: no subordination of the concrete to the abstract universal but, instead, finding the universal in the concrete. Benjamin called his take on Leibniz's monad simply 'the Idea', which, like the monad, is not mental-istic but unmediatedly felt, carnal, direct. Or, as Adorno also says: 'Therefore, Benjamin does not weave a relation to the absolute out of concepts, but rather seeks it through corporeal contact with the material' (1955/1988a, p. 4). Yet, at the same time, Adorno writes that 'there was something incorporeal' about Benjamin himself, that his 'thinking constitutes the anti-thesis of the existential concept of the person, he seems empirically, despite extreme individuation, hardly to have been a person at all, but rather an arena of movement in which a certain content forced its way, through him, into language' (1966/1988b, p. 329, p. 330). What better way to model the ongoing processes by which critical thought and everyday life fold and unfold into and out of each other? An arena of movement, the collective insistence of a world (contrary to the solitary, separate existence of a being), a touch of/for concreteness with a simultaneous sense of how such concrete tactility taps incorporeal universes of experience (in both their persistent and coming potentials): wherever the utopics of everyday life appear, they will nearly always traverse these critical ingredients.

The contemporary import of Leibniz's monad – and the complex related-ness of monadic aggregates through the 'vinculum substantiale' [substantial link or bond] – might register with greatest insight on those theoretical approaches that focus on the rhythmic everyday interpenetration of corporeality and incorporeality (combined as 'virtuality'), or, from one other angle of approach, the terrain of biopolitics. Although, of course, Lefebvre never made use of the term 'biopolitical', his theory of moments and his rhythmanalysis – because of the way that they go beyond classical ontology (since he always maintained that there is more to 'being' than the actual), beyond existentialism (since, Lefebvre notes, one must also account for 'essences'), and beyond phenomenology (since everything eliminated as outside conscious experience must be reinstated) [1961/ 2002, pp. 349–350] – might have much to offer the increasingly frequent invocation of the biopolitical.

In this regard, it might be instructive here to re-read (again) one of Lefebvre's earliest and best known statements on everyday life. From the first volume of his *Critique of Everyday Life*, written in 1947, Lefebvre writes:

> Everyday life, in a sense residual, defined by 'what is left over' after all distinct, superior, specialised, structured activities have been singled out by analysis, must be defined as a totality. Considered in their specialization and their technicality, superior activities leave a 'technical vacuum' between one another which is filled up by everyday life. Everyday life is profoundly related to *all* activities, and encompasses them with all their differences and conflicts; it is their meeting place, their bond, their common ground. And it is in everyday life that the sum total of relations which make the human – and every human being – a whole takes its shape and its form. In it are expressed and fulfilled those relations which bring into play the totality of the real, albeit in a certain manner which is always partial and incomplete: friendship, comradeship, love, the need to communicate, play, etc.
>
>   The substance of everyday life – 'human raw material' is its simplicity and richness – pierces through all alienation and established 'disalienation.' If we take the words 'human nature' dialectically and in their full meaning, we may say that the critique of everyday life studies human nature in its concreteness.
>
> (1947a/1991, p. 97)

Among numerous uptakes from this oft-quoted passage, everyday life has been made to appear variously as 'lack', as dialectical grace note, as shadowy and irrecoverable disintegration, as unconscious, as null or empty set, and so forth. But what if Lefebvre's striking appeal, through these words, tends in a different, less vacuous (despite the mention of a 'technical vacuum') direction?

Not surprisingly, we think that there is another (less-travelled) direction as echoed by the notion of 'bond' in paragraph one and, then, by 'substance' in paragraph two of the above passage from Lefebvre. Nothing, in the everyday, ever truly falls away, gets lost, goes lacking, turns to zero, is rendered null and void (though maybe full and void is another story). As Lefebvre notes: 'When determinations fall outside one another they only do so relatively, momentarily and partially' (1961/2002, p. 192). Partial and incomplete, while adhering to their own concreteness: the variously indeterminate is as crucial as what is determined and, in fact, offers up a more profoundly aggregate 'something' (even if it might come to pass as barely anything, or, almost nothing).[7]

> *Something*, we will say, which is not easy to define, precisely since this 'something' is not a thing, nor a precise activity with determined outlines. So what is it? A mixture of nature and culture, the historical and the lived, the individual and the social, the real and the unreal, a place of transitions, of meetings, interactions and conflicts, in short a *level* of reality.
>
> (Lefebvre 1961/2002, p. 47)

The residual is, then, its own kind of differential (it is worth remembering too that 'differential space' was Lefebvre's way of talking utopia). This residual is rarely a neatly defined fall-off (perhaps better conceived anyway, in its own light, as immanent bleed-up rather than fall-off). Invariably, its edges are unevenly contoured. As such, in the oscillation of materialities and incorporeal-ities and their rough-hewn intermixtures (where the everyday serves as common ground, as bond), rhythms emerge (rhythms which need not literally be 'heard' but might, also, belong to some other manner of sonority). In fact, the everyday retains the rhythmic, transitional flip itself [the vibratory differen-tial as a whole] as on-going part of the process, and the vinculum su]bstantiale serves as sticky palimpsest for these shuffling superpositions of everyday moments (it is the adhesive surface of their transitions, meetings, interactions, and conflicts).

Blanchot, long the best reader of Lefebvre around several of these points, captures it in this way:

> To live it [the everyday] as what might be lived through a series of separate, technical acts (represented by the vacuum cleaner, the washing machine, the refrigerator, the radio, the car), is to substitute a number of compartmen-talized actions for this indefinite presence, this connected movement (which is however not a whole [that is, less a whole than a 'becoming']) by which we are continually, though in a mode of discontinuity, in relation with the indeterminate totality of human possibilities.
>
> (1959/1993, p. 244)

Indefinite presence, indeterminate totality, and connected movement: Leibniz's *vinculum substantiale* plays a similar, though widely disputed, role with regard to the monads of his own philosophy.[8] The vinculum substantiale was Leibniz's attempt, admittedly not without some amount of hesitancy and controversy, to think how the real (corporeality) and the ideal (mental phenomena) fold together, in inseparable union and continuous extension, through the super-added force relayed from adherent monads-as-resonating-aggregate. Here Leibniz's infamous pre-established harmony as divined through God finds its correlate in the decidedly more discontinuous yet equally 'divine will' of matter (where, instead of harmony, the matter of lived existence beats with the alternating punctual and a-punctual rhythms of grace, chance, accident, process, and recurrence).[9] Or as Lispector, in *The Passion According to G.H.*, effuses:

> Oh, the violent amorous unconsciousness of what exists surpasses the possibility of my consciousness. I am so afraid of so much matter – matter resonates with attention, resonates with process, resonates with inherent nowness. What exists beats with strong waves against the unbreakable grain that is I, and that grain tumbles among the abysses of tranquil billows of existence, tumbles and does not dissolve, that seed-grain.
>
> (1964/1988, p. 132)

When Lefebvre says that the basis for his theory of moments is found in Leibniz's *vinculum substantiale* and that the substantial link between monads is itself a monad, the monad becomes then 'the moment' (the undissolvable seed-grain of experience surpassing the possibility of consciousness) in Lefebvre's theory of moments, and the substantial linkage of these everyday monadic moments is knotted with the rhythmic foldings or becomings of matter and passion.[10]

This dynamism of mattering has become a key focus of recent critical work around the biopolitical, turning attention to the matter of life itself, nakedly so (as in Agamben's 'bare life') and increasingly molecularized.[11] As Rose has summarized:

> Politics now addresses the vital processes of human existence: the size and quality of the population; reproduction and human sexuality; conjugal, parental and familial relations; health and disease; birth and death. . . . It [biopolitics] has given birth to techniques, technologies, experts, and apparatuses for the care and administration of the life of each and all, from town planning to health services. And it has given a kind of 'vitalist' character to the existence of individuals as political subjects.
>
> (2001, p. 1)

Perhaps inevitably, then, the accent in the term 'everyday life' must, on occasion and particularly now, fall slightly more heavily on the vitalistic fourth vowel (and of course, when placed upon other tongues, life precedes the everyday). Life itself is the supple line in the everyday between the living and the lived (Lefebvre 1961/2002, p. 217). It is this 'life' of the everyday that

Lefebvre wanted to bring to the vocabulary of Marx, to rethink the everyday in a new dialectic that 'allows for the analysis of becoming, that is to say, of time, more or less connected to space' and where music ('the art of time') could arise within the everyday through melody, harmony, and rhythm (1988, p. 86). Such a music could almost never be fully pre-established in its melody, harmony and rhythm (indeed, Leibniz's *vinculum substantiale* concedes as much too, by departing from the 'divine intellect' of God), and must, thus, remain continually open to its outside, to risk, to occasional near-stasis, and to total transformation (and to ugliness as well as beauty). It was Lefebvre's way to imagine, through Marx,

> the total person of the future, being deployed as a body, as a relation between the senses, as thought. These investigations converge toward the supreme and final question that goes beyond classical philosophy. It is not a matter of understanding what the verb 'to think' signifies, as Heidegger did, but of responding to the question, *What remains to be thought now?* . . . To understand this in Marxist terms we need to reformulate the conflictual relations within the triad: nature/matter/human. If a person is first and foremost an earthly being and a human body, how do we relate the person to a representation of the world that includes the recent contributions of all the sciences, including cosmology, astrophysics, and microphysics? These types of knowledge extend from infinitely small to infinitely large. What, then, is the relationship of human beings to the world of which they continue to be a part?
>
> (1988, p. 87, emphasis added)

Certainly, it seems self-evident that such questions, sets of concerns, and means of approach (to the becomings of nature/matter/human) might offer themselves as potential links to a variety of ongoing biopolitical projects, and one could, indeed, productively dilate along any of these numerous lines of pursuit almost infinitely. Let us, then, by way of drawing this introduction to its more finite close (even if it might actually be more akin to throwing it into the open), touch briefly on a small feature, drawn from out of this preceding discussion, that could have rather profound importance to the practices of cultural studies.

Soft tissue and supple articulations

We are thinking specifically here (or rethinking as the case might be) of Jameson's response to the doorstop volume *Cultural Studies* published in 1988 (edited by Grossberg, Nelson and Treichler): even more specifically, the section of his essay 'On "cultural studies"', entitled 'Articulation: a truck driver's manual'. Jameson claims that, although for cultural studies, the concept of articulation seems to be '[d]erived, like organic, from the body as a reference, it rather designates the bony parts and the connections of the skeleton, than the soft organic organs' (1993, pp. 30–31). There is, as Jameson implicitly advises, another route that can be taken through Marx's rather figural conception of the organic [and 'organs'] and, particularly, his notion of 'metabolism'. Once meant to designate the separate functionings of the various organs, when run through the cultural studies' (truck driver's manual of) articulation, this more fluidified conceptualization of the 'organic' has been lost in transposition – *from* the diverse and divergent functionings of the body's organs *to*, now, become indistinguishable parts of one and the same thing: an identifiable and organized body with its organs always presumably in their appropriate location and proper arrangement. Further, the term 'organic' itself has regularly come to serve as modifier preceding the word 'intellectual' – embracing, in this way, the main divergence allowed to such a body: the splitting of its pessimistic intellect from its less fatalistic will (as the latter tries to turn in a decidedly sunnier direction). However, Marx brings more into the mix than the severing and reconnecting of intellectual heads and wilfully optimistic bodies; a whole diverse ensemble and polyrhythm of bodies, organs, brains, and value-generating machinery are caught up in the circulations of capital. As Marx writes in the *Grundrisse*: '[I]n the human body, as with capital, the different elements are not exchanged at the same rate of reproduction, blood renews itself more rapidly than muscle, muscle than bone, which in this respect may be regarded as the fixed capital of the human body' (1973, p. 670). It is the 'fixed capital' of the body's skeletal structure that cultural studies' concept of articulation (with its mapping of contexts – wherein the entirety of the body itself often becomes one more bony connecting node among the other non-necessary linkages) – captures in its own way: by turns, successfully but also ultimately limited in its suppleness (as organs resolve into a hierarchy of function, as bones lock into place). The knee bone's connected to the thigh bone, the thigh bone's connected to the hip bone . . .

But what if the concept of 'articulation' was able to offer a better accounting of 'soft tissue' and those other, more inconspicuously supple kinds of circulation, mobile differentiation, and implicate connectedness? Taking on board the immanence and vitalism of 'life' from philosophies of the everyday certainly places different demands upon cultural studies (whilst also, fortunately, offering up several suggestive and road-tested directions in response to these demands). That is, there cannot be any mere substituting of 'everyday life' in the place of 'culture' without, of course, drawing upon and redrawing new (and old) constellations of concerns (not to mention, among other things, subsequent shifts and reconfigurations in conceptions of praxis itself). In the space of this ground still to be covered, cultural studies is not yet, if it wants to be, synonymous with the study of everyday life, and its theory of articulation will have to be one crucial site of rethinking.

Felski takes notes some of this distance-to-be-covered in a recent essay on cultural studies and method, marked by her own (implicit) ambivalence to the idea of articulation. She writes that, against more symptomatic reading strategies, cultural studies' theory of articulation

> refuses to see the world in a grain of sand [or] to proceed as if a text were a microcosmic representation of social relations that, if deciphered correctly, will yield the hidden truth of the social whole. By contrast, cultural studies seeks to detotalize the social field and hence rejects the assumption that any individual work can represent that field. The political pulse of a culture is not to be found in the depths of a single work but rather in a mobile and discontinuous constellation of texts as they play off, influence, and contradict each other.
>
> (2003, p. 512)

However, needless to say, this is precisely what Leibniz's monadology (as modified by the vinculum substantiale) and, hence, what Lefebvre's theory of moments and rhythmanalysis set out to do: to remind us of and to revive, in their own ways, totalization (albeit 'open totality') as critical tool, to find the world in a seed-grain of matter, to rhythmically scale up/down from intimate to immense in a single bound. None of this 'everyday' approach necessarily works to deny the 'political pulse' that cultural studies takes from discontinuity and non-necessary correspondence, but, further, superadds the immanence of 'life' as connective (soft) tissue, as substantial and saturative bond: affectively over-determined and permeable to the contingent.

The main political pulse of the 'bios' is, most certainly, found in the super-additive of immanence as the 'moving substrate of force relations which is the condition of possibility of power' (Cheah 1996, p. 126). While cultural studies' theory of articulation can work *across* diverse elements, as Felski also notes, and make certain linkages, it is less apparent how, in its current state, it might begin with a visceral, substantial bond always already in place (not always to-be-made by critical practice itself) and, then, how rapidly it might traverse, more vertically than across (a dash less cartographer's fever-dream and a dash more insomniac's virtual time-unravel), the life ground that opens up – in a straight shot of immanence – from molecular membrane to cosmic forces. That is, without feeling silly (though likely getting dizzy). This would mean taking seriously Lefebvre and Regulier when they write (echoing in part Marx's *Grundrisse* moment):

> Without knowing it [. . .] human beings appropriate at the center of the universe movements that are consonant with their own movements. The ear, the eyes, the gaze, the hands – these are far from being passive organs that do little besides record or execute. What is shaped, formed, and produced is part of this scale which, it must be emphasized, has nothing accidental or

arbitrary about it. It is the scale of the planet, of accidents, of the surface of the earth, and of the cycles that recur.

(1985/1999, p. 11)

What would cultural studies look like (sound like) (feel like) if it was to work at this scale, if it was to fully bring the 'life' of everyday life on-board, with its moments, monads, movements, multiplicities and matter? It is hard to predict, but perhaps worth the try. Time to get supple.[12]

Turning the kaleidoscope

We will not attempt to sum up the special double issue that follows (like one of those bravura performances by a conference panel respondent who tenuously demonstrates how all of the papers just presented 'truly' shared a common thread). To undertake such a task here would be next to impossible. Simply put, we have gathered some people together whose writing on everyday life we admire: whether long sustained as a life's distinguished work or as promising start to a career just underway. In our initial entreaty to each of our contributors, we posed the following series of questions (contributors' names, in brackets, are attached to those questions that give shape to particular thematics of their essays, though needless to say, nearly any bracketed name can slip from this particular attachment to migrate to other sets of concerns as well):

- What is everyday life? What are its central (and ambient) qualities, properties and dynamics? (Sandywell)
- How is everyday life transformed under the conditions of modernity and, as some would now have it, postmodernity? How is everyday life manifested (similarly and/or differently) on the peripheries and semi-peripheries of the capitalist world-system? What does an accounting of everyday life have to contribute the current discourse of globalization? (Harootunian & Maffesoli)
- How can the nascent critical or 'redemptive' elements of everyday life be identified and understood? How are the emancipatory possibilities inscribed in everyday practices, relationships and events taken up and realized concretely by specific individuals and groups (often taking the form of new potentials for autonomy, collectivity, dissent/culture jamming, accommodation, etc.)? (Burkitt & Gardiner)
- What are the central intellectual traditions of a critical approach to the analysis of everyday life? To what extent are these traditions influenced by local and national conditions and specific contexts of intellectual production, or is there the possibility of constructing a broader, more synthetic theory? How might the pursuit of different intellectual pre-histories of the contemporary 'everyday' subsequently yield altogether new and perhaps contrasting

sets of questions, critiques and strategies for everyday living? (Ganguly & Pickering)

- What implications do recent transformations (and continuities) in the nature of everyday life hold for analyses of subjectivity (and the conceptual status of 'the object' for that matter), gender, embodiment, race, ethnicity, socio-ocultural identity, sexuality, the concept of 'experience', transnational capitalism, the conditions of collectivity/belonging, and so on? (ffrench)

- What are the ethical and aesthetical qualities of everyday life? Are these elements in contradiction, or do they dovetail in important respects? (Highmore & Probyn)

- How does the very study of everyday life itself conjure up a different sense of the relationship between theory and practice? How does one's understanding of everyday life transform the movements of critique and, thus, produce new strategies for writing (e.g. increasingly fabulative, poetic, evocative, experimental, explorative, polyrhythmical, processual, sensuous, etc.) for otherwise conveying the insights of intellectual work? How is pedagogy (and the role of the university) transformed in the light of such understandings? (Game/Metcalfe and Gregg)

- Social relationships are increasingly technologically mediated by ubiquitous consumer culture and digital/virtual modes of communication, which blur the line between the social and the cultural, and between formerly differentiated institutions and spheres of activity. How have the lived space-times of everyday life been affected by these sorts of processes? (Galloway, Poster & Wise)

- What implications might follow for our understandings of everyday life if we attempt to grasp, not only those inconspicuous aspects of everyday life (as derived from the various inadequacies, habitual tendencies, and distractions of human consciousness), but also such sidereal realms as: the inorganic, the incorporeal, the impersonal, the nonhuman, the non-representational, the affective, and the bio-political? (Shotter & Thrift)

Some contributors, as readers will discover, address one or more of our questions directly.[13] Others approach our series of questions more obliquely or presume different sorts of catalysing problematics about everyday life. Many of the essays that follow speak to one another (without necessarily acknowledging their conversation), and a few may even interrupt each other (though again, not by explicit design). However, all told, herein are seventeen different essays about one thing (for once, that one thing is not sex or, then again, maybe sometimes it is): everyday life. Multiple, monadic, mobile. Turn this issue like a kaleidoscope in your hands, and the various, unevenly contoured pieces will fall into new patterns. Everything is in everything and nothing is in anything other than itself – and, then, nothing turns itself inside out. That is everyday life. That much we know.

Notes

1   To our knowledge, only Harvey, in his *Justice, Nature, and the Geography of Difference*, has explored, to some extent, the debt that Lefebvre's work owes to Leibniz. However, it also seems to us that Harvey, at times, often chooses to read Leibniz's monadology uncharitably (at least, less charitably than Lefebvre) by turning the monad too plainly idealist and too literally inward (as 'hermetically sealed' in its windowlessness) and, thus, removed from 'social and political life' (1996, p. 74). Needless to say, this presents a problem that Harvey must then endeavour to solve – and he illustrates one proposed solution by mapping, rather awkwardly, the apparent inadequacies of Leibniz's philosophy on to the *processual* circuit of Marx's political economy, and, thereafter, casts any Leibnizian-inspired approach as one that could, at best, only grasp each node of the process in isolation, and, at worst, come to serve as indication of a 'political practice that made retreat into the windowless world (his study) . . . a particularly attractive proposition' (1996, p. 75). There is a minor irony about this latter flourish of Harvey's and his mention of 'his [Leibniz's] study'. In 1870, Karl Marx is thrilled to receive a very fine present from his friend Ludwig Kugelmann: tapestries that had once hung in Leibniz's study! On 10 May 1870, Marx even writes to Engels of his delight at this gift: 'You know my admiration for Leibniz'. What Harvey misses (as we will later touch upon) is the undulating linkage of Leibniz's monadic moments (not always so firmly set in twinkling motionlessness) as 'vinculum substantiale' (substantial bond) – which, indeed, become the basis for Lefebvre's rhythmanalysis and his concomitant theory of moments. Leibniz's monadology remains to be better cast in light of Marx's discussion of 'living' labour and the circulatory processes of the body, as well as the human body's ongoing absorption into the 'body' of capital itself (for potential points of resonance, see Dienst 1994, Negri/Hardt 2000, Dyer-Witheford 2002 and, yes, even Harvey (2000, pp. 97–130) himself on the body as an accumulation strategy and Marx's 'species-being').

2   Although it is a witty aside from his *The Production of Space*, Lefebvre is probably more than half-kidding when he writes: 'The beach is the only place of enjoyment that the human species has discovered in nature' (1974/1991b, p. 384). Following this, he then launches into a discussion of the body itself as a 'differential field'.

3   Pessoa offers this lovely account: 'At a certain level of written cogitation, I no longer know where I have my attention focused – whether it's on the dispersed sensations I'm trying to discover, as if they were unknown tapestries, or on the words into which I plunge right in, get lost, and see other things in my desire to discover my own description. There form within me associations of ideas, of images, of words – everything lucid and diffused' (1998, p. 219).

4   Lispector's *The Passion According to G.H.* conveys this quality (indeed, qualia!) of consciousness better than anyone (with the possible exception of Maurice

Blanchot). The beatings and resonances of matter, the will to accretion, the neutrality of love, the impersonal soul, the 'greater reality' of the nonhuman, the energetics of indifference, and, in a few sentences that point ahead to our discussion of Leibniz's 'vinculum substantiale', she writes: 'I am trying to tell you how I came to the neutrality and inexpressivity of myself. I don't know if I am understanding what I say, I feel – and I very much fear feeling, for feeling is merely one of the styles of being. Still, I shall go through the sultry stupor that swells with nothingness, and I shall have to understand neutrality through feeling. Neutrality. I am speaking of the vital element linking things' (1964/ 1988, p. 92). Or, as Lefebvre says, the substantial link between monads is itself a monad: vital and neutral.

5   For more on correspondences, see Bachelard (credited by Lefebvre as the originator of the term 'rhythmanalysis') who writes of Baudelaire: 'immensity in the intimate domain is intensity, an intensity of being, the intensity of being evolving in the vast perspective of intimate immensity. It is the principle of "correspondences" to receive the immensity of the world, which they trans-form into the intensity of our intimate being' (1958/1969, p. 193).

6   See, for instance, the passage in Leibniz's *Monadology* where he writes: 'Consequently every body is sensitive to everything which is happening in the universe, so much so that one who saw everything could read into each body what is happening everywhere, and even what has happened or what will happen, by observing in the present the things that are distant in time as well as space' (1973, p. 189). See, also, Deleuze's *Foucault* and its last chapter on 'Foldings, or, the inside of thought (subjectivation)' (1986/1988, pp. 94–123).

7   A detailed consideration of Lefebvre's conceptual 'something' could be reveal-ing in this regard: 'Something – which is certainly not a thing – is encountered once again. . . . It vanishes, and at the same time it makes itself known' (Lefebvre 1961/2002, p. 342). The notion that there is always, in every relation, 'something that is not a thing' (an ambiguous whole or totality residing alongside any singular, lived space-time) is important to Lefebvre; it is his 'whatever', his Leibnizian indiscernible. See, for further example, his relation of 'something' to ambiguity (contra 'ambivalence') and totality (1961/2002, p. 84, p. 220) and the flashes of the mobile concept of 'some-thing' across his masterwork *The Production of Space*, especially during its brief appearances in the discussion of Leibniz in the 'Spatial Architectonics' chapter (1974/1991b, p. 169) and in its concluding chapter 'Openings and Con-clusions' (1974/1991b, p. 403)

8   The majority of Leibniz interpreters – most notably, Bertrand Russell – have greatly downplayed the role of the substantial bond in Leibniz's system of thought, if not denied it any importance whatsoever (thus, making it all the more interesting that Lefebvre should have alighted upon it). The vinculum substantiale is discussed by Leibniz almost exclusively in his correspondence, from 1712–1716, with a Jesuit scholar, Bartholomew Des Bosses, in the final years of his life. It receives no mention in any of his formally published works;

for instance, his *Monadology* was published in 1714, two years before Leibniz's death, and makes no mention of the vinculum substantiale. This concept's life of ill repute is chronicled rather thoroughly in Adams' *Leibniz: Determinist, Theist, Idealist* (1994, pp. 299–307). For further background on the vinculum substantiale and other details, see also Rescher (1979), Woolhouse (1993), Fenves (2001) and Deleuze (1988/1993).

9   See Massumi on the rhythm and beats of existence (1997, pp. 748–750). Additionally, see Lefebvre for more on musically-derived approaches to dialectics and worn-out ontologies (1961/2002, pp. 244–263).

10 Negri's 'kairos' [the singular and indeterminate time defined by life itself] transpires around this same fold of matter and passion. In fact, he describes 'subjectivity' as something that does not subsist but is produced in the 'connection of monads of kairos' and, later, that their 'plane of association [is] the material fabric of the common predication of the being of the world' (2003a, p. 173, p. 180). All of which sounds, probably not accidentally, like Leibniz's vinculum substantiale. Thus, when Negri translates 'kairos' from heavy-duty philosophizing to more everyday discourse (in an interview from 2003), he could easily be mistaken for Lefebvre: 'Everything is constructed each time, at each instant. Nothing is predetermined, because everything is determined, in the void of reality, by the infinity of wills that open up at each moment. And this is the richness of life, of a life that can modify itself through and through, that can completely reinvent itself at any moment' (2003b, p. 97). See also Maffesoli's poetic invocation of 'kairos' in this issue of *Cultural Studies*.

11 Cheah's extended review-essay 'Mattering' (1997, pp. 108–139), of Butler's *Bodies That Matter* and Elizabeth Grosz's *Volatile Bodies*, is perhaps one of the best recent essays at clearly spelling out what is at stake in debates over the dynamisms of matter itself.

12 Latour rehabilitates 'articulation' by thinking it outside of subject-object relations (in a sense, thinking 'articulation' on the life-ground of the event and not of phenomena, or what Massumi has called 'the being of relation' versus the relatedness of beings (2002, p. 70)). A theory of articulation that starts with relatedness as first condition (not secondary analytical construct) takes it away from the realm of the (only) human and makes it, instead, as Latour says: 'an ontological property of the universe' (1999, p. 303).

13 In the initial stages of this project, Professor of Sociology Stephen Crook of James Cook University, Australia – a superb scholar with a long-standing interest in the issue of everyday life – had committed himself to contributing an essay. Stephen, however, became very ill in the interim with cancer and passed away in September 2002. The current issue of *Cultural Studies* is very much poorer for not being able to include his planned essay. The editors would like to dedicate this special issue to the memory of Stephen Crook, and to direct readers to the memorial essay in his honour by Barry Sandywell at the end of the present volume.

References

Adams, R. M. (1994) *Leibniz: Determinist, Theist, Idealist*, Oxford University Press, New York and Oxford.

Adorno, T. (1988a [1955]) 'Introduction to Benjamin's *Schriften*', in *On Walter Benjamin*, ed. G. Smith, The MIT Press, Cambridge, MA and London, pp. 2–17.

Adorno, T. (1988b [1966]) 'Benjamin the letter writer', in *On Walter Benjamin*, ed. G. Smith, The MIT Press, Cambridge, MA and London, pp. 329–337.

Bachelard, G. (1969 [1958]) *The Poetics of Space*, trans. M. Jolas, Beacon Press, Boston.

Berlant, L. (2003) Untitled, [online] Available at http://www.uchicago.edu/research/jnl-crit-inq/typewriter.html

Blanchot, M. (1993 [1959]) 'Everyday speech', in *The Infinite Conversation*, trans. S. Hanson, University of Minnesota Press, Minneapolis, pp. 238–245.

Cheah, P. (1996) 'Mattering', *Diacritics*, vol. 26, no. 1, pp. 108–139.

Deleuze, G. (1988 [1986]) *Foucault*, trans. S. Hand, University of Minnesota Press, Minneapolis, MN.

Deleuze, G. (1993 [1988]) *The Fold: Leibniz and the Baroque*, trans. T. Conley, University of Minnesota Press, Minneapolis, MN.

Dienst, R. (1994) *Still Life in Real Time: Theory After Television*, Duke University Press, Durham and London.

Felski, R. (2003) 'Modernist studies and cultural studies: reflections on method', *Modernism/Modernity* vol. 10, no. 3, pp. 501–517.

Fenves, P. (2001) *Arresting language: from Leibniz to Benjamin*, Stanford University Press, Stanford, CA.

Foucault, M. (1977 [1970]) 'Theatrum philosophicum', in *Language, Counter-Memory, Practice*, trans. D. Bouchard & S. Simon, Cornell University Press, Ithaca, NY, pp. 165–196.

Hardt, M. & Negri, A. (2000) *Empire*, Harvard University Press, Cambridge, MA and London.

Harvey, D. (1996) *Justice, Nature, and the Geography of Difference*, Blackwell Publishers, Cambridge, MA.

Harvey, D. (2000) *Spaces of Hope*, University of California Press, Berkeley, CA.

Highmore, B. (2002) *The Everyday Life Reader*, Routledge, New York and London.

Jameson, F. (1993) 'On "cultural studies"', *Social Text*, vol. 34, pp. 17–52.

Latour, B. (1999) *Pandora's Hope: Essays on the Reality of Science Studies*, Harvard University Press, Cambridge, MA.

Lefebvre, H. (1988) 'Toward a leftist cultural politics: remarks occasioned by the centenary of Marx's death', in *Marxism and the Interpretation of Culture*, eds C. Nelson & L. Grossberg, University of Illinois Press, Urbana & Chicago, IL, pp. 75–88.

Lefebvre, H. (1991a [1947]) *Critique of Everyday Life: Volume One*, trans. J. Moore, Verso, New York and London.

Lefebvre, H. (1991b [1974]) *The Production of Space*, trans. D. Nicholson-Smith, Basil Blackwell, Cambridge, MA and Oxford.

Lefebvre, H. (2002 [1961]) *Critique of Everyday Life: volume II*, trans. J. Moore, Verso, New York and London.

Lefebvre, H. & Régulier, C. (1999 [1985]) 'The rhythmanalytical project', trans. M. Zayani, *Rethinking MARXISM*, vol. 11, no. 1, pp. 5–13.

Leibniz, G. (1969) *Philosophical Papers and Letters*, 2nd edn, ed. & trans. L. E. Loemker, D. Reidel Publishing Company, Boston.

Leibniz, G. (1973) *Philosophical Writings*, trans. G. H. R. Parkinson & M. Morris, Everyman's Library, London.

Lispector, C. (1988 [1964]) *The Passion According to G.H.*, trans. R. W. Sousa, University of Minnesota Press, Minneapolis.

Marx, K. (1973) *Grundrisse: Foundations of the Critique of Political Economy*, trans. M. Nicolaus, Random House, New York.

Massumi, B. (1998) 'Involutionary afterward', *The Canadian Review of Comparative Literature*, vol. 24, no. 3, pp. 745–782.

Massumi, B. (2002) *Parables for the Virtual: Movement, Affect, Sensation*, Duke University Press, Durham, NC.

Negri, A. (2003a) *Time for Revolution*, trans. M. Mandarini, Continuum, London and New York.

Negri, A. (2003b) 'N for Negri: Antonio Negri in conversation with Carles Guerra,' *Grey Room 11*, pp. 86–109.

Perec, G. (1997) *Species of Spaces and Other Pieces*, ed. & trans. J. Sturrock, Penguin, New York.

Pessoa, F. (1998) *The Book of Disquiet*, trans. A. MacAdam, Exact Change, Boston.

Rescher, N. (1979) *Leibniz: An Introduction to His Philosophy*, Rowman and Littlefield, Totowa, NJ.

Rose, N. (2001) 'The politics of life itself', *Theory, Culture, and Society*, vol. 18, no. 6, pp. 1–30.

Virno, P. (1996) 'The ambivalence of disenchantment', trans. M. Turtis, in *Radical Thought in Italy: A Potential Politics*, ed. M. Hardt, University of Minnesota Press, Minneapolis, pp. 13–34.

Woolhouse, R. S. (1993) *Descartes, Spinoza, Leibniz: The Concept of Substance in Seventeenth-Century Metaphysics*, Routledge, London and New York.

Yo La Tengo (2000) 'Everyday', *And Then Nothing Turned Itself Inside Out*, Matador Records, New York.

Barry Sandywell

THE MYTH OF EVERYDAY LIFE
Toward a heterology of the ordinary

In Memoriam Steven A. Crook (1950–2002)

The aim of this paper is to contribute to the rethinking of everyday life as a central, if highly diverse and problematic, theme of modern philosophy and social theory. The focus of the essay concerns the uncertain ontological status of 'the everyday' within the human sciences. An initial exploration of the ambiguity of the expression 'everyday life' points to a more consequential type of undecidability once it is fully recognized how the ideology of 'everyday life' functions to suppress the materiality, contingency, and historicity of human experience. This can be seen in the contrast between powerful atemporal conceptions of everyday life and more critical under-standings of the lifeworld framed in temporal categories. The distinction between everyday life and lifeworld proves useful as a marker for two very different approaches to the ordinary. The paper claims that the ordinary has been systematically deni-grated in the very act of being theorized as 'everyday life'. A tradition of binary and dichotomous theorizing is uncovered as one of the fundamental sources of the myth of an ahistorical, unmediated everyday life. After mapping a range of more reflexive perspectives toward the investigation of ordinary life, the paper concludes on a positive and reconstructive note by suggesting that any attempt to go beyond the dualisms and antinomies of contemporary theory must first abandon this mythology to reveal the histor(icit)y and alterity of lifeworlds in their rich natural, incarnate, political, and reflexive imbrications.

Keywords   everyday life; the ordinary; historicity; lifeworld; alterity; heterology

Introduction

The aim of this paper is to contribute to the rethinking of 'everyday life' as a central, if highly diverse and problematic, theme of modern philosophy and social theory. The focus of the essay concerns the uncertain ontological status of 'the everyday' within the human sciences. An exploration of the ambiguity of the expression *everyday life* points to a more consequential type of undecidability

Cultural Studies Vol. 18, No. 2/3 March/May 2004, pp. 160–180
ISSN 0950-2386 print/ISSN 1466-4348 online   © 2004 Taylor & Francis Ltd
http://www.tandf.co.uk/journals   DOI: 10.1080/0950238042000201464

 Routledge
 Taylor & Francis Group

once we recognize how the term has functioned ideologically to suppress the *historicity* of human experience. This can be seen in the contrast between powerful *atemporal* conceptions of everyday life and more critical understandings of the lifeworld framed in temporal categories. The distinction between *everyday life* and *lifeworld* proves useful as a marker for two very different approaches to the ordinary. For example, across a range of philosophical perspectives everyday life has been theorized as the sustaining *ground*, *matrix* and *foundation* for other social practices, while on the other hand the ordinary is seen as an unfinalizable *force-field* of living history and novel forms of selfhood. However, even this binary divide between synchronic and diachronic perspectives is seen to be mapped onto much more ancient binary oppositions that still operate as debilitating dichotomies of modern thought (*essence/appearance*, *theoria/praxis*, *universalism/particularism*, *abstract/concrete*, *objective/subjective*, *form/content*, *cognitive/pragmatic* among the more notable of these). I argue that the ordinary has been systematically denigrated in the very act of being theorized *as* 'everyday life'. This dichotomous *theorizing* has helped sustain the myth of an ahistorical, unmediated everyday life. I conclude by suggesting that any attempt to go beyond the antinomies of contemporary theory must first abandon this mythology to reveal the *histor(icit)y* and *alterity* of *lifeworlds* in their rich material, incarnate, political, and reflexive imbrications.

The essay is divided into four parts. First, a brief review of the grammar of 'everyday life'. Second, an analysis of some of the persistent antinomies associated with the myth of everyday life. Third, a sketch of alternative accounts of everyday experience aspiring to overcome the antinomies that accompany the very idea of a theory of the pretheoretical. Finally, the essay will conclude with observations about the prospects of a more reflexive approach to the heterology of ordinary life.

The grammar of 'everyday life'

Given a larger canvas, an exploration of the disparate meanings of 'everyday life' would require a critical deconstruction of different approaches to the analysis of everydayness (for example, in the work of such figures as Dilthey, Wittgenstein, Simmel, Husserl, Schutz, Heidegger, Dewey, Lefebvre, Kosik, Bakhtin, Benjamin, Bloch, Habermas, Garfinkel, Debord and de Certeau, among others). Given the limitations of a short essay, our sights are confined to a prolegomena to this larger project. We first need to explore the ways in which the 'ordinary' and the 'everyday' have been imagined in mainstream/malestream philosophy and social theory before assessing the limits of these approaches. We begin by asking 'what is meant by the expression *everyday life*'? What, in other words, are the meanings implicated in this polysemic term? We can set the scene by asking where and when 'the everyday' entered modern discourse.

To begin with the word *ordinary*: from the Latin *ordinarius* (*ordo -dinis*, order, arrangement, system), *ordinary* implicates a cluster of significations indexing the habitual, customary, regular, usual, or normal. What is ordinary is 'real'. Terms for stability thus tend to borrow from Middle and Shakespearean English words for order (*order-ly*, *order-li-ness*, *order-ing*, *ordin-ance*, *ordin-ate*, *ordin-al*, *ordin-ar-y*, *co-ordin-ate*, *sub-ordin-ate*, and so forth). Like the dualism '*real/unreal*', the *ordinary* contrasts with the *exceptional* or *unusual*. Thus we say that something is *commonplace* (and perhaps even *mediocre* or 'of middling quality') in contrast with the shock of the *extra*ordinary. The latter experience is literally 'outside' or 'beyond' the usual order or normal course of things (cf. Skeat 1963, pp. 205–206, p. 414). Where the ordinary is exemplified by commonplace phenomena that are taken for granted and unnoticed, the extraordinary marks the disturbing eruption of the rare and the highly valued. Like other forms of *extravagant* experience, the extraordinary exceeds the limits and boundaries of ordinariness.

Ordinariness is also one of the key features of 'custom' and 'tradition', the 'non-place' where 'nothing happens' (since 'the real world' is precisely *that* order that guarantees that nothing extraordinary will happen). In this respect, the 'ordinary' prepares the way for ideological interpretations of the related idea of stable *tradition* (and thereby of traditional *communality*) as a timeless sociality of the now (or in the watchword of modern capitalism, 'business as usual'). In social thought, this allows the dangerous elision between *moral* order and *social* order. Thus, in medieval culture where routinization, customary work patterns and status hierarchies codify the moral norm, periods of disruption – for example, in carnival – are the times when the 'world is turned upside down', when once-ordered things wander beyond their limits, when class, gender and sacred hierarchies are inverted, where everyday prodigality is overthrown in bouts of excessive expenditure, where the seriousness of the established moral and political order is suspended in a temporary utopia of irreverence, festivity and scatological laughter (Bakhtin 1984). What is ordinary is subject to the 'orders that be', protected by the denizens of official culture. What is extraordinary prefigures the 'effervescence' of social orders rendered fluid and mobile. In this way, Bakhtin famously counterposes carnivalesque temporality to quotidian time as the possible to the actual. Without exploring this theme further, we can already see a whole metaphysics condensed in the grammatical contrast of *ordinary/extraordinary* – or its sociological equivalent, *tradition/modernity*.

In a related vein, *ordinary language* is seen as the unnoticed, but ever-present discourse of everyday usage. Unlike the 'extraordinary' idiolects of specialisms and professional discourses (the differentiated domains of law, science, philosophy, theology, aesthetics and so forth), ordinary language is the realm of mundane speech practices that predate the differentiated idioms of modernity. Conversational usage operates as a pseudo-eternal form of life whereas 'extraordinary' speech acts can be compared to the carnivalesque moments within ordinary language, for example, the moment where traditional discourse gives way to 'the philosophical discourses of modernity'.

Similar associations and dualities cling to the term *everyday*. *Everydayness* connotes the normal run of things, the usual and the commonplace. Everyday experience is what happens in typical form today as it has done yesterday and will do tomorrow. Everydayness is the positive continuity of endless repetition, the 'bad infinity' of mundane temporality, to borrow Hegel's idiom. For this reason, the standing *present* – the present stripped of its possibilities – is the grammatical tense of the everyday. Everydayness characterizes experiences that appear to be firmly embedded in the known rituals of practical life separated from the open realm of events and temporal flux. In their detachment from change such experiences become *mundane* (Latin *mundanus*, from *mundus*, the world). Things that are mundane are thus this-wordly, earthly, confined to the horizon of commonsense knowledge and its presentist categories. Like the Greek word *kosmos*, mundanity frames the order of daily life denuded of its ambiguities as eternally the same. Depending upon the features we highlight this might be variously described as a *presentist*, *substantive* or *ontological* conception of everyday life.

These ancient senses are still preserved in the concept of *Lebenswelt* or *lifeworld* that first appears in the philosophy of Husserl. The lifeworld is the world of mundane knowledge presupposed by all scientific knowledge, a prelogical realm composed of everyday experiential typifications and interpretive schemes by means of which habitual patterns of social interaction are practically managed. In contrast with extramundane 'provinces of meaning', the world of everyday life is represented as a coherent intersubjective or public 'domain' of consciousness shared by all members of society. Once reified into *existential presuppositions*, the 'structures of the life-world' can be said to sustain the 'paramount reality' of social coexistence and co-ordinated world-work (Schutz 1967, 1971). Phenomenology sometimes identifies and sometimes separates 'the world of work' (or 'world of working' (*Wirkwelt*) with the 'world of everyday life' as the *sphère de la vie pratique* (Schutz/Gurwitsch 1989, p. 226). The commonality of *la vie pratique* is ensured through its unproblematic and taken-for-granted status as an experiential 'ground' for other 'provinces of meaning', 'practices' and life-world structures (Schutz & Luckmann 1973). Phenomenology thus both substantializes and conflates 'everyday life', 'the world of work', 'the ordinary' and 'quotidian experience'. Another polemical and contrastive term is the specialized cognitive 'attitude' of science or philosophy that suspends the 'natural attitude' of everyday life in order to thematize and describe previously taken-for-granted assumptions and horizonal presuppositions: 'The concept "life-world," world of daily existence, etc., is after all a polemical concept. It signifies the world in which we live and which for us – or for some other group – constitutes reality in contrast to the "world" which science constructs'.[1]

Irrespective of their provenance – whether embedded in ordinary language or reformulated as theorists' categories – the same insistent image of everyday life as a static and 'timeless' sphere, a sustaining *matrix*, or *ahistorical* fundament of repetitive behaviour is evident. Whether we speak in terms the *le monde vécu* (*le mode comme il est vécu*), the pre-predicative realm of the lifeworld, the 'paramount reality' of mundane relevances, the 'natural attitude of everyday life' or the microsociology of ordinary conversation that artfully produces 'ordinariness' makes little difference. Social *reality* as a *cohesive identity* is securely 'anchored' in prosaic assumptions, typifications, and members' collaborative, methodic work of ordinariness. This is where essentialism and presentism actively occlude the possibility of a more radical understanding of heterological *experience* (*vécu*), obstructing the exploration of experience unhindered by received metaphysical dualisms. Let us briefly itemize some of the sources of this *ontologization* of ordinariness.

To condense a complex story we can simply assert that both ancient and modern philosophy has, with notable exceptions, treated the ordinary as the phenomenal world of *doxa* – of opinion, dogma, illusions and unreflexive thinking that obstructs the efforts of philosophical reflection (and thereby truth-saying). From Parmenides onwards, the complexities of everyday life are denigrated as 'that' which has to be abandoned or transcended in order to engage in true *theoria* and to live the *vita contemplativa*. In the Eleatic vein, ordinary experience understood as a sphere of illusory 'knowledge' has to be suppressed as a negative obstacle to the positivity of 'genuine' *theoria, philosophia, science*. This cultural amnesia is most visible in the tenacious hold of Platonic and Cartesian 'specular' theories of knowledge which translate the *essence/appearance* dualism of certain knowledge and dubitable experience – the Way of Truth and the Way of Seeming – into the language of modern culture (Sandywell 1996, 1999). Indeed, orthodox philosophical traditions can be viewed as different phallocentric attempts to *escape* from ordinariness into a pure realm of truth-saying. Thus in the crucial century between 1750–1850 ordinariness formed one of the epistemological adversaries of the Enlightenment project; the everyday came to be projected as the target of radical scepticism, the source of 'superstition' and 'prejudice' (the modern form of denigration which represents every-dayness as an adversary of what Habermas calls 'the philosophical project of modernity'). Closely associated with the devaluations of radical Enlightenment is the image of everydayness as a bounded *domain* of 'merely' pragmatic interests and fallible knowledge (of *commonsense* contrasted with *science* with its promise of secure foundations and absolute self-certainty). In a more immediate way, everydayness was simultaneously identified with the secular realm of 'practical activity' and transmuted into the *action* pursued by 'ordinary people' (this-worldly activity anchored in the rational subject as the sphere of practical life).[2] Both movements involved a type of 'reality-stripping' in which the material mediations of modernity (including the ravages of capitalist exploitation, gender oppression and colonial violence) were suppressed to secure the pseudo-transparency of 'mundane' life.

An important chapter in this process coincides with the democratic politics of modernity where ordinariness comes to be contrasted with 'revolutionary' periods of sudden change and transformation. Where the everyday is habitual and static, political and social change is depicted as fluid and mobile (a contrast that is still embedded in the expression 'social movements'). More generally, everydayness is frequently understood as the *popular*, the universal sphere of the 'common good', the 'common wealth' or even 'common humanity' expressed in the activities of daily life as a cultural invention of democratic modernity (privileging the popular as a source of authentic will-formation and societal purpose). In this sense, 'the everyday' is a construction of modernity, following the philosophical and institutional transformations of late-enlightenment Europe. In the late nineteenth and through the first part of the twentieth century, everydayness as *commonality* is reconceptualized as *mass experience* (providing a key presupposition for accounts of popular experience couched in terms of the commercialization, trivilization and banalization of experience as a consequence of the new technologies of cultural (re)production and dissemination bewailed by cultural critics of the right (from Arnold to Leavis) and the left (Adorno). As 'low' to 'high' culture, the 'popular' is whatever is common to or shared by a collectivity, typically presented in terms of mass population groupings (implicit in terms such as 'the people', 'popular culture' or the forms and practices of 'ordinary people' tacitly understood in terms of the large population-centres of urban-industrial nation-states).

In sociological discourse, these meanings were incorporated into the category of 'community' (*Gemeinschaft* in Ferdinand Tönnies terminology) contrasted with the imposed and 'artificial' organization of 'society' (*Gesellschaft*), 'mechanical solidarity' displaced by 'organic solidarity' (Durkheim), substantively rational action displaced by formal-instrumental action (Weber). In these imaginary schemas, the associations and organizations of 'society' are represented as abstract systems arising upon a substructure of vital forms of face-to-face community (thus, in Weber the forms of action associated with traditional authority are systematically replaced by rationalized forms geared to more impersonal, abstract and instrumental forms of social organization). More recently, everyday life has been presented as the 'object' of managerial systems (the response of governmental authorities to the crisis of liberalism, corporatism, welfare-state capitalism and the triumph of legislative reason; Bauman 1987). From here, it is a short step to theories of the state regulation and colonization of everyday life (in both the liberal capitalist spheres and the eastern-bloc communist states) framed in terms of the demise or disappearance of 'community' before the bureaucratic juggernauts of corporate capitalism and the modern state. Once these distinctions are in place, we can move from images of eroded community, colonization and domination to a view of everyday life as an 'object' of political administration and reconstruction (the processes through which the welfare/warfare state has reconstructed the basic terms of reference of everyday life in the twentieth century).

These variant forms of devaluation have long been incorporated into the fabric of modern social thought. Here everydayness is the *habitual*, the *local* and the *routine* or, more generically, the domain of *taken-for-granted* practices and assumptions shared by a 'mass public' (as in the expression 'public opinion' and, of course, efforts to take the temperature of the public through 'opinion research'). This becomes the unquestioned premise of both normative sociology and the 'mass-observation' studies in the 1930s and 1940s (see Adorno 1998, Highmore 2001). Even more poignantly, in the tradition of Romantic anti-capitalism, the everyday is troped as 'fallenness': the quotidian nihilism of ordinary vacuity and banality (the 'being-forgetful' *Weltanschauung* of 'the They', or in less guarded terms the hegemony of mass-popular taste and mass-market consumer culture that follows in the wake of 'the revolt of the masses').

The world we have lost

> How has everyday life been viewed through these interpretations? What is the question to which 'everyday life' is the answer?
>
> (Crook 1998, p. 534)

In reality, there are a number of questions to which everydayness has been commended as an answer. We have already noted one of the most pervasive attitudes toward the everyday in the repression of ordinary life that forms a presupposition of the quest for absolute wisdom (*sophia*) and the modern project of cognitive foundationalism. We refer, of course, to the ancient dualisms of *essence/appearance* and *theory/practice* (*vita contemplativa/vita activa*). A related attitude is exemplified in the condescension of historical and descriptive social science that views everyday life as a *domain* of banal popular culture. Finally, and overlayered on these prejudicial images, the idea of everyday life is framed as depoliticized *private life*, the affective realms of intimate sociation counterposed to the public world of consequential, organized social action (typically divided into the 'spheres' of *work* and *politics*). This topographical imagery is routinely formulated in gendered terms where the private is the sphere of the 'feminine' and the public the sphere of 'masculine' interests.

Antinomies of everyday life

Sustained by these negative and formal conceptions of ordinariness, we should not be surprised to find a series of persistent, if spurious, antinomies characterized by a relentless drift toward universal, asocial and atemporal models of everydayness. These can be briefly sketched under the following headings:

Ontologized dualism

The conceptual dichotomies of *theory and practice* (or *theory over practice*, when troped into disinterested 'knowing' as against mundane 'doing', a putatively extramundane realm of 'pure cognition' versus the mundane constraints of 'action'). This either/or thinking is, of course, the root of the terminological contrast between scientificity and 'mere practice', of abstract reflection vs. habitual opinion, of rational versus non-rational 'forms of life'. Once these dichotomous frames are turned into transcendental schemas, the everyday inevitably becomes the repressed 'other' of rational modernity.

Homogenization

The phenomenological concept of an aboriginal '*Lebenswelt*' functions as a barely disguised nostalgia for the sustaining source of meaning, of primal significances occluded by the rise of modern science and technology. This forms the basic premise for a 'phenomenology of the social world' and theories of the lifeworld contrasted with the colonizing logics of systems (Schutz 1967, Habermas 1987). In this approach, the *Lebenswelt* is a paradoxical 'no-place', a 'horizon' or ground-less site for all other practices. In Gurwitsch's phrase: 'It is hopeless to start from any place other than from the "life-world". The whole question of the existence of the sciences must be posed as a question of the transition from the order of the "life-world" to the "Pythagorean" order'.[3]

The result is an originary, unitary and homogeneous 'lifeworld' set against multiple, differentiated 'spheres' that announce the inception of modernity (the Kantian triumvirate of *science*, *morality* and *art* as *Lebenssphären* ('spheres of life') being the most influential differentiation paradigm in social theory).

Unity/plurality

This raises the question of whether there is one everyday world or many. Both everyday language and philosophical discourse would have us talk of 'everyday reality', as though it were a shared, homogenous and universal *domain of experience*; but reflection discloses plurality and multiplicity (everydayness as a field of manifold cultures segmented and differentiated in terms of occupation, age, class, gender and related sociological parameters): the everyday world of youth (again sub-differentiated into agrarian, industrial, black, third world young, etc.), the everyday world of professionals, the world of high politics, the world of shopping and consumption, and so on. Hence the postmodernist antipathy toward this kind of totalization: away with 'the world' and its legitimating metanarratives and welcome to the multiple, nomadic universes of polycentric significance.

Essentialism

Speaking in dualist and essentialist terms of appearances, 'masking' essence tends to support the institutional divide between things public (the political) and things private (the domestic). The phallocentric binary of masculine/feminine is also valorized in semiotic terms as a general 'economy' of images and representations through which essence-talk is culturally reproduced.

Naturalization

The older metaphysical distinction between outer and inner (public/spiritual) lends itself to naturalization into a cluster of related couplets: universal and particular, ordinary and extraordinary, mundane and heroic (cf. Featherstone 1992).

Scientism

Resonating with the older terminology of appearance and reality scientism posits an epistemological division between the 'world of commonsense' and 'the scientific world view'. Conflating the two as diachronically discrete domains, phenomenology can then depict itself in totalizing terms as the 'ultimately grounding science', which explores the prelogical lifeworld (Husserl 1970, p. 131, Schutz 1971). In this way the theme of the *Lebenswelt* acquires mutually exclusive scientistic and vitalist meanings as a changeless foundation of 'lived' intentionalities.

Fetishization of the immediate

This includes populism or the fetishization of the ordinary (for example as 'popular culture') and the valorization of the vivid and direct moments of 'lived' experience (overcoded in such dualities as immediate/mediate, local/general, communal/societal, same/other where the opposites are tacitly valorized in a spurious judgemental contrast between *authenticity/inauthenticity*. For phenom-enological thought, the lifeworld functions as a symbol for the loss of originary meaning, the world we have lost in the triumphant march of modernization, urbanization, and globalization. For other theorists it operates like a normative utopia and occasionally quite openly as a kind of post-theological nostalgia for ontological security in a chronically indeterminate universe. It is, therefore, not surprising that the theme of everyday life should reassert itself in critical diag-noses of the postmodern age of' totally *mediated* culture (Crook 1998, Chaney 2002, Lash 2002).

Reclaiming the ordinary

However we 'rethink' the everyday, it is evident that answering the question 'what is everyday life, how is it to be known and studied?' involves an interweaving of complex ontological, epistemological, methodological and cultural questions. We have suggested that recent social theorizing is characterized by at least three conceptions of everyday life. First, everyday life as an empirical research problematic where 'doing being ordinary' is framed as a foundational level or ground in the edifice of social science knowledge. This is the grass-roots orientation of the many sociologies of everyday life that project 'the everyday world' as a substantive *domain* stripped of history, conflict or ethicopolitical relations; second, everyday life as a way of 'transcending' or 'deconstructing' philosophy (in its speculative and metaphysical variants in powerful currents of ordinary language philosophy, phenomenological, and post-phenomenological theory); and third, everyday life as a vital source of transgression in contemporary culture (the ordinary as a recalcitrant existential surd exposing the limits of specialist disciplines, institutions and orthodoxies). The third orientation has been associated with a tradition of poststructuralist and postmodernist thought that includes such names as Bataille, Foucault, Derrida, Deleuze, Debord, Virilio, Bakhtin and Benjamin, among others.

Yet, the disquieting question remains: if 'theorizing' is partially responsible for the denigration of everyday life, are we not inevitably involved in similar *aporiae* in speaking of revisionary 'theories' of ordinariness? The problematic nature of systematic reflection upon prereflective and pre-categorical experience that was already a theme of classical phenomenology returns in the paradoxes associated with theorizing everyday life (see Gardiner 2000, Highmore 2001). How can theory articulate the pre-categorical and pre-theoretical? Can we 'recover' a strong notion of everydayness while avoiding the *antinomies* of theorizing? Can we demystify everyday life without rendering it into an 'object' or 'topic' of high-altitude inquiry? An incomplete list of contemporary efforts to rethink everyday experience would include the following six perspectives.

Phenomenological theories of everyday life

In phenomenological philosophy, everyday life is framed as the pre-interpreted world or *Lebenswelt*, the forgotten realm of sedimented lived meanings whose recovery through painstaking phenomenological 'archaeology' might resolve the 'crisis of the European sciences' (and, by implication the crisis of European culture and 'European humanity') diagnosed by Husserl, Schutz, Gurwitsch and others in the 1930s (Schutz 1967, Husserl 1970, Schutz & Gurwitsch 1989; see also Pollio *et al.* 2001).

Microsociological theories of everyday life

Phenomenological sociology approaches everydayness as a topic of descriptive social science. Here we think of the empirical sociologies of everyday life and the intersubjective structures of organized daily activities (from the Schutzian phenomenology of the natural attitude to phenomenological sociology of knowledge (Berger & Luckmann 1966), the dramaturgical interactionism of Goffman (1969, 1974), and the ethnomethodological programmes of Garfinkel and Sacks and their students). Let us simply index this strategy as the empirical thematization of everday life as a series of 'methodic appearances' through which 'doing being ordinary' is mundanely, methodically and reflexively accomplished (Garfinkel 1952, 1967, Sacks 1992).

On a more interdisciplinary plane, everydayness operates as a kind of 'basement' for the micro/macro duality in orthodox sociology (Truzzi 1968). Here the micro is typically interpreted as the interactional order in which daily life is pursued, a web of interrelationships that sustains the macro institutions power, authority and societal organizations. The everyday is then viewed as an extraordinarily complex *realm* of micro interactions and interpretive reflexivities through which the practices of everyday life and organized sociality are constructed and maintained. Here mainstream sociology and ethnomethodological studies converge in seeing the interactive processes of 'doing being ordinary' as the foundation of social worlds.

Everyday life as ordinary language

Another 'foundational' reading of everydayness can be found in the tradition of 'ordinary language philosophy'. The descriptive recovery of the foundational grammars of everyday language is a common rhetorical strategy in the pragmatic critique of philosophy as epistemology and 'philosophy of mind' (in such diverse writers as Wittgenstein, Dewey and Heidegger). As Cupitt has observed: 'if there is anything that stands upon its own feet, it is everydayness. Everything else is derivative, including all expertise' (1995, p. 29).

The critique of everyday life

The 'critique of everyday life' refers to a tradition that stems from Marx's, Lukács' and Simmel's critique of commodify reification to the situationism of Debord and ideology-critique of Lefebvre. Debord's *Society of the Spectacle* centres on the claim that a grand 'theory of the ordinary' is a contradiction in terms as the everyday is what eternally antedates and evades all theoretical language. For Debord, everydayness is the sphere of commodity reification *par excellence* and thereby the central target for a critique of the commodity spectacle. The 'revolution in everyday life' is, in turn, part of a larger critique of mainstream social science and its inattention to the contingencies and situated 'reality-work' that produces mundane social orders of degradation, violence and injustice (Lefebvre 1991). It is somewhat ironical, given their very different political assumptions, that the central de-reifying epistemological strategy of Situationist critique is shared by the sociology of knowledge (Berger & Luckmann 1966), ethnomethodology (Garfinkel 1967), social constructionism (Potter 1996), reflexive ethnography and sociology (Bourdieu & Wacquant 1992), feminism (Smith 1987, Butler 1997), SSK (Gilbert & Mulkay 1984, Woolgar 1988, Collins & Pinch 1993), actor network theory (Law 1991) and conversation analysis (Sacks 1992).

Critical cultural theories of everyday life: from cultural studies to the ethnography of everyday cultures

In critical theory, everyday life appears as the occluded material substrate of the sciences, modern technology and capitalist socieconomic systems driven by instrumental reason (Kosik, Adorno, Horkheimer, Heller, etc.). In its political orientation, it shares a great deal of common ground with the theory of the 'crisis of everyday life' mentioned above. However, there has been a significant shift from the tradition of French and Italian Marxism (Althusser and Gramsci) to the empirical investigations of the lived experiences of subcultural groups and modes of counter-cultural resistance associated with the cultural studies programme of the Birmingham Centre for Cultural Studies (Hall & Jefferson 1976, Hebdige 1979, Tudor 1999). For cultural studies, everyday life is the site of the dominant hegemonies and differential inequalities of class, age, sex/gender, race and ethnicity. The recent ethnographic turn in cultural studies takes everyday life as a site of sociotechnical transformations driven by global capitalism (or *techno-capitalism* in Kellner's (1989) terminology). Under this rubric, we can also include investigations of everyday life as totally information saturated or *media-tized* domain (Kellner 1989, Poster 1990, Lash 2002) and also the new sociology of everyday artefacts that approaches everydayness as the central topic of an enlarged and more critical cultural hermeneutics focusing upon the existential and cultural functions of everyday objects, artefacts, technologies and material complexes. More recent contributions to this critical ethnography present an important alternative to mainstream sociology and philosophy.[4]

Globalized perspectives toward postmodern everyday culture

Theorists of late modernity and postmodernity have explicitly reassessed the place of everyday life in modern societies dominated by the city-scapes of global capital, media technologies, and the information revolution. In the 'condition of postmodernity' daily life has become 'disembedded' and 'glocalized' (the theme of time-space compression (Giddens, 1990, 1991)), consumerized (Featherstone

1991, 1992), decentered, deracinated and detraditionalized (Harvey 1989). The politics of pleasure displaces the politics of class struggle (Harris 1992). Post-modernism abandons substantive and ahistorical conceptions of tradition and everyday life to embrace the multiplicity of digitally driven quotidian lifeworlds. We shift from substantive, vitalist and metaphysical conceptions of 'life' to functional and post-metaphysical images of lifeworld heterology as one conse-quence of global communications and capitalist 'mediatization' (with a conse-quent shift toward ethnographic explorations of emergent virtual lifeworlds brought into being by global cybersociety – for example, Hine (2000) and Miller and Slater (2000)).

Ordinary, everyday experience is no longer denigrated as a sphere of illusions nor posited as a universal foundational realm of 'life-world structures' and 'methodic sense-making practices', but is reconceptualized as a zone of transformations in which every aspect of individual existence has been refigured through global mediatization. Individuals are not prisoners of the mass-mediate pleasure dome of consumption but agents in a centrifugal universe of life-style experimentation, emergent practices, and experiences that resist and contest the generalized sign values of consumer society. We need to think of the *dialectics* of privatization and colonization of the lifeworld by the logics of the state and big business: everyday life as both the site of media-ted power and surveillance and of cultural forms that potentially disturb and resist the encroachment of the entertainment industries and 'information culture' (Durrschmidt 2000, Lyon 2001, Chaney 2002).

In very broad terms, the essentialist concept of 'everydayness' (and everyday identity) has been dilated, mediated and politicized as the point of intersection of major economic, social, technological and political force fields. This is itself part of a more generalized critique of culture in the age of mass-mediated (re)production (leading to retrospective investigations of modernity in terms of the geographical, political and sociotechnical transformations of everyday life over the past two centuries). The result is a reappraisal of the complexity of the sites of quotidian experience as these have become incorporated in the mediated image-worlds of late modernity. On a philosophical plane, this paradigm shift marks the intersection between postdeconstructionist heterology and critical methodologies of the oppressed (Sandoval 2000).

Toward a heterology of everyday life

Accepting the tenacity of dichotomous thinking and shifting definitions we return to the question, what exactly is 'everyday life'? Like the omnipollent term 'community', 'everyday life' is in continuous use within lay and theoretical discourse and yet continuously evades definition. Perhaps in the wake of globalization and total commodification we should ask 'where is everyday life'?

We seem compelled to answer: everywhere and nowhere? Every human science that strives to resist objectivism and scientism appeals to 'life', every minimally reflexive hermeneutic study invokes 'lived experience', every critical theory finds its ground in the liberation of reified socialities. Yet, the term has no unequivocal meaning or fixed referent. How then can we overcome the disembodied and essentialist view of everyday life common to philosophy and mainstream sociology?

Epistemologies of everyday life

Given the aporetic nature of everyday life, it is not surprising that alternative epistemologies of everyday life are now in circulation. By abandoning the *appearance/essence* distinction, most of these positions have been inevitably linked with postmodernism as the new cultural paradigm (Sim 2002). In passing, we might note the following 'postmetaphysical paradigms': postphenomenological, structuralist/culturalist, pragmatic, critical, ludic, dialogical and heterological orientations:

- *Postphenomenological*: the descriptive recovery of personal lifeworlds, sedimented horizons of meaning, subjectivity, intersubjectivity, the differentiation of 'multiple realities' and 'finite provinces of meaning' mediated by technology and science (e.g. Ihde 1995);
- *Structuralist* and *culturalist programmes* exploring the interplay of linguistic, textual and societal structures/textual processes informing the fabric of everyday experience (from Barthes to cultural studies);
- *Pragmatic 'postempiricism'*: the lifeworld as a domain of *pragma*, contingency and world openness; philosophy's recovery of the complexity of the ordinary (Wittgenstein 1958, Rorty 1989, Cavell 1990, 1995, Mulhall 1994, Critchley *et al.* 1996);
- *Critical*: everyday reality as a domain of materializations and incarnate practices; technologically mediated interactions between lifeworld and systems; technoscience as a powerful force in late modern societies (e.g. Lyon 2001);
- *Ludic*: the everyday as the play of *différence* (in signifiers, language-games and signifying practices in the writings of Derrida, Lyotard and Kristeva respectively);
- *Dialogical*: the complex heteroglossia of daily life articulated in speech genres and cultural forms (Bakhtin); sociological hermeneutics investigating the reflexivity forms in which different individuals and groups live out their relationships to their everyday activities (Bauman 1990, Gadamer 1998, Lafont 2000);
- *Heterological investigations* of 'molecular' power, the micropolitics of everyday social practices, the multidimensionality of the ordinary (in the work of Deleuze, Guattari, de Certeau, Maffesoli, and others).

Lifeworlds and temporality

Each of these paradigms claims to provide a framework for studying everyday experience free from the metaphysical presuppositions of traditional theorizing. This is evident in a shared rejection of fixed, static and foundational presuppositions with regard to 'ordinariness' and an awareness of the complex mediated nature of 'ordinary life' situated in class, gender, ethnic and sexual differences. We have been misled by grammar. There is no such thing as 'everyday life'. 'Everyday life' as a homogeneous entity or as a veil of illusory experience has never existed. In fact, *this* view is one of the myths sustaining the Eurocentric social-imaginary universe (Crook 1998). The homogeneous category of 'lifeworld' (and lifeworld subjectivity) is no longer seen as a simple identity, but is redefined as a complex site of contestation and difference. Postmodern obsessions with *plurality* and *différence* have effectively destabilized the identitarian metaphysics of 'everyday life'. The task of thinking after postmodernism is to imagine more constructive projects of alterity studies, to invent new kinds of heterology in response to the mutations of globalized experience. This can best be illustrated through the recognition of the historicity of change and transformation as this operates within the texture of everyday life worlds and microcultural practices of globalized, postcolonial and decolonizing formations (with the metropolitan-peripheral dynamics of these processes taking centre stage). Ordinariness turns out to be the hybridized 'non-place' where collective memory, the struggle for the meaning of sociality, identity and history are represented and performed on a day-by-day basis across a spectrum of social and political struggles and conflicts. In this sense, there can be no pure *domain* called 'ordinary life' separated from other spheres of struggle and contestation. In reality, everyday experience is a wholly mediated, contested, and processual site of material and ideological struggles, a screen of unsatisfied hopes, desires and dreams as well as a nostalgic icon of value and order.[5]

What survives this demystification is a version of 'ordinariness' as an exemplary site of otherness or alterity processes in sociocultural life. This is reflected in a renewed awareness of the awesome complexity of everyday experience and the ways in which the dense interweaving of memory, identity and power relations has become an insistent theme across a range of recent critical problematics.[6] In abandoning the traditional antinomies, the realm of mundane experience can be revealed in its full contingency and complexity.

Conclusion

One of the recurrent themes in this brief essay is the inherent undecidability of the category of *everyday life*. We have suggested that 'everydayness' has operated as an equivocal signifier and an ideological category in many of the most important cognitive and political programmes of modern social life. Another theme is the millennial-long denigration of ordinary experience ('the devaluation of the most valuable'). In one of its prominent meanings, *everydayness* is manifestly a product of the rhetorics of modernity constructed upon the denigratory dualisms of *élite* world-views that can be traced back to classical antiquity. A third is the nostalgia for origins symbolized by 'lifeworld' theory. A fourth is the persistent contrast of the ordinary with the symbolic icons of modernity. In sum, the *everyday* remains an essentially contested concept (Gallie 1955/6). Like a sociological inverse square law, the more everyday community appears to retreat, the more theorists invoke the language of 'communality'.

The chronic ambivalence of the everyday, however, does not remove the place of the ordinary in ethicopolitical discourse. Quite the reverse. Once the myth of everyday life has been placed 'under erasure' and fully concretized, pluralized and historicized in terms of material relations and power networks, it may be withdrawn from the categorical framework of 'objects', 'topics' or even 'sites' and 'fields', and recovered as an immense domain of defeasible practices and transgressive experiences that are continuously in play as individuals and groups construct and reconstruct the configurations through which they reflexively make sense of their lives. We need to abandon the false security of *everyday life* to reveal the complex play of decentered, heterological lifeworlds (and their associated discourses and forms of subjectivity). From this perspective 'everyday life' is no longer an object of social analysis, but an index of 'the undecideable' that resists *theorizing*, a recalcitrant ordinariness through which bureaucratized and technocratic worlds and discourses are put in question and transformed. 'Ordinariness' becomes a generic index of hitherto uninvestigated processes through which people make sense of their lives given the material and cultural resources available to them. In this respect it is the transhistorical field *par excellence*, the very crucible of historicity in which social worlds are constructed and transformed (Sandywell 1996).

For the human sciences, this rethinking of one of its basic categories promises a far-reaching shift of orientation away from its metaphysical legacy and toward alternative ways of thinking beyond the canonical terminologies of social theory. Where the grammar of everyday life intoned universality, homogeneity and passivity, the heterology of ordinariness opens the way for a more radical politics of experience informed by an agonistic conception of culture and sociocultural change (Sandywell 2000a). It also foregrounds a more radical analysis of the intertwining of the 'natural' and the 'cultural' – the organic and the inorganic realms of existence – that destabilizes the traditional binarism that organize our thinking about nature and the social. Thinking beyond the limits of ethicopolitics and ecological thought in this way means recovering the everyday in its dual aspect as both the incarnate locus of social experience and as the irreducible source of transhuman reflexivities that are always-already at work in transforming the world. From being a denigrated 'topic' or an investigative 'object', ordinary experience reasserts itself as another name for *historicity* itself as the medium of experimental forms of selfhood. But here, 'historicity' must be rethought in terms of the dialectic of materiality and technicity, the interminable play of the natural and the cultural in human affairs. The devalued practices of the common life may then be reclaimed as an ethicopolitical force field that holds open the possibility of new types of relationships, alternative visions of the natural and the artificial and more humane forms of history.

Notes

1   Aron Gurwitsch to Alfred Schutz, in Schutz/Gurwitsch (1989, p. 235). For a systematization of this theme of *reality constitution* into a full-blown 'sociology of reality' see Berger and Luckmann (1966). Gadamer describes the term *'Lebenswelt'* as 'one of those rare and wonderful artificial words . . . that have found their way into the general linguistic consciousness, thus attesting to the fact that they bring an unrecognized or forgotten truth to language' (1998, p. 55). We might also add Wittgenstein's *Lebensformen* ('forms of life') and *Sprachspiele* ('language-games') to Gadamer's category of 'wonderful words'.

2   A more detailed reconstruction would need to document the convergent transformations of Protestantism, the bourgeois political revolution, capitalism and the industrialization of society, and the longer-term disenchantment of the medieval world view as a constellation of conditions for the contemporary construction of the *world-as-mundane-reality* and the mundane subject as a *centred-rational-self*.

3   Aron Gurwitsch, letter to A. Schutz, 3 September 1945, in Schutz and Gurwitsch (1989, p. 75).

4   From the growing literature, we can mention Bennett and Watson (2002), Chaney (2002), Highmore (2001), Gardiner (2000), Miller and McHoul (1998), Osborne (2000) and Sandoval (2000).

5   On the grammar of 'nature' (and I would also suggest 'life', 'culture', 'identity' and 'creativity') as related screen memories and allegories of loss and redemption (see Sandywell 2000b, note 1, p. 117). Crook traces the mythology of everyday life to three moments: 'the unity of the social, of its inexhaustible vitality and of its ineradicable capacities for resistance and renewal' (1998, p. 537). He observes that: 'the myths of the everyday ensure that organic processes, technical artefacts, bodies, texts, weather patterns, musical sounds and all the threatening legions of otherness remain safely outside "the social"' (1998, p. 524).

6   Among these: power/discourse problematics (Foucauldian models extended to the micro-sociology of power networks as these operate in the fabric of ordinary life): the work of de Certeau on the dialectics of everyday life or Bakhtinian dialogics as a sociology of the democratizing and de-democratizing processes of ordinary existence (Gardiner 2000); feminist critiques of power

and relations of domination as constitutive processes within everyday life experience (Smith 1987, Haraway 1991, Butler 1997); investigations of everyday life mediated through advanced digital technologies (for the digitalization of everyday life, see Winston 1998, Bull 2000, Hand & Sandywell 2002); the global political economy of 'everyday life' dominated by transnational corporations and cybercapitalism (everyday life transformed and restructured through the effects of the mass cultural industries; the erosion of active public spheres and the construction of fragmented 'phantom public spheres' under the combined impact of new forms of mass leisure, tourism, mass consumerism and globalization (Habermas 1987, Urry 2001); the McDonaldization of civil society (Ritzer 2000, 2001), the tribalization of communities (Maffesoli 1996); work on the transgressive dialectics of everyday life: Lefebvre, de Certeau, Maffesoli (see Gardiner 2000, Chaney 2001, Highmore 2001); alterity paradigms: hybridized and heterological conceptions of experience, new ways of writing the texts of history and sociality (Bakhtin 1984, de Certeau 1988, Sandywell 1996, 1998, Gardiner 2000), everyday experience as the *Jetztzeit* of unanticipated possibilities, subversive change and transformation (Sandywell 2000b).

References

Adorno, T. W. (1998) *The Stars Down to Earth*, Routledge, London.

Adorno, T. W. (2000) 'Lecture 13', in *Metaphysics. Concepts and Problems*, Polity Press, Cambridge.

Bakhtin, M. (1984) *Rabelais and His World*, Indiana University Press, Bloomington, IN.

Bauman, Z. (1987) *Legislators and Interpreters*, Polity Press, Cambridge.

Bennett, T. & Watson, D. (eds) (2002) *Understanding Everyday Life*, Blackwell, Oxford.

Berger, P. & Luckmann, T. (1966) *The Social Construction of Reality*, Allen Lane, London.

Bourdieu, P. & Wacquant, L. J. D. (1992) *An Invitation to Reflexive Sociology*, Polity Press, Oxford.

Bull, M. (2000) *Sounding out the City: Personal Stereos and the Management of Everyday Life*, Berg, Oxford.

Butler, J. (1997) *The Psychic Life of Power: Theories in Subjection*, Stanford University Press, Stanford, CA.

Cavell, S. (1990) *Conditions Handsome and Unhandsome*, Open Court, La Salle, IL.

Cavell, S. (1995) *Philosophical Passages: Wittgenstein, Emerson, Austin, Derrida*, Blackwell, Oxford.

Chaney, D. (2002) *Cultural Change and Everyday Life*, Palgrave, Houndmills.

Collins, H. & Pinch, T. (1993) *The Golem: What Everyone Should Know About Science*, Cambridge University Press, Cambridge.

Critchley, S., Derrida, J., Laclau, E., Rorty, R. & Mouffe, C. (1996) *Deconstruction and Pragmatism*, Routledge, London.

Crook, S. (1998) 'Minotaurs and other monsters: "everyday life" in recent social theory', *Sociology*, vol. 32, no. 3, pp. 523–540.

Cupitt, D. (1995) *The Last Philosophy*, SCM Press, London.

de Certeau, M. (1984) *The Practice of Everyday Life*, University of California Press, Berkeley, CA.

de Certeau, M. (1988) *The Writing of History*, Columbia University Press, New York.

Debord, G. (1961) *Perspectives for Conscious Alterations in Everyday Life*, 17 May 1961, Center of Sociological Studies of the CNRS.

Durkheim, E. (1976) *The Elementary Forms of Religious Life*, Allen and Unwin, London.

Durrschmidt, J. (2000) *Everyday Lives in the Global City*, Routledge, London.

Featherstone, M. (1991) *Consumer Culture and Postmodernism*, Sage, London.

Featherstone, M. (1992) 'The heroic life and everyday life', *Theory, Culture and Society*, vol. 9, pp. 159–182.

Featherstone, M., Lash, S. & Robertson, R. (eds) (1995) *Global Modernities*, Sage, London.

Gadamer, H.-G. (1998) 'The idea of practical philosophy', in *Praise of Theory: Speeches and Essays*, trans. C. Dawson, Yale University Press, New Haven and London, pp. 50–61.

Gallie, W. B. (1955–1956) 'Essentially contested concepts', *Proceedings of the Aristotelian Society*, vol. 56, pp. 167–198.

Gardiner, M. E. (2000) *Critiques of Everyday Life*, Routledge, London and New York.

Garfinkel, H. (1952) 'Perception of the other', PhD dissertation, Harvard University.

Garfinkel, H. (1967) *Studies in Ethnomethodology*, Prentice-Hall, Englewood Cliffs, NJ.

Giddens, A. (1990) *The Consequences of Modernity*, Polity Press, Cambridge.

Giddens, A. (1991) *Modernity and Self-Identity*, Polity Press, Cambridge.

Gilbert, N. & Mulkay, M. (1984) *Opening Pandora's Box*, Cambridge University Press, Cambridge.

Goffman, E. (1969) *The Presentation of Self in Everyday Life*, Penguin, Harmondsworth.

Goffman, E. (1974) *Frame Analysis: An Essay on the Organization of Experience*, Northeastern University Press, New York.

Habermas, J. (1987) *Moral Consciousness and Communicative Action*, MIT Press, Cambridge, MA.

Hall, S. & Jefferson, T. (1976) *Resistance Through Rituals*, Hutchinson, London.

Hand, M. & Sandywell, B. (2002) 'E-topia as Cosmopolis or Citadel: On the democratizing and de-democratizing logics of the Internet, or, towards a critique of the new technological fetishism', *Theory, Culture & Society*, vol. 19, no. 1–2, pp. 197–225.

Haraway, D. (1991) *Simians, Cyborgs and Women*, Routledge, London and New York.

Harris, D. (1992) *From Class Struggle to the Politics of Pleasure: The Effects of Gramscianism on Cultural Studies*, Routledge, London.

Harvey, D. (1989) *The Conditions of Postmodernity*, Basil Blackwell, Oxford.

Hebdige, D. (1979) *Subculture: The Meaning of Style*, Routledge and Kegan Paul, London.

Heller, A. (1984) *Everyday Life*, Routledge and Kegan Paul, London.

Highmore, B. (2001) *Everyday Life and Cultural Theory: An Introduction*, Routledge, London.

Hine, C. (2000) *Virtual Ethnography*, Sage, London.

Husserl, E. (1970) *The Crisis of European Sciences and Transcendental Phenomenology*, Northwestern University Press, Evanston, IL.

Idhe, D. (1995) *Postphenomenology*, Northwestern University Press, Evanston, IL.

Kellner, D. (1989) *Critical Theory, Marxism and Modernity*, Polity Press, Cambridge.

Lafont, C. (2000) *The Linguistic Turn in Hermeneutic Philosophy*, MIT Press, Cambridge, MA.

Lash, S. (2002) *Critique of Information*, Sage, London.

Law, J. (ed.) (1991) *A Sociology of Monsters: Essays on Power, Technology and Domination*, Routledge, London.

Lefebvre, H. (1991) *Critique of Everyday Life*, Verso, London.

Lyon, D. (2001) *Surveillance Society: Monitoring Everyday Life*, Open University Press, Buckingham.

Maffesoli, M. (1996) *The Time of the Tribes*, Sage, London.

Miller, D. & Slater, D. (2000) *The Internet: An Ethnographic Approach*, Berg, New York.

Miller, T. & McHoul, A. W. (1998) *Popular Culture and Everyday Life*, Sage, London.

Mulhall, S. (1994) *Stanley Cavell: Philosophy's Recounting of the Ordinary*, Oxford University Press, Oxford.

Osborne, P. (2000) *Philosophy in Cultural Theory*, Routledge, London and New York.

Pollio, H. R., Henley, T. B. & Thompson, C. J. (1997) *The Phenomenology of Everyday Life: Empirical Investigations of Human Experience*, Cambridge University Press, Cambridge.

Poster, M. (1990) *The Mode of Information*, Polity Press, Cambridge.

Potter, J. (1996) *Representing Reality: Discourse, Rhetoric and Social Construction*, Sage, London.

Ritzer, G. (2000) *The McDonaldization of Society*, Sage and Pine Forge Press, London.

Ritzer, G. (2001) *Explorations in Social Theory: From Metatheorizing to Rationlization*, Sage, London.

Rorty, R. (1980) *Philosophy and the Mirror of Nature*, Princeton University Press, Princeton, NJ.

Rorty, R. (1989) *Contingency, Irony, Solidarity*, Cambridge University Press, Cambridge.

Sacks, H. (1992) *Lectures on Conversation*, Blackwell, Oxford.

Sandoval, C. (2000) *Methodology of the Oppressed*, University of Minnesota Press, Minneapolis.

Sandywell, B. (1996) *Logological Investigations, Volume 1, Reflexivity and the Crisis of Western Reason*, Routledge, London.

Sandywell, B. (1998) 'The shock of the old: Mikhail Bakhtin's contributions to the theory of temporality and alterity', in *Bakhtin and the Human Sciences*, eds M. Mayerfeld Bell & M. Gardiner, Sage, London, pp. 196–213.

Sandywell, B. (1999) 'Specular grammar: the visual rhetoric of modernity', in *Interpreting Visual Culture: Explorations in the Hermeneutics of the Visual*, eds I. Heywood & B. Sandywell, Routledge, London and New York, pp. 30–56.

Sandywell, B. (2000a) 'The agonistic ethic and the spirit of inquiry: on the Greek origins of theorizing', in *The Sociology of Philosophical Knowledge*, ed. M. Kusch, Kluwer, Dordrecht, pp. 93–123.

Sandywell, B. (2000b) 'Memories of nature in Bakhtin and Benjamin', in *Materializing Bakhtin: The Bakhtin Circle and Social Theory*, eds C. Brandist & G. Tihanov, Macmillan and St. Martin's Press, London and New York, pp. 94–118.

Sandywell, B. (2003) 'Metacritique of information', *Theory, Culture and Society*, vol. 20, no.1, pp. 109–122.

Schutz, A. (1967) *The Phenomenology of the Social World*, Northwestern University Press, Evanston, IL.

Schutz, A. (1971) *Collected Papers, vol. I*, ed. M. Natanson, Martinus Nijhoff, The Hague.

Schutz, A. & Gurwitsch, A. (1989) *Philosophers in Exile: The Correspondence of Alfred Schutz and Aron Gurwitsch, 1939–1959*, Indiana University Press, Bloomington & Indianapolis, IN.

Schutz, A. & Luckmann, T. (1973) *Structures of the Lifeworld*, Heinemann, London.

Shapin, S. & Schaffer, S. (1985) *Leviathan and the Air Pump*, Princeton University Press, Princeton, NJ.

Sim, S. (2002) *Irony and Crisis*, Icon Books, London.

Skeat, W. W. (1963) *An Etymological Dictionary of the English Language*, Clarendon Press, Oxford.

Sklair, L. (2002) *Globalization: Capitalism and its Alternatives*, 3rd edn, Oxford University Press, Oxford.

Smith, D. (1987) *The Everyday World as Problematic: A Feminist Sociology*, Open University Press, Milton Keynes.

Storey, J. (1999) *Cultural Consumption and Everyday Life*, Sage, London.

Truzzi, M. (ed.) (1968) *Sociology and Everyday Life*, Prentice-Hall, Englewood Cliffs, NJ.

Tudor, A. (1999) *Decoding Culture: Theory and Method in Cultural Studies*, Sage, London.

Wagner, P. (2001) *Theorizing Modernity: Inescapability and Attainability in Social Theory*, Sage, London.

Winston, Brian (1998) *Media, Technology and Society: A History from the Telegraph to the Internet*, Routledge, London.

Wittgenstein, L. (1958) *Philosophical Investigations*, 2nd edn, Basil Blackwell, Oxford.

Woolgar, S. (ed.) (1988) *Knowledge and Reflexivity: New Frontiers in the Sociology of Knowledge*, Sage, London.

Harry Harootunian

SHADOWING HISTORY
National narratives and the persistence
of the everyday

The issue this paper wishes to address is how history, as encoded in historiography of history-writing, is actually based upon its capacity to conceal, disguise and indeed suppress the everyday. This is especially true when you consider that most history is really driven by the nation state and that far from envisaging a history free or rescued from the nation, most history-writing ends up reinforcing it. In other words, history's primary vocation has been to displace the constant danger posed by the surplus of everyday life, to overcome its apparent 'trivia', 'banalities' and untidiness in order to find an encompassing register that will fix meaning. With Hegel, narrative was given the role of supplying the maximal unity by which to grasp the meaning of history. What immediately got privileged was, of course, the nation state in the making of world historical events or and ultimately class, subjects who can claim world historical agency. By the same measure, the surplus or messy residues of modern life, especially its immensely staggering complexities, its endless incompletions and repetitions – all irreducible – are repressed or in some instances the microcosmic is sometimes mobilized to reinforce macrocosmic meaning. (This has frequently been called history from below and what Germans have called Alltagsgeschichte.) What I would like to do is explore the category of everydayness, ushered in with the masses and the appearance of the subaltern, as a minimal unity that provides its own principle of historical temporality that easily challenges the practice of history-writing as we know it.

Keywords   colonialism; everyday life; history; Japan; memory; modernity

Everyday life, policed and mystified by every means, is a sort of reservation for good natives who keep modern society running without understanding it – this society with its rapid growth of technological powers and forced expansion of its market. History – the transformation of reality cannot presently be used in everyday life because the people of everyday life are the product of history over which they have no control.

(Guy Debord)

Cultural Studies Vol. 18, No. 2/3 March/May 2004, pp. 181–200
ISSN 0950-2386 print/ISSN 1466-4348 online   © 2004 Taylor & Francis Ltd
http://www.tandf.co.uk/journals   DOI: 10.1080/0950238042000201473

Routledge
Taylor & Francis Group

Past presents/present pasts

One of the interesting recurrences throughout Asia during the interwar period was not simply the evident material transformation of societies under the impact of capitalism and colonialism but the way these societies came to understand this modernizing and modernist experience. Owing either to the accelerated destruction of long standing received cultures of reference inflicted by the implementation of new modes of production and the introduction of commodity consumption or, in some instances, to enforced colonial domination which, in cities like Shanghai or Bombay, dramatized the incongruence of politics and culture, the common response was to find an optic through which to account for the experience of a phenomenal present, as such, rather than resort to the 'knowledge' offered by an historical representation of the past. In this fateful encounter – experienced, I believe, more intensely in societies like Japan, which came late to capitalist modernization, or India and China (not to forget Africa and Latin America), which had it forced upon them through the violent agency of colonization than their EuroAmerican counterparts – the spectacle of the present, condensed and accelerated, took precedence over the past and history's knowledge. Often the rate of change inflicted by the forces of capitalism and colonialism was so rapid and fierce, that not even the immediate past was accessible to historical consciousness, prompting Fanon's observation of the brutal destruction of 'systems of reference . . . matched by sacking cultural patterns . . . values are flaunted, crushed emptied' (1970, p. 33, p. 41). This is not say that societies in Asia were not interested in historical representation. But when history in these places was written to bridge the great 'epistemic violence' caused by capitalism and colonialism, it was invariably bonded to the nation form, if there was one, or the idea of the nation yet to come after the demise of colonialism, thus replicating established historiographical practice in EuroAmerica. As in the industrialized world of the interwar period, the Asian periphery especially, and I suspect parts of Africa and Latin America, identified history and its narrative with the story of a particular group or folk and the heroic formation of the nation-state. If history writing served to catalyze, if not sanctify, the new nation form in the nineteenth century, nation and narrative increasingly functioned to unify diverse populations and to secure the guarantee of civil order through the often fictive agency of common identity and the more or less voluntary assent of the people to work and die for one's country. This particular lesson was learned early by Japanese, who happily escaped foreign domination only to become colonizers, to achieve nationhood before colonized and semi colonized societies like India and China. With India, its peoples were seen as subjects of the Crown – albeit second class ones – who were enlisted to work for the Raj and fight Great Britain's enemies. When, at the time of World War II, the anti-colonial Indian National Army was formed and threw in its lot with the Japanese, its adherents were instantly branded as traitors. Yet even in these colonial sites, the nation constituted the principal category for historical representation. So powerful was this association that the Indonesian nationalist Soetomo spoke of the nation's history in his *Autobiography* long before there was one (see Anderson 1998 and Harootunian 1999).

However, after World War I – and a first phase of 'globalization' that transported capitalism and commodity consumption to Asia, Africa and Latin American – the problem was how best to account for (and represent) what was occurring in the present, not what had happened in the past. This entailed forging a present of one's own that would become a past in place of a practice in which another's past dominated the present. The experience of capitalist penetration under the sign of modernization and a new temporality called 'modernity' meant that the lived reality of the everyday by the masses was different from the nation and its narrative telling people how to fulfil its requirements for national subjectivity and citizenship. If the nation composed a narrative of enactment by the people, the everyday of the masses wrote a vastly different history of its own. The immense upheavals that sent mass migrations from the countryside to the new industrial sites of the cities prompted a growing awareness of a different life in kind among those national subjects who entered new labour markets and the world of commodity consumption. The perception of this transformation was registered early by thinkers throughout the emerging capitalist world in places like Germany, France, Japan, Brazil and then later in India and China, who began to examine the specific texture of the everyday lived by the urban classes – especially workers – and the consequences of commodity culture. With the Bolshevik Revolution this new everyday began, for the first time, to make possible the envisaging of history in such a way as to foreground the present – the now – in contrast to the past of national narratives that ultimately implied an identity with both present and future. The effect of this emphasis on the present was to disclose the recognition of the existence of different temporalities between history (especially 'national history') and the everyday, where the former looked to an indeterminate past leading to the present and capable of both shaping the future and securing the identity of each moment (periodization and stages in a trajectory), while the latter saw in the present a break with all antecedents and thus a new way to envision the relationship between the present and the past. By the same measure, this new perspective resulted in rehierarchicizing the event and reordering the relationship between the significant and insignificant by showing that what now counted as a force of disruption and change was no longer the large scale happenings but the micro-occurrences of the everyday. (This strategy was not only later promoted by the Situationists in the 1960s but put into brilliant documentary practice by film makers like Imamura Shohei in his memorable 'History of post-war Japan as told by barmaid'.) It is in this sense that the everyday, marking a different kind of historicity, shadowed the narrative of national history and the putative movement of world historicality, just as Asia, Africa and even Latin America existed in the eclipse cast by EuroAmerica but whose very negativity enabled the claims of universality associated with History. The turn to the everyday meant fixing on the present and was not simply seen as the site of punctual events but rather as the location of a durational moment and its subsequent ontologization. It is this relationship I would like to explore further in order to see if there is some way we can restore to historical practice the everyday which, according to phenomenology since Husserl, has constituted the kernel of the historical world and designated the identity of the *lebenswelt* as the sign of historicality itself. In pursuit of this programme, I will first consider how, momentarily, the idea of everyday life appeared as the basis of history in Hegel was abandoned for the more expansive conceptualization of world history that fixed the primacy of the nation state as the sign of true historicity. This notion was subsequently reinforced by the further development of the nation-state in nineteenth-century Europe, especially, and its vocation for capitalist accumulation that not only demanded of new national subjects unwavering willingness to sacrifice their lives but also, as a penultimate service, to work for it. The organization of work time closely matched the progressive sequentiality that figured the national narrative and seemed to have inspired its smooth and seamless linearity. In this way, the capitalist nation state reduced different, co-existing temporalities lived by diverse groups within different realms of the social formation to constitute variations of segmented and cumulative time that opened the door to an historical consciousness rooted in evolutionary and progressive plot lines. This sense of historicity was challenged in the twentieth century by the formation of mass society in new industrial sites whose lived experience in the present – making their own history – collided politically with the claims of the national narrative, just as their privileging of the everyday or now time clashed with the temporal presumptions of a completed national past. I will end this examination of how everydayness supplied new principles for a history of the present and produced the forms appropriate to it by reconsidering its meaning for the current practice of cultural studies.

Historicizing the everyday

According to Kracauer, writing in his last book, *History, the Last Things Before the Last*, there was a moment in the early nineteenth century when history and the everyday encountered each other through the mediation of photography. He recalls how, in 1840, Friedrich von Raumer's contemporary histories were 'praised for resembling daguerreotypes' in that they captured the 'fleeting shadows of the present' on the wing (Kracauer 1995, p. 58). Kracauer was concerned with drawing out a shared structure of history and the everyday, which he called the *lebenswelt*, since 'camera reality' paralleled 'historical reality', as both were amorphously 'patterned' on the 'half-cooked state of our everyday world'. (It is important to recognize that this coupling of history and everyday sealed by photography actually contradicted an earlier view Kracauer had proposed in the *Mass Ornament* that argued for their difference and separation.) In this new kinship, he discerned, nevertheless, the contingent nature of the material, random events, 'transient and unforeseeable encounters' (1995, p. 58). However, history, especially national history in the nineteenth century, was never seen as the locus of contingent events but rather as the arena of purposefulness and destiny. From this perspective, it is safe to say that the contingent was associated with the precinct of the 'half cooked state' of the everyday. While Kracauer acknowledged how photography invariably precluded any chance for achieving completion, he failed to recognize that historical reconstruction always (until recently) aspired to completeness since it was about a past that was long over. Only the isolated traces of a long national history could be caught in the photographic lens. The present, the site of the everyday, could never claim completion until it became past, while the past was over and done with, ready to be definitively reconstructed. Although this separation between a completed past and an incomplete present partially explains why photography and history prematurely ended what might have become a productive relationship for both, Kracauer seemed more interested in liberating the 'life-world' from its relationship to philosophy (and science) and realigning it with history, with which it supposedly shared a structure. By contrast, we know that Benjamin saw in photography a model for history, but one built on images signifying the now time of everyday life that recognizes in the concept (*Begriff*) of history proposed in the 'Theses on the Concept of History' an interchangeability between the operation of how thought seeks to bring history within the grasp of a concept and the camera's ceaseless fixation on a moment of history (Benjamin 1999; see also Cadava 1997, p. xviii). In his quest for a materialist historiography, Benjamin was convinced that there could be no thinking about history without at the same time thinking about photography.

Yet, the separation between a completed past and an incomplete present had already been accomplished earlier by Hegel. In the *Aesthetics*, Hegel early identified the everyday with what he called the 'prose of the world'.[1] For Hegel, the prose of the world was concretized in the endlessly multifarious activities of the everyday. 'This is the prose of the world', he wrote, 'as it appears to the consciousness both of the individual himself and of others: a world of finitude and mutability, of entanglements in the relative, of the pressure of necessity from which no individual is in a position to withdraw' (Hegel 1975, p. 150). Everydayness constitutes both the temporality and the unity of the prose of the world. It is the present in which intersubjective relations are carried out, pointing to a future on whose path the past – the history of each individual based on a priori experiences – acts as a steady guide. At this moment in Hegel's thinking, history would thus be conceived as the multiplicity of individual experiences, an inexhaustible tableau of actions and events, and its subject matter would seek to comprehend the entirety of the human condition itself. (While no actual history ever came close to approaching this truly global ideal, a trace of this aspiration is still visible in Balzac's monumental desire to map the world of early nineteenth-century France.) Nothing would be excluded from this history of the human condition, no culture, class, ethnic group would be ineligible. Yet, not too long after Hegel abandoned this breathtakingly heroic task to comprehend and represent the totality of human experience, he decided to narrow the compass and re-identify history with the nation-state, transmuting the prose of the world into Spirit's unfolding in world history. By discerning in history the patterning of Providence and the itinerary of Spirit's unfolding plan, Hegel not only linked significant eventfulness to a 'higher necessity', he also banished (apparently as insignificant) entire cultures and continents from the achievement of historicality. It is ironic to observe that, more than a century afterwards, the world of the excluded that had once been eliminated from History turned to the everyday, as if it were the return of the repressed, to mark the historicity of its experience with the modern present and perhaps rescue the promise of Hegel's original vision of an all encompassing history of the human condition. With this move, it was able to call into question the universalistic claims of History's narrative at the same time it began to supply the resources for envisioning, especially among the colonized, new political projects for the future. In fact, the appeal to the everyday was to become the primary method to rehistoricize the present.

The Hegelian model of evolutionary development is too well known to recount in any detail. But what is important about it is the recognition that Spirit moves through stages as it 'actualizes' itself and that each actualization is expressed in the form of a national spirit that progressively, and I should add, purposefully acquired knowledge of the 'movement of its own activity . . . and frees its consciousness from natural immediacy' (Guha 2002, p. 26). Along Spirit's route, 'nations' have achieved partial actualization in emancipating themselves from nature and consciously affirming such freedom, only to stall and become stranded in permanent 'standstill'. The development of the state – revealing the fullness and completion of Spirit's self-consciousness – fulfils the vocation of freedom and thus finds for a people a place in world-history, that is, history itself now differentiated from pre-history. We know, of course, Hegel's Oriental World – China and India, especially – failed the test and remained fettered to nature's immediacy and far from the realization of true freedom. By the same token, these 'nations', or as he called them 'forms of nations' were destined to become 'people without history'. Marx's 'Asiatic mode of production' and Weber's confident identification of rationality in a specific religio-cultural endowment later merely reinforced the great divide Hegel's providential plan had produced. Both, moreover, were persuaded that Asia – and presumably the rest of the world outside EuroAmerica – could free itself from the lockstep and rejoin History through agencies of capitalism and scientific rationality. The

Japanese folklorist, Yanagita Kunio, commenting on H. G. Wells's *Outline of World History* after World War I, observed how whole continents like Africa and entire peoples had simply vanished from the screen of world history. History, the world historical thus came to mean only those 'nations' which had, as in Europe, managed to develop a state – thus sealing the kinship between history and historiography and the category of the nation-state as its true object and 'rational content'. Hence, the nation state became the principal vocation of history since it was history that recorded the development of the state, (a theory of develop-ment we have not yet overcome) as Spirit's self-objectification and the content of historical writing. It was precisely this totalizing identity between reason, history and nation-state that eliminated the space of the everyday, or, at the very least, consigned it to the domain of contingency. Consequentially, the everyday was reduced either to the status of a repressed remainder or ethnographic atemporality – to those aspects of life that had not yet been assimilated to the nation form or which, somehow, had been able to resist its hegemonizing templates of behavior and conduct. (In Durkheimian social theory, nation-state was replaced by the category of society based on organic solidarity and the capacity of the division of labour to ultimately find a place for everybody.) Kracauer, it is important to recall, wanted to show both the linkage of photog-raphy and history, whose promise had not been realized, and history and the 'life-world', whose necessary mismatch he failed to grasp. However, historians early rejected the partnership of history and photography by dismissing the latter as mere 'reproduction' of the immediate, despite the Rankean dictim to see 'how things actually are'. Instead, they saw in history the form of 'reconstruction' and even representation of the 'nature of things', much like a painting, according to one prominent historian (Kracauer 1995, p. 51). Above all else, history was concerned with the past of the nation rather than the experience of the present – how the nation came into existence – whereas photography and the everyday it captured in its particularity were too fastened to the present and rooted in an indeterminate temporality not yet completed. Because the past was completed, it was the time and place history had been made, whereas the present could only reaffirm its identity with it and recall its exemplars by designating places of memory but not remake it. It would have to wait for the moment it became past, itself requiring a distancing operation, which would have made it past and eligible for historical status. Owing to the process of commodification, this distancing would eventually be objectified in the collective temporalization of events, by distinguishing between a 'then' and the 'now' (Feather 2000, p. 134). Commodifi-cation would further result in placing other times beyond the grasp of a frozen and seemingly endless present. Ultimately, the past would have to find perma-nent expression in the reformulation of national history as heritage. In fact, it was Benjamin who observed how history in its historicist inflection transmuted the phenomena of the past into enduring manifestations of their value as 'heritage' and 'cultural treasures' for the nation. It was this distrust of historicism that, in part, induced him to turn the 'focus of historiography away from narrative forms of historical totalization to montage', from story to image, quotation, anecdote (Osborne 1995, p. 115). Japanese, on their part, not only envisaged and implemented the project of national history to eternalize the accomplishment of nationhood but also established a classification system in the 1930s that organized and designated artefacts from the past as 'national treasures' 'cultural property' and ranked artisanal/artists who were still working as 'living national treasures'. There were even attempts to assimilate the everyday into 'living culture', (*seikatsu bunka*) founded on the survival of vestiges now config- ured as 'heritage'. The importance of this valorization of national history into heritage (long before the British turned to it after World War II), is the identity of a distancing trope that demanded not only forgetting the role of the present in historical memory but also everything in the past which continues to resist transmission as national heritage (Osborne 1995, p. 140). Yet it is important to recall that one of the principal purposes of national history and its reliance on narrative form was to not only flatten out time, literally reducing temporality to a timeless space, but also to remove all of those sediments from different pasts that if engaged in the present would prevent a closure of the future. It is interesting to recognize, in this connection, the parallelism between national narratives and dominant narratives of modernity.

In the nineteenth century, the everyday and the now, according to Bakhtin, thus left the domain of history writing and historical knowledge to become the content of the realist novel – inadvertently yoking experience to the task of fiction and opening the way to overcome the authoritative univocal narrative of national history for polyvocal enunciations signifying different plots, plural political perspectives and differing temporalities. The everyday, thus, was increasingly seen as the place where events were transformed into a mass article through the process of commodification and instantaneous transmission that made possible the repeated experiencing of the image-event. It was the act of recognizing reproducibility that prompted people like Benjamin to conclude that experience was being removed from both traditional and spatial determinations, resembling most the commodity form. By contrast, the events that continued to configure historiography could only be recalled and remembered but not expe- rienced. Benjamin saw these 'recurrences' as the sign of a repressed history, its watermark, perhaps, the repeated production of the image that constituted for him the fundamental event of modernity. This is why he famously proposed in the 'On the concept of history' (Thesis No. 5) that the 'true picture of the past flits by' and can only be 'seized as an image which flashes up at the instant it can be recognized and is never seen again'.

By proposing that in modern times nation-state and history formed an original alliance, a vocation for each other, I am not implying that such an arrangement excluded other kinds of historical representation. The dramatic example of Jacob Burckhardt discloses the possibility of envisaging a different kind of history not constrained by the nation form. I am suggesting that the form of the nation-state constituted the primary category through which historical writing 'reconstructed' the past for the present. Its content usually concentrated on the origin and development of a specific group or people and their realization of a state entitling them to occupy a place in world history. It is interesting to recall how Japanese thinkers in the late 1930s saw the coming of a war with the West as an affirmation of the Japanese state's 'world-historical mission'. The task of the national history was to recuperate this achievement of the past in the present in order for the nation-state to accomplish the principal goals of unity, wealth and power. Historical practice meant discovering a 'timeless truth' of the nation's past, a fixed ' "eternal" image of the past'. When we look at the later refractions of nationhood in Asia, we see the replication of this model, despite differences of time, place and political circumstances, and the repetitive appeal to pastness intimately linked to the creation of national subjects who at an abstract level collectively shared a common identity that was intended to secure the prospect of unity and social order to be realized in their willingness to work and die for the nation. The hyphenated nation often approximated the commodity form itself, inasmuch as its mystical and spiritual side remained concealed yet was unfailingly recruited to interpolate subjects to work and sacrifice themselves. The constitution of people as subjects, emblematized by appeals to race, language and timeless national culture, were employed as the forms through which to objectify the hidden spiritual and mystical side of the nation that accompanied the continuous creation of the past. A subject for the nation also worked, at least initially, to displace or subsume subject positions demanded by the new division of labour. In this regard, Chaterjee reminds us that the national dichotomization of inner and outer aimed to shift national subjectivity away from bourgeois liberal notions of universal humanity to forms of particularity and difference – to the recognition of the 'national community as against other communities' (1993, p. 75). In other words, nation formation always presupposed a principle of inclusion and exclusion, based upon a presupposed givenness, for its effectiveness and sought through abstract emblems of identity to unify, if not actually homogenize, a population into a fictive ethnos. While this impulse was directed to penetrate and permeate daily life through the staging of punctual rituals, ceremonies, holidays, fixing places of national memory etc., it rarely succeeded in completely assimilating the everyday to its protocols. Even in the daily life of workers and colonial labour, especially migrants to the metropolis like Koreans in Japan, who constituted a virtual Industrial Reserve Army ready for capital bonded to the insecurities of day work, there were still areas in the lived experience that were capable of resisting assimilation to the structures of domination. This was especially the case in the twentieth century with massive industrialization and the formation of mass society, persuading Weber to entrust state bureaucracy with the task of 'dominating everyday life', which meant eliminating precisely the excess or surplus that remained unassimilated. In this regard, the everyday appeared as a repressed and irreducible remainder of the nation-state, what was left over, surplus, which, in the eyes of Japanese, Chinese and Indian observers in the interwar period, came to constitute the zone of non-everyday life. What seems clear is that the domain of everyday life possessed its own complex mix of temporalities (Mariategui's prescient sense of what we might today call mixed temporalities in Peru) and routines that often clashed with national time and behavioural expectation.

Investment in the nation form promised a solution to the problem of smoothing out or levelling the ground of society for the accomplishment of capital accumulation and its continuous reproduction, that is to say, removing the fetters to its installation and implementation, even though the necessity to create unevenness was inscribed in the social formation of the new nation states. Hence, it was the desire of nation-states, everywhere, to present the picture or image of an even, unblemished surface, capable of concealing its enabling conditions of existence. Yet, this effort to secure a smooth surface, hiding nothing, and polish the rough edges of unevenness in order to achieve unity, common sense through shared identity, coherence was powerfully mediated by received temporal and spatial matrices deriving from earlier modes of production (Poulantzas 2000, p. 104ff). The new meanings of territory and history were reinscribed in more fundamental changes underlying the conceptual matrices of space and time whose rhythms were now regulated by significant shifts in the mode of production. A new spatial configuration fixed boundaries between inside and outside, within which the reproduction of capital was able to take place. The state thus acted to monopolize the organization of social space in such a way as to materialize its various apparatuses – army, schools, central bureaucracy, penal system – and patterned, in turn, the subjects over whom it exercised power. While this space split the labour process into capitalist units of production and reproduction, the uneven development of capitalism in its spatialized dimension was actually coterminous with this 'discontinuous morphology' (Poulantzas 2000, p. 104). In other words, the state was imbedded in a spatial matrix implied by the labour process and ultimately in the circulation of commodities and consumption. Because of this arrangement, production, especially as it was augmented by machine power and the factory system, entailed further segmenting, serializing and dividing a cumulative and irreversible time. This practice stood in marked contrast to received pre-modern conceptions of temporality that were usually considered as reversible. The nation-state's objective was thus to master time in such a way as to secure a standard single and homogenous measure – clock time – capable of reducing the different, co-existing temporalities lived by diverse groups within different domains of the social formation by acknowledging a distance between each. For the first time, then, the temporal matrix of the capitalist nation state mapped out the particular moments as different temporalities and construe them as variations of segmented and cumulative time. These different temporalities, in turn, were totalized into a procession of moments following one another that would make way for the construction of modes of historical consciousness rooted in narratives of evolutionary and progressive plotlines (Poulantzas 2000, p. 111, p. 113). With relentless linearity, each moment led to and produced the next to represent yet a further move in an irreversible series. The awareness of this linear movement provided a perspective for envisaging a before and after, a then and now – differentiating the present from what preceded it and comes after. Here, in any case, was a model for national history and the construction of a continuist and totalizing narrative capable of explaining how the folk – in time and space – had managed to create the nation-state and how the history of this achievement revealed a progressive unfolding which materialized or objectified the fusion of idea and reason. The combining of spatial and temporal matrices of capitalism disclosed how spatial unevenness of diverse spheres of the social formation and the respective co-existence of different temporalities constituted a function whose relationship between history (time) and space (territory) was articulated by the nation-state. The modern nation form supplied the occasion for the interaction of these matrices to produce a 'historicity of territory' and a 'territorialization of a history', both the calling and the content of the national narrative (Poutlantzas 2000, p. 114).

Quotidianizing the present

While the task of the national narrative was to concretize the link between history and territory, and to exceptionalize the particular story that had been carried out by the folk, this did not mean that the idea of the national was able to reach and permeate the space-time matrices of everyday life. If the national culture failed to become the end point of everyday life but only its 'ground' that would continuously be reworked and recoded, it was also the case that everydayness was expected to lift itself up to the dignity of the nation (and thus reason). In other words, everyday life was supposed to be colonized by the national idea yet it too often escaped this colonizing impulse to exist as a remaindered excess outside of its reason. Even though the spatial and temporal matrices of the capitalist nation-state were supposed to be articulated through the forms of everyday life, to perform the national narrative, so to speak, it – everydayness – invariably resisted this assimilative process to become an other to the form of historical representation. The presumed subsumption – more formal than real – of the everyday to the consensus producing demands of the nation and national identity was never complete. In a sense, it was the emphasis on the nation's pastness, rather than its present, and its meaning for the future, and the necessity to homogenize time that provided the everyday with both the identity of social space – the world – and the temporality of the now to remake life in the twentieth century.

The re-emergence of the everyday as an active concept demanding political, social and cultural transformation occurred in the twentieth century conjuncture whose co-ordinates were marked by the Bolshevik Revolution and the accelerated and technological modernization during and after World War I. If the Russian Revolution unveiled the power of the masses to determine, momentarily, their own everyday for the first time in history, the unprecedented move to capital industries, massive urbanization and the subsequent production of consumer commodities and the global expansion of capitalism signalled the figuration of a new kind of mass society. By the same measure, the new everyday itself was transformed, in turn, under the impact of fascism and Stalinism in the 1930s. Accompanying this profound change in the social topography – one the nation-state form was hardly prepared to meet – was the formation of a new hermeneutic which, with thinkers like Georg Simmel, sought to concretize philosophic understanding by constituting metropolitan life and its complex of social interactions into an object of inquiry. Under the impact of social and economic transformation, the everyday was thus 'denaturalized' into a domain of common experience whose hidden significance, as Freud proposed at the outset of the century in *The Psychopathology of Everyday Life*, was already manifest in the countless slips and mistakes encountered in daily speech. At the same time it was also seen as the spatial and temporal location of social contradictions, as perceived by Georg Lukacs, signified by the 'reified reproduction of immediacy' (Roberts 1999, p. 17). In 1920s Japan, the thinker Tosaka Jun called for the 'quotidianization of philosophy' and turned to examining both custom – a code for the commodity form – as a symptom that concealed lived history and the practice of journalism that reinforced the reified surface of daily life. Throughout the inter war period the category of the everyday had become the ground of an analytic minimal unity. Moreover, it would be seen as the empirical place for staging social and cultural transformations seeking to reclaim it for the masses (Marxian Communism, non-Marxian socialism) or contain them (fascism). If, as proposed earlier, the image was envisaged as the central event of modernity (Benjamin), its locus was the everyday, now grounded in the commodity form. But its identification with the global expansion of capitalism and the virtual transformation of the older nation-state system into an expanded version consisting of new states, colonies, and semi-colonies already challenged the received division between centre and periphery. More importantly, it contributed to the further exhaustion of an excluding national narrative and its effort to historicize spatial unity and homogenize time. In conception and experience, the everyday dramatized both diversity and temporal unevenness within an immanent framework and the existence of a world that no longer was simply divided between EuroAmerica and its 'shadow'. It also began to offer the possibility of another kind of history that was capable of recognizing how the working masses had been able to separate the collective experience of the dominated from 'religious and cultural fatalism' invariably employed by the ruling classes (Roberts 1999,

p. 16). Hence, the appeal to the everyday would now mean accounting for the active relationship of custom and commodity and new forms of representation promised by technological invention and innovation. This implied not simply a change in the putative content of history and the addition of new social constituencies to the story as subunits of the national subject (simply filling out a consensual order). Rather, it promoted a change in form that would appeal to new verbal and visual devices. It would also lead to a reconsideration of the question of subjectivity and social agency itself resulting from the replacement of the folk by the collective power of the working masses, who saw in the everyday the 'entangling pressures of necessity' Hegel observed a century earlier. While Lukacs constructed a critique of everyday life in the figure of the 'reified reproduction of the immediate', it was Walter Benjamin – in Europe – and Miki Kiyoshi in Japan who looked to the dissolution of art in the everyday and Tosaka Jun who saw in the day to day routines and frozen countenance of custom the necessity for representing them in their rehistoricization. However, it was a rehistoricization of what had been forgotten, despised, remaindered – in short the microscopic content of everyday life – now fused with what escapes the totalizations of reason and the nation-state. In fact, this effort to see the everyday as the site of rehistoricization, envisaged by a range of thinkers in the 1930s, referred to the observation that even though everyday life appeared as endless routine it was still marked by temporal unevenness. Under the achievement of a putatively smooth and even surface, different temporalities would manage to break through to emit significations of co-existing or co-eval modes of production and class affiliation. It was the place where the constant braiding of different temporalities took place. Benjamin, who referred to these temporalities in the shape of an arabesque, was prepared to trade the smooth, even surface of historical continuity, what he called historicism, for a remembrance which modernity had made into a form of cultural unconscious. National history was nothing if not an abstracted continuity with the past, cast in the form of a natural and naturalizing chronology. The present, now constituting the temporality in which the momentous concurrence of the past in the present was occurring, signalled the great drama of unevenness, staged and sharpened by the specific location of societies, like Japan, China, India and Brazil, which only recently had plunged into the process of capitalist modernization. What I am referring to is the role played by temporally rooted forms in the present and what Ernst Bloch identified as non-contemporaneous synchronisms, where past and present are not necessarily successive but simultaneously produced or co-exist as uneven temporalities, just as the then and now of modernity are co-eval, even though the former is invariably forgotten or repressed. In this drama of uneven temporalities – the contemporaneity of the non-contemporaneous – the past will be seen to break into and gathered up in the seemingly eternal present in the form of memoration, often acting as a revenant or ghostly spectre of the past bent on haunting and destabilizing the present, exacting its retribution for having been forgotten. The critical recovery of this memory from the surface of immediacy constituted an interruption – history as arrest – and provided both an occasion for reassessing the present's links to the past and thus the opportunity for historical experience. With this move, the everyday appears as a spectral precinct of time/space. The shadows of another life – sedimented temporal conditions – constantly act upon and are acted upon by the new. In this way, the now – Toska's *ima* or Benjamin's *jetzt* – could become the site for a qualitatively different experience of the now as an *historical* present. But this present would henceforth be grasped as an historical rather than simply a natural temporality, even though its very instantaneity made the everyday appear as nothing more than a static figure fusing nature and history into the image of atemporal eternity (Osborne 1995, p. 143). (In a certain sense, this might conceivably be the only way to 'experience' history since it is impossible to imagine how anybody could experience a national history that had already been made in the distant past, even by those who were presumably making it then, apart from declaring identity with it, what more properly has been called patriotism.) It was for this reason that Tosaka Jun argued that the everyday supplied the principles of historical temporality, even though nothing *seemed* to happen from one day to another.

The rejection of the identity of the everyday with immediate reality required the necessity to actualize the now for its repressed historical memories. The present actively conjuring up a past looms in sharp contrast to the national narrative that favoured the past over the present or a social scheme that simply conflated the present with the way things are. It should be pointed out that while this interpretative strategy calling for actualization was supposed to serve the cause of social transformation, the everyday and the observable co-existence of different temporalities during the 1930s was often enlisted for other, less progressive political agendas. Nothing better illustrates how the everyday embodied the symptoms of alienation, repressed revenants summoning a lost and forgotten past discounted by capitalist modernization and unfulfilled desire than those societies that either came late to capitalism or encountered it through the agency of colonization. Here, too, is a dramatic reminder of how the everyday structurally resembled the colony. In these societies, the constant concurrence of past in present was lived and experienced in the everyday which the national narrative had originally tried to eliminate by making the present continuous and identical with the past and the future. Throughout Asia in the 1930s, the everyday was often identified with an unchanging essential history, housing irreducible cultural characteristics or enduring folk custom. Both of these perspectives converged on the projection of an eternal everydayness and its capacity to summon the real. In India, Gandhi utilized these resources to construct a non-Marxian communitarian movement aimed at enlisting the peasantry who could recognize their everyday lives in its program. At the same time, Rabindranath Tagore, in one of his last essays, celebrated an enduring everydayness that had continued to escape imperial and national histories, the Japanese critic Kobayashi Hideo looked to literature, especially what he called the 'classics of life', to show how a certain commonness characterized the everyday in contrast to history. Folklorists in both Japan and China punctually fastened onto unchanging custom lived and reproduced over the long duration as the surest sign of an eternal everyday. In our time, the historian Ranajit Guha has looked back to a form of common and unchanging everydayness, revealed by Tagore, as the alternative to a history founded on the nation-state (Guha 2002, pp. 48–94). In other words, while some saw in the everyday the figure of incompletion and the occasion for remaking the world, others saw it as a completed reservoir of unchanging custom, irreducible experience and timeless value. In both cases, we can see the discrowning of the narrative of nation-state. In other instances, the phenomenology of the everyday was (and still is) elided with ethnography, or some form of native ethnology, as a way of reducing the remainder to the object of observation and description, atemporalization and dehistoricization. Yet all of these appeals to an atemporal and unchanging everydayness too often raised the risk of slipping into or inviting appropriation by fascist calls for an auratic community and its authentic culture.

The opportunity for rehistoricization promised by the everyday was often indistinguishable from the new cultural practices made available by technology and consumption culture. Hence, the category of the everyday, which had appealed to realism (recast by thinkers like Lukacs) as its epistemology, announced an unprecedented expansion of new cultural and representational forms supplied by new technologies, diverse artistic experimentation, film, photography, photomontage, documentaries and novels depicting the experience of daily life and more that called attention to both an historical moment and the foregrounding of everyday life as the ground of history. In this inventory photography was able to renew its lease on history by serving as the quintessential technique and art capable of interrupting the seemingly atemporal present and calling a momentary pause to it in the interest of critically recovering objects and events from it and reconsidering their contemporary significance and relationship to its concealed past. This ground, therefore, referred not simply to how images were indexed according to whether or not they belonged to a 'specific time', but rather how they 'entered into the legibility' of that time, what Benjamin called the 'Now of a specific recognizability' that momentarily brought past and present, then and now together in a configuration best expressed in the form of the collage. The new forms through which the everyday found expression also began to mark the path through which everyday life sought to historicize its present. In this way, the documentary that played such an important role in Soviet culture of the 1920s sought to construct the category of the everyday, while the documentary narratives based on direct observation on the streets of Tokyo by Kon Wajiro chronicled how modern life was remaking the world at the level of everyday consumption patterns, gestures, ways of dressing, etc. (Kon called his practice 'modernology' as against mere ethnographic reporting of the present urbanscape). At the same time, we can observe how new novelistic forms in Japan (the daily life novels of Kikuchi Kan and the detective stories of Edogawa Ranpo) and China (Zhang Henshui's *Shanghai Express*) were transcribing the textures and pace of urban life in serialized form in mass circulating dailies; the increasing use of montage for narrative, whether photographic or verbal, indeed a cinema in Shanghai itself devoted to producing 'vernaculization', performed both as the representational forms through which the masses were able to recognize themselves and the distractions of their everyday and the means that offered how best to imagine it as the place of constant remaking. Nakai Masa-kazu, an activist in the Japanese popular front in the 1930s, early recognized in the documentary the means to represent the real despite subsequent efforts to mediate its facticity. In his view, facticity, however fictionalized and recoded, is clearly still able to sustain its status as a recorder of fact as social reality, owing to the technology of reproduction. He also recognized in montage an entirely different kind of 'narrative' signifying a difference of everyday life and its sepa-ration from the linear story telling characterizing the feature films that captured spectators. But his most interesting innovation was to initiate a weekly magazine called 'Saturday' (*Doyobi*), which sought to vocalize and provide a voice to mass cultural aspiration. Through this newspaper, Nakai was convinced that the masses could give expression to their own everyday in such a way as to resist the encroachments of fascism and its desire to penetrate daily life. In Colonial Korea, Ch'oe Myongik's short stories employed the technology of detail to explore the bourgeois self and its claims to autonomy, while Yi T'aejun recalling Tagore and Kobayashi Hideo, imagined an Asian space outside of commodity culture that still embodied the material past in the present.

In many ways, this promise of rehistoricization prompted by the appeal to everydayness was momentarily actualized in action discourses produced by colonial Marxisms in the wake of decolonization after World War II. While time and space does not allow for a full treatment of how colonial Marxisms moved beyond the static forms of Western Marxism and its culturalist lock step, even the most cursory examination of early anti-colonizers will remind us of the timefulness of their analyses and how a temporalizing present, embarked upon a new itinerary from a disabling past to reach future expectations, recognized a process whereby a non-locational time generates imminent production through space to give it its 'objective' givenness. Any reading of Cesaire's 'Discourse on colonialism' will immediately recognize its moment and the world it speaks to and about. What characterizes Cesaire's almost paradigmatic discourse is how deeply it is imbedded in a specific spatio-temporality, suggesting further the relationship between the production of certain textual forms concerned with the labour of practice and organization and its capacity (desire?) to signify a specific project mediated by its durational present of everyday life in Martinique (Cesaire 2000, pp. 31–78). Cesaire's text marks a significant departure from more conventional and received forms of Marxian analysis by situating its authority (if not authenticity) in the everyday, the lived experience and what it could offer for tactics, organization and strategy. Similarly, Frantz Fanon moved uneasily between a ceaselessly dialectic tension attended by the immediate and specific moments of the colonial world – contingencies of a lived history, with all of the socio-economic structures it had created with the decolonization it had re-provoked and the desire to remember the 'universally human', the formations of human commonness. In this regard, this oscillatory position is what marked the colonial Marxism of the 1950s and 1960s and undoubtedly derived from the colonial experience before World War II which had already been foreseen by writers and activists like M. N. Roy, Jose Carlos Mariategui, C. L. R. James, Ho Chi Minh and others. Yet to suggest this difference with a putative Western Marxism is to not saddle a new metaphysical necessity on a Marxism deeply devoted to assessing and seeking to engage the 'current situation'. With Fanon, it is true that he unmasked a fugitive universalism of Europe (like the Japanese Takeuchi Yoshimi) and its destruction of whole peoples everywhere. However, it is also the case that he was convinced that the lived political experiences of the colonial world would disclose a new conception of humanity he called 'new humanism'. Already in *Black Skin, White Mask*, Fanon prefigured a program based on the temporal present and its capacity to reveal the shape of a future (Fanon 1968, p. 134). In the *Wretched of the Earth* he underlined the importance of 'examining' the conditions of the 'colonial context' at 'close quarters', that is, in its immediacy in order to make 'intelligible' the nature of the domination in its spatial compartmentalization – a world locked in space, much like a prison – timeless, even though it is a temporal moment that will be succeeded, its nowness, that permits him to grasp it and see beyond it (Sekyi-Oto 1996, p. 16, p. 18). A broken world, whose culture of reference has been violently shattered through ambivalent and often self-destructive consequences of 'spontaneity' leading to 'self-repudiation' and 'everyday, practical realism' replacing the 'effusion' of the day before, it manages only to 'substitute itself for the illusion of eternity' (Fanon 1968, p. 134). What must come forth is the work of 'national culture' consisting of the 'whole body of efforts made by a people and . . . through which that people has created itself and keeps itself in existence' (Fanon 1968, p. 232). Such a labour, Fanon announced, is neither a 'delving into the past', as such, nor a folklore or 'abstract populism' revealing the secret nature of people but actions attached to the 'ever present reality of the people' that 'prepares the ground where vigorous shoots are already springing up' (Fanon 1968, p. 253). If Fanon was riveted to the temporal immediacy of the now, Amilcar Cabral went a step further to define this arena as the 'everyday'. What Cabral meant by the scene of everydayness referred to a specific reality that signified History. 'The colonialists usually say', he wrote, 'that it was they who brought us into history: today we show that this is not so. They made us leave history, our history, to follow them, right at the back, to follow the progress of their history' (cited in Young 2001, p. 288). National liberation demands the rejection by all the people of their current social and economic circumstances. But it also requires acknowledging what had been taken away by the colonizers, 'their land' and the 'return of history'. History, in this sense, meant the culture of everyday life, which constituted for Cabral 'daily contact with the mass of people' (Cabral 1980, p. 145).

Finally, it is important to acknowledge how the everyday and its production of new forms of representation actually prefigured and supplied a different mapping of historical consciousness and history writing which, as Hayden White called for thirty years ago, were able to free themselves from the models of nineteenth-century art and science that held the former hostage to an unyielding formalism and the latter to a single truth – romantic art and positivist science – co-extensive with the formation of the national narrative that employed the exemplars of both (White 1978, pp. 27–50). However, White was, understandably, only partially correct in advising historians to look to newer models of art and science for imagining a different kind of history. What he overlooked was the crucial relationship between the form of the national narrative as the principal template for history's content and the temporality of the everyday, between the history of a specific national past – other people's past – and the rehistoricization of the present, a 'knowledge' of the past and the 'experience' and 'memory' of the present, and a completed then and a forever incomplete now.

Epilogue: the spatial continent of cultural studies

In the post World War II era, the everyday and its critique were momentarily refigured by thinkers like Lefebvre, Bachelard, Schutz and Goffman. Fleetingly, they also provided the basis of what we might call Third World or colonial Marxisms, as distinct from a unitary 'Western Marxism' locked in the immediacy of its geopolitical place and a constraining culturalism, now virtually museumified, which disclosed sensitive attention to uneven temporalities and unequal development to figure new strategies for liberation and political agendas in the wake of decolonization. In the industrial states of EuroAmerica, there were brief attempts to actualize the promise of social transformation pre-war writers had once identified with everyday life. However, that possibility was rapidly eclipsed by the wave of modernization and the global expansion of consumption and commodity relations. Moreover, new forms of modernization inaugurated by the state invariably altered the relationship between the everyday and the nation to ultimately fuse consumption with national citizenship and subjectivity. Under these circumstances, the concern for the everyday eventually passed into the practice of social history and ethnographic reporting that expanded the boundaries of its content to include new social constituencies and its entailing range of eventfulness, all within national borders and the temporal framework of a 'natural' and 'naturalizing' chronology. In the USA especially, cultural studies overtook and even displaced the vocation of social history and ethnography by appropriating their exemplars in the cause of further dehierarchization and all-encompassing inclusion promised by the move to multiculturalism. Hence, everyday life was assigned the new task of recoding the signifying system of bourgeois culture (reflected in the work of de Certeau) to ultimately become a postcolonial discourse that 'insinuates' the voice of the colonized other into the bourgeois text – its other half – to show how 'imitation' and 'mimicry' of the powerful signal resistance. Here, too, all objects – virtually everything, perhaps an exhausted attenuation of the 'trivia', and 'trash' Benjamin refused to 'inventory' but wished only to 'use' – are seen as potentially significant resources for possible resistance, aligning the practice of cultural studies itself with the 'older history from below' at the same that it embraces self-referentiality and self-representation and the 'free creativity of the enunciating subject' (Roberts 1999, p. 24). Above all else, the practice of cultural studies has come to be grounded in the supremacy of lived immediacy, 'the creative powers of the consumer' inhabiting a timeless, spatial continent and what Ranciere (1999) has called 'postdemocracy', where everyday life is automatically expanded with the greater differentiation and proliferation of social subjects – identities – where nothing is left out, and where even the victims of modernity are finally assimilated to their proper place in the consensual community and thus accounted for.

Notes

1   My thanks to Ranajit Guha (2002, pp. 20–21) for putting me on to Hegel's earlier appeal to the everyday. I have, however, moved in an entirely different direction from Guha's desire to fix experience in the site of an essentialized everyday, free from the corrosions of historical change. See also Hegel (1975, pp. 149–150).

References

Anderson, B. (1998) *The Specter of Comparisons, Nationalism, Southeast Asia and the World*, Verso, London.

Benjamin, W. (1999) 'A short history of photography', in *Walter Benjamin, Selected Writings, Vol. 2*, ed. M. W. Jennings, Harvard University Press, Cambridge, MA, pp. 507–530.

Cabral, A. (1980) *Unity and Struggle, Speeches and Writings*, trans. M. Wolfers, Heinemann, London.

Cadava, E. (1997) *Words of Light*, Princeton University Press, Princeton, NJ.

Cesaire, A. (2000) *Discourse On Colonization*, Monthly Review Press, New York.

Chaterjee, P. (1993) *The Nation and Its Fragments*, Princeton University Press, Princeton, NJ.

Fanon, F. (1968) *Black Skin, White Mask: The Experience of Blackman in a White World*, Grove Press, New York.

Fanon, F. (1970) *Toward the African Revolution*, Penguin, Harmondsworth.

Feather, H. (2000) *Intersubjectivity and Contemporary Social Theory: The Everyday as Critique*, Ashgate Publishing Company, Brookfield, VT.

Guha, R. (2002) *History at the Limit of World History*, Columbia University Press, New York.

Harootunian, H. (1999) 'Ghostly comparisons: Anderson's telescope', *Diacritics*, vol. 29, no. 4, pp. 146–148.

Hegel, G. W. F. (1975) *Aesthetics*, Clarendon Press, Oxford.

Kracauer, S. (1995) *History, The Last Things Before the Last*, Marcus Weiner Publishers, Princeton, NJ.

Osborne, P. (1995) *The Politics of Time*, Verso, London.

Poulantzas, N. (2000) *State, Power, Socialism*, Verso, London.

Ranciere, J. (1999) *Disagreement*, University of Minnesota Press, Minneapolis.

Roberts, J. (1999) 'Philosophizing the everyday', *Radical Philosophy*, Nov–Dec, 98.

Sekyi-Oto, A. (1996) *Fanon's Dialectic of Experience*, Harvard University Press, Cambridge, MA.

White, H. (1978) *Tropics of Discourse*, Johns Hopkins University Press, Baltimore, MD.

Young, R. (2001) *Postcolonialism*, Blackwell, Oxford.

Michel Maffesoli

EVERYDAY TRAGEDY AND CREATION
Translated from the French by
Karen Isabel Ocaña

In this essay, Michel Maffesoli exalts the poetry of the everyday, and a way of being that, paradoxically, opens one up to life through rituals that smack of a quest for divine nothingness. 'Everyday Tragedy and Creation' traces a series of connections: between Benjamin's particular form of empirical mysticism and the notion of messianic time, the vitalism of Nietzsche (and tangentially his rediscovery of the Greek notion of tragedy and destiny), that of Bergson with his concept of duration, as well as the sociological hermeneutics of Dilthey. In the course of his discussion, Maffesoli invokes Verlaine, Rimbaud, street theatre and Eliot, and proposes a Zen-like approach to everyday happiness. More generally, Maffesoli rejects the temporality of modernism and drama and celebrates instead the 'non-time' of the tragedy of living in the present within a medium of communal images and practices.

Keywords   drama/tragedy; everyday life; modernism; popular culture; prophesy; the sacred

I

It is always interesting to lend an ear to what mystics, dreamers and storytellers have to say, as they are often in tune with the natural forces secretly tapping into a given era. Their messages are naturally ahead of established facts yet largely in accord with everyday social life. They are also *paroxysmal* with respect to prevailing social conformism, hence marginal.[1] And yet, from the moment one wishes to be attentive to things in their nascent stages, it is important to know how to appreciate their true value. This is a good 'method' since these *creations* illuminate the paths taken by all practices, ways of being and thinking that, in a non-conscious manner, reject established values and other dogmatic representations in an era that has become alien for most people.

In this sense, the prophetic message is a highly pertinent one. Contrary to what is generally said in order to invalidate it, prophecy is not given to foretelling the future. In terms closest to its etymological roots as *pro phemi*, a prophet

Routledge
Taylor & Francis Group

speaks 'before' rather than 'ahead of' the people. He is content to voice the experiences that others keep to themselves. To select just a few examples among many, one may recall that for the mystics of the Kabbalah, the progressive temporality of modernism makes little sense. All that matters is the *moment* when eternity can be gathered in its plenitude. This insight has often been highlighted. Benjamin's *Theses on the Philosophy of History* reflect on the claim that for Jews 'every second of time constituted the strait gate through which the Messiah might enter' (1968, p. 264). In *messianic time*, this moment only matters, inasmuch as it offers self-fulfilment through a ritual of communion transcending the limits of the small self, hemmed in by time and all of its constraints and contingencies.[2]

It would be easy to conceive of this moment as nothing but a succession of moments: good or bad moments, as the case may be, but moments that one strives to live with qualitative intensity and that are, for want of anything better, accepted for what they are. Such a popular concern may, further, be compared to that of another mystic, Eckhart, for whom fulfilment consists in passing from the realm of *pure possibility* to that of *eternal actuality*. Such is the natural force of the eternal moment!

To connect with the subject at hand, I would say that the *drama* of history – be it individual or social – consists in being a perpetual possibility. It is characterized by an ideological tension, and its essential trademark is the 'project', or *pro jectum* tending towards the future. *Tragedy*, on the other hand, is of the present, and is nothing but a series of actualizations: passions, thoughts and creations that exhaust themselves in action, in acts of instantaneous expenditure, without reserve. There is a mythical vision – of which there are many contemporary illustrations – whereby each moment possesses, in some sense, the potential to express the manifold possibilities at the disposal of each person, individually, or of every social group, collectively. Time stands still, becomes intensified, to allow each individual and every situation to give the best of itself.

Let the world turn, events unfold, catastrophes strike, politics make a spectacle of itself; all that matters is a still point where what exists can be fully enjoyed. As T. S. Eliot put it: *at the still point of the world*. An aristocratic attitude, you might say. Yes, but a popular one, befitting the man without qualities, whose existence (conscious or not), is but a succession of fixed moments, whose concatenation constitutes the vital flow. In Bergsonian terms, one remembers the *duration* of such moments more than their *historical* connection.

II

This is the issue with respect to the moment and the present, since both lead back to life and experience, more than to representation or a theory of life with some kind of all-encompassing and rigid system. Life in its banality, in its cruelty too, and its mixture of light and shadow: this is what terrifies those who give voice to life or who have taken it upon themselves to make life speak. Vitalism and the diverse strands of a philosophy of life (Nietzsche, Simmel and Bergson) have received rather poor press, having always been under suspicion of corruption, by association with dubious influences. What cannot be controlled or rationalized is always disquieting, especially in the Western tradition, where the primacy of the cognitive functions and of reason has always been maintained.

It would be simple to establish a parallel between reason and the future on the one hand, and image and the present on the other. By image – as indicated earlier – is meant an image insofar as it presents or *actualizes* things immediately and directly. In any case, it is striking to note the coincidence of two phenomena: the forceful return of the image, and the multifaceted reinvestment of the present. Add to this, the renewed interest for the vitalist authors cited above.

What is most important though is the relation between life and the present, and both of these issues are generally left unspoken, or relegated to the category of things that are so self-evident, it is pointless to commit them to theory. To illustrate this nexus of ideas, there is a passage from the work of poet and novelist Julien Gracq, which reads: 'Nine tenths of our lived life – of the time when, after all, nothing is uninteresting for literature – takes place in a world without past or future. This is the world that Paul Eluard called *immediate life*, a world which is largely off limits to history, and where the drive for action and accomplishment has no purchase' (Gracq 1969, p. 878).[3]

This insightful analysis aptly underscores the atemporality of immediate life and the eternity of the lived moment as well as its intensity. It would appear that these *nine tenths* of life are what so interest literature, and theory even more so. Indeed, it is all of existence, all of those mundane elements that make up the ground of culture and the social tie. This plenitude is the conservatory, in the long run, of our being together – a surprisingly resilient togetherness, if you consider the many estrangements and impositions affecting it. Strength of the everyday!

I have said that one could give pride of place to poets. Verlaine comes to mind here: 'The humble life with its simple and repetitive tasks is a choice labour, deserving much love' (1964, pp. 146–147).[4] This is it, exactly: 'immediate life', non-theorized, non-rationalized, with no finality nor aim, but entirely invested in the present. It is this that calls for love; in other words, intensity. In this way, I repeat, giving these terms their strictest sense: no longer *tending towards* something (*ex-tendere*), but *tending inwards*, to what founds and constitutes being together (*in-tendere*). Investment in the present, *intensity*, is what ties me to others in order to live this mutual investment. A *choice labour* allows me to understand, at certain moments, the importance of the qualitative, the suspension of time, rituals of all kinds, and the uses and customs that in fact ensure the framework of the body social. Life without qualities is just what ensures, in a mysterious manner, the preservation of society. This leads us to the heart of everyday sociality, of banality, but also *survival* in the long run.

In a mysterious manner: meaning in the manner that is closest to the sort of mystery found in traditional initiation rites, allowing individuals to congregate and commune in something that surpasses them. Indeed, over and above any strictly religious form, perhaps what is truly sacred resides in this: an unfathomable connection ensuring a no less solid bond. And is it not in this sense that one can comprehend, on the level of the day-to-day, what ethnologists have called the *aura*, what historians of certain secret societies have named the *egregore*, and what theologians and philosophers refer to as the *habitus*? In brief, a way of being, based on a close relationship to the natural and social environment, lived before it is thought or theorized.

On the whole, everyday situations are thus a kind of naturally occurring founding ritual. The places and games of childhood, the circumstances of early enthusiasms, the apprenticeship of ways of thinking, the internalization of bodily postures, the assimilation of linguistic forms, and foremost, all sorts of non-verbal communication – all of these rituals – through successive layerings, create the framework of an organic solidarity without which society would fall apart.

There are times when these fundamental uses and customs are rejected, or at least relativized, through historical movements. Modernity belongs to this class of events, tending to erase or minimize all of the effects and contingencies of rootedness. At times, however, rootedness returns with a vengeance. Things such as territory, space, and symbolic values again make sense. The local and its nostalgic associations, its fragrances and flavours 'structure' individuals and groups. All of this is what gives the present its power of assemblage. One could say that a philosophy of becoming makes way for an anthropology of being, or, to repeat a statement of Durand's, the abstraction of history is replaced by the *density of the present* (1980, p. 157), or what may also be called the *labyrinth of the lived* (Moles & Rohmer 1972, cf. also Maffesoli 1979).

In this context, it is interesting to recall the etymology of the term *concrete*: meaning what stimulates growth or 'increase' with (*cum crescere*); that is, a time lending itself to being that is shared with others. It is an increase that, mirroring the surrounding flora, raises itself by taking root and nourishment from all of those trifling things making up common life. Consider this an ethic (*ethos*): the place that unites me with the other, the other that is at hand, the other that is the distant tamed.

That is what I am calling the sacred. However, this sense of sacred is not overarching, nor does it imply an abstract God or a rational state. Instead, this sense of sacred relates to an *immanent transcendence* that is constituted by the feeling of belonging, by shared passion or by a quasi-mystical sense of correspondence to one's surroundings. Consequently, it is no longer the universal that matters, but the particular in all of its carnality, affectiveness and essentially symbolic properties. Indeed, if one sees the *presentist* ambience in this light, it is what enables self-knowledge as well as the knowledge of others. Is this not what constitutes a symbol *stricto sensu*? It implies knowing oneself and acknowledging the other, but not as a purely rational, autonomous abstract entity. That is, not as a modern individual who separates himself from nature and distinguishes himself from his neighbours, and makes of this separation and distinction the basis of a well-known logic of domination and mastery. Rather, it implies a knowledge and acknowledgement lived by someone in a community framework: that of a group, a tribe, of *elective affinities*, all things of which tradition speaks, and which seem to be coming back before our very eyes. It is this very *feeling* that lends the present moment all of its tragic intensity.

At the same time, it is all of this that makes the present so alien to our modes of analysis, based as they are on and upon the universal. In fact, as modernist theories would have it, everyday life, insofar as it is concrete and rooted, is essentially alienated. As modernists, we are urged to overcome ordinary life and to liberate it from all of the constraints in which it is steeped, in order to attain a surplus of being. We are told that it is in history and the dialectics that drives it, that the modern individual will find fulfilment. All that links us to space and habits is more or less potentially damaging. We must, through rational and consciously assumed struggles and conflicts, dramatically break loose from everything that binds us.

III

One may recall, at this point, the work of Henri Lefebvre, who in his unique critical way of thinking, with all of the nuances bestowed upon it by his erudition, could nevertheless not desist from being critical of ordinary life. He must be praised for taking it into consideration, but he regards daily life only as something that should be overcome, that must, in a sense, be freed from itself. The title of his work is instructive in this regard: *The Critique of Everyday Life*. In this case, the critique consists in considering everyday life as the 'non-tragic' par excellence. For Lefebvre (1991, p. 169), kitsch objects and interior design in general serve to create an armature against the feeling of tragedy, which is to say against our consciousness of death and the inevitable finitude of life. The work of Moles (1971), on the contrary, shows how a 'psychology of kitsch' is entirely an *art of happiness*.

Lefebvre's stance is characteristic of an intellectual attitude incapable of grasping what imbues the everyday with its poetry. This *poetry* is clearly not present as such, but is nonetheless at work in such things as the ironic stance toward any grandiloquent moral certainties, the humour suffusing run-of-the-mill conversations, and most of all in the body language expressing our passion for all things social.

Evidently, each of these instances bears the stamp of the stereotypical; this is the reason, moreover, why they are so often overlooked, and yet it is important to realize that the stereotypes in question are rooted in founding archetypes. I would even say that it is precisely this dialectic between the everyday and the archetypical that constitutes the poetry of the everyday, and again it is this everyday poetry that becomes the wellspring from which, soon after, works of culture will emerge. In effect, this everyday poetry is where the richness of cultural experience can be found, the source of its longevity.

IV

As opposed to the dramatic, which tends to overlook it, the conditions of everyday life are ideally suited to the tragic; our task is to provide a theoretical account of this situation. If we take Dilthey's hermeneutics, for example, we see that it places its emphasis squarely on lived experience. On Dilthey's account, 'taking life as the starting point and maintaining a permanent connection with it forms the primary feature of the structure of the cultural sciences, based as they are on experience, understanding and acquaintance with life' (Habermas 1978, p. 178). What Dilthey proposes is an entire programme. This includes learned comprehension, but also a theory of empathy or *Einfühlungstheorie*, a theory that sees in 'poiesis' the basis of creation par excellence. *Poiesis* is not to be confused with a goal to be attained, nor with an end to be reached, but should be understood as the rooted sense, the lived sense, the sense that is exhausted *in actu* – in the act itself.[5] This is what founds the triadic relation of 'tragic/lived/ experience'. It is also the key to understanding what Moles (1995) refers to as the *science of the imprecise*.

If hermeneutics takes such a connection seriously, it provides a way to understand the many contemporary expressions of being open to the world and the tranquil raging of the present. That is, it can shed light on the need to live here and now, and the desire to enjoy whatever presents itself. It can explain, as well, the current disillusionment with all of the ideological and political agendas, and the extreme scepticism with which many abstract beliefs and representations are viewed. In a word, an amazing empiricism is afoot, placing its trust only in the presentation of the world, and appreciating only the world such as it is, not worrying about how the world should be or might be. Everyday experience is geared to living life as it is, to accommodating what exists, to making sense 'anyway' of an experience awash with vicissitudes and imperfections, seeing as it is the only life we are given to live. While it is clearly not the case in every epoch, it appears that in certain eras the collective unconscious is constituted by and for such an *immanentism*.

I would like to insist on this point; there is a poetics of banality, a poetics harbouring a high degree of intensity. I would tend to view it as a wellspring of societal energy, a watertable (so to speak), hidden from view but crucially important to collective survival. In a different context, Callois comments on what he calls the 'adventure of greyness' (Cioran 1986, p. 140). The expression fittingly describes this repository that is everyday life. A treasure is buried there, although it must be revealed to itself *within the framework of an organic knowledge and solidarity*. It should therefore not be disdained *a priori*. In keeping with the mysterious cycle of human history, the fascination of the future or the search for lost origins is sometimes superseded by the adventure of the present. And, one may well wonder whether the postmodern knights of the Holy Grail are not actually the adventurers of the everyday, who no longer speculate about faraway hypothetical ideals, but expend their energies living in the here and now, day by day, with a kind of existential intensity.

Simmel considered a key trait of this adventure to be precisely this focus on the 'here and now', life in its immediacy, 'the upsurge – he said – of the vital process in a point that has neither past nor future' (1989, pp. 319–320). The expression is paradoxical, yet it captures the intensity of the moment, that of Zen archers focusing more on their inner balance than on their aim, with the end result being given as a bonus. It is interesting to note that adventure as a concentration of the vital process is presented by Simmel as a form of experience. One could say as the 'ethics of aesthetics', inasmuch as it creates sociality.

When one is aware of the importance of 'form' as per Simmel (form being that which reveals and brings about the advent of being), one cannot but be attentive to the reversibility, the intimate connection, in a word to the cross-fertilization between adventure and experience. By keeping this in mind, one can understand how, more and more, an adventurous life goes hand in hand with a spiritual experience lived as a relationship with destiny – a relationship that must be counted on, but of which one is not entirely in control.

In this sense, the contemporary attitude connects with that of the tragic hero, especially as incarnated in the Greek tradition. The Greek tragic hero does not question; instead, he is proud to accept the dictates of fate. Cioran distinguishes between this type of heroism and that embodied by Job. The latter harasses the Almighty, demands explanations, and absolutely rejects what is and what happens, although his fate is out of his hands. Job's is a good example of the dramatic spirit, hounded by an obsession with the future, the project, the action – in a word – mastery of life. This sums up all of Judaeo-Christian culture. Tragedy, on the contrary, accepts destiny and acknowledges existence for what it is: precarious, finite, always submitted to the inexorable law of mortality, the finitude of every thing and every one.

As paradoxical as it may seem, the accentuation of the present is simply another way of affirming one's acceptance of death. To live in the present is to live one's death in the everyday, to confront it, and to assume it. The terms intensity and tragedy convey exactly this: the only things that matter are those that one knows will cease. Certain eras fight against this certitude and, therefore, will, action and projections for the future predominate. Other ages adapt, accommodate and adjust to finitude and give preference to the contemplation and enjoyment of the world, and to the present serving as their vector. Yet, such contemplation and pleasure are fleeting, shot through as they are with feelings of finitude, consuming with intensity everything that gives them life.

We may recall, for example, the difference between civilizations that bury their dead, and those that cremate them (Spengler 1973). The former express a desire for duration over time. Burial is a kind of negation or denial of death. It is a simulacrum of lasting life, the tomb being in a sense a second abode which, depending on the culture, may be decorated or where one may leave nourishment and other manifestations of the kind in the hope of a return to life. Cremation, on the contrary, enacts the fact that what is over is definitely over. The lapsing of life is affirmed and even constitutes through appropriate ceremonies an exaltation of the end. The force of destiny goes hand in hand with the force of oblivion. This ritual does not mimic rebirth, but rather recognizes that death is an integral part of life. This amounts to a paroxysmal display of immanentism, of a present that suffices unto itself and wants no truck with the illusions and comforts furnished by long-term aims.

Death and the present are at the heart of any number of contemporary phenomena. The music scene surely offers numerous examples, but painting does so as well, highlighting through various forms the 'minimalism' and the everyday banality of art that in the best of cases resembles the quest of mystics for divine nothingness. Street theatre is no less important, offering the moving spectacle of the vibrant new tribes living innocently in excess and chaos, in a surprising alliance where the closeness of death is coupled with a voracious zeal for life. Such an alliance brings to mind Rimbaud's invocation to a 'mysterious death', his 'sister of charity'. Actually, from the moment one makes one's life into a work of art, that is, makes one's existence into something all-encompassing, life contains its opposite and will strive to accommodate it.

Presentism and its incarnation in everyday life tends to give rise to a kind of intensity that, conscious or quasi-conscious of the ephemeral nature of all things, chooses to enjoy them to the fullest, at full speed, here and now. Consequently, the linear time of modern calculation, the mechanical time of industrial production and the time clock, the empty and homogeneous time of drama, make way for the discontinuities of lived time – the time of duration. The powerful moments or the banal events of the everyday are all that matter. One might say that only the banal is eventful. Thus the *kairos* of ancient philosophy meets up with a sense of opportunity, a generalized *savoir vivre*, a 'situationism' for all of those events that occur along the path of one's existence.[6] Contemporary research on cinema and advertising stresses the fact that the success of a given movie or advertising campaign hinges, precisely, on whether or not they express the eventfulness or the *adventitiousness* of life without qualities (Moles 1981).[7] In this sense, the image is definitely a medium for symbolic communication. It creates culture.

We are speaking here of *popular* culture in the strongest terms, by which I mean to say something that founds or creates society. That is, culture expressing a collective experience that, in the final analysis, thumbs its nose at any and all moral, political or economic imperatives issued by power in the abstract and overarching sense. The phrase 'in the final analysis' has to be uttered because there must exist, beyond a doubt, an apparent submission to the established order. What choice is there? But, above and beyond this apparent submission, there exists a substantial force of resistance, that of aloofness or that of dropping out, not causing a stir but expressing itself in a thousand little ironies, versatilities and revolts that come to light regularly in societies called democratic.

It may be possible to compare this ruse or anthropological duplicity with the fundamental immanentism or 'instinctive phenomenism' with which the cultures of the Far East, as well as the diverse religious philosophies that have constituted them, have been credited (Pons 1988, p. 43). This immanentism succeeds in expressing a relationship with nature and with others that compose what is finite, derelict and mortal in everyday life. Transcendent power, whether religious or political, may be exercised, but is considered no more than an illusion that is not to be trusted, or as a force that can be tempered by the much more precious demands of the everyday, of concrete existence expressing itself in the infinity of rites and customs – exacting, minutious, constraining – that make up a culture. A strange reversal of fortune, whereby the hegemony of Western thought, underscored by a linear conception of time, is now ceding to the 'mythical Orient' whose revenge it is to impose, through an accentuation of the present, an openness to the world, to its pleasures and its joys, as well as its cruelties and sorrows.

Is ordinary life becoming oriental? Perhaps not consciously, but certainly unconsciously, precisely to the extent that only the present lived moment exists, with others, in a given place. This is immanentism. Living that is transmitted through the medium of communal images, the bodies that one intensifies, the environment that one reinvests in, all things found under the aegis of the 'instinctive phenomenism' of empirical life. Life without qualities, the everyday life that in the strongest terms is 're-orienting' the world – giving it its profound sense.

Notes

1   Trans. Note: Maffesoli uses this term throughout his work to mean 'extreme' or 'acute'.

2   Cf. the analysis of Löwy (1992, pp. 95–126); also Eckhart (1942, p. 158).

3   Trans. by Karen Isabel Ocaña.

4 Modified trans. by Karen Isabel Ocaña.
5 For those with etymological knowledge of ancient Greek, the sense of *poiesis* would be very close to that of the creative act.
6 Trans. Note: *Kairos* in Maffesoli's usages means right or proper time; that is, the propitious moment for performing an action.
7 Cf. Durand (1982, p. 254); also Maffesoli (1993, 1996).

References

Benjamin, W. (1968) *Illuminations*, ed. & introduction H. Arendt, trans. H. Zohn, Fontana, London.

Cioran, E. M. (1986) *Exercices d'admiration: éssais et portraits*, Gallimard, Paris.

Durand, G. (1980) *L'Âme tigrée, les pluriels de la psyche*, Denoël, Paris.

Durand, G. (1982) 'Le génie du lien', *Eranos Jahrbuch*, vol. 51, p. 254.

Eckhart, M. (1942) *Traités et sermons*, Aubier, Paris.

Gracq, J. (1969) *Préférences*, vol. I, Pléiade, Paris.

Habermas, J. (1978) *Knowledge and Human Interests*, trans. J. J. Shapiro, Heinemann Educational, London.

Lefebvre, H. (1991) *Critique of Everyday Life*, trans. J. Moore, Verso, London and New York.

Löwy, M. (1992) *Redemption and Utopia: Jewish Libertarian Thought in Central Europe: A Study in Elective Affinity*, trans. H. Heaney, Stanford University Press, Stanford.

Maffesoli, M. (1979) *La conquête du present*, Re-ed, Desclée de Brouwer, Paris.

Maffesoli, M. (1985) *La Connaissance ordinaire: précis de sociologie comprehensive*, Librairie des meridians, Paris.

Maffesoli, M. (1993) *Éloge de la raison sensible*, Grasset, Paris.

Maffesoli, M. (1996) *The Contemplation of the World: Figures of Community Style*, trans. S. Emanuel, University of Minnesota Press, Minneapolis.

Moles, A. (1966) *Information Theory and Esthetic Perception*, trans. J. E. Cohen, University of Illinois Press, Urbana, IL & London.

Moles, A. (1971) *Le Kitsch; l'art du bonheur*, Mame, Paris.

Moles, A. (1981) *L'image communicationalle fonctionelle*, Casterman, Paris.

Moles, A. (1995) *Les sciences de l'imprécis*, Seuil, Paris.

Moles, A. & Rohmer, E. (1972) *Le Labyrinthe du vécu*, Méridiens, Paris.

Pons, P. (1988) *D'Édo à Tokyo: mémoires et modernités*, Gallimard, Paris.

Simmel, G. (1989) *Philosophie de la modernité*, Payot, Paris.

Spengler, O. (1973) *The Decline of the West*, The Modern Library, New York.

Verlaine, P. (1964) *Selected Poems*, trans. C. F. MacIntyre, University of California Press, Berkeley and Los Angeles, CA.

Ian Burkitt

THE TIME AND SPACE OF
EVERYDAY LIFE

This article argues that everyday life is related to all social relations and activities, including both the 'official' practices that are codified and normalized and the 'unofficial' practices and articulations of experience. Indeed, everyday day life is seen as the single plane of immanence in which these two forms of practice and articulation interrelate and affect one another. The lived experience of everyday life is multidimensional, composed of various social fields of practice that are articulated, codified and normalized to different degrees and in different ways (either officially or unofficially). Moving through these fields in daily life, we are aware of passing through different zones of time and space. There are aspects of everyday relations and practices more open to government, institutionalization, and official codification, while others are more resistant and provide the basis for opposition and social movements. Everyday life is a mixture of diverse and differentially produced and articulated forms, each combining time and space in a unique way. What we refer to as 'institutions' associated with the state or the economy are attempts to fix social practice in time and space – to contain it in specific geographical sites and codify it in official discourses. The relations and practices more often associated with everyday life – such as friendship, love, comradeship and relations of communication – are more fluid, open and dispersed across time and space. However, the two should not be uncoupled in social analysis, as they are necessarily interrelated in processes of social and political change. This is especially so in contemporary capitalism or, as Lefebvre called it, the 'bureaucratic society of controlled consumption'.

Keywords   everyday life; institutions; official; production; space; time; unofficial

Everyday life is profoundly related to *all* activities, and encompasses them with all their differences and their conflicts; it is their meeting place, their bond and their common ground. It is in everyday life that the sum total of relations that make the human – and every human being – a whole takes its shape and form. In it are expressed and fulfilled those relations that bring into play the totality of the real, albeit in a certain manner which is always

Cultural Studies Vol. 18, No. 2/3 March/May 2004, pp. 211–227
ISSN 0950-2386 print/ISSN 1466-4348 online   © 2004 Taylor & Francis Ltd
http://www.tandf.co.uk/journals   DOI: 10.1080/0950238042000201491

R Routledge
Taylor & Francis Group

partial and incomplete: friendship, comradeship, love, the need to communicate, play, etc.

(Lefebvre 1991, p. 97)

It seems to me that this statement from Lefebvre is so important because it
captures most of the things that everyday life is about. Everyday life must relate
to *all* daily activities because it is here that our social relations are produced and
reproduced. However, the term everyday life is often taken to mean the life we
all lead when the official forms of relations and activities are taken away, leaving
behind the residual relations of family and friendship – the more unofficial
relations of social life. Yet, this definition cannot be correct for, as Lefebvre points
out above, everyday life is related to all activities and is the sum total of relations
that constitute the human – and every human being – in terms of our collective
as well as our individual experience. In that sense, the everyday world is very
much about the activity of production, of *praxis* and *poiesis* (Lefebvre 2000/1971,
p. 31). These terms are taken from Aristotle, for whom *praxis* meant the attitude
that involves doing, transaction, and practical activity in general, while *poiesis* is
the productive, manipulative, and uncovering attitude of humans. For Lefebvre
these two terms are important because they refer to the everyday world of
production, which not only involves the making of products, but also

the term signifies on the one hand 'spiritual' production, that is to say
creations (including social time and space), and on the other material
production or the making of things; it also signifies self-production of a
'human being' in the process of historical self-development, which involves
the production of social relations.

(Lefebvre 2000/1971, pp. 30–31)

Thus, in order to produce, humans enter into the relations of everyday life and
bring into play the totality of the real, even though this is always incomplete and
open to further production and reproduction. We produce social time and space,
and we also produce the very basis of humanity, the processes of historical self-
development, as in the various cultural forms. In this way, the production of daily
reality does not occur somewhere beyond our reach in, say, the 'higher' echelons
of the state, and is then imposed upon us. Rather, the reality of everyday life –
the sum total of all our relations – is built on the ground, in daily activities and
transactions. This happens in our working relations but also in friendship,
comradeship, love, the need to communicate and to play.

The question of what constitutes everyday life, then, must be centrally
concerned with how these relational fields of human experience are produced
in time and space. However, to underline what I am saying here about the
different dimensions of everyday life, Lefebvre points out that there is not one
single system of the everyday; 'there are only sub-systems separated by

irreducible gaps, yet situated on one plane and related to it' (2000/1971, p. 86). Taking this idea further, what I want to argue here is *that the experience of everyday life is multidimensional,* even though it takes place on a single plane. It is multidimensional because it involves different social fields that are separated by irreducible gaps, yet which are permeable and, in their interaction, create a series of effects. These social fields are also produced in everyday life in ways that give them the appearance and feel – in our perceptions – of differentially materialized forms. Social time and space is combined in them in different ways to give some relations the feeling of more permanence and resistance to change than others. This gives the sense of a more fixed and stable 'structure' to these particular social fields. However, to develop this argument further, I need to first define more clearly what I mean by a social field.

Social fields and relations of power

Pierre Bourdieu defines the social field in terms of power, in that the field is the space of the relations of force between different types of capital, or between agents who possess differential amounts of one of the types of capital (1998, p. 34): economic, cultural or informational, symbolic and military capital (1998, p. 41). The state is the holder of meta-capital in that it possesses a monopoly of some of these forms of capital (especially that of physical force) and possesses all the forms of capital in a unique combination. The state and its various institutions also carry out the work of normalization and codification: of setting laws or regulations that clearly outline the legitimacy or illegitimacy of certain practices and what the forms of these practices are. For Bourdieu, the production of social space and the field of power involve the production of difference – the positions of distinction of the differential holders of capital and the relations between them. These relations are a series of gaps or of differences and distinctions between social agents, be they institutions, corporations or individuals in everyday life. Bourdieu tends to define social space in this invisible sense, existing as gaps and differences in a network of relations.

However, I would claim that this also involves a concept of space in a geographical sense as social relations and the fields of power are often produced and reproduced at specific institutional sites. Many of these are specially built to organize a specific set of relations and the differential positions within them. Thus, social space – the differences between agents – and geographic space – the built environment in which certain practices and relations take place – coexist but are not identical. We can understand social space as the power relations and differences between agents, without this being made manifest in geographic space. Yet, at the same time, these relations of difference are instantiated in social practices that are located in certain times and actual spaces in their social production and reproduction.

However, Bourdieu makes the point that although power works through a network of relations, nevertheless it is the most real reality (1998, p. 31). That is, because a field of power is the relational space of force between different types of capital, it acts as the principle of behaviour of the individuals and groups (the holders of capital) within it. Because social space as a relational field is invisible, it does not mean that its influence upon us is only imaginary – in fact, it is one of the most real determinate forces that we experience. Having said this, I feel that we must carefully define the different social fields that converge on the single plane of everyday life because, as I will explain throughout this piece, we experience them in diverse ways. Because we produce and reproduce social fields differently, whereby time and space is uniquely combined within them, some social fields feel to be more open to change and influence than others, although all are interrelated on the single plane of everyday life and change over time at different paces.

All of this, however, is fairly abstract until we begin to examine these definitions in more detail and ask how they work in practice. I want to begin to do this by looking at the different ways in which time and space is produced in various social fields, with specific reference to how the practices within them are officially or unofficially codified.

The official and the unofficial in everyday life

As Bourdieu pointed out, the state and its institutions carry out the work of normalization and codification of social practices, outlining the legitimacy or illegitimacy of certain forms of behaviour. However, the state and its institutions are not the only agents involved in this, for the explicit codification or articulation of social practices and ideas can occur in any social field. Following the ideas of the Russian linguist Voloshinov (1986), we can begin to understand how the process of official and unofficial forms of codification and articulation work. There are established or official systems of ideas to be found in the social fields of science, art, religion or ethics, some aspects of which may have the backing of the state in terms of funding or support. Ideas from these social fields may also influence state policy and legislation. In contrast, unofficial forms of social practice and articulation could be seen as the living tissue of everyday relations and activities that are less systematized and explicitly codified. The relations of love, intimacy and friendship, for example, are social practices of a less codified, explicitly rule bound nature. The social rules that bind such relations are more implicit and, as such, these daily activities feel as though they have a less fixed quality to them: rather, they feel to be more open, fluid, and emergent.

However, the official and the unofficial are not two separate realms: rather, they are open, permeable and necessarily interdependent. The unofficial realm is the living tissue of social life upon which official social life rests and, indeed, official ideas and ethics are often a crystallization of unofficial ideas and practices. In turn, official codification exerts a powerful influence on the unofficial aspects of daily life, setting the tone and the parameters of activity. Take, for example, the family, perhaps one of the most private and intimate spheres of everyday life, which rests on the emotional bonds between its members. Even here, in the private realm, we are subject to official ideas of what the family should be and how family life should be lived. State policy and legislation shape the types of families we live in and, along with religious authorities, seek to define exactly what families are. The recent debates over whether gay couples should be allowed to marry or to adopt children is an illustration of this. However, much of the social pressure that has led to such debates comes from the unofficial spheres of everyday life, where more gay couples are living together more openly and wanting social, legal and, in some cases, religious recognition of their union. There are also many more single parent families. All of this is calling into question and leading us to redefine what a family is. It is also a good example of the ways in which the official and the unofficial interact in everyday life to call established ideas into question and generate new ones.

It seems to me, though, that most social theory and philosophy overlooks this necessary relation between the official and the unofficial realms of everyday life. Instead, the focus is drawn towards *either* the official codification and normalization of practices and the institutional apparatuses of the state *or* to the emergent properties of daily life, as if these are two uncoupled realms (Shotter 1993, p. 80). An example of the former trend is to be found in some of Foucault's works, which have concentrated on disciplinary power and its employment in institutions such as asylums and prisons, or in the official discourses of science, medicine, and ethics. According to Foucault (1977, 1979), disciplinary power has as its focus two main entities – the body of the population and that of the individual – and it operates according to the discursive codification and regulation of practice through observation and description. Interestingly, in the quotation below, Foucault contrasts this to past forms of power where the everyday or ordinary individual and their practices were not so carefully scrutinized.

> [F]or a long time ordinary individuality – the everyday individuality of everybody – remained below the threshold of description. To be looked at, observed, described in detail, followed from day to day by an uninterrupted writing was a privilege ... The disciplinary methods ... lowered the threshold of describable individuality and made this description a means of control and a method of domination.
>
> (1977, p. 191)

It is interesting to note from the above that while Foucault believes that the threshold of describable individuality has lowered under disciplinary forms of power, he does not say that he feels this has disappeared altogether. However, in other writings, Foucault suggests that 'the individual' is not just opened up to greater levels of description and codification by power, but that he or she is 'one of its prime effects' (1980, p. 98). Thus, the individual is no longer the subject of a form of power but is produced by that very power. The clash between these two contrasting positions is, I believe, a product of Foucault's concentration on institutions and their official discourses and the neglect of the unofficial aspects of everyday life. Surely, as individuals, we are the products of the way in which official and unofficial discourses and social practices interweave within the single plane of immanence that is everyday life?

This makes the lived experience of everyday life multidimensional, because it is related to all activities and to all the different social fields. Moving through these fields in daily life, we are aware of passing through different zones of time and space. As Harvey puts it, our lives are composed of 'a variety and hetero-geneity of socio-ecological and political-economic conditions' (2000, p. 244) that make the very experience of life heterogeneous or multidimensional. Just as there are social fields in which practices and relationships are made more open to government and official codification, so too are there social fields that are constituted as spaces of hope and resistance. As de Certeau puts it, unofficial practices 'continue to flourish in the interstices of the institutional technologies' (1986, p. 189). Commenting on Certeau's position, Gardiner says:

> whereas the procedures and techniques (or what Certeau terms 'strategies') that Foucault describes are visible manifestations of power, and occupy an identifiable physical space (the academy, the clinic, the prison), unofficial or marginal practices ('tactics') operate without such a fixed locus.
>
> (2000, p. 168)

In such unofficial and marginal practices, the symbolic and material products of official institutions can be transformed into something quite different than that intended by official powers. Also, because the unofficial practices, or tactics, do not colonize a specific space, they are more dispersed and hidden as well as being 'improvised in response to the concrete demands of the situation at hand' (Gardiner 2000, p. 172). Rather than seeking a space to colonize they are more temporal in nature, relying 'on the art of collective memory, on a tradition of popular resistance and subversion passed on from generation to generation since time immemorial' (Gardiner 2000, p. 172). However, as we shall see shortly, I think such practices do have their spaces, as they must be instantiated in both time and space. It is the way that time and space is combined in such practices that is the key to their difference from official practices.

Officially and unofficially codified social practices can be further defined by arguing that the official is based on a 'game' form of association, while the unofficial is based on play. One could say that a game employs strategies, in that the efforts of players have to be co-ordinated into an overall move or formation within the rules of the game. For Mead (1934), the role of games in childhood was that they allow us to master more formal, rule-like behaviours, and involve the internalization of collective rules as a generalized other – a kind of super-ego that is a psychic understanding of the laws within a social field. People also need to develop the necessary skills to be able to participate properly in the game. In contrast, play is less formal interaction in which people take the part of the other and empathize with their position and perspective. In play, we can be more experimental using our imagination to construct scenarios, stepping into many and varied roles, even changing such supposedly 'fixed' attributes as gender. Here people – especially children – develop all-round human capacities as opposed to skills: capacities such as empathy, understanding, and fellow feeling. These aspects of human relations – of leisure pursuits, hobbies, the sharing of pastimes, enthusiasms, intimacies, emotions and the morals and ethics of care and concern – are more related to play forms of interaction than games, which seem more synonymous with the rule-bound and the official. These different forms of activities, along with their times and places, are mixed in varied ways in everyday life. Play and games are not just stages in child development, as Mead thought; they are the basis for different forms of interactions throughout life.

However, this also means that they serve as bases for the formation of individual selves, so that the individual is not just constituted in the realms of official social practice and discourse. In fact, the root of modern forms of individuality is in play during the years of childhood and although this area of practice and the self may be curtailed in later years, it still remains a formative influence on the self. I therefore believe Foucault is wrong to suggest that the individual is only the effect of disciplinary power, for the source of what he referred to at one point as 'everyday individuality' is still to be found in those activities of daily life that are less officially codified.

The mixing of the official and unofficial, the game-like and the playful, can be seen in all aspects of everyday life and is also reflected in discourse. As Bourdieu illustrates, state institutions are often involved in the formal codifica-tion of 'proper' ways of speaking and in the teaching of correct grammar. However, one could look at an unofficial, yet popular, speech genre like rap as a more playful genre, evolving its own patois and playing with formal grammat-ical structure. Indeed, Saussure's distinction of language and speech follows the contours of official and unofficial discourse, with language being more of a codified structure, whereas speech is the more fluid and mobile use of language in everyday life. As Certeau says, speech is the unmarked, existing primarily in time, rather than being the codified and formal language of official discourse. Whereas the official is more monologic in form and is often explicitly codified as rules of grammar and correct usage, speech is not objectified in such a way. Unofficial speech is more dialogic and changes more quickly (Harvey 2000). It is reliant on oral traditions of public discussion, debate and storytelling.

However, the two are necessarily interrelated to such a degree that one would not survive without the other and, thus, there is constant transmutation between official and unofficial speech genres. For example, official texts are interpreted and works are consumed, including art and novels, by people reading their own meanings into texts. Voloshinov (1986, p. 91) has shown how official discourse needs unofficial discourse in order to stay a living language as opposed to a dead one, as it is in everyday speech that official discourse is interpreted and, in some cases, critiqued and opposed. In turn, aspects of unofficial speech styles, such as elements from rap or slang, enter the official language or change it in some subtle way.

However, this assumes the continuation of a living tissue of informal relations in everyday life to which speech refers and in which it is made significant. While I emphasize the importance of this aspect of everyday life, I also realize that less formalized and unofficial networks of practice and relationships are under threat. This comes not only from institutions that aim at the disciplinary governance of various social fields, but also from the current bureaucratized form of consumer capitalism that is colonizing everyday life. As Lefebvre remarks, in such a society the leisure time that was once a reward for labour, which was spent in celebration and in revitalizing social ties, now becomes a generalized display for the passive consumer. Advertising and consumerism dominate leisure time as signs for consumption and for the production of difference. As in Baudrillard's work, signs are seen to lose their referent and float free in an endlessly circulating sea of signs. Everyday life becomes an object of social organization, the 'bureaucratic society of controlled consumption' where the scope and limits of rationalization are set, and the object of its organization becomes consumption rather than production. Is the threshold of the description of everyday life and individuality lowering, as Foucault thought, opening this field up to rational control and new techniques of government? This could be taken as read in the shift from what Lefebvre refers to as signs to signals. The latter (which include codes, such as the Highway Code) are not just referential signs; they are systems of compulsion, 'practical systems for the *manipulation* of people and things' (Lefebvre 2000/1971, p. 62).

Yet it is the displays of reality in modern consumer capitalism that have the most notable implications for Lefebvre. This is because all referent, all substantiality fall away from the symbolic system, destroying the certainty human groups once had that signs possessed some referent external to the symbolic system. Now we have form without content. Taken together with the spread of signals, this means that the bureaucratic society of controlled consumption aims 'to cybernetize society by the indirect agency of everyday life' (Lefebvre 2000/ 1971, p. 64). Foreshadowing Baudrillard, Lefebvre writes,

> The 'cool' prevails. Everything is ostensibly de-dramatized; instead of tragedy there are objects, certainties, 'values,' roles, satisfactions, jobs,

situations and functions. Yet there are powers, colossal and despicable, that swoop down on everyday life and pursue their prey in its evasions and departures, dreams and fantasies to crush it in their relentless grip.

(2000/1971, p. 65)

Thus, there is an aim to create the perfect closed system of controlled consumption that encapsulates everyday life, systematizing thought and structuring action. However, unlike Baudrillard who, in my view, seems to say that this project is complete, so much so that his own understanding of contemporary society itself mirrors the cybernetics that attempts to enclose it, Lefebvre believes that something intervenes to prevent this occurring. This is not a certainty, however, for 'time alone will reveal whether it will be possible for those who are willing to recapture . . . the lost harmony of language and reality, of significant actions and learning' (Lefebvre 2000/1971, p. 73). As soon as people wish for something different, they short-circuit the system, no matter how temporarily. But why should we do this? Why dream of something beyond a society of controlled consumption that aims to satisfy our every need? I will argue that such wishes and dreams are the products of everyday individuals who still reside in the interstices of institutional technologies and in some of the more unofficial networks of everyday life. However, this will form the conclusion of the piece and, for now, I want to move on to discuss the time and space of everyday life.

The production and articulation of everyday life in time and space

For Williams (1977), time was the most important aspect in our everyday experience of society. It is only when we look back in time that we experience the social world as an objective formation of fixed and stable institutions and ideologies that are somehow separate from subjective experience. Thus,

> relationships, institutions and formations in which we are still actively involved are converted, by this procedural mode, into formed wholes rather than forming and formative processes. Analysis is then centred on relations between these produced institutions, formations, and experiences, so that now . . . only the fixed explicit forms exist, and living presence is always, by definition, receding.

(Williams 1977, p. 128)

Contrasted with this, the subjective sense of social life in the here and now, as we live it, has a more fluid and open feel: it seems like a reality still to be made rather than one that is already made. Everyday life as it is currently being lived often feels as though it is disordered and formless, while institutions appear to stand over and against us as something already made, not even by our own hand. For Williams, then, society is clearly composed of time and this runs like a river through our everyday lives. The problem that social theorists have often referred to as the division of subject and object is not, then, one of two separate locations of experience composed, on the one hand, by the 'internal' mental and emotional experience of life and, on the other, the 'external' nature of social institutions. The subject–object split is an appearance that occurs through time rather than being an ontological reality. It is an appearance constituted in time because we always think of the social in the past tense as already formed 'structures', which seem divorced from the current 'subjective' moment of the everyday where we are engaged with social life as it is emerging around us. This emergence feels in part responsive to our actions, because it is yet to be fully formed and therefore open to shaping. It also engages us in its still-to-be openness in a way that the past does not (although, as Mead (1934) pointed out, the past is also open to reconstruction).

Williams is not trying to divorce present from past and to say that the conception of society and self as objective is a false idea. He wants to account for the influence of the past in terms of social formation and ideology and the pressures these exert on us in the present. Humans never act as a blank slate, even when we act impulsively, as our actions are always connected in some way to the past. The present moment, too, soon becomes the past, and we make sense of it by connecting it to what we already know, articulating it in relation to some already formed ideology. While that ideology may be changed in the process, past and present are linked in a continuity of practical consciousness and discursive or ideological articulation of present experience. Nevertheless, the feeling of an open and fluid present is an important moment in the social process.

It would be wrong, though, to suggest that the present moment of action is uniformly experienced as open and fluid, while the past is understood as composed of objective, already formed institutions. Everyday life is more complex and nuanced than this. In everyday life, our experience ranges daily from encounters with institutions that have more fixed and stable form and are located usually in an identifiable geographical space, to more unstable and fluid experiences of open and permeable relationships. Indeed, what are institutions if not an attempt to fix in geographical space and in codified language the relational forms and activities of the past? However, these institutions confront us in the present as actual realities that are hard to change, even though as produced realities they are open to change over time. Change happens in official institutions because they are open to the influence of unofficial practices and articulations of feeling, the difference being that, in official institutions, the social practices or ideas that compose them change more slowly. This is because institutions and customs are relations and activities that, although they have developed over time, are codified forms of practice that sediment in two ways: in geographical spaces and in human bodies.

Firstly, in a geographical sense, institutions are often associated with special buildings that are designed to regulate set practices according to codified rules. These rules are often written down as codes of practice or as more formal constitutions that outline peoples' rights and duties. We have already noted how Foucault studied various institutions in this light, such as the asylum, the clinic, the school and the prison. Secondly, in a bodily sense, the rules governing various institutions, and of social life more generally, are embodied in each of us as individual persons throughout our lives within particular social fields. These relations and activities sediment in, and expressed as, habitual practices or customs wherein the rules and codes disappear from consciousness and practices are produced unconsciously by each of us, who 'simply know' how to 'carry on' in social life. The aim of institutional practices is to make themselves official, accepted, and, ultimately, 'second nature'. Time and space are relatively solidified here, as these practices take on a more explicitly codified and enduring form. As Williams puts it, 'social forms are evidently more recognizable when they are articulate and explicit' (1977, p. 130).

Yet, Williams is surely right in that there is another side to everyday life, which is the experience of living presence in which things are not so formalized but are, at the extremes, emerging, indistinct, yet to be articulated experiences. The awareness of such experiences is described by Williams as 'practical consciousness', which is 'always more than a handling of fixed forms and units. There is frequent tension between the received interpretation and practical experience . . . Practical consciousness is almost always different from official consciousness' (1977, p. 130). In fact, the relations between practical consciousness and the already articulated official consciousness are always exceptionally complex. Changes in style or presence 'do not have to await definition, classification, or rationalization before they exert palpable pressures and set effective limits on experience and on action' (1977, p. 132). These are what Williams refers to as changes in 'structures of feeling', in that they are sensed before being consciously articulated and reflected upon, combining thought as felt and feeling as thought in a living and interrelating continuity. Once these have fully formed, a new structure of feeling will have begun to appear. Forms of art and literature are prime examples of the emergence of structures of feeling, where the style and ideas expressed appear to be new and cannot be reduced to established belief systems or institutions. It also can include elements of social and material (physical or natural) experience that may lie beyond articulate systemic beliefs.

Those aspects of everyday life that could be described as more informal or unofficial relations and activities are produced in a very different way to the more official and fixed structures, being more dispersed across time and space. Because of this, they are less evident as they do not rely on institutional space and clearly codified rules, but materialize in the more informal spaces of the home, the streets, playgrounds, cafes, bars, restaurants and other such spaces in the modern urban landscape. These are the places where friends and comrades meet and talk and laugh and think. It is no surprise that in the last 200 years or more, the place of revolutionary ferment has stereotypically been the drinking den and the cellar. However, in the less formal sphere, relations are constituted largely over time and are less reliant on space, although various spaces are needed in which they can materialize. What bind these relations into a formation are not institutionalized spaces and codified sets of rules, but human emotions such as loyalty, mutual needs, and interests. These relations are then produced temporally more than spatially and can exist in a number of domains, even those not specially designed for their purpose (if they have an explicit purpose). They rely on memory and feeling and the desire to constitute them again in a future time and place. In this sense, they are also registered in the human body, but not so much as fixed habit (although even informal relations can become that) as much as open possibilities fuelled by shared desire, need, and interest.

What this illustrates is that in the contemporary world the lived experience of everyday life is rich, complex and multidimensional: it is an experience of diverse and differentially produced and articulated forms, each combining time and space in a unique way. Although there are irreducible gaps and differences between these social fields, nevertheless they overlap with one another on the single plane of everyday life to create a series of effects. As such, the past and the present (or what we have traditionally thought of as objective and subjective experience) are not so clear cut in the lived moments of everyday life. In these lived moments, the various social fields feel as though they invite and guide our actions in different ways, some exerting power in a looser and less determinate form. This is because they are produced differently depending on the time and space combinations within them. As Melucci has said with respect to time:

> Everyday time is multiple and discontinuous, for it entails the never-ending wandering from one universe of experience to another: from one membership network to another, from the language and codes of one social sphere to those of another, semantically and affectively very different from it.
>
> (1996, p. 43)

We can, of course, say the same thing about space for, as both Melucci and Giddens (1991) have shown in their different ways, we now live in a globalized world where new information and communication technologies allow for the compression of space (and thus time also). One can now communicate instantaneously with people who live on the other side of the world and receive television images of events from the farthest flung places in a second. Global space is thus a routine datum of everyday life, alongside the more local aspects of relations, activities, and communications that were its traditional basis. Space as well as time is now multiple and discontinuous. Thus, as Melucci (1996) points out, today a well-adjusted person must be able to make flexible transitions between different planes of experience in living their everyday life.

This gives to subjective experience a highly variegated formation. In the early decades of the last century, Voloshinov began to unravel the complex relation between structures of feeling and fully articulated discursive forms of consciousness. For Voloshinov (1986), the 'higher' levels of social conscious-ness were formed from the official levels of institutionalized and codified social practices in which past social activities and ideas are crystallized. This forms a consciousness of 'reality', of what already exists, which is often hard to change as it is supported by institutions that attempt to structure the possible field of action in geographical space, and by dispositions and habits instilled in the body. However, below this strata of consciousness is another level of awareness of the structures of feeling, which are supported by the dimensions of behavioural emergence, responsiveness to change and innovation, and the articulation of new forms of living. This reflects the more unofficial and less systematized dimension of social and inner speech. In any one moment of subjective experience, our thoughts and feelings range from the lowest level where the social articulation of an experience may be indistinct, haphazard or ephemeral, to the upper strata that are more vividly and exactly articulated. The former thoughts, feelings and semi-articulated ideas are more fleeting and transitory, whereas the latter are more clear and vital. At the lower level, thoughts and feelings are also more mobile and sensitive, conveying social changes more quickly and vividly, as in popular culture. Here emerge the creative ideas that act to restructure and re-articulate official discourses and practices, although in the process they undergo the influence of official discourses (Voloshinov 1986, pp. 91–93).

In contemporary society, where people must cope with regularly crossing into new social fields of activity, and where the pace of change is more rapid, individuals must rely less upon fixed and habitual forms of practice and discourse to reflexively monitor their behaviour. Giddens (1991) has charted the growing importance of the reflexive monitoring of behaviour in late modernity. However, his work can be criticized for the view that reflexive consciousness is now freed from all cultural constraints and habits (Adams 2001). It is not so much that we are now living in a post-traditional society where all customs and habits that once controlled behaviour are called into question. Rather, it is more to do with the complex interweaving of social fields, in which occurs a clash of dispositions towards habitual behaviour (Dewey 1922/1983). It is where such dispositions clash that reflexive consciousness is drawn upon to assess the social contexts and the various dispositions towards action in order to decide upon the best course. Although Dewey outlined this process 80 years ago, one can say that this subjective experience is now more acute then ever. It is not that the habitual dispositions towards action, backed by official institutions, customs and discourses, are losing their power, more that there is in everyday life such a divergent yet overlapping array of social fields that reflexive consciousness is forced to play a greater role.

What we are talking about here, in terms of the constitution of subjective experience in modernity, is also interlinked with the complex interweaving of time and space through social life and through the self. There are the more slowly changing official aspects of social life and consciousness, the ones that seem more objectified and to stand as objects over and against us. Then there are the more quickly changing strata of unofficial experiences, which are fleeting or ephemeral in their constitution. In modernity there are perhaps more of these experiences, where not only time but also space feels to evaporate before our very eyes, as 'all that is solid melts into air' (Marx 1848/1977, p. 224). Within everyday life, some practices are fixed more in geographical space and relatively frozen in time, while other more fleeting experiences are quick to pass and do not have such a substantial materialization in geographical space.

Everyday life can then be viewed as a complex relation between fluid, open processes and relatively more permanent forms of belonging and association, both official and unofficial. In it, there is a heterotopia of spatial form just as there is a heteroglossia of linguistic forms (Harvey 2000, p. 240): a variety of official and unofficial spaces and the interaction of their different discourses and social practices. While the official and monologic are more formal and less easy to change, they are nevertheless in a necessary relation with the unofficial practices and discourses, which are playful and more fluid, dynamic, and rapidly changing.

Because of this, in the process of social change, the unofficial sphere of everyday life often forms the basis for political opposition. Melucci (1989) has stressed that it is in the unofficial networks of everyday social relations and activities that group meanings are formed which provide a basis for the politics of opposition. These informal networks become 'experimental laboratories' for alternative lifestyles and a free range for the more playful side of the self. Again, then, we find in Melucci's work, as in Certeau's and Lefebvre's, the idea that the official, institutional realm has its limits. Although its tentacles have extended into all aspects of everyday life, especially in the bureaucratic society of controlled consumption, it still cannot control every aspect of every social field. Of course, not everyone is living a daily life of political opposition and many are seduced into the world of bureaucratically controlled capitalist consumption. Yet, there still exists the time and the space in the everyday world for those who are willing to recapture the lost harmony of language and reality, of significant actions and learning, to work out some alternative lifestyles (Lefebvre 2000/1971). It is on the basis of such lifestyles that those social movements, which oppose capitalism and certain aspects of the bureaucratic state, rise up and draw their strength. In consumer societies where power works through seduction rather than repression (Bauman 1991), relations of power become more heterogeneous and less obvious. It is part of the work of those who practice alternative lifestyles, or hold alternative values, to occasionally manifest themselves as a social movement and, in so doing, make what they oppose also manifest as power.

However, in the bureaucratic society of controlled consumption, where individuals are seduced rather than repressed by power, what is it that makes people want to resist, to practice alternative lifestyles and generate alternative meanings? Lefebvre has claimed that, paradoxically, in order to keep selling new products to fulfil the promise of satisfying every need, consumer capitalism must produce dissatisfaction. If satiety of every need were achieved, people would no longer buy. To buy, people must want. In the bureaucratic society of controlled consumption, not only must satisfaction be produced and manipulated, so too must dissatisfaction. Thus, the satiety of needs

> cannot provide an end, is devoid of finality and of meaning. For a distinction must be made between satisfaction, pleasure and happiness. Pleasure was once the prerogative of the aristocracy who knew how to give it a meaning-ful place in their lives; but the bourgeoisie can, at best, only achieve satis-faction; and who will discover happiness?
>
> (Lefebvre 2000/1971, p. 80)

The last comment above is extremely pertinent for in recent years many social surveys in Britain have shown that while, on the whole, many people feel themselves to be wealthier than they were twenty years ago, nevertheless they feel themselves to be less happy. This is largely because, in order to earn the money to participate in consumer capitalism, people are working longer hours and have less free time than they once had. The leisure time people are left with is often of such small duration that it has to be 'time managed' to get the most out of it. There is a loss of time for some of the more valuable things in human life – for meaningful work and hobbies, family and friends, love and play. Also at work, tighter management control of task and time adds to the feeling of a society under pressure and less happy. There is then an increase in the kind of leisure pursuits aimed at the 'prospect of departure' (Lefebvre 2000/1971, p. 85), which include things like tourism as well as the use of recreational drugs.

Indeed, a focus for the political activities of new social movements is often the control of time and space, as well as the control over the production of social meanings. For example, the squatters' movement is about the reclaiming of social spaces from private property owners and speculators, and the 'reclaiming the streets' campaigns are about taking back the streets as public spaces for celebration, protest and self-expression, as opposed to the current consumer capitalist function of the streets. It is no coincidence that during the recent anti-globalization protests in countries all over the world, the targets for vandalism during these protests are the large global corporations like McDonalds and Starbucks that are currently colonizing our city streets. Furthermore, those social groups whose lifestyles form the basis for new social movements – such as squatters, travellers, trade unionists or religious groups – are also involved in the issue of the control of time, either by dropping out of the world of work altogether, or by resisting attempts to constantly rationalize the time and space of work and life. As Melucci has said, social movements have their roots in a dimension other than the managed time of work and consumption, 'in the everyday network of social relations, in the capacity and will to reappropriate space and time, and in the attempt to practice alternative lifestyles' (1989, p. 71). This makes collective conflicts increasingly personal as they revolve around the meanings through which certain social individuals organize their lives and mobilization rests on 'the capacity of individuals to initiate action and to control the space, time and interpersonal relations that define their social existence' (Melucci 1989, p. 71).

In this way, everyday life forms the time and the space in which some individuals address the issue of the loss of value in the bureaucratic society of controlled consumption. In this world of endlessly circulating signs that act primarily to sell the latest consumer goods, there are still referents that have a meaning for humans, which can be found in the relations of everyday life. Everyday life is the arena for an effort towards 'disalienation', making a contribution to the art of living and forming a critique of everyday life (Lefebvre 1991, p. 40, p. 66, p. 199). This is because the desire to escape everyday life, no matter how distorted this desire becomes as expressed in the needs of consumer capitalism, is still nevertheless a real desire to transcend the routine of the everyday. Alongside this desire, the attempt of the society of bureaucratically controlled consumption to colonize the space of everyday life ultimately fails. As Gardiner has said of Lefebvre's conclusion:

> [he] suggests that although modernity attempts to homogenize and commodify space, this state-sponsored project of 'normalization' ultimately provokes opposition and negativity. A plurality of what [Lefebvre] calls 'differentiated' spaces continues to persist under neo-capitalism, where difference is registered and 'linked to the clandestine or underground side of life'.
>
> (2000, p. 97)

A truly revolutionary social transformation, then, must express itself not only through language, in transformed meanings, but also in a transformed urban space that can sustain social activity as play (Lefebvre 2000/1971, p. 135). In the varied fragments of everyday life as it is currently lived, individuals have to play many and varied roles. In this, we communicate with one another and, in acting in the various fields of power, we are constantly affirming both similarity and difference with others. However, if resistance to the bureaucratic society of controlled consumption is to be successful then the urban spaces most of us inhabit will have to be reclaimed and transformed into spaces where the more playful aspects of social relations can thrive. Only in such a context can relations that rely on commonality as well as difference find in that difference the marks of the social development of humanity as a whole as opposed to the signs of status marked out by consumer capitalism.

References

Adams, M. (2001) 'The reflexive self: a critical assessment of Giddens's later work on self-identity', PhD thesis, Nottingham Trent University, Nottingham.

Bauman, Z. (1991) *Modernity and Ambivalence*, Polity Press, Cambridge.

Bourdieu, P. (1998) *Practical Reason*, Polity Press, Cambridge.

de Certeau, M. (1986) *Heterologies: Discourse on the Other*, trans. B. Massumi, Minnesota University Press, Minneapolis.

Dewey, J. (1922/1983) *Human Nature and Conduct. The Middle Works, 1899–1924. Volume 14: 1922*, ed. Jo Ann Boydston, Southern Illinois University Press, Carbondale and Edwardsville.

Foucault, M. (1977) *Discipline and Punish: The Birth of the Prison*, trans. Alan Sheridan, Penguin, Harmondsworth.

Foucault, M. (1979) *The History of Sexuality, Volume One: An Introduction*, trans. Robert Hurley, Penguin, Harmondsworth.

Foucault, M. (1980) *Power/Knowledge*, ed. Colin Gordon, Harvester, Brighton.

Gardiner, M. E. (2000) *Critiques of Everyday Life*, Routledge, London and New York.

Giddens, A. (1991) *Modernity and Self-Identity: Self and Society in the Late Modern Age*, Polity Press, Cambridge.

Harvey, D. (2000) *Spaces of Hope*, Edinburgh University Press, Edinburgh.

Lefebvre, H. (1991) *Critique of Everyday Life: Volume One, Introduction*, trans. J. Moore, Verso, London.

Lefebvre, H. (2000/1971) *Everyday Life in the Modern World*, trans. Sasha Rabinovitch, Athlone Press, London.

Marx, K. (1848/1977) 'The Communist Manifesto', in *Karl Marx: Selected Writings*, ed. David McLellan, Oxford University Press, Oxford.

Mead, G. H. (1934) *Mind, Self and Society, From the Standpoint of a Social Behaviourist*, Chicago University Press, Chicago.

Melucci, A. (1989) *Nomads of the Present: Social Movements and Individual Needs in Contemporary Society*, Hutchinson Radius, London.

Melucci, A. (1996) *The Playing Self: Person and Meaning in the Planetary Society*, Cambridge University Press, Cambridge.

Shotter, J. (1993) *Conversational Realities: Constructing Life through Language*, Sage, London.

Voloshinov, V. N. (1986) *Marxism and the Philosophy of Language*, trans. L. Matejka & I. R. Titunik, Harvard University Press, Cambridge, MA.

Williams, R. (1977) *Marxism and Literature*, Oxford University Press, Oxford.

Michael E. Gardiner

EVERYDAY UTOPIANISM
Lefebvre and his critics

The strategy of sociocultural critique through the 'problematization' or 'defamiliarization' of the habitualized character of everyday life is one that is well-established in the literature, especially for adherents of various neo-Marxisms. However, in recent years, several prominent critics have taken issue with the concept of defamiliarization, arguing that the habit-bound, 'distracted' and routinized character of the everyday cannot be easily contrasted with, or superceded by, the exceptional or the extraordinary. Such a position, it is suggested, both denigrates the integrity of daily life and promotes a kind of incipient transcendentalism. The work of Henri Lefebvre is often taken to be representative in this regard, and various phenomenologies or pragmatisms are promoted in his stead. In this article, I take issue with such critics, by analyzing Lefebvre's writings on such key points as his treatment of routine in everyday life, as well as his concepts of totality, dialectics and critique. I end up asserting that, contrary to what is often said, Lefebvre does not promote a dualistic transcendentalism in which daily life is denigrated, but rather an 'everyday utopianism' in which routine and creativity, the trivial and the extraordinary, are viewed as productively intertwined rather than opposed. As such, I seek to defend the notion of 'critique' vis-à-vis the everyday, and to demonstrate the on-going relevance of Lefebvre's work, as well as that of the 'counter-tradition' that is loosely associated with his name.

Keywords   critique; dialectics; Lefebvre; routine; totality; utopia

> It is not true that life is one damn thing after another – it's one damn thing over and over.
>
> (Edna St Vincent Millay)

Introduction

In a narrative voice-over that begins the recent film *One Hour Photo*, the central character Sy Parrish, an anonymous, middle-aged everyman working in a department store photo-processing lab, reflects on the skewed vision of daily

Cultural Studies Vol. 18, No. 2/3 March/May 2004, pp. 228–254
ISSN 0950-2386 print/ISSN 1466-4348 online © 2004 Taylor & Francis Ltd
http://www.tandf.co.uk/journals DOI: 10.1080/0950238042000203048

Routledge
Taylor & Francis Group

life projected in family snapshots. Such photographs inevitably portray the happier and more exceptional moments in our lives, such as holidays, weddings and birthday parties. Hypothetical observers of such images, from some alien world perhaps, might well conclude that 'we had led a joyous, leisurely exist-ence, free from tragedy'. A more accurate view, Sy muses in a later narration, would not consist exclusively of such atypical moments of festivity, leisure and celebration, but off-kilter and out-of-focus photographs of dusty lampshades, faded wallpaper, the back of people's heads, or the facades of buildings – that is, images that better reflect the unnoticed backdrop that saturates our everyday lives.

To a large extent, what has come to be known as 'everyday life studies' concerns itself with the supposition that to focus exclusively on the memorable, highly visible or extraordinary events of the sociocultural world is something akin to a category mistake, because to do so universalizes the atypical and ignores the overlooked norm. As Perec notes in his short but intriguing rumination 'Approaches to What?': 'What speaks to us, seemingly, is always the big event, the untoward, the extra-ordinary: the front-page splash, the banner headlines'. Daily newspapers, Perec observes humorously, are misnamed because they are concerned with virtually everything except what actually occurs in daily life, in the ebb and flow of our quotidian, mundane existence. This is a world that we are so inured to that we often inhabit it as if anaesthetized, in which we wander about distractedly whilst in a kind of 'dreamless sleep'. But how, asks Perec, can we turn up the volume on the murmuring 'background noise' of the everyday, which lies at the very threshold of metaphorical and conscious 'audibility'? How do we wrest the commonalities of our daily existence from the mental refuse-heap onto which they are more or less automatically discarded, so as to give these things a 'meaning, a tongue, to let them, finally, speak of what is, of what we are'? (Perec 1999, p. 210).

In developing a distinctive methodology to illuminate what Perec's contem-porary de Certeau would refer to as the 'operational logic' of the everyday in his influential study *L'Invention du Quotidian* (later rendered in English, albeit inaccu-rately, as *The Practice of Everyday Life*), we can ascertain the lineaments of what Perec describes as a sociology of the 'endotic' rather than the 'exotic'. This endotic sociology would encourage us to pose questions to such hitherto silent interlocutors of daily life as 'bricks, concrete, glass, our table manners, our utensils, our tools, the way we spend our time, our rhythms' (Perec 1999, p. 210). One of its central elements would be to render visible the overlooked, to reverse figure and ground, in order to supercede the blind-spots we usually have *vis-à-vis* the habitualized aspects of daily life. Indeed, this is precisely the strategy championed by Wayne Brekhus, a founding editor of the online publication *Journal of Mundane Studies* (http://www.mundanebehavior.org), one of the few scholarly periodicals devoted specifically to the topic of everyday life. In an article that became the template for the manifesto of this journal, Brekhus outlines a technique that he calls 'reverse marking', in which the 'negative space' that exists at the margins or in the interstices of socially 'marked' phenomena – such as 'whiteness' with respect to a sociological discourse about race that tends to focus almost exclusively on relatively distinct and visible racial or ethnic minorities – is brought to the foreground and treated as analytically interesting. This methodology provides a 'useful way to problematize the taken-for-granted elements of our world and make them more "visible". [It] allows us to look at the "morally relevant" from the perspective of the negative case' (Brekhus 1998, pp. 43–44).

This technique of 'problematization', along with such related concepts as *Verfremdung*, the 'alienation effect' and, in particular, defamiliarization, is a relatively commonplace one in sociocultural analysis.[1] Whilst its utility has been widely acknowledged, for many the notion of problematization is itself problematic. For it would seem to conform to the familiar Enlightenment strategy of 'unmasking' that which is obscured, and thereby abstracting the truth-imparting 'deep essence' of things from the confusing tangle of mere phenomenal appearance. In short, strategies of defamiliarization or 'making strange' seem to fall prey to an 'ocularcentric' metaphorics characteristic of mainstream social scientific inquiry, one that accords the 'seeing' of intellectuals a privileged epistemic status (see Jay 1993). Folk knowledges of everyday life might have a certain quaint or exotic appeal, but ultimately they must be superceded by social-scientific description and analysis. But, as Foucault (1980) in particular has demonstrated, this 'sociological gaze' suppresses, like a guilty conscience, how formal regimes of knowing are bound up with wider dynamics of power and social control in ways that circumscribe and de-legitimate a range of unofficial 'micro-knowledges'. In contradistinction to this mainstream approach, many have argued that the everyday is a mode of living or way of relating to the world in which not every facet can be opened up to reflexive understanding, and to presume so is to align oneself with the forces of technocratic authority in opposition to local knowledges and practices (see Smith 1987, Bauman 1992). Yet, at the same time, daily life evinces a 'slippery', elusory quality that evinces a not insignificant degree of resistance to the technologies of power, largely because its very presence is often not registered by the panoptic sweep of bureaucratic surveillance, indexing and control. The everyday remains an inchoate and heterodox mix of fluid, multiple and symbolically-dense practices and ways of feeling and knowing, a 'black rock that resists assimilation' (de Certeau 1984, p. 60). As Felski puts it:

> much of the unthought of our thought must remain opaque, recalcitrant and beyond the reach of understanding and critique. One's own form of life is never fully available for retrieval and analysis, thanks to the irreducible embeddedness of thought and action, the impossibility of turning all of one's background into foreground. The life-world in this sense offers a stubborn

resistance to the mastery that is implied in the intellectual's claim to penetrate the veil of illusion.

(2000, pp. 614–615)

Arguably, then, a strong and recurring trend in contemporary writing on this
topic is an attempt to get beyond some of the perceived ethico-political, ontological and epistemological lacunae and dualisms that are widely felt to have
hobbled our understanding of daily life, particularly with respect to the
question of 'knowing' or representing the everyday through various critical
interpretive strategies. The discussion that follows will examine some of the
more salient recent developments *vis-à-vis* the issue of routine, as this bears on
the study and critique of everyday life. As a prefatory remark, it could be
argued that much theoretical work in everyday life studies over the last few
decades has been largely polarized between two sharply divergent approaches.
The first of these can be described as an overtly political project that aims to
interrogate daily life in a critical fashion, to identify the various alienations and
subjectifications felt to be located at the heart of our experience of capitalist
modernity, as well as to realize as fully as possible the 'emancipatory' potential
that is felt to inhere in the everyday. This 'critical-dialectical' view has been
closely aligned with the neo-Marxist wing of cultural and social criticism,
which is broadly humanistic and trans-disciplinary in scope, and that includes
such iconic figures as Walter Benjamin, Guy Debord and Henri Lefebvre.[2] The
second approach is a relatively more straightforwardly academic (and hence
ostensibly less politicized) one, and has sought to counter the overly abstract
and deterministic bent of much quantitative social science in order to better
understand the realm of lived, immediate experience. This would include sociologists and philosophers inspired by European *Geistewissenschaften* thinkers like
Dilthey, Schütz and Weber, as well as American pragmatists like Dewey or
Mead. It might be said to include the social phenomenology of Berger and
Luckmann, Goffman's dramaturgical sociology, and the ethnomethodology
pioneered by Garfinkel. The central premise in this latter group, regardless of
specific intellectual influences, is that investigators of the social world must
articulate an interpretive understanding of how actors develop an 'insider's
knowledge' of particular social processes and utilize this so as to act in a
voluntaristic and creative fashion.[3]

These two rival traditions have largely operated in isolation from each
other, for only rarely have there been productive cross-fertilizations between
them. In any event, from the 1960s through to the 1980s, especially in the early
phases of the emergence of cultural studies in the UK, North America and
Australia, the neo-Marxist wing was arguably the most influential and widely
cited. However, what we seem to be witnessing more recently is a turn away
from the critical, dialectical orientation of Benjamin or Lefebvre in order to
embrace more fully the phenomenological and pragmatist traditions. The desire

to acknowledge what Burkitt calls (in the present volume) the 'multidimensional' aspect of everyday life, to supersede what are viewed as a series of false polarities (such as between authentic versus inauthentic existence, or everyday and specialized knowledges), and to challenge the perceived essentialism that marks much theorizing about the everyday, has led to many valuable insights and developments (see Harrison 2000, Ireland 2002). But at times it seems to have come at the cost of abandoning the project of a theoretically-informed analysis of mundane social existence, and to sever the link between the utopian impulse and daily life that has been the hallmark of what I have elsewhere characterized as the 'counter-tradition' of critical everyday life studies (Gardiner 1995, 2000a). Much of the current debate, as highlighted by the Felski quote above, seems to turn on the degree to which some measure of critical distanciation from the more routinized and opaque qualities of the everyday is possible or desirable. Critical-dialectical theories advocate a relatively high degree of distanciation through various techniques of defamiliarization, insofar as they subscribe to the belief that the potential and vitality of daily life has been debased by the forces of capitalist modernity. Felski and others challenge this supposition, arguing instead that routinization has its own merits and that the capacity for critical reflection to shed light on all aspects of everyday life is strictly delimited.

In what follows, I will treat Lefebvre as an iconic and hence representative figure within the critical-dialectical school, and focus on some recent criticisms of his work that rehearse the aforementioned shift towards phenomenology and away from neo-Marxism. These include: (1) Felski's desire to 'make peace with the ordinary' by rehabilitating the role of routine and the mundane in sociocultural life, by way of her argument that Lefebvre privileges the exceptional and implicitly denigrates the everyday, thereby subscribing to a kind of dualistic transcendentalism; (2) the suggestion advanced by John Frow that Lefebvre's notion of 'totality' is an example of a holistic romanticism, and hence partakes of a largely-discredited theological discourse of sin and redemption; and (3) Claire Colebrook's assertion that dialectical-critical theories such as Lefebvre's view the everyday as a site of unbridled positivity, and do not sufficiently take into account the forces of negativity and 'non-life' that are equally part and parcel of the everyday.[4] I will then examine Lefebvre's work more closely in order to ascertain whether these critiques hold up to scrutiny. What I hope to establish is that Lefebvre in fact adheres to positions that in many ways anticipate, and hence largely undermine, the force of such criticisms – or at the very least, the arguments developed by Lefebvre and the critical-dialectical school more generally are more complex, variegated and nuanced than its critics are often willing to acknowledge. This will in turn prompt us to revisit the issue of defamiliarization or critical distanciation.

Criticisms of Lefebvre

In a couple of important articles, Felski (2000, 2002) has argued that much discussion of everyday life has been subordinated to certain theoretical and political agendas, especially involving a number of questionable assumptions about gender, whereby the everyday is not so much analysed for what it is, but rather for what it could or should be. In such approaches, which for her marks the work of Marxist radicals like Debord or Lefebvre, but paradoxically reactionaries such as Heidegger as well, daily life is thought to be exceptional precisely because of 'its lack of distinction and differentiation' (Felski 2002, p. 79). As such, everyday life is typically contrasted with that which it lacks: such more visible and distinctive qualities as aesthetic experiences, extraordinary events and historically-significant happenings, as well as the human capacity for abstract, critical thinking which allows such phenomena to be comprehensively investigated and understood. The fixation on apparently trivial concerns that characterizes much of daily existence, of a sort marked by unreflexive and highly routinized action, inures us to a life of mindless drudgery and contributes to the stifling of creative possibilities. Whether the repetitive and dehumanizing aspects of everyday life is something that is intrinsic to the process of capitalist modernization (as Lefebvre might be said to argue), or a more obscure metaphysical quality that permeates mundane existence *per se* (as Heidegger appears to suggest), does not obviate an overarching desire for transcendence.[5]

Central to Felski's argument is her treatment of the issue of defamiliarization. For Lefebvre, according to her, the reification of everyday life through technocratic programming, and the concomitant internalization of routines of wanton consumption and compulsive deference to authority, must be disrupted through various strategies of critical problematization.[6] Whereas dominant ideological mechanisms define and sanction certain patterns of life as 'natural' or 'inevitable' – which helps to gives the everyday the unreflexive and 'taken-for-granted' quality that phenomenologists attribute to it – such defamiliarizing moments problematize, 'make strange', and thereby subvert the ideological and bureaucratic structuring of everyday life. In Eugene Lunn's words, these moments 'freshen perceptions and cleanse the senses and language of routine, habitual, and automatic responses, to "defamiliarize" expected and ordinary connections between things in favour of new, and deeper ones' (1982, p. 34). When such disruptions of daily conventions occur, and individuals no longer need to rely quite so extensively on commonsensical notions and typified behavioural responses, we are able to examine more critically prevailing traditions and received ideas, and our receptivity to alternative ways of being, or what Bakhtin (1984, p. 73) called the 'buds and shoots of new potentialities', is heightened dramatically.

For Felski, however, the strategy of defamiliarization is symptomatic of a certain avant-gardism that runs though much everyday life theorizing, particularly that of French providence. It involves the fetishization of untrammelled novelty and ceaseless creativity at the expense of the more prosaic and habit-bound aspects of ordinary life. 'Influenced by modernist ideals of innovation and irony, contemporary theorists have tended to either excoriate the everyday for its routine, mundane qualities, or celebrate the everyday by pretending that such qualities do not exist', she writes. 'It is time, perhaps, to make peace with the ordinariness of daily life' (Felski 2000, p. 95). Although Felski acknowledges that ingrained dispositions and routinized behaviours can in certain circumstances promote a passive acquiescence to the status quo, and that critical reflection informed by theoretical work can play an important role in countering this, Felski is nonetheless adamant that it is misguided to reject habit and routine out of hand, for the following reasons. First, it is wrong to equate our devotion to habit and routine as dehumanization, a loss of individuality or subjective uniqueness. On the contrary: such personal quirks and ingrained dispositions, which are accumulated over a considerable period of time through first-hand experience (roughly corresponding to Pierre Bourdieu's *habitus*), are very much a part of who we are, and provide an anchor of personal meaning in a world that seems increasingly fraught with risk and incoherence. This is what social theorist Giddens (1984) terms 'ontological security': the need to develop a relatively stable sense of selfhood and an intersubjective sense of trust in the context of a world that must appear to be reasonably predictable. Whatever their drawbacks, habits and routines, especially as they emerge from within the domestic and other intimate spheres, can provide individuals with a bulwark of affective and emotional support. In a more collective sense, the *habitus* can also provide groups with considerable cultural resources for resisting, for example, the shock of continuous socioeconomic restructuring on an increasingly global scale, or myriad forces of political domination. Of course, suggests Felski, such cultural formations can have deeply conservative, even reactionary elements, but it would be foolish to ignore their at least potentially resistant and progressive aspects.[7] Secondly, Felski feels that it is erroneous to suppose that everyday life can be identified with particular groups and understood as a discrete subset of activities marked by 'immediacy' or 'concreteness'. Rather, the everyday represents a 'lived process of routinization that all individuals experience' (2000, p. 95). It is a quality that inheres (albeit to greater or lesser degrees) in all sociocultural practices, from the utterly banal, such as brushing one's teeth, to the most apparently rarified and 'conceptual', which might include highly technical scientific research. All such apparently disparate undertakings partake of what phenomenologist Schütz (1967) once described as 'stock knowledge at hand' – the nebulous, taken-for-granted frame of reference through which social actors attribute significance to the world of objects, events and other people that they pragmatically engage with on a daily basis.[8]

Hence, according to Felski, Lefebvre and his 'fellow-travellers' believe that the transformative promise embedded within everyday life can only be redeemed fully via aesthetic (or quasi-aesthetic) techniques and gestures, through which the 'the all too prosaic [is] made to reveal its hidden subversive poetry' (2002, p. 608). In other words, for all his talk of respecting the integrity of everyday life, as against those who would either ignore or denigrate it, Lefebvre falls prey to the same sort of transcendentalist errors. Felski therefore seeks to promote a questioning of what she views as certain elitist and theoreticist currents within everyday life studies, and to sketch out a more recognizably populist and empirically-sensitive approach. This method would be concerned to acknowledge that the mundane practices and routines of ordinary people are skilled accomplishments irreducible to the abstract conceptual schemas and political agendas of social and cultural theorists, and to affirm instead that the everyday is a mode of relating to the world acquired in specific contexts and eventually sedimented in individual and collective habits and bodily dispositions. As such, everyday life does not constitute an identifiable region of the social world or a fixed ontological essence. The democratic-populist implications of Felski's argument should be clear: that all of us, even intellectuals, cannot arbitrarily transcend everyday life by ideological fiat (although particular groups might well be more closely identified with the everyday for a host of socioeconomic and cultural reasons than others). For, as Gramsci (1971) pointed out long ago, all of us are fully capable of constructing complex and meaningful interpretations of the world around us and engaging practically with and shaping our environment, regardless of the fact only relatively few of us are actually allotted the social role of 'intellectual'. Felski would therefore doubtless concur with John O'Neill's assertion that we cannot overlook 'the massive fact of the *already known* everyday world', unless we wish to be complicit with a project of technocratic domination. The 'defence of everyday life, of common-sense knowledge and values . . . requires that sociologists be prepared to set aside their narcissism in order to work as the under-labourers in the world of everyday life with which in all other respects they retain kinship' (O'Neill 1995, p. 174).[9]

In his article '"Never draw to an inside straight": on everyday knowledge', Frow also sets out to deconstruct what he sees as the false dichotomy between everyday and specialized knowledges and practices. The notion that everyday life is an unreflective, corporeal, and heterodox way of being that is obsessively attuned to the minutiae of the passing moment, as opposed to the abstract and decontextualized cast of formal, conceptual reasoning and technical procedures, is for him a distinction that operates to essentialize these two spheres and maintain a distinct hierarchy of value between them. According to Frow, Lefebvre is a fairly typical representative of the tendency to think of the everyday as a kind of 'negative space', the residue that is 'left over' after all the more formal and specialized knowledges and practices have been accounted for, and as such constitutes a realm of intuitive, spontaneous immediacy. He interprets Lefebvre as saying that whereas modernity is linear, progressive and goal-oriented in its temporal organization, the everyday involves a cyclical time that is associated with nature and the related activities of premodern life (consumption, biological reproduction and suchlike) (see also Osborne 1995). The unified culture (or 'style of life') that Lefebvre identifies with the premodern era, and which imparted to every object and activity a distinct, integral meaning, is increasingly fragmented by the extreme division of labour and pervasive commodification that accompanies modernity. Frow construes Lefebvre's solution to the problem of alienation as crucially involving the enlightened intellectual, who helps to lead humankind from a present-day state of debasement to one of liberation in which the unfulfilled potential of the everyday is realized completely through a revivified totality. As such, he regards Lefebvre's project as one that is fundamentally allegorical in nature, because it expresses a profound nostalgia for the lost unity and plenitude of premodern society, a desire that is projected into a utopian future. The Marxism of Lefebvre is hence a 'classically theological discourse' conforming to a 'narrative of grace, alienation, and redemption which structures its account of the loss of significant totality, the fall into repetition, and the promise of a future advent of a life again become meaningful' (Frow 2002, p. 632; see also Colebrook 2002, p. 700). The everyday cannot, in short, be inserted into an overarching sociohistorical *telos* that gives it meaning and purpose: daily life, to a significant extent, simply is what it is, and as such should be left, by and large, to its own devices.

Colebrook's contribution to this debate involves her claim to have detected a certain bifurcation in the literature, in which everyday life is seen as either the site of triviality, inauthenticity, or mindless repetition, or else as a wholly positive repository of subterranean vitality, resistance and authenticity. Lefebvre ostensibly supercedes this dichotomy by subscribing to a view that sees 'the ambivalence of everyday life in a necessarily dialectical relation between immediate existence and transcendent ideas of existence' (Colebrook 2002, p. 695). Yet, Lefebvre is only apparently in opposition to what Colebrook calls the 'immanent' school of Bergson or Nietzsche, the latter in her opinion cleaving to the notion that everyday life should be seen as a pure elemental life-force existing beyond all idealist metaphysics and all mediation. This is because in actuality Lefebvre adheres to a monolithic and universalistic vision of 'redemption' or 'liberation'. By interpreting the everyday as part of an integrated totality that has a 'generic', holistic and entirely positive quality, he betrays the promise of the dialectical position. The 'life' in everyday life for such thinkers as Lefebvre, that is to say, is something that has a certain potentiality (especially through its link to the immediate and the concrete, as opposed to the spectral abstractions of high theory), and which can be realized *in toto* under the appropriate sociohistorical conditions – totality lost and totality regained, if you will. Negativity drops out of the equation because it is incompatible with the quasi-theological or messianic cast of his thinking. Lefebvre's account of the everyday therefore represents the affirmation of the force and productivity of proper life. This is so even when this everyday is regarded as that which requires the demystification or illumination of theory to realize its inherent potential. . . . Life must arrive at itself in a univocal conception of subjectivity, humanity, or 'man.' . . . Lefebvre sees the redemption of everyday life only in the recognition of life as a whole. In all cases everyday life realizes itself in collective appropriation; what must be refused is an everyday life that remains, in itself, separate from the collective comprehension of life.

(Colebrook 2002, p. 688, p. 701)

For her part, Colebrook wants to argue instead that everyday life is 'always-already' permeated by non-life, by negation, and is therefore not just a self-constituting positivity that evinces some sort of inherent *telos* towards the universal self-realization of humankind. As such, she advocates a turn to such thinkers as Irigaray and Derrida, who would presumably agree with Colebrook (2002, p. 704) that the 'political is not the realization of life so much as the recognition of all the ways in which an inappropriable non-life traverses bodies from the beginning'.

Lefebvre on routinization and totality

To summarize the preceding discussion: from the perspective of critics like Felski, Frow and Colebrook, Lefebvre is typical of a particular way of thinking about the everyday, and hence can be regarded as representative of the critical-dialectical school. This tradition ultimately fails to appreciate everyday life on its own terms, preferring to subordinate it to various intellectual, political and quasi-theological projects. These end up undermining the integrity of everyday life and promoting the viewpoint of the critical intelligentsia at the expense of the 'folk' accounts of the ordinary people who inhabit it. At the same time, Lefebvre *et al.* are held to portray the intellectual as a figure whose capacity for critical reflection and insight is magically exempt from the dull compulsions and hide-bound modes of thinking characteristic of the everyday – a position that, for Felski and company, is perversely anti-democratic.

There is considerable value in many of the positions staked out by these writers, particularly their desire to deconstruct various dualisms, to go beyond the sort of essentialist tendencies that do admittedly crop up in much writing on everyday life, and to introject a certain cautionary note into the more extravagant claims made by some theorists about the transformative or emancipatory potential of the everyday. However, there is a danger that their stance, which dovetails in many key respects (though is at odds in other, sometimes curious ways), ends up undercutting the very *raison d'etre* of the critique of everyday life.[10] I suggest, by contrast, that Lefebvre's own work can be read against the grain of such received interpretations in ways that affirm many of the more salient critical points they make, whilst at the same time continuing to uphold the notion of critique in defensible ways, so long as we regard this project as one that abjures the Messianic hubris of some critiques of everyday life, as I believe it does. To begin with, Lefebvre's work is consistently informed by the realization that everyday life cannot be understood solely at the phenomenal level nor reduced to the properties of macro-level systems. Nor does he starkly counterpose the mundanity of the everyday with the transcendental qualities of fulfilled potentiality. Rather, Lefebvre strives to overcome such dualisms, particularly with respect to the various forms of knowledge that tend to coalesce around these different (but not ontologically separate) spheres of activity. He argues, for instance, that we need to transform abstract thought, the prototypical mode of Western philosophical and scientific reasoning, into a 'dialectical consciousness of life, in life: unity of the mediate and immediate, of the abstract and concrete, of culture and natural spontaneity' (Lefebvre 1991a, p. 76). All phenomena necessarily partake of the interacting forces of the material and the ideal. Consequently, genuinely dialectical thought always concerns itself with what Lefebvre calls 'concrete universality': it must embrace both form and content, the distant and near-at-hand, sensuous and abstract. 'The specific does not preclude the formal', Lefebvre (2002, p. 180) makes it clear, 'and the particular does not preclude the general'.

Accordingly, Lefebvre does not hold an unfavourable view of everyday knowledges and practices with respect to their more specialized counterparts: again, dialectical understanding grows out of the constant and active interaction between them, which must always understood as part of a complex, overlapping continuum and not a dichotomy. We 'should not reject *savoir* (knowledge) but integrate it into the lived (*vécu*)', as Lefebvre scholars Kofman and Lebas put it (1996, p. 21). We cannot detect an adherence to some sort of theoreticist transcendentalism in Lefebvre's work – but neither is there a cult of the immediate or the pre-reflective, the defining feature of Colebrook's 'immanent' school. Furthermore, as a thinker who in many respects fits into the 'process philosophy' mould, Lefebvre is cognizant of the fact that real, dynamic social and natural processes will always slip through the cracks of pre-conceived theoretical categories or generalizations. In common with Adorno and others, Lefebvre argues for the existence of a constitutive but 'open' dialectic between subject and object in which each retains its specificity and distinctiveness, and wherein the material world cannot be fully absorbed into reflexive consciousness, or vice-versa (see Clucas 2000, p. 15). In particular, Lefebvre believes that there is always something about the bodily processes, desires and intersubjective relations, which inhere in the often obscure rhythms and activities of daily life, that escape the gravitational pull of theoretical discourses. For Lefebvre, this is in many respects a good thing, because the languages of institutionalized power, which are an integral part of what he calls the 'bureaucratic society of controlled consumption', aim at the homogenization and purification of the social world.

For Lefebvre, then, the critique of everyday life as he understood it concerned our ability to grasp daily existence in all its complexity and ambiguity, to fathom its shifting and nebulous qualities as well its more enduring and stable elements, its stultifying routines together with its open-ended and creative aspects (see Sheringham 2002). The notion that Lefebvre regards the everyday as the sphere of mindless, dehumanizing routine to be contrasted unfavourably with exceptional events and experiences, whereby daily life must be 'liberated' through a transformative praxis that ushers in some sort of idealist utopia, is therefore a distorting caricature.[11] Such arguments do not, tellingly, engage with his writings on 'rhythmanalysis', a major focus of his later work. By rhythmanalysis, Lefebvre meant the study of the multiple and cross-cutting rhythms (or polyrhythms) and temporalities that imbue and structure all social and natural phenomena. Particular bodies and entities, each composed of various and distinct rhythms, coalesce and are sutured into more complex wholes (or 'ensembles') consisting of constantly reciprocating elements. However, these wholes are not self-contained and homogeneous – what Lefebvre would call 'closed' totalities. Rather, they are 'open' totalities that exist in a state of 'metastable equilibrium' and are prone to constant changes, internal and external shifts, and realignments (Lefebvre 1996, p. 230). The concept of rhythmanalysis is relevant to our understanding of everyday routines especially in the following sense: as alluded to above in the brief discussion of Frow, Lefebvre advances a key distinction between two forms of temporality, cyclical and linear. In his essay 'Rhythmanalysis of Mediterranean cities', Lefebvre highlights their differences as follows: cyclical rhythms are largely those of the organic flows and movements of nature, whereas the linear is 'defined by the consecutiveness and the reproduction of the same phenomena, identical or almost at more or less close regular intervals' (1996, p. 231). So, whilst the former is modelled on (in particular) the endless growth, death and rebirth of biological forms, as well as geological or climatological phenomena, examples of the latter might include the repetitive hammer blows of manual labour, or the regular ticking of a metronome.[12]

The first point to make about this distinction between cyclical and linear temporality is that, *contra* Frow, Lefebvre never intended to portray them as a binary pair, and nor does he unambiguously identify the cyclical with premodern society and linearity with modernity. On the contrary, Lefebvre takes great pains to point out that 'If therefore the cyclical and the linear can be clearly distinguished, the analysis which has separated them must rejoin them, for they enter into a perpetual interaction and are even relative to each other, to the point that one becomes the measure of the other' (1996, p. 231). Both linear and cyclical are found in all societies. The mathematical exactitude and precise repetitions associated with the linear is an intrinsic component of the human labour process, and hence necessary for our physical survival. Likewise, cyclical time does not disappear entirely in even the most technologically-advanced societies. Of course, in a relative sense, linearity is associated more with modernity because instrumental rationality increasingly predominates over the rhythms and processes of the natural world, so that time is structured (especially on a day-to-day basis) more by economic and technical imperatives rather than, say, planetary movements or climatic changes. Secondly, the notion of multiple rhythms and temporalities helps to defend Lefebvre from the charge (advanced by Felski and others) that he privileges unhindered creativity and innovation at the expense of inherently alienating and dehumanizing everyday routines. This, in turn, sheds light on the ambiguous and contradictory character of routinization, which is something Lefebvre fully acknowledges and appreciates. That is, in his work on rhythmanalysis Lefebvre makes it clear that his target is not routine or repetition as such – which, as mentioned, is central to the daily life (and especially the labour process) of all possible societies. But whereas the habits and routines that are tied to organic cycles and rhythms (including of course those of the human body) are an important (and unsurpassable) aspect of social existence, under Western modernity our activities are colonized progressively by the imperatives of the expansion and accumulation of capital. These latter forces operate in such a way as to 'empty out' the more sensuous and qualitative aspects of lived temporality. It is only when routine becomes effectively 'routinized' by capitalist socioeconomic processes, when it becomes an 'obligation or an external imposition' (what he calls 'everydayness') rather than a 'self-creation', that it must be subjected to critique (Lefebvre & Regulier 1999, p. 8). The eminently dialectical connection between habit and innovation, cyclical rhythm and linear repetition, constitutes what Lefebvre terms a 'conflictual unity' rather than an opposition. What this means, in particular, is that we cannot think of habit or routines separately from wider political and economic forces. Insofar as it is not insulated from the logic of the commodity, the everyday is never simply 'that which is'. 'By becoming the time of everydayness', write Lefebvre and Régulier, linearity has

> subordinated to the organization of work in space all aspects of the everyday: the time for sleeping and waking up, the time for eating and for private life, the relationship between parents and children, leisure and entertainment, and other domestic interactions. At the same time, biological rhythms persist; everyday life is traversed by great rhythms that are both cosmic and vital, such as the days and nights or the months and seasons. As a result, the everyday revolves around a *conflictual unity between these biological rhythms and the repetitive process associated with homogeneous time.*
>
> (1999, p. 5, emphasis added)[13]

This brings us to the concept of 'totality' as it figures in Lefebvre's writings. As mentioned above, for many critics the notion of totality (especially the ideal of the 'total person') is indicative of a misguidedly nostalgic conception of an integrated human culture and concomitantly unified selfhood that Lefebvre allegedly believes existed in some past era and that he wants to see reconstituted in a future utopia. However, this is a rather serious misreading of Lefebvre. For he did not regard totality as a homogeneous and *sui generis* whole, akin to the belief of the ancient Greek philosopher Parmenides that reality was monolithically homogeneous and indivisible, and hence did not contain any hint of its negation. Rather, reality for Lefebvre is complex and internally divided; a fractured mosaic of positive and negative forces that partakes of otherness as well as sameness, difference no less than identity. It is more analogous to the flowing river of Heraclitus, which travels along certain discernable conduits even as it erodes its banks or forges new channels, than the inert sphere of Parmenides. Totalities are therefore radically *pluralistic*, inasmuch as they are generated out of the ceaseless alterity of opposing forces and processes, consisting of multiple determinations and diverse elements that each retain 'a certain independence and relative autonomy' (Lefebvre 1996, p. 152). Any equilibrium they achieve can only be a relative and contingent one. 'Totality for Lefebvre could be an endless chain of everyday particularities and plural differences', as Ben Highmore usefully puts it, 'linked in ways that neither obliterate them nor abandon them to isolation' (2002, p. 14).[14]

Lefebvre's concept of totality therefore resembles far more closely the 'open system' of Merleau-Ponty than Lukacs' 'expressive totality', the latter constituting the *bête noire* of structuralist critics like Althusser.[15,16] Closed totalities for Lefebvre are monolithic and static postulates, and conceptualizing phenomena from the point of view of this sort of totality, which is symptomatic of dominant strains in Western philosophy going back to ancient Greece, tends to 'absorb particularities and specificities, and therefore to neglect differences and types'. Open totalities, by contrast, are 'perpetually in the process of being transcended', and a given totality (such as the city), is not autonomous and self-contained but partial in nature and which must be related dialectically to wider totalities, up to and including 'the world, history, "man"' (Lefebvre 2002, p. 185, 1968, p. 111, 1996, p. 92). Thinking about (and with) open totalities is not about the production of grand abstractions in which concrete specificities and distinctions are lost, but represents instead a 'meditation on *differences*', which makes complete sense inasmuch as Lefebvre describes totalities as '*ensemble[s] of differences*' (1996, p. 88, p. 109). Whilst totalities are always open towards the future, Lefebvre emphatically does not advance a teleological view of history in which the 'fallen' present is redeemed in full in some post-messianic time. There is no final closure to the historical dialectic, which manifests itself in unpredictable and often unfathomable ways, and no overarching goal of liberation or self-realization towards which it is necessarily propelled. From Nietzsche, Lefebvre borrows the notion that the human and natural worlds involve multi-voiced narratives that have no ending (except via arbitrary closure), that are forever being written and re-written. Nonetheless, although history certainly cannot transcend all alienations and separations, it does have a certain relative coherence. History is not completely random or formless, for even Heraclitus' flowing river can be mapped, as long as we understand such a map as an heuristic tool, and not an exhaustive representation that is isomorphic with the external world in every detail. As such, Lefebvre continues to argue we should strive to think of history as a totality, without ever suggesting (*pace* Merleau-Ponty's argument in *Adventures of the Dialectic*) that we can never theorize it in its entirety by reducing it to simple, inexorable 'stages' and so forth. And, contrary to what Frow or Colebrook say about his wish to return humankind to a simpler and less fragmented premodern culture, Lefebvre specifically acknowledges the irreversibly complex and pluralistic character of late modern societies, and consciously rejects the possibility or desirability of reconstituting some imaginary lost totality (see Kofman & Lebas 1996, p. 27). As he puts it in volume two of *Critique of Everyday Life*, dialectical reasoning seeks to grasp the central aspects of the 'total human phenomenon' as

> a theoretical structure [i.e., as a totality]; at the same time their practical relations and interactions will constitute the basis of a process of becoming; and a historicity. Within this frame of reference we will observe active differences, relations and conflicts. By determining them we will be able to define historical and social particularities without assuming the supreme (and always illusory) power of capturing the universal and of exhausting 'being'.
>
> (2002, p. 189)

To Lefebvre's way of thinking, as might be expected, everyday life also constitutes a totality. Frow correctly points out that Lefebvre describes the everyday as the 'residue' that remains after other, more specialized activities and ideological constructions are identified and accounted for. But Lefebvre also goes on to say (and Frow fails to mention this) that 'Everyday life is profoundly related to *all* activities, and encompasses them with all their differences and their conflicts; it is their meeting place, their bond, their common ground. And it is in everyday life that the sum total of relations which make the human – and every human being – a whole takes its shape and its form. In it are expressed and fulfilled those relations which bring into play the totality of the real' (1991a, p. 97). In other words, everyday life is not to be defined strictly as an 'absence' in opposition to the 'presence' of other allegedly 'higher' human activities and knowledges. Rather, the everyday is part and parcel of all human practices; it is the 'connective tissue' of the social world. But nor does everyday life represent pure 'positivity' *à la* Colebrook's interpretation of the critical-dialectical school. Totalities are structured in difference, constituted by the opposing forces of presence and absence, concentration and dispersal, positivity and negativity.

Lefebvre argues at one point that totalities have at their centre 'a hole which is sacred and damned, inhabited by the forces of death and life, times dark with effort and ordeals, the *world*' (1996, p. 88). Again, the reduction of the inherent complexity of the world to abstract categories – such as the homogenization and purification of space/time attempted (if not perfected) by global capital and the nation-state – was for Lefebvre an exercise of hegemonic power that had to be actively resisted in order to preserve such concrete differences.[17]

So, the key is not to privilege either the mundane or the exceptional, linear or cyclical temporalities, but to grasp how they interrelate on the terrain of the totality that constitutes everyday life. A useful way to clarify this is to focus briefly on Lefebvre's theory of 'moments'. For Lefebvre, moments are flashes of perception into the range of historical possibilities that are embedded in the totality of being, but which cannot be disentangled from the activities of everyday life. Not unlike Bloch's *novum*, they are manifestations of what could be termed *immanent transcendence*, or perhaps *everyday utopianism*. As Shields (1999, p. 58) astutely puts it, such moments represent 'those times when one recognizes or has a sudden insight into a situation or experience beyond the merely empirical routine of some activity [and hence into] the wider significance of some "thing" or "event" – its relation to the whole, and by extension, our relation to totality'. Put differently, moments are themselves partial totalities that reflect and refract larger wholes; they constitute a crucial point of linkage between the immediacy and particularity that inheres in the fine grain of everyday life, and the broader sweep of sociohistorical change. By temporarily disrupting the relatively unreflective and 'distracted' state that generally marks our being-in-the-everyday, Lefebvrean moments bring to consciousness the rich and manifold possibilities that are presented to us at given historical conjunctures. It is a tragic consciousness because most of these potentials, of course, will remain tantalizingly unfulfilled or only partially realized. But, again, there is no ultimate synthesis of these fragments or moments into some unified whole that is purged of opposition or difference. Moments do not represent negations of the everyday, but are organically connected to it and intensify the 'vital productivity' of daily life. 'The moment is born of the everyday and within the everyday', Lefebvre (2002, p. 351) notes. 'From here it draws its nourishment and its substance'.

Critique, routine and everyday life

To recapitulate the central argument thus far: many critics of Lefebvre often miss their mark because they have failed to read Lefebvre carefully enough, or else have not ranged widely enough in his (admittedly large and variegated) *oeuvre*.[18] They misconstrue Lefebvre in a manner that paradoxically confirms the strength of many of the positions they stake out. These would include, as a partial list, their desire to deconstruct various binary oppositions (extraordinary/mundane, figure/ground, and so on), to de-reify everyday life in order to see it as a contingent ensemble of living relations and open-ended processes, and to draw our attention to the limits of abstract reason, especially when it comes to acknowledging our own embeddedness in the commonplace routines of daily life. This is because Lefebvre's own works broadly affirm virtually all of these arguments. But he does so in a manner that does not abandon critique by surrendering the field of everyday life studies to a descriptive phenomenology. Looking more closely at this issue brings us full-circle to the question of defamiliarization and the nature of the relationship between everyday and (relatively) more theoretical knowledges and practices.

Lefebvre would acknowledge that we cannot, and should not aim to, comprehend phenomena in some sort of totalizing sense. As such, he clearly participates in 'the refusal of the modern project of Truth (the ideology of a totalizing identity or Sufficient Reason) which seeks to unify the limitless plurality of meanings that make up language and our world' (Kearney 1991, p. 172), a renunciation that has preoccupied many prominent intellectuals in the second half of the twentieth-century. Again, recall Lefebvre's preference for the tactile metaphor of 'grasping' living entities and processes, rather than striving to dominate things via the forced imposition of sterile and abstract concepts onto the world. 'The totality we have defined does not purport to exhaust man's "being," or to define it', asserts Lefebvre (2002, p. 193). 'It does not preclude other determinations and other dimensions, i.e., other degrees of freedom. On the contrary, it invokes them; it is a necessary and non-sufficient condition for them'. However, rejecting totalization does not preclude the very existence of totalities or the importance of striving to comprehend them, of the need to investigate the everyday dialectically and articulate a critical understanding of its central elements and dynamics. In particular, 'routine' *per se* is not the target of Lefebvre's critique of everyday life. Phenomenologically-speaking, the acquisition of habits and routines performed in the 'distracted' mode of profane existence, as mentioned in the opening paragraphs of the present article – Perec's 'dreamless sleep' – is, as Felski rightly points out, an intrinsic part of our experience of the life-world. But *enforced* routinization in the service of the reproduction of global capital, in a manner that increasingly alienates us from the rhythms and desires of the human body, the moral fabric of our intersubjective relations, and the cycles of the natural world, and that inures us to the *status quo* by effectively short-circuiting our ability to envisage and enact different ways of living, is something that needs to be understood critically and ultimately transformed. Lefebvre sought to 'expose' – but not surmount or negate – the ambiguities and contradictions of daily life, to grapple with 'its baseness and exuberance, its poverty and fruitfulness, thereby releasing the myriad forces and energies that are an inherent part of it' (Clucas 2000, p. 19).

In this dialectical intertwining of routine and creativity, the trivial and momentous, as mediated by the Lefebvrean 'moment', the everyday is not negated or absorbed into a 'higher' level of development. It should be noted that this oscillation crucially involves the Hegelian term *aufhebung* (sometimes rendered in English as 'sublation'). But *aufhebung* for Lefebvre does not mean an idealist transcendence of the real, which it is all too often interpreted as. Rather, it is best understood as a spiralling movement in which destruction is necessarily bound up *with* preservation, in the sense of the 'storing' or 'saving' of something, usually for later use. (Or, even more interestingly, *aufhebung* can mean taking something from the ground in order to examine it sensuously and ultimately return it.)[19] Lefebvre is not promoting a cult of 'newness' for its own sake, or continual innovation, of a sort favoured by various modernist avant-gardes (as well as postmodernism), mainly because highly creative or extraordinary moments inscribe difference and negativity in ways that always emerge from, and eventually devolve back to, the ground or 'humus' of everyday life. As such, Trebitsch (1991, p. xviii) points out, Lefebvre's critical strategy resembles in many respects the 'negative dialectics' of Adorno, insofar as both develop their understanding of modernity by focussing on 'the way the negative is at work in present reality, acknowledg[ing] that this negativity embodies another "colour" – a difference in what is possible which will allow us to stand back from the greyness of the "already there" in order, precisely, to criticize it'.

This critical strategy highlights an important element of Lefebvre's utopianism, which is not concerned with the construction of purely speculative ideal societies in a manner bereft of practical ramifications – what is often called the 'blueprint' model of utopianism.[20] This sort of appeal to utopian transcendence, often through the vehicle of some kind of 'technological fix' unmediated by human intervention, and without reference to concrete forms of social and cultural life, merely reconciles the existing contradictions and antimonies of modern society into what Adorno once called a 'spurious harmony'. But this position, which helps to explain much of the current hostility to utopian thinking, cannot be associated legitimately with Lefebvre, because he sought to grasp the complex skein of negative and positive forces embedded in the dense textures and rhythms of everyday life, and with how these relate to wider totalities in a manner which provides us with tangible clues and signs *vis-à-vis* the possibility of alternative modes of being – roughly what Bloch designated as the 'concrete utopia'. Again, a heightened awareness of utopian possibilities is for Lefebvre generated largely through defamiliarizing processes (in the form of his theory of moments or the festival, for instance). Yet, these are 'not situated outside the everyday, but can be seen articulated with it by uniting with critique in order to introduce into it what is lacking to its richness. It can thus be seen as tending to overcome at the heart of the everyday, in a new form of particular pleasure united with the whole, the old oppositions of lightness and heaviness, the serious and the lack of seriousness', as Lefebvre writes (2003, pp. 175–176).

A better understanding of Lefebvre's thoughts on everyday utopianism might well be gleaned from a brief consideration of McCracken's article 'The completion of old work: Walter Benjamin and the everyday'. McCracken points out that phenomenologically-informed accounts of the everyday do not leave their object of study untouched, as its adherents so often suggest. Phenomeno-logical description, that is to say, is no less bound up with extant regimes of power than other discourses of social theory; its inherent biases and motivating interests are simply more veiled. The Wittgensteinian conceit of leaving everyday life 'as it is', which could be said to inform the work of Felski and others, is ultimately vulnerable to the charge of naïveté. It is naive because Benjamin fully understood, following Simmel, that the shocks and vicissitudes of modern urban life, combined with the commodification of virtually all facets of daily existence, tend to induce habitualized and highly stereotypical behavioural reactions to our environment that in many ways ultimately support the structures of domination, albeit not in all respects, or in wholly irreversible ways. The study of the everyday cannot exclude a comprehension of extant socioeconomic forces or the material culture of urban space simply because these extensively and profoundly shape the former. Accordingly, the task for the social critic is to investigate 'the points of rupture in the everyday, its cracks and fissures', inasmuch as 'the everyday is not just *what is*, because what exists is made up of the complex social relations that constitute collective living. It is at the fractures and joins of the everyday that the possiblities [*sic*] of *what might be* emerge' (McCracken 2002, p. 151). McCracken argues that Benjamin cleaves to the possibility of a dialectic between routine and innovation – as does Lefebvre, it should be clear by now – one that does not seek to neutralize or supersede the everyday, but to nourish and enrich it. Benjamin's methodology is not content to view everyday life as something that is merely 'there', but to 'to suggest that indeed what has been, might, at the same time, contain the possibility of transfiguration' (McCracken 2002, pp. 146–147). In Benjamin's case, this possibility turns on the interrelation between immediate experience (*Erlebnis*) and a more distanciated and reflective state of mind (*Erfahrung*). Through such productive juxtapositions, the habitualized 'dreaming' that constitutes the everyday life of modernity is disrupted and jolted into a state of relative wakefulness, albeit one in which the dust of sleep is never entirely absent from our eyes. So long as we understand the metaphors of 'cracks' or 'fissures', not as surface imperfections on an otherwise perfect whole (Parmenides' inert sphere), but as constitutive of the complex and incomplete totality that is the everyday, McCracken's analysis is a pertinent and useful one it the present context.[21]

This emphasis on the continual interaction and slippage between 'sleep' and 'waking', habit and creativity, is echoed in another important article authored by Paul Harrison. He argues that we build up habits and embodied routines through a process of 'enfolding' memory, in a manner that helps to 'filter out' the background noise of everyday life and provides us with a degree of shared ontological security a la Giddens. Yet, there is no singular, overarching life-world in late modern societies within which such a process of enfolding occurs. Rather, there are a multiplicity of overlapping and often antagonistic forms of life, which is one reason why the Wittgensteinian ethos of Felski *et al.* is open to question. In engaging with multiplicity and difference, we not only 'sense' in a relatively passive way, but more actively *make sense*, and we do so in a way that can partially unravel habits and precipitate different reconfigurations *vis-à-vis* our way of living. What allows for such reconfigurations, of new assemblages of sense and meaning, is what Harrison terms 'style', which (comparatively speaking) is a more spontaneous and open-ended process than that associated with the usual flow of everyday routine. Whilst both improvisation and repetition are equally necessary to the constitution of social life, each considered on its own, in isolation from the other, as they so often are in the everyday life literature, is deeply problematic. As Harrison writes:

> habits are sets of techniques for on-going coping *of* and *within* given forms of life, in relation to this style operates by drawing out the potential of such contexts. Style operates by liquefying (molecularizing) some of the consistency habit. Habits set boundaries for forms of life and so ways of seeing and saying, delineating a field in which certain moves are sensible. . . . Style always refers to life, always to a 'style of life', as it is always an embodied doing. The term 'style of life' should not mislead, it does not refer to a complete survey of a life, but to movements in living. . . . To invent a possibility of life is to make sense: to operate a detournament [*sic*] within the conditions of sensation and so synthesize a new difference.
>
> (2000, pp. 512–513)

Conclusion

Thinking about the points raised above by Harrison and others helps us to better grasp the nature and limits of critique, and to acknowledge that we need to comprehend daily existence as a mode of being that is neither wholly about stultifying routine or untrammelled invention, but something that lies on the 'threshold between the ordinary and the extraordinary, between what is and what might be. The extraordinary is never the "truth" of the everyday, but neither is it its untruth' (McCracken 2002, p. 164). The critique of everyday life should not be about denouncing the habitualized illusions and foibles of daily life as a form of 'false consciousness', so as to proffer an unequivocal and universal truth through some definitive flash of insight. The 'bad' everyday is, after all, always bound up with the 'good' everyday – which is not to say that we cannot exercise analytical and value judgements about the differences between them. Rather, critique as Lefebvre understands it is about opening ourselves up to multiple possibilities, in order to embrace a myriad of alternative ways of thinking and living. It does so by subverting the 'naturalization' of dominant viewpoints and ideologies via the 'making strange' of daily life, but in a manner that relies on a productive juxtaposition of creative play and habitualized routine, and that does not project a monolithic and essentially theological vision of a transcendent, utopian society. Lefebvre therefore participates in the construction of a critical (and self-critical) discourse that is best understood as a 'seditious expression of social change and popular sovereignty carried on in a permanently open process of envisioning which is not yet' (Moylan 1986, p. 213). Accordingly, his legacy is one that, so I would argue, retains its crucial importance *vis-à-vis* the perennial project of 'changing life', and hence of continuing relevance to the study and critique of the everyday.

Notes

1   For more on 'problematization', see Gardiner (2000a), Highmore (2002) and Felski (2000, 2002).

2   The phrase 'critical-dialectical' is taken from Colebrook (2002).

3   As Tacussel (1989, p. 61) notes, however, the story is somewhat more complicated than this. Everyday life studies can also take their cue from various philosophical currents (Kant, Hegel, Heidegger, Wittgenstein), novelists like Proust or Musil, and cultural movements like Dada or Surrealism. More recently, also, cultural studies and postmodernism have claimed a fidelity to the 'everyday' as part of their central interests and orientations (see Gardiner 2000a, pp. 8–9). However, for the purposes of this article, we can talk about a broad division between materialist and critical-dialectical approaches on the one hand, and more interpretive-textualist ones on the other – although of course some figures, like Maffesoli (see his contribution to this *Cultural Studies* issue), often straddle this divide.

4   See, for instance, Heller and Feher (1988) on 'messianic Marxism'; also Gardiner (1997).

5   Yet, Felski goes even further than this, suggesting that more populist approaches which strive to challenge the perceived intellectualism of such quasi-transcendental theories and the thinly-veiled denigrations of the everyday they supposedly evince – a good example being the highly influential work of de Certeau – still paradoxically cling to the view that everyday life harbours emancipatory qualities that escapes the everyday *per se*. The main difference is that, for the likes of de Certeau, the 'masses' are not engaged in any deliberate project of social transformation. Rather, through the course of their daily lives, individuals engage in various non-conscious activities that are not subordinated to the criteria of instrumental success or performative efficacity, and hence inadvertently confound the operation of centralized power. De Certeau therefore ends up subscribing to a 'ludic vision of mystical spaces of affirmation created by those who turn their back on politics and its

games of power', as Ross describes it, a 'mystical celebration of localisms and quartierismes [that] comes to resemble the path taken by the "user," the pratiquant, the ordinary man' (1997, p. 22). As such, the apparently opposing categories of what Ross refers to as the 'sociologist' vs. the 'priest' are not so different as might be supposed with respect to the status of everyday life. This is a conclusion with which Felski would likely concur, insofar as she holds that de Certeau does not properly appreciate the mundane and repetitive qualities of daily life (see Felski 2002, p. 612).

6   It is worth noting that different theorists of everyday life have divergent terms for of such phenomena: the Surrealists, for instance, looked at the 'marvellous', poetic flashes that irrupted into everyday life in the most unexpected situations and defied our habitualized expectations. Lefebvre evoked the 'festival' as an example of a spontaneous, ecstatic and collective affirmation of transfigured social relationships, in a manner that both transcended and enriched everyday life, as did the Situationists, who also referred to such pre-modern forms of celebratory sociality as the potlatch. Bakhtin, likewise, found succour in the 'carnivalesque', which for him revealed the arbitrariness of not only established linguistic or literary conventions, but also of a whole range of institutional arrangements and social roles. Yet all such techniques of defamiliarization are examples of what Bloch called the *novum*, by which he meant the periodic introjection of the radically new into the apparently stable, and that makes its appearance in different forms and unexpected historical junctures. For more on this topic, see Gardiner (2000a).

7   Equally, as Felski (2000, p. 611) rightly points out, it would be wrong to assume that techniques of defamiliarization will translate automatically into effective and progressive political action, rather than, say, postmodern irony or cynicism.

8   It is important to point out that, *pace* Felski, not only do 'specialized' knowledges partake of mundane habits and routinizations, the everyday itself is not immune to innovation and novelty. Thus, the 'unquestioned' and cognitively opaque nature of daily life is a relative, rather absolute quality, and the desire to drawing stark dividing lines between specialized and ordinary knowledges is futile (see also Frow 2002).

9   It might be pointed out that other approaches to the everyday, such as cultural studies, have always regarded themselves as 'underlabourers' *vis-à-vis* the mundane sociocultural world, whatever the success or failure of this identification understood as theoretical intervention/political praxis. O'Neill's quote, then, might well reflect certain obsessions and identifications peculiar to sociology, as opposed to other disciplines or transdisciplinary approaches. I thank Greg Seigworth for suggesting this.

10   It is interesting to note, for instance, that whereas Felski regards Lefebvre *et al.* as archetypal avant-garde modernists, Frow portrays Lefebvre as a nostalgic romanticist who pines for the supposed totality and unified culture of the pre-modern. And whilst Felski argues that Lefebvre denigrates the everyday and

sees positivity elsewhere, located instead in 'higher-order' aesthetic or intellectual phenomena, Colebrook sees him as interpreting daily life as suffused with a pure positivity that is in opposition to the reifications of high culture or formal institutions. Such divergent readings belie a failure to grasp the entirety of Lefebvre's project, and to appreciate fully the complex and nuanced qualities of his work.

11   In this context it is worth mentioning that Lefebvre's criticism of the Surrealists hinged to a large extent on the latter's focus on exceptional events and phenomena to the neglect of everyday life. That is, Lefebvre finds fault with the Surrealist tendency to interpret the 'marvellous' as an escape or transcendence of everyday life. For Lefebvre, the notion of the marvellous, which predates the Surrealists and can be found in such nineteenth-century artistic and literary movements as Symbolism and the Decadents, expresses a 'transcendental contempt for the real' (Lefebvre 1991a, p. 29). Hence, to his mind Surrealism reinforced rather than overcame the perennial bourgeois separation between spirit and matter, mind and body, ideal and reality. Lefebvre suggests the Surrealists were right to believe that, under modernity, myth and ritual are written off as manifestations of 'irrationality', and sublimated into lesser domains like 'play', 'art', or 'dreams'. However, rather than develop a theory of *poesis*, and come to appreciate the rich and manifold character of human experience, Surrealism preferred to cultivate irrationality and the 'bizarre' as an escape from the everyday. Hence, to remain at the level of the aesthetic rather than grasp the 'total person' (i.e. all the multifaceted aspects of human existence) was for Lefebvre (as it was for Benjamin) a profound mistake. The goal for Lefebvre, as Trebitsch puts it, was the develop a 'theoretical method capable of reconciling thought and life . . . of producing one's life as the "revolutionary way", as opposed both to the "poetic" way embodied by the Surrealists and the Heiddeggerian-style "metaphysical" way' (1991, p. xx). It is worth noting that Lefebvre's critique of Surrealism dovetails in many respects with that of Benjamin – on the latter, see the contribution by Ganguly in this issue of *Cultural Studies*.

12   Interestingly, Lefebvre mentions that the natural system of measurement for the cyclical is based on duodecimals, because it 'extends itself to living matter in direct providence from nature' (Lefebvre 1996, p. 231), whereas the metric system, based on multiple of ten, is better suited to the linear. For more on the birth of the metric system and its erasure of local and experiential forms of measurement in eighteenth-century France, see Alder (2002).

13   For more on Lefebvre and rhythmanalysis, see Highmore's contribution to this issue of *Cultural Studies*.

14   Jay usefully points out that Lefebvre's notion of totality borrowed much from the Surrealists, especially the idea (*contra* Hegel) that totality is best understood as a juxtaposition of dispersed and contradictory elements that does not evolve towards some final synthesis (Jay 1984, p. 287; see also Baugh 2003, pp. 55–56).

15   For Merleau-Ponty, the dialectic is not an abstract, mystical force that propels
      history inexorably down a preordained path. Rather, it must be understood as
      an 'intra-ontology' that allows us to think of relationality as a complexly-
      mediated and mutually-conditioning process that occurs simultaneously at a
      number of different levels of reality and orders of being, and is not marked by
      an inherent *telos* towards ultimate resolution. Positive and negative forces
      interpenetrate each other, are contained as 'seeds' within their ostensive
      opposites, in a manner that will eventually germinate into something unex-
      pected. Moreover, dialectical moments represent contingent transformations
      that can only occur in and through the medium of concrete human bodies,
      minds and actions, in concert with other individuals, within the context of a
      shared lifeworld. Consequently, totalities for Merleau-Ponty are 'open'; they
      are manifestations of identity *and* difference, unity *and* diversity, and contain
      within themselves multiple and often conflictual temporalities. For more on
      Merleau-Ponty's interpretation of totality and dialectics, see Gardiner
      (2000b).

16   Indeed, in an untranslated essay entitled 'The notion of totality in the social
      sciences', written in 1955, Lefebvre explicitly upbraids Lukács' *History and
      Class Consciousness* for advancing an image of a closed totality, especially when
      it came to class consciousness. For more on this, see the discussion in Jay
      (1984, pp. 276–299).

17   It should be pointed out that Lefebvre's conception of 'difference' is radically
      at odds with that espoused by postmodernism. Whereas the latter tends to
      equate difference with particularity or uniqueness, or mere symbolic contrast,
      for Lefebvre it emerges out of living practice and conflict. Differences, in
      other words, cannot be presumed to exist. They are always part of a larger
      ensemble, or series of ensembles; they have to be fought for, against the forces
      of homogenization; and they crucially involve the realization of alternative
      ways of living, which is not reducible to the production of discourses *per se*
      (see Kofman and Lebas 1996, p. 27). As Lefebvre writes:

>   One might suppose that little argument would be required to establish
>   that the 'right to be different' can only have meaning when it is based on
>   actual struggles to establish differences and that the differences generated
>   through such theoretical and practical struggles must themselves differ
>   both from natural distinguishing characteristics and from differentiations
>   induced within existing abstract space. The fact remains that the differ-
>   ences which concern us, those differences upon whose future strength
>   theory and action may count, can only be effectively demonstrated by dint
>   of laborious analysis.
>
>   (1991b, p. 64)

18   See the extensive Lefebvre bibliography in Shields (1999).
19   See http://www.hegel.net/general/dict/sublation.htm

20   Moylan sees this sort of utopianism as indicative of the rationalistic desire to contain the world within an homogeneous conceptual whole, to impose order and system-ness upon a messy and recalcitrant reality and to thereby exclude difference and diversity. He contrasts this with another form of utopian discourse that can function in a more oppositional and subversive manner, and can hint at the possibility of a less oppressive and exploitative form of social organization. The latter is what Moylan refers to as the 'critical utopia', a hypothetical mode of being which 'bases its drives in the personal experience of unfulfilled human need, rather than in instrumentally rational systemic requirements'. Critical utopias reject domination, hierarchy and 'identity-thinking' in order to explore 'emancipatory ways of being as well as the very possibility of utopian longing itself' (Moylan 1986, p. 212, p. 12). They are not merely imaginary projections of ideal cities or societies, in that they are linked to actual sociohistorical movements and the activities and desires of particular social groups. Moreover, they are reflexive in the sense that they are aware of the limitations of the dominant utopian tradition, but also in that they are self-critical and deconstructive. Accordingly, they attempt to realize the contours of a desired future society in their very textual and narrative form via the incorporation of elements of contradiction, ambiguity, and openness. In so doing, they disrupt the unified and homogeneous narrative of the traditional utopia and demonstrate the multiplicity of possible futures. Lefebvre's work, I suggest, adheres fully to Moylan's conception of the critical utopia.

21   See, for instance, the discussion of Lefebvre's treatment of Leibniz's concept of 'viculum substantiale' in the introduction of the present volume. Thanks again to Greg Seigworth for this observation.

References

Alder, K. (2002) *The Measure of All Things: The Seven-Year Odyssey and Hidden Error That Transformed the World*, Simon and Schuster, New York.

Bakhtin, M. (1984) *Rabelais and His World*, trans. H. Isowolsky, The MIT Press, Cambridge, MA.

Baugh, B. (2003) *French Hegel: from Surrealism to Postmodernism*, Routledge, London and New York.

Bauman, Z. (1992) *Intimations of Postmodernity*, Routledge, London and New York.

Brekhus, W. (1998) 'A sociology of the unmarked: redirecting our focus', *Sociological Theory*, vol. 16, no. 1, pp. 34–51.

Clucas, S. (2000) 'Cultural phenomenology and the everyday', *Critical Quarterly*, vol. 42, no. 1, pp. 8–34.

Colebrook, C. (2002) 'The politics and potential of everyday life', *New Literary History*, vol. 33, pp. 687–706.

de Certeau, M. (1984) *The Practice of Everyday Life*, trans. S. Rendall, The University of California Press, Berkeley, CA.

Felski, R. (2000) 'The invention of everyday life', in *Doing Time: Feminist Theory and Postmodern Culture*, NYU Press, New York, pp. 77–98.

Felski, R. (2002) 'Introduction', *New Literary History*, vol. 33, pp. 607–622.

Foucault, M. (1980) *Power/Knowledge: Selected Interviews and Writings 1972–77*, Pantheon Books, New York.

Frow, J. (2002) '"Never draw to an inside straight": on everyday knowledge', *New Literary History*, vol. 33, pp. 623–637.

Gardiner, M. E. (1997) 'A postmodern utopia? Heller and Féher's critique of messianic Marxism', *Utopian Studies*, vol. 8, no. 1, pp. 89–122.

Gardiner, M. E. (2000a) *Critiques of Everyday Life*, Routledge, London and New York.

Gardiner, M. E. (2000b) '"A very understandable horror of dialectics": Bakhtin and Marxist phenomenology', in *Materialising Bakhtin: The Bakhtin Circle and Social Theory*, eds C. Brandist & G. Tihanov, Macmillan, Basingstoke.

Giddens, A. (1984) *The Constitution of Society*, University of California Press, Berkeley, CA.

Gramsci, A. (1971) *Selections from the Prison Notebooks*, eds Q. Hoare & G. Nowell-Smith, International Publishers, New York.

Harrison, P. (2000) 'Making sense: embodiment and the sensibilities of the everyday', *Environment and Planning D: Society and Space*, vol. 18, pp. 497–517.

Heller, A. (1979) *A Theory of Feelings*, Van Gorcum, Assen.

Heller, A. & Ferenc Fehér, F. (1988) *The Post-Modern Political Condition*, Columbia University Press, New York.

Highmore, B. (2002) *The Everyday Life Reader*, Routledge, London and New York.

Ireland, C. (2002) 'The Appeal to Experience and its Consequences - Variations on a Persistent Thompsonian Theme', *Cultural Critique*, Fall, vol. 52, pp. 86–107.

Jay, M. (1984) *Marxism and Totality: Adventures of a Concept*, University of California Press, Berkeley, CA.

Jay, M. (1993) *Downcast Eyes: The Denigration of Vision in Twentieth-Century French Thought*, University of California Press, Berkeley, CA.

Kearney, R. (1991) *Poetics of the Imagination: From Husserl to Lyotard*, Harper Collins, London.

Kofman, E. & Lebas, E. (eds and trans.) (1996) 'Lost in transposition - time, space and the city', in *Writings on Cities*, ed. L. Lefebvre, Basil Blackwell, Oxford.

Lefebvre, H. (1968) *Dialectical Materialism*, trans. J. Sturrock, Jonathan Cape Ltd, London.

Lefebvre, H. (1991a) *Critique of Everyday Life Vol. I: Introduction*, trans. J. Moore, Verso, London.

Lefebvre, H. (1991b) *The Production of Space*, trans. D. Nicholson-Smith, Basil Blackwell, Oxford.

Lefebvre, H. (1996) *Writings on Cities*, eds E. Kofman & E. Lebas, Basil Blackwell, Oxford.

Lefebvre, H. (2002) *Critique of Everyday Life Vol. II: Foundations for a Sociology of the Everyday*, trans. J. Moore, Verso, London.

Lefebvre, H. (2003) *Henri Lefebvre: Key Writings*, eds S. Elden, E. Lebas & E. Kofman, Continuum, New York and London.

Lefebvre, H. & Regulier, C. (1999) 'The rhythmanalytical project', *Rethinking Marxism*, vol. 11, no. 1, pp. 5–13.

Lunn, E. (1982) *Marxism and Modernism: An Historical Study of Lukács, Brecht, Benjamin, and Adorno*, The University of California Press, Berkeley, CA.

McCracken, S. (2002) 'The completion of old work: Walter Benjamin and the everyday', *Cultural Critique*, Fall, vol. 52, pp. 145–166.

Moylan, T. (1986) *Demand the Impossible: Science Fiction and the Utopian Imagination*, Methuen, London.

O'Neill, J. (1995) *The Poverty of Postmodernity*, Routledge, London and New York.

Osborne, P. (1995) *The Politics of Time: Modernity and Avant-garde*, Verso, London.

Perec, G. (1999) *Species of Spaces and Other Writings*, Penguin, Harmondsworth.

Ross, K. (1997) 'The sociologist and the priest', *Journal of Contemporary French Studies*, vol. 1, no. 1, pp. 17–30.

Schütz, A. (1967) *The Phenomenology of the Social World*, trans. G. Walsh and F. Lehnert, Northwestern University Press, Evanston.

Sheringham, M. (2002) 'Attending to The everyday: Blanchot, Lefebvre, Certeau, Perec', *French Studies*, vol. 54, no. 2, pp. 187–199.

Shields, R. (1999) *Lefebvre, Love, and Struggle: Spatial Dialectics*, Routledge, London.

Smith, D. E. (1987) *The Everyday World as Problematic*, Open University Press, Milton Keynes.

Tacussel, P. (1989) 'Criticism and understanding of everyday life', *Current Sociology*, vol. 37, no. 1, pp. 61–70.

Trebitsch, M. (1991) 'Preface', in *Critique of Everyday Life Vol. I: Introduction*, H. Lefebvre, trans. J. Moore, Verso, London.

Keya Ganguly

PROFANE ILLUMINATIONS AND THE EVERYDAY

The historical movement of surrealism continues to influence contemporary theories of everyday life even if its project of bourgeois self-transformation proved to be an epochal failure. The melancholic subjectivity associated with surrealist experiments is often regarded as a form of resistance against objective conditions of capitalist domination. This essay looks at Walter Benjamin's and Theodor Adorno's arguments about surrealism's radical attempts to transform the everyday. It reflects on the similarities and differences between the views of these two Frankfurt School thinkers, showing how Benjamin found surrealism to be ultimately inadequate to the purpose of social critique, while Adorno still located in its vision a source of possibility for overcoming the alienation of subject and object. Both Benjamin and Adorno took surrealism to be the site of an epistemological and political crisis, but they had differing interpretations of its critique of commodity culture. Benjamin emphasized surrealism's 'montage-like' strategies of estranging the familiarity of the everyday world but concluded that the 'profane illuminations' of surrealism never managed to transcend the realm of the imagination, or to serve as a call to action. Adorno, by contrast, saw in surrealism the potential to mobilize subjective aesthetic experience against the rationalizing imperatives of daily life, although he did not think the lessons of surrealism could be duplicated or reduced to a dogma about the efficacy of the unconscious. For Benjamin, particularly, the limitations of surrealism as a political and aesthetic movement revealed the ongoing necessity of organized political struggle, even as he understood its 'intoxicating' appeal. In this, he remains distant from contemporary modes of criticism that celebrate the ineffability of cultural margins and the oppositionality of subjective modes of being.

Keywords   aura; dialectics; Frankfurt School; historical materialism; profane illumination; surrealism

For the German philosopher Walter Benjamin, the concept of 'aura' applied not only to artworks but also to ideas themselves and, in his collected writings, he credited his Weimar contemporary, Karl Kraus, with having captured the essence of aura as follows: 'The closer you look at a word, the more distantly it looks

Cultural Studies Vol. 18, No. 2/3 March/May 2004, pp. 255–270
ISSN 0950-2386 print/ISSN 1466-4348 online   © 2004 Taylor & Francis Ltd
http://www.tandf.co.uk/journals   DOI: 10.1080/0950238042000201509

Routledge
Taylor & Francis Group

back'.[1] Benjamin's use of a proposition that he borrowed from Kraus (although it has come to be associated with him alone) as well as the relay between the entire framework of Weimar thought and the discourse of cultural studies, gives us some indication of the distances – and misunderstandings – that today separate critical theory's materialist emphases from our own scholarly conversations. The problematic of everyday life represents one site of both distance and convergence, especially to the extent that the idea of everyday life has become self-evident and, at the same time, elevated into a concept-metaphor for social existence. The objective of this essay is to work out an adequate understanding of how their perspectives on the historical movement of surrealism informed, in particular, Benjamin's and later, his younger colleague Theodor Adorno's theorizations of the everyday. This objective is in keeping with ongoing efforts to provide an adequate historicization of the philosophical antecedents of cultural studies (as exemplified, for instance, by the Frankfurt School's social philosophy).

Recent cultural studies of consumption and lifestyle often privilege everyday life as the terrain of oppositional expression (a position I find conceptually vacuous and ultimately unrelated to the project of serious critique). Rather than addressing that literature, I will focus on Benjamin's and Adorno's powerful formulations regarding the necessity to *overcome* the charge of the everyday, with the hope that the 'unforced force of the better argument' – as Jürgen Habermas once put it – has something more (and still) to offer in the ongoing struggle to transform the present. Benjamin's 1929 essay, 'Surrealism: The Last Snapshot of the European Intelligentsia' and Adorno's brief 1956 retrospection entitled, 'Looking Back on Surrealism' provide most of the bases for this discussion (although there will be occasion also to make reference to other writings that bear on the problem).[2,3] The phrase, 'everyday life', invoking as it does the inimitably important ideas of Henri Lefebvre (and, to a lesser extent, Michel de Certeau) has more commonly been traced to various traditions of French Hegelian thought of the twentieth-century, so it may be useful – if only as an exercise in genealogy – to recall the ways in which Gallic formulations about *la vie quotidienne* come together with an older German tradition of 'natural history' that took its formative cues from Marx, received its most productive elaboration in the thought of Georg Lukács, and culminated in the still-unsurpassed theorizations of *Alltagsgeschichte* produced by Weimar critics such as Adorno, Benjamin and others.[4]

To return to the conceptuality of the phrase itself: in so far as 'everyday life' seems transparent, it is misleading and betokens just that auratic quality of words and ideas Benjamin wanted to capture with the proposition from Kraus (cited at the beginning of this essay). That is to say, the more closely one looks at the phrase and its intended objects, the more distantly and obliquely they look back: the idea of everyday life as well as the practices it refers to conjure up a certain mysteriousness that needs to be unmasked rather than aestheticized or valorized.[5] At the very least, it is difficult to enlist the likes of Benjamin in such aestheticization – although, by the same token, there are any number of critics who deploy Benjamin to support textualist readings of aestheticist values (looking to reinforce the early Benjamin invested in the legacy of German idealism as opposed to the mature critic who took many of his leads from Brecht and Marxism). Nonetheless, if one examines the overall span of his writings and more particularly at his ideas in *One-Way Street* (the volume of writing immediately preceding the surrealism essay), he firmly abjures the idealization of the mysteries of the everyday. In that venue, he writes: 'histrionic or fanatical stress on the mysterious side of the mysterious takes us no further; we penetrate the mystery only to the degree that we recognize it in the everyday world, by virtue of a dialectic optic that perceives the everyday as impenetrable, the impenetrable as everyday' (Benjamin 1978, p. 237).

Both *One-Way Street* and the surrealism essay represent Benjamin's attempts to unveil the mysteries of the everyday, although the latter study is more explicitly taken up with strategic questions, in so far as it reflects on the dilemmas confronting radical intellectuals in the late 1920s. The essay on surrealism, published in 1929, was in fact composed in the previous year (that also saw the publication of *One-Way Street*). Benjamin's interest in surrealism dated back to 1925, the year Breton's first 'Manifesto of Surrealism' appeared. In a letter to Rilke, he wrote 'in particular what struck me about surrealism . . . was the captivating, authoritative and definitive way in which language passes over into the world of dreams' (Wolin 1994, p. 126). The surrealist fascination with dream life was endorsed by Benjamin and in his 1935 outline of the (unfinished) Arcades project, he would raise his obsession with the emancipatory potential embodied in dreams to the level of a methodological axiom. But for him the endorsement was also the basis of an immanent critique of the dream world – in line with Marx's understanding of the commodity as a dream form. In this, as in many other instances, Benjamin's conceptual investments reflect his debts more to Marx than Freud; his emphasis on the world of the everyday aimed at 'dissolving' myth into the space of history, just as his interest in dreams stemmed from the imperative to unearth the aspirations and desires that humanity is denied in the sphere of material life.

The problem of penetrating the everyday's mysteries relates to the concept of 'aura', which Benjamin (following Kraus) elaborated as the 'unique phenomenon of a distance, however close it may be' (Benjamin 1968, p. 222). Providing its most picturesque enlargement in his famous 'Artwork' essay, Benjamin uses an utterly everyday activity or scene of relaxation to formulate it: 'If, while resting on a summer afternoon, you follow with your eyes a mountain range on the horizon or a branch which casts its shadow over you, you experience the aura of those mountains, of that branch' (Benjamin 1968, pp. 222–223).[6] Of relevance to us is that, for Benjamin, the philosophical programme of dialectics and historical materialism represented the key to getting beyond the lure of auratic discourses; it also was the key to politicizing all aesthetics, including the aesthetics of the everyday. This, we may recall, was the central challenge of an era in which Fascism had, according to him, aestheticized politics – a mode with which we ourselves have become all too familiar in the context of the over-the-top theatrical stagings of George Bush *fils* as superhero of America. Aura, as an aspect of perception (rather than of the art object), does not disappear altogether under the regime of mechanical reproduction but is transposed onto mass-produced representations such as films and other 'phantasmagoric' forms; moreover, as we can glean from Benjamin's description of a mountain scene on a summer afternoon above, it pertains to everyday experience as well. Thus, despite its appeal, aura is in fact constitutive of 'cult value' (with all connotations of Fascism's mode of address intended here) and for this reason the aura of the everyday world needs to be undermined, not reinstated – first, through the painstaking and fraught work of criticism, but above all, by the 'energies of the revolution' (Benjamin 1978, p. 190).[7]

Only in the context of this overall framework of ideas do the specific arguments of the surrealism essay come into clear focus. Read out of place or too hastily, the essay may seem to endorse the propensities and worldviews associated with surrealist strategies of estranging and defamiliarizing the everyday as capable of bearing the burden of a radical aesthetic and political practice. Read together within Benjamin's general predilection for *Denkbilder* ('thought-images'), he appears quite far from suggesting that the recuperation of the quotidian can take place in the name of validating a space of subjective practice where the vicissitudes of capitalist existence are somehow bypassed or escaped. To lead with this contention is to agree entirely with Gilloch's estimation that 'Benjamin's essay on Surrealism is not a paean to its "heroic phase" . . . but rather, a critical intervention in its brief afterlife so as to tease out and redeem its own revolutionary truth content' (Gilloch 2002, p. 110). Benjamin (unlike many of his latter-day, poststructuralist interpreters) was invested in the aesthetic outlook of surrealism only to the extent that it provided him with a theory of revolutionary practice – as opposed to a theory of subjectivity that contented itself with gazing inward upon subjective or cultural fragmentation. Along these lines, Pensky has suggested that 'much of Benjamin's "materialist" work – above all his appropriation of the surrealists – was the attempt to articulate a methodology that could appropriate the mode of insight peculiar to melancholy subjectivity while avoiding its paralyzing effect' (Pensky 1993, p. xi).

Even the title of Benjamin's essay gives away something of his intentions: 'Surrealism: the *last* snapshot of the European intelligentsia' (emphasis added). Evoking the Hegelian sensibility of Minerva's owl only taking flight at dusk, Benjamin charges the surrealists with belatedness and decadence: they are what *remains* of the European intelligentsia, of its pretensions to a genuine liberatory movement. As an aside, we may note that such a charge is hardly a celebration; on the contrary, it is what ultimately prevents the surrealists from embodying much more than the effete sensibility of the outsider (as opposed to the organic imperatives of the revolutionary). Immediately into the essay, Benjamin adduces himself as 'the German observer', who understands the true stakes of surrealism's endeavour for, he says, 'he has had direct experience of its highly exposed position between an anarchistic *fronde* and a revolutionary discipline, and so has no excuse for taking the movement for the "artistic", "poetic" one it superficially appears' (Benjamin 1978, pp. 177–178). Caught in the ambivalent position between avant-garde posturing and the disciplined *work* involved in organizing a political transformation of the bourgeois order, the surrealists can retrospectively be seen as (perhaps unnecessarily) surrendering to the melancholia of an aestheticized subjectivism in the face of objective political constraints. Surrealism, in other words, must be reckoned with in terms of what it has to teach those who are situated down the stream of time from it about consolidating 'a matter-of-fact, profane struggle for power and domination' (Benjamin 1978, p. 178). And, based on their historical example, this includes lessons in both how to and how not to wage those struggles – since in the end surrealism proved to be a 'false overcoming' (Habermas's phrase). The 'profane illumination' (Benjamin 1978, p. 179) that Benjamin suggests as the precise method by which 'a materialistic, anthropological inspiration' can be arrived at for theorizing experience, represents, as Pensky clarifies, 'the only alternative that offered the possibility of relating the act of critical construction immediately to the prospect of revolutionary practice' (Pensky 1993, p. 189). But it is also important to emphasize that this prospect of an alternative suggested by the profane illuminations of surrealism were reckoned by Benjamin to be ineffective and unrealised – an emphasis that Habermas captures best in his famous retrospection on one of his predecessors at the Institute for Social Research:

> In the nonsensical acts of the surrealist, art was translated into expressive activity; the separation between poetic and political action had been overcome ... Nonetheless, the illustrations of pure violence offered by surrealism found in Benjamin an ambivalent spectator. Politics as show, or even poeticizing politics – when Benjamin saw these realizations, he did not want after all to close his mind to the difference in principle between political action and manifestation: 'This would mean the compete subordination of the methodical and disciplinary preparation for revolution to a praxis oscillating between training for it and celebrating its imminent onset'.
> (Habermas 1991, p. 119)

This talk of revolutionary theory and practice may well sound passé, accustomed as we have become these days to hearing about the alleged subversiveness of everyday practices such as shopping, reading romance novels, rap music or whatever, and, similarly, about the oppositionality of everyday existence (particularly when it comes to the 'consuming passions' of female or queer subjects).[8]

Likewise, the language of dialectics appears so old-fashioned and stodgy when compared to its borrowings in the pages of cultural studies journals as 'theory lite' – which, in the words of the advertising jingle, tastes great but is less filling.[9] Nonetheless, the form and substance of Marxist dialectics, however pre-post-modern it may sound, is the language to which we must have recourse. More pertinently, it colours the utterances of the Frankfurt School thinkers – not in some flatly nihilistic or elitist way (as has sometimes been caricatured) but as the hallmark of a genuine materialist criticism that cannot be satisfied merely with esoteric theory but with *actualizing* the potential for remaking the world that everyday objects hold out but do not guarantee. For Benjamin, then, surrealism could not provide a model for revolutionary thinking and it is quite surprising to find latter-day enthusiasts who, in reprising the idea of 'profane illumination' exemplified by surrealist strategies of defamiliarization and aesthetic *dégonflage*, use him to authorize their proclamations about cultural subversion.[10] According to Benjamin, however, 'This profane illumination did not always find the Surre-alists equal to it, or to themselves, and the very writings that proclaim it most powerfully, Aragon's incomparable *Paysan de Paris* and Breton's *Nadja*, show very disturbing symptoms of deficiency' (1978, p. 179). One might, with some justification, muse on the irony of our own theoretical milieu in which it is no longer uncommon to write off all attempts to conceptualize political praxis in terms of class struggle or organized opposition as the stuff of a 'vulgar' Marxism or as Judith Butler has accused, of 'Left Conservativism'. By any attentive (rather than ideological) measure, Benjamin would certainly be equally guilty of exem-plifying such a tendency, especially in his later writings. Habermas goes on in his essay to show how, from the point of his encounter with Brecht onwards, Benjamin in fact 'regarded the relationship of art and political praxis primarily from the viewpoint of the organizational and propagandistic utility of art for the class struggle' (Habermas 1991, p. 119).

If there remain any quarters of intellectual opinion in which cultural theo-rists retain the responsibility to submit their theoretical arguments about aesthetics and culture to the test of political accountability (and by that I mean of course oppositional political accountability), the deficiencies of surrealism are surely only magnified by history. The movement's strategies of disruption – the slogan, manifestation or counterfeit – are revealed as failures in relation to their political goals to the precise degree that they ended up being institutional-ized within the canon of modernist art practice and, one might equally add, those versions of populist cultural theory in which the distinctions between high and low art are removed by fiat (so that, for instance, Disney can be regarded as equivalent to Proust). Yet, for Benjamin the point was not to fixate either on the means or ends that surrealism might have reached, but on the possibilities that remained in shadow within the very medium of its failures. According to him, what continues to be valuable as a model for materialist criticism is the outlook of surrealism, an outlook that sought to trace 'the revolutionary energies that appear in the outmoded: the first factory buildings, the earliest photos, the objects that have begun to be extinct'. Indeed, he took this commitment directly from Louis Aragon, one of the most influential figures in the surrealist movement – who, in his novel, *The Peasant of Paris*, makes a claim on behalf of 'places that were incomprehensible yesterday and that tomorrow will never know' (quoted in Abbas 1989, p. 48).[11] Taking the surrealists as his conceptual point of departure – but, crucially, *not* as his point of arrival – Benjamin proposed that the most seemingly trivial phenomena could be used, once reassembled in the 'dialectical image', to deduce the most profound aspects and the innermost truths of bourgeois society. Wolin has persuasively argued that 'the purpose of this intention was not to attempt to discover rudiments of archaic life in the modern per se, but to unmask the idea of the modern itself – i.e. the idea of an endless stream of consumer goods or fashion – as that of eternal recurrence or the always-the-same' (1994, p. 129). The modern, characterized as eternal recurrence, in turn revealed its coalescence with the idea of mythical repetition, which dominates life in prehistory. Paraphrasing Adorno's recollections of Benjamin's own description of his interest in such a 'materialist anthropology', Wolin says: 'Thus prehistory returns to dominate the modern era under the mythical guise of commodity exchange, in which the self-identical perpetually presents itself as the new' (1994, p. 129). The surrealism essay constitutes Benjamin's first significant attempt to delineate this theoretical problematic, and it continued to represent the core of his intellectual project throughout his life ultimately terminating in the unfinished study of the Parisian arcades.

The line of thinking I have been tracing so far in relation to Benjamin's arguments about surrealism is consistent with more historically attentive discussions of his project, albeit contrary to the ways in which they have been read by critics invested in promoting a view of Benjamin as, so to speak, a post-structuralist *avant la lettre*.[12] By contrast, Howard Caygill's theoretical enlargement of Benjamin's arguments about experience is among the more careful and comprehensive assessments of Benjamin's writings. Caygill suggests that the convolution of memory Benjamin traced in his essay on Proust, finds its complement in the convolution of objects in his surrealism essay (Caygill 1998, p. 66). Acknowledging that it is 'perhaps one of Benjamin's most ambivalent essays', Caygill adduces Benjamin himself as stating that 'it at once celebrates the surrealist intoxication with 'the revolutionary energies that appear in the outmoded' while seeing them as remaining 'enmeshed in a number of pernicious Romantic prejudices' (1998, pp. 66–67). Quoting this statement from a letter Benjamin wrote to his friend, Gershom Scholem, Caygill underscores Benjamin's critique of the remnants of a Romanticist worldview within surrealism's own tendencies, noting that Benjamin described his relation to the surrealist movement as that of a 'philosophical Fortinbras' (Fortinbras, we may recall, is the figure who remains on the stage of Shakespeare's *Hamlet* at the end of all the destruction). Thus, what we are left with, what we have to recognize, is Benjamin's self-designation as the inheritor of surrealism's legacy *after* its destruction; a destruction that can only be regenerative *après coup*. In summing up Benjamin's historical evaluation of surrealism Caygill states:

> The surrealists' insight into how 'not only social but architectonic [destitution], the poverty of interiors, enslaved and enslaving objects – can suddenly be transformed into revolutionary energy' was very close to Benjamin's own concept of experience, *but for him their insight remained auratic. . . .* By casting himself as a 'philosophical Fortinbras', Benjamin gives a negative answer to the question he put to surrealism: 'are they successful in welding this experience of freedom to the other revolutionary experience that we have to acknowledge because it has been ours, the constructive dictatorial side of revolution?' Just as Fortinbras takes on the heritage of a court devastated by spectres, and commences its reconstruction so Benjamin sees himself entering into the heritage of auratic phantasms of surrealism, and recommencing their reconstruction in epic recognition.
>
> (Caygill 1998, p. 67, emphases added)

Let me turn now to the second of the major points of contact for this discussion: Adorno's later views of his friend (and sometimes intellectual opponent) Benjamin's meditations on surrealism's potential for rethinking questions of art and politics. However, before I do so, it may be instructive to have at least one indication of exactly how far we have travelled down the road of idealist, recuperative readings of Benjamin's work on the issue of surrealist practice. In a book that specifically takes up this topic, Cohen has argued that Benjamin's thought can be read as an attempt to reconstruct a 'surrealist Marxism' (1993, p. 3). She asserts that underlying Benjamin's writings is the influence of 'modern materialism', itself a derivation of Andre Breton's desire to 'reconcile Engels and Freud' and Engels's own nineteenth-century critique of mechanical materialism. However, according to her, in Benjamin's hands, this modern materialism becomes even more hybrid – a project of integrating 'the psychological, sensual, irrational, and often seemingly trivial aspects of life during the expansion of industrial capitalism which such monolithic Marxist categories as base and superstructure tend to obscure' (Cohen 1993, p. 4). Cohen's enterprise is to recuperate Benjamin's use of psychoanalytic language and surrealist conceptions from the criticisms of his colleagues at the Frankfurt School as well as Brecht – who, as she puts it, regarded this as 'the place where he [Benjamin] substitutes the smoke and mirrors of writerly technique for critical analysis' (1993, p. 8). Elevating writerly technique itself *into* critical analysis – in keeping with much of the tenor of contemporary textualist criticism – Cohen ends up producing a portrait of Benjamin who, far from being associated with any sort of revolutionary Marxism, is rendered a *surrealist* Marxist, an appellation Cohen uses to describe his interest in issues of interiority and subjectivity, mingled with his attempts to recombine a theory of art and experience. Against the grain of his own writings, Benjamin is transformed from a thinker concerned with both the theoretical and practical applications of a revolutionary Marxism (which he himself credited to his reading not only of Marx, but also Lukács's *History and Class Consciousness*) to being the bedfellow of Jean Baudrillard and post-Marxism (Cohen 1993, p. 11). Cohen's book is a virtuoso exercise in abstracting much of Benjamin's preoccupation with the conceptual terrain of the constitution of social relations under capitalism – the 'untranscendable horizon' of Marxist thought as Fredric Jameson has put it – to elaborate notions about what one of the blurbs on Cohen's book lauds as 'the historicity of the imagination'.[13] What she also, and symptomatically, leaves unaddressed is the question of why we should be persuaded that Benjamin is closer to Althusserian and post-Marxist apologetics than to his associates at the Frankfurt School (Leo Lowenthal, Eric Fromm, Herbert Marcuse and Ernst Bloch among others) all of whom had a great deal to say about psychoanalysis and materialism (modern and otherwise), not to mention the irrational aspects of modern life – without having to renounce or revise their Marxist affiliations and, moreover, precisely because the historical materialism of Marx and Engels (to name only the principals) was already capacious enough to encompass their arguments.[14]

Adorno cannot, of course, be mistaken for the intellectuals inspired by post-war French ideas – despite aspects of his work (the emphasis on subjective experience, the embrace of an aesthetic sublime, and so on) that seem to resonate with poststructuralist motifs. In his estimation, the difficulty in assessing Benjamin's oeuvre has less to do with a vexed relationship to Marxism than that we encounter with Benjamin a thinker whose 'thought sought again and again to free itself of all impulse to classify, the prime image of all hope for him [was] the name, of things and of men, and it is this that his reflection [sought] to reconstruct' (Adorno 1995, p. 231). Notwithstanding this difficulty in classifying Benjamin's overall work, his allegiance to the Hegelian-Marxist tradition was abundantly clear. As Adorno says, 'The Hegelian concept of "second nature", as the reification of self-estranged human relations, and also the Marxian category of "commodity fetishism" occupy key positions in Benjamin's work' (1995, p. 233). Reification, estrangement, commodity fetishism: these are all concepts that suffuse Benjamin's later writings and both *One-Way Street* and the surrealism essay represent key points in his turn away from philology and the philosophy of language to the mature and more complex terrain of historical materialism. By the time of his writing, this body of ideas, far from the supposed 'monolith' of Marxism's dependence on base-superstructure relations, was developed to a very nuanced extent (under the auspices of Marxism itself) by the likes of Lenin, Lukács, Bloch, Karl Korsch, Siegfried Kracauer and others in the German tradition. Benjamin was intimately familiar with this tradition, to say nothing of work done in Italy, England or France, with which he was less well acquainted.

Contrary to the ways that Benjamin has sometimes been rendered – as a thinker who elicited an aesthetic sublime from the everyday banalities of 'mere' history and economy – Adorno makes it clear that the fetish of subjective aestheticism had very little appeal for Benjamin in his mature phase (an aestheticism that was associated with the revelation or unconcealment of being ushered in by Heidegger and his followers). The subject of an entirely different discussion, let me simply note here that the Heideggerian return to 'being' was proclaimed under the sign of a revitalized attention to the concrete aspects of existence and to the essences of daily life – that took the psychoanalytic 'subject' out of the equation while reinstating it as *Dasein*. Adorno represents Benjamin as completely opposed to such philosophical moves: 'He saw through them [phenomenology and the ontological schools] as the mere mask of conceptual thinking at its wits [*sic*] end, just as he also rejected the existential-ontological concept of history as the mere distillate left after the substance of the historical dialectic had been boiled away' (1995, p. 231). Adorno goes further to state forcefully that, 'His [Benjamin's] target is not an allegedly over-inflated subjectivism but rather the notion of a subjective dimension itself' (1995, p. 235). So, finally, in Adorno's reading of Benjamin's theory of the everyday, he portrays the latter as 'drawn to the petrified, frozen or obsolete elements of civilization, to everything in it devoid of domestic vitality' (1995, p. 233). Within this overall perspective, surrealism was the tinderbox that lit the flame of Benjamin's 'conceptual liquidation' of the everyday, which he regarded as the scene of objective petrification rather than subjective salvation.

There are differences in interpretation between Adorno's own view of surrealism and that of Benjamin, in the place given to the importance of surrealist shocks. This emphasis is vividly brought home in the image Adorno uses in 'Looking back on Surrealism', to characterize the surrealists' artistic technique: 'The house has a tumor, its bay window. Surrealism paints this tumor: an excrescence of flesh grows from the house' (Adorno 1991, pp. 89–90). For Adorno, surrealism, coming as it did on the eve of the catastrophe of World War I, emblematized both the prefiguration of this catastrophe, as well as its aftermath – thereby including within it the kernel of a prospective vision of the future because the catastrophic event, in laying bare the destruction of everything in its wake, also makes renewal possible. Consequently, surrealism is to be 'looked back on' as a Janus-faced, double-sided movement, simultaneously betokening attempts to awaken from the nightmare of the nineteenth century and to penetrate the realities of twentieth-century daily life. In his words, 'After the European catastrophe the Surrealist shocks lost their force. It is as though they had saved Paris by preparing it for fear: the destruction of the city was their center. To conceptualize Surrealism along these lines, one must go back not to psychology but to Surrealism's artistic techniques' (Adorno 1991, p. 87). Putting more distance (than did Benjamin) between psychoanalytic modes of understanding subjectivity and surrealist practice, Adorno says: 'Reducing

Surrealism to psychological dream theory subjects it to the ignominy of some-thing official' (1991, p. 86); and further: 'Surrealist constructions are merely analogous to dreams, not more' (1991, p. 87). In other words, even though Adorno held in esteem the surrealist principle of returning art back to ordinary life, he did not think that this was because surrealism – like psychoanalysis – provided insights into the processes of the unconscious (or embodied them). Rather, Adorno upheld the conventional modernist belief that the artistic tech-niques of the surrealists, based on the principle of cinematic montage, intensified the fossilized terrain of everyday life – 'gathering up', as he put it, 'the distortions [that] attest to the violence that prohibition has done to the objects of desire' (1991, p. 90). In so doing they not only 'salvaged' (a word Adorno uses to describe the surrealist act) what is out of date but looked forward to a future in which the subject could once more experience authentic forms of art and life. This opinion, representing a kind of homeopathic theory of experience, is of course in line with his interpretation of lyric poetry, Schöenberg's music or Kafka's fiction, all of which he sought to interpret as resisting the reification of everyday life.[15]

Perhaps a secondary point for us to remember is that the contemporary critical warrant, first, for subjecting all social and discursive forms to psycho-analytic readings and second, for making wide-ranging associations between these expressions and the artistic explosions of the surrealists does not receive much support from Adorno. For him, '[t]his kind of decoding would force the luxuriant multiplicity of Surrealism into a few patterns and reduce it to a few meager categories like the Oedipus complex, without attaining the power that emanated from the idea of Surrealism if not from its works of art' (1991, p. 87). If Adorno disparaged the idea that any kind of analogue exists between the image-language of the unconscious and either theory or practice of surrealism, it likewise followed that for him a responsible theory of interpretation had to avoid the temptation to reduce the historical successes and failures of surrealism to programmatic formulations about the effectiveness of the unconscious. This is stated very clearly towards the beginning of his essay:

> Were Surrealism in fact nothing but a collection of literary and graphic illustrations of Jung or even Freud, it would not only duplicate, superflu-ously, what the theory itself says rather than giving it a metaphorical garb, but it would also be so innocuous that it would hardly leave room for the scandal that is Surrealism's intention and its lifeblood.
>
> (Adorno 1991, p. 86)

Moreover, although Adorno and Benjamin both shared a critique of the ways that the nineteenth-century embodied *par excellence* an era of bourgeois 'inwardness', itself highlighted by the over-abundance of decorative and ornamental elements in everyday objects (the velvet and plush of furnishings and the carapaces and coverings of everything from shaving kits to Fabergé eggs), Adorno regarded surrealism's lessons as a form of sociohistorical critique that looked both back-wards *and forward* in time. It is in their specific understanding as to whether surrealism's images were hieroglyphs of an archaic past (the terrain of psycho-analysis) or montage-like encapsulations of the futural dimension of sociohistory that Adorno and Benjamin differed in their efforts to resurrect the 'world-rubble of Surrealism' (Adorno 1991, p. 87). In the end, though, Benjamin was perhaps the better dialectician – despite the fact that Adorno accused him of being inadequately dialectical – because he had less faith in surrealism's prospective capacities, a position amply evident in the way he assessed the overall place of the movement:

> In just how inconspicuous and peripheral a substance the dialectical kernel that later grew into Surrealism was originally embedded, was shown by Aragon in 1924 – at a time when its development could not yet be foreseen – in his *Vague de rêves*. Today it can be foreseen. For there is no doubt that the heroic phase, whose catalogue of heroes Aragon left us in that work, is over. There is always, in such movements, a moment when the original tension of the secret society must either explode in a matter-of-fact, profane struggle for power and domination, or decay as a public demonstration and be transformed. Surrealism is in this phase of transformation at present.
>
> (Benjamin 1978, p. 178)

By contrast, Adorno continued to uphold the 'negative vision' by means of which surrealism mounted its attack on bourgeois life: 'Surrealism is akin to photog-raphy. Surrealism's booty is images, to be sure, but not the invariant, ahistorical images of the unconscious subject to which the conventional view would like to neutralize them; rather, they are historical images in which the subject's inner-most core becomes aware that it is something external, an imitation of something social and historical' (Adorno 1991, p. 89). Notwithstanding Adorno's faith in the power of forms of aesthetic practice (such as that of the surrealists) to overcome the limits of everyday reification through intensifying the sociohistor-ical contradictions of capitalist existence, we have still to understand that this was never a matter of the personal becoming political or of the individual escaping the command of capital to become the expression of a free multitude.[16] In the context of the growing popularity of hypostatic theorizations of the supposed spontaneity of the masses, we would do well to recall one of the more memorable propositions in Adorno's revaluation of the historical role of surrealism: 'The dialectical images of Surrealism are images of a dialectic of subjective freedom in a situation of objective unfreedom' (Adorno 1991, p. 88). As one can readily agree, in many ways this statement continues to be at the crux of the dilemma we face as oppositional cultural critics in that it is difficult to come to grips with the ineluctability of our predicament under capitalism: our private expressions of protest (whether as social actors or as critics) are subject to the fate of all efforts at rescuing 'subjective freedom in a situation of objective unfreedom'. To say this is neither to bemoan our paralytic existence nor is it to escape responsibility by admitting complicity with the 'system' (though that too has become something of a critical commonplace). Rather, it is to acknowledge that the search for adequate models of cultural and political, not to mention analytic, opposition can neither reside nor be dressed up in the guise of the failed gestures of yesterday. Attempting to replicate the 'shock' of surrealism's original intentions in the hope that, somehow, it will prove to be the escape hatch – at the level of the body and technologies of the self – that takes us beyond capitalist domination partakes not only of the effeteness of historical surrealism, it redoubles our error. For, in doing so, we are perhaps more guilty of 'freezing the moment of awakening' (Adorno 1991, p. 89). Instead of learning from the example of their obsolescence, we wrap ourselves in the illusion that in surrealist conceptions lie the kernels of our own critical agency. However, derailing or deranging the familiar, whether through the tactics of shock (rendered less shocking through repetition) or the aesthetics of *flânerie* does nothing to undermine the structure of social relations. If this is seen as the stuff of contestation, as a redoubt against power, this is only because we live in a historical moment in which the inherited categories of transformative social analysis – of class struggle, exploitation, reification – are smugly rejected as 'determinist' or 'reductionist' (against the anarchistic, ambiguous, and polysemic potentialities of the 'event'). At best, this is an aestheticist solution to historical problems; at worst, it betokens the self-satisfied politics and poetics of conservatism masquerading as the rhizomatics of a new radicalism.

Notes

1   From Benjamin's *Gesammelte Schriften* (1.2: 647 n; 200, n. 17), quoted in Weber (1996).

2   'Surrealism', in Benjamin (1978), and 'Looking Back on Surrealism', in Adorno (1991).

3   Although my discussion does not take up this essay, many of Benjamin's propositions about surrealism are also expressed his 1931 meditations on photography entitled, 'A short history of photography' (Benjamin 1972).

4   In addition to German and French elaborations of the concept of everyday life, there is also the Russian notion (and related discussion) of *byt*, which captures the sense of the everyday as banal and commonplace, above all else. An interesting, historical (though somewhat tendentious) enlargement of *byt* can be found in Boym (1994).

5   See, for instance, the sublime preoccupations of Chambers in his 'Signs of silence, lines of listening' (1996).

6   'The artwork in the era of its technical reproducibility' (Benjamin 1968).

7   Weber's essay (cited in note 1) elaborates on the ways that Benjamin counter-poses the decay of aura in the 'traditional' work of art with its continuation within the image-sphere in general.

8   I am referring less to the book by Williamson, with the title *Consuming Passions* (1991) – which provides a trenchant critique of popular cultural mores – than to the annual conferences designated by this name where much of this brand of scholarship is on display.

9   I owe this usage to James Kavanagh (who was the first to use it to describe the new pop culture studies, though the idea of 'theory lite' has travelled quite a bit since then and seems to have lodged itself as the mode *du jour* in many cultural studies departments).

10   See, for example, many of Taussig's vertiginous (and quite inapposite) formu-lations in *The Nervous System* (1992) and more moderate (though perhaps equally dehistoricized) renderings of surrealism's potentialities in Clifford's (1988) 'On ethnographic surrealism'.

11   See Abbas's (1989) stimulating essay, 'On fascination: Walter Benjamin's images'.

12   Cadava's book *Words of Light* (1998) seems to me to be a typical representative of this tendency; a somewhat earlier iteration of it would take us back to Nägele's (1988) *Benjamin's Ground: New Readings of Walter Benjamin*. Readers may also be interested to look at Agamben's (1988) 'Language and history in Benjamin'.

13   From a blurb by George Steiner on the back cover of Cohen's book.

14   In this, as in so much else in the book, Cohen falls into what can only be called the 'vulgar poststructuralist' formula of reducing the complex heritage of modern Marxism to the '68ist shibboleths first proclaimed by the likes of Louis Althusser, Michel Foucault and Gilles Deleuze and now recited as articles of faith by the literary-critical establishment in the name of 'critical theory'. This is a symptom, as Brennan (2001) has argued, of the 'transform-ism' of radical Left thought into contemporary anti-Communist theoretical reaction.

15   The best discussion of Adorno's theory of aesthetic experience is by Nicholsen (1997).

16   See the important criticisms of this strand of thinking in the special issue on empire and imperialism in *Interventions: International Journal of Postcolonial Studies*, particularly the theoretical dismantling of contemporary post-Marxist thought offered by Parry (2003).

References

Abbas, A. (1989) 'On fascination: Walter Benjamin's images', *New German Critique*, vol. 48, Fall, pp. 43–62.

Adorno, T. (1991) 'Looking back on surrealism' [1956], in *Notes to Literature*, trans. S. Weber Nicholsen, Columbia University Press, New York, pp. 86–90.

Adorno, T. (1995 [1967]) 'A portrait of Walter Benjamin', in *Prisms*, trans. S. Samuel & S. Weber, The MIT Press, Cambridge, MA.

Agamben, G. (1988) 'Language and history in Benjamin'. *Differentia*, Spring.

Benjamin, W. (1968) 'The artwork in the era of its technical reproducibility' (translated as 'The Work of Art in the Age of Mechanical Reproduction'), in *Illuminations*, trans. H. Zohn, Schocken Books, New York, pp. 217–256).

Benjamin, W. (1972 [1931]) 'A short history of photography', trans. Stanley Mitchell, *Screen*, vol. 13, no. 1, pp. 5–26.

Benjamin, W. (1978) *One-Way Street* [1928 under the German title of *Einbahnstrasse*], partially reprinted in *Reflections*, trans. E. Jephcott, Schocken Books, New York.

Benjamin, W. (1978 [1929]) 'Surrealism', in *Reflections*, trans. E. Jephcott, Schocken Books, New York, pp. 177–192.

Benjamin, W. (1991 [1974]) *Gesammelte Schriften*, eds R. Tiedemann & H. Schweppenhäuser, Suhrkamp Verlag, Frankfurt am Main.

Boym, S. (1994) *Common Places: Mythologies of Everyday Life in Russia*, Harvard University Press, Cambridge, MA.

Brennan, T. (2001) 'Antonio Gramsci and postcolonial theory', *Diaspora*, vol. 10, no. 2, pp. 143–187.

Cadava, E. (1998) *Words of Light*, Princeton University Press, Princeton, NJ.

Caygill, H. (1998) *Walter Benjamin: The Colour of Experience*, London, Routledge.

Chambers, I. (1996) 'Signs of silence, lines of listening', in *The Post-Colonial Question: Common Skies, Divided Horizon*, eds I. Chambers & L. Curti, Routledge, London, pp. 47–62.

Clifford, J. (1988) 'On ethnographic surrealism', in *The Predicament of Culture*, Harvard University Press, Cambridge, MA, pp. 117–151.

Cohen, M. (1993) *Profane Illumination: Walter Benjamin and the Paris of Surrealist Revolution*, Princeton University Press, Princeton, NJ.

Gilloch, G. (2002) *Walter Benjamin: Critical Constellations*, Polity, Cambridge.

Habermas, J. (1991) 'Walter Benjamin: consciousness-raising or rescuing critique', in *Walter Benjamin: Critical Essays and Recollections*, ed. G. Smith, MIT Press, Cambridge, MA, pp. 90–128.

Nägele, R. (1998) *Benjamin's Ground: New Readings of Walter Benjamin*, Wayne State University Press, Detroit.

Nicholsen, S. W. (1997) *Exact Imagination, Late Work: On Adorno's Aesthetics*, MIT Press, Cambridge, MA.

Parry, B. (2003) 'Internationalism revisited or in praise of internationalism', *Interventions: International Journal of Postcolonial Studies*, vol. 5, no. 2, pp. 299–313.

Pensky, M. (1993) *Melancholy Dialectics: Walter Benjamin and the Play of Mourning*, University of Massachusetts Press, Amherst, MA.

Taussig, M. (1992) *The Nervous System*, Routledge, New York.

Weber, S. (1996) 'Mass mediauras; or, art, aura, and media in the work of Walter Benjamin', in *Walter Benjamin: Theoretical Questions*, ed. D. S. Ferris, Stanford University Press, Stanford, CA, pp. 27–49.

Williamson, J. (1991) *Consuming Passions*, Marion Boyars Publishing House, London.

Wolin, R. (1994) *Walter Benjamin: An Aesthetic of Redemption*, University of California Press, Berkeley, CA.

Michael Pickering

EXPERIENCE AS HORIZON
Koselleck, expectation and historical time

This article explores and develops the concept of the horizon as a figurative and analytical device used to negotiate the relations between experience, everyday life and historical time. Its central focus is Reinhart Koselleck's application of the concept, though it also draws on the work of Karl Mannheim (through his distinction between conjunctive and communicative experience) and Raymond Williams (through his concept of structure of feeling) in order to add to and refine Koselleck's use of the term in examining the temporal structures of experience and expectation. Our sense of historical time is generated through the tensions between experience and expectation, everyday life and social process. These are, of course, historically variable and contingent. During the course of modernity and late modernity, experience and expectation have become increasingly divergent. Their separation has profoundly affected how we think about historical time in relation to everyday life and the span of a generation and a lifetime. It also turns the conception of history as historia magistra vitae on its head, with modernity increasingly forced to fund itself ethically out of its own transient present. The article discusses the main aspects of these changes and how they have altered the balance between the space and horizon of experience and expectation. It attends both to the need to examine historical concepts in terms of their various meanings and implications, and to the ways in which the particular concept of the horizon can help illuminate the consequences of accelerating time in the conditions of modernity and late modernity. The diminution of historical understanding in relation to everyday life is seen as among the most serious of these consequences.

Keywords experience; expectation; everyday; modernity; history; horizon

Introduction

The image of the horizon is commonly used in everyday life to signify a broadening of experience and outlook, whether through education, travel or some other

Cultural Studies Vol. 18, No. 2/3 March/May 2004, pp. 271–289
ISSN 0950-2386 print/ISSN 1466-4348 online © 2004 Taylor & Francis Ltd
http://www.tandf.co.uk/journals DOI: 10.1080/0950238042000201518

R Routledge
Taylor & Francis Group

means of transforming how we see and think. This is considered desirable because it means moving beyond the confines of everyday life. It means expanding our experience and knowledge in ways not available to us in our existing or immediate situation. The image encapsulates this aspiration by providing us with an extremely strong metaphor of what we seek to embrace, and, in this way, it mediates the distinction between exploration and fulfilment.

The metaphorical strength of the term derives from the exhilaration we feel when we look at the horizon, particularly at the pure, unbroken, panoramic line of the horizon on the open sea, for it is there that the magnitude of the earth and sky meet in an uninterrupted vastness. The joy and trepidation we experience in this are created by the absence of intervening objects that meet our gaze in cityscapes or the landscapes of mountain ranges. The scope of our vision as we look at the open horizon at sea becomes synonymous with a sense of the future as open and unlimited, inciting us to conceive beyond what we can actually see.

It is because of this that the horizon is the supreme locus of promise and possibility. It stands for the potential to transcend our present limits, to enlarge our view, to explore, to go beyond the boundaries of what we know. It tantalizes with the knowledge of what is unseen beyond it even as it traces a limit. The sea horizon symbolizes a limit that is not fixed, that is potentially always to be pushed further on and moved beyond, as we seek forwards towards what is unseen. In this way, the line that defines the reach of our vision acquires the expressive quality of our desire to exceed it, in experience, outlook and knowledge.

While the semantic power of the term 'horizon' is taken over from the image of the sea horizon, it is quite different to the image itself because of its high degree of abstraction. The horizon marks the boundary between earth and sky where the sun rises and sinks, but when the term is used in relation to experience or knowledge the reference has no immediate correlate in *what* we experience or know. It is because of this that it is important to examine how the term is being deployed in any particular application.

In this article, I want to examine Koselleck's work in clarifying and sharpening its conceptual meaning as a historical category. This work is closely related to the long-term editorial project on which Koselleck was engaged in the 1960s and 1970s, a six-volume dictionary of historical concepts. Out of this project, certain themes emerged as central to his own historical and theoretical writings. It is these as collected in the book *Futures Past*, rather than the earlier *Critique and Crisis*, derived from his doctoral thesis, that I draw on here. My particular concern is with his conceptual use of horizon as a way of bringing together the three major dimensions of historical time, and within the resulting framework, dealing with the varying investments we make in our conceptions of their complex interrelations within the course of everyday life (see Koselleck 1985, 1988).[1]

Koselleck is notable in German historical scholarship for his exacting philological attention, his acute historical insight, and his broad theoretical understanding of the relations of past, present and future. In *Futures Past*, where these are characteristic strengths, Koselleck keeps his sights throughout on two major questions. The first of these concerns the ways in which the temporal dimensions of past and future are related in any particular present. In pursuing this question, he outlines how the old ideal of history as a supreme form of instruction, directing our everyday lives in the present by means of exemplary cases, models and types, has been eroded. This view derives from Cicero's conception of history as the school of life – *historia magistra vitae*. Thinking of the past in that way helps to connect history and everyday life, but it depends upon an assumption of the constancy of human nature and the human condition. In modernity, this assumption is untenable since succeeding times are experienced as new temporalities, and as breaks or ruptures with what has gone before, so that it is not only the finitude of personal life which becomes relativized into different structures of temporality, but also the relations of past and future more generally, in our understanding of social and historical change.

Our heightened awareness of historical singularity and historical discontinuity in modernity relates to Koselleck's second major question, which is concerned with the specific kinds of experience in everyday life generated by modern conditions. These include a historically new experience of time itself in which time has attained its own quality of historicality. The consequence of denaturalized time, and the separation of history and chronology which it entails, is that our experience of the temporal gradations of 'now' and 'then', 'earlier' and 'later', become sharply differentiated from each other in our historical awareness. They can no longer be understood in terms of any simple linearity of chronological time. This is a familiar feature of the experience of modernity, but what is not so much noticed is its necessary corollary. It is not only the discovery of historically specific temporality that turns the Ciceronian view on its head. This happens also because our investment in the future increases in proportion to the decline in our connection with the past. Having eyes only for the wide-open horizon ahead, rather than for the one that is receding behind us, we lose track of the route that we historically travel. Everyday modernity continually distances itself from the past in an effort to fund itself entirely out of its own transient present, with 'time as a scarce resource for mastering the problems that the future hurls at the present' (Habermas 2001, p. 132). Crisis and critique thus become paradigmatic for modern consciousness.

Experience and expectation

The value of attending closely to the meaning of historical concepts lies in the simple fact that the terms we use to talk about the past have consequences for the way we understand it, both in itself and in its relations with the present and future. Our understanding of history in terms of these relations is inseparable from the categories we use in making sense of it. Sometimes these categories are embedded in historical sources, while at others they exist only in the historian's lexicon and interpretive framework of understanding. In both cases, they are based in language and require sensitivity either to past uses of language or to contemporary terminology and concepts in their application to historical objects of study. This need is especially acute when we are dealing with categories that do not relate to particular events, episodes or procedures, such as the bombing of Pearl Harbour, the Crusades or the Nuremberg War Crimes Trial, or with the contemporary resonance that these examples have acquired as a result of historical contingencies.

More broadly, we should think carefully about the categories and concepts we use in historical analysis and interpretation because without them analysis and interpretation are not possible. As Koselleck puts it: 'No event can be narrated, no structure represented, no process described without the use of historical concepts which make the past "conceivable"' (1985, p. 112). Such concepts themselves have horizonal qualities. In creating the means with which to comprehend past events, structures and processes, they provide the conditions by which our historical understanding becomes possible. These conditions have their limits in what they permit us to see, or in what they allow us to understand of particular historical events, structures and processes, but our intellectual investments in them are based on the possible ways in which they may help us extend how we perceive and comprehend the past. So, in this way we hope that they will show us what is singular as well as suggesting what extends beyond such singularity, in far wider connections where different spatial occurrences across time are simultaneous with different temporal occurrences across space. Their promise lies in helping us to ascertain the interrelations of event and structure and in taking us beyond the simple temporal succession of chronology into alternative conceptions of historical process.

The formal categories that Koselleck uses in relation to the horizon as a term for referring to historical time are experience and expectation. These are formal in that the content of what is experienced or expected at any one time cannot be deduced from them. They are metahistorical concepts in the same way as time and space, to which they are fundamentally connected as conditions for possible histories. They can be applied to particular historical events and circumstances, but taken in themselves, or in tandem, they have no direct or tangible referentiality. They are all-inclusive terms and so distinct from what is historically specific and contingent, although at the same time what is historically specific and contingent about, say, the experience of Japanese Americans and Japanese Canadians during and after World War Two, presupposes their conceptual use, both in themselves and in tandem. This remains the case regardless of whether we are discussing the different representation of the expansion of their historical experiences and the constriction of their social expectations in the fictional accounts of Kogawa (1983) and Guterson (1995), or in the letters, documents, oral testimonies and historical studies from which these accounts of mid-twentieth century racism are drawn.[2]

Experience and expectation are concrete and directly known, and at the same time abstract and indirectly conceived. In their abstract forms, they can seem true but without any relation to reality, whereas in their concrete forms they can seem real but without any relation to what is true. It is in this way that their relations are conceptually characteristic of the formal categories of historical time. In general terms, experience can absorb whatever it is taken to mean. This is equally true of expectation as the general term that Koselleck pairs up with experience. Together, they not only escape any necessary relation to, say, peace or freedom, but also conceptually redouble on each other, becoming twinned in a necessary interdependence, as are time and space. Hence Koselleck's dictum: 'No expectation without experience; no experience without expectation' (1985, p. 270).

Koselleck's conceptual extension of this couplet produces the historical categories of 'space of experience' and 'horizon of expectation'. From a naturalist standpoint, the validity of this extension would be denied: 'There is no temporal field of vision corresponding to a spatial field of vision – it's a false analogy – since events which are earlier and later than one another, by definition, do not coexist' (Gale 1967, p. 154). Strictly speaking, this is true, but exceptional cases aside, understanding is hindered rather than helped by speaking strictly. Among other things, it means ignoring the powerful metaphorical current in conceptual thinking. It is through metaphorical reasoning that such thinking advances, and the experiential and historical condition of understanding is constituted.

Conceptually, horizon is related to the term 'field of vision', which is itself a founding orientational metaphor derived from our spatial experience where the boundary of a territory or open expanse is defined by what we can see (Lakoff and Johnson 1981, p. 30). Its metaphorical encapsulation of that experience provides the ground for further metaphorical extension into our temporal experience, as, most simply, with the 'distant past' or 'the past behind us', but also, more significantly, with the wider spatial and temporal intersections opened up by modernity, which Koselleck captures in the phrase 'the contemporaneity of the noncontemporaneous' (1985, p. 279). Metaphorical extensions based around the organising principles of proximity and distance inform our conceptual understanding of the temporalities of experience, and particularly of the dialectical relationship between situated and mediated forms of experience, so that 'the contemporaneity of the noncontemporaneous' is now commonplace in everyday life, whether we are watching the news on TV at home or glancing through CDs in our local music store.

Similarly, boundary and perspective are other metaphors taken from the field of vision. A perspective gives us a different view according to the place where we are standing, whereas the horizon defines the boundary of our broadest possible perspective at any particular point. That point may be either spatial or temporal. Thinking of the horizon in a temporal as well as a spatial sense is precisely what characterizes the hermeneutic uses to which Koselleck and Gadamer put the term, so that the perspective we develop as historical subjects is formed and transformed by the confrontation of horizons occurring in our present engagement with the past: 'The horizon is something into which we move and which moves with us' and 'understanding is always the fusion of horizons only supposedly existing by themselves' (Gadamer 1996, pp. 304–306). Engagement with historical 'difference' makes us more aware of our own 'lived' historicality – it 'makes visible that from which something is fore-grounded' (Gadamer 1996, p. 305) – but the term 'fusion' is unfortunate in suggesting that it is possible to merge our own historical horizon with that of an inherited tradition or past time. This would result in a reduction or loss of awareness of our own historicality. The term also implies a rather naive sense of empathy, and while Gadamer's conceptual use of the horizon is more sophisti-cated than this, he does not critically dispatch the images of integration, consen-sus and non-contradictory synthesis that easily arise from the notion of 'fusion'. Bakhtin supplies the necessary corrective in rejecting the 'false tendency toward reducing everything to a single consciousness, toward dissolving in it the other's consciousness (while being understood)'. The condition of distance between historical horizons means that 'one cannot understand understanding as emotional empathy [*Einfühlung*] as the placement of the self in the other's position (loss of one's own position)' (Bakhtin 1986, p. 141; see also Pickering 1999, pp. 186–194).

In view of the distance between historical horizons, we can say that history's concern is threefold: with short-term events, which have their own diachronic structure; with longer-term structures, which persist through the successive flow of events; and with the diverse temporal extensions and connections that follow both events and structures. So, to take another example, in its conceptual grasp of the experience of cyberspace, William Gibson's term 'event horizon' – beyond which we cannot see the longer-term structures, or even middle-term extensions and connections – gains its force through its metaphorical conjunc-tion of two words which have both concrete and abstract applications (Gibson 1986, p. 288). The suggestive power of the term for our understanding of cyberspace derives precisely from these applications in their mutual interaction. This is also the case with more commonplace uses of the term, where it attains a more direct specificity through being coupled with a particular case (as, for example, in Ruskin's phrase 'the entire horizon of man's action' or, by way of contrast, in Jefferson's reference to the 'lowering aspect of our political hori-zon'). When that to which it is connected is particularized, as in the experience of a specific war or a definite form of servitude, we tread the grounds of what seems starkly actual to us. These condition-specific experiences, as with the terms used to refer to them, are, as Koselleck puts it in a memorable phrase, drenched in reality. As such they presuppose alternatives (peace and freedom, though again only as alternatives to what is, in finite terms, historically experienced) and exclude other meanings since they refer to definite semantic fields.

There is no need to fuss about this any further since Koselleck's conceptual history [*Begriffsgeschichte*] relies upon the recognition of the imaginative potential of thinking in metaphors. In the light of this recognition he notes that experience, in its 'space', can change over time, for various specific experiences may overlap and influence each other while lived experience itself, being reality-drenched, 'binds together fulfilled or missed possibilities' which enter into it and act back on it, thus changing it after the fact: 'This is the temporal structure of experience and without retroactive expectation it cannot be accumulated' (Koselleck 1985, pp. 274–275). While expectation has a different temporal structure since it consists of what 'is not to be had' as yet, directly within the present, new experiences are born out of the surprise of the unexpected: 'The gain in experience exceeds the limitation of the possible future presupposed by previous experience' (Koselleck 1985, p. 275). This seems fine, but what is involved in these and various other directions of movement beyond what has become a given line of attainment could just as fittingly be covered by referring to the 'horizon of experience' as a finite limitation which is exceeded, and to the 'space of expectation' which is thereby reconfigured as the space in which an experiential possibility is realized, moving us beyond the limit of what has already been attained.

Shifting the elements of Koselleck's categories in this way expands their analytical value, as for instance when we consider horizon as a background of intelligibility in everyday life against which people define themselves and others, in terms of their experience or knowledge. It is in this way that we speak anthropologically of culture and psychologically of cognition. However, expanding the applicability of the categories has historiographical consequences too. Changing the terms of Koselleck's conceptual couplet for the experience of historical time shifts the theoretical balance from possible stasis to possible change. It allows possibility and change a fuller presence in the ways the couplet may be analytically applied. Koselleck points to a fulfilled possibility as a condition for changing experience 'after the fact', yet he elides this with expectation. While this is partly a consequence of linguistic horizons, we need to take some steps to obviate the confusion and to accommodate the surprise of the unexpected and the promise of the yet to be reached.

In English, the word 'expectation' can be used to express the strongest hope, as in 'fervent' or 'high' expectation, but its more prevalent association is with good prospects, legitimate entitlement, and everything that we feel will happen in all likelihood. This applies regardless of whether one is on tiptoes in anticipation of something happening, or cast down in disappointment at a broken promise, when expectation is dashed.[3] We should thus distinguish more strongly between expectation and possibility. If to expect is to foresee, it is the familiar that is expected. Possibilities are not expected to the extent that they diverge from the familiar, from the normal recurrent patterns of everyday life. Unless they are strong, they are beyond expectation. Possibilities are more to do with aspiration than expectation. Where expectations are almost guaranteed their fulfilment, possibilities are, as it were, expectations without guarantees.

Experience as horizon engages with both, but in terms of this distinction, involving structures of continuity in the present and articulations of change in the future. Expectation accommodates itself to the horizon of existing social relations and practices in everyday life; possibility aspires to horizons beyond them, where relations and practices might operate otherwise. Everyday experience as a temporal horizon is lived in both senses, and it is only in both these senses, conceived as mutually dependent, that they connect with the politics of historical time. This connection reveals the everyday as more differentiated and less elusive than we may commonly think. In many ways, everyday experience occurs in the realm of what is familiar and easily recognized. It falls in with our usual ways of categorizing, classifying and giving meaning to what goes on. This is quite different to perception where it breaks through everyday recognition and produces a reconstruction of meaning and value, giving direction and imparting some new significance to our action in the world. Recognition remains within the horizon of what is known; perception crosses this horizon in the interests of what is knowable. So it is that within the everyday we are able to move beyond an existing space of expectation and recognition, and so extend the horizon of our experience and our sense of the possible.

Taking Koselleck's four main co-ordinates as conceptually interchangeable, we can move this further in distinguishing between different horizons of expectation in different spaces of experience, as these are manifest in everyday life. So, for instance, in relatively subdued times our habitual experience of the media is readily accommodated in everyday life. Writing in the 1930s, the German sociologist, Karl Mannheim (1887–1947), noted how this happens. He observed first of all a horizon of expectation resting on a relative constancy of social experience, and on certain social guarantees of continuity, thus enabling it to readily integrate novelty within a structure of normality:

> When we eagerly take up a newspaper, we are already prepared for the occurrence of certain kinds of events that interest us for the very reason that we cannot foresee in detail what they will be. Although we always leave a gap in our horizon for unforeseen facts, that certainly does not mean that we are prepared for anything – that we have an equally intense and concentrated attitude towards all categories of events. We think it probable that the newspaper will report a case of robbery or that the cabinet has fallen, or that certain commodity prices fluctuate in a certain area. In other words, we are prepared to perceive facts and complexes of facts of a certain type, of a certain order of significance, which we expect as 'normal' and relevant.

The single facts may vary; the framework and the system of co-ordinates into which they must be dovetailed remains more or less constant as long as the whole social situation is stable, and its development is continuous.

(Mannheim 1960, p. 179)

If this kind of horizon is characterized by its expectation that things will fall into a settled pattern within everyday life, so needing only to accommodate what we might call the foreseen unforeseen, it is quite different from the horizon of expectation of someone who is caught up in an unstable social order, or who lives through a time of intense and tumultuous change. The framework and its accompanying co-ordinates seem rapidly to lose their validity. 'In such times we may speak of discarding an earlier, more limited, horizon for a broader range of expectations' (Mannheim 1960, p. 180). Easier said than done, of course, for the need to discard what has become a relatively limited horizon of understanding that has been outstripped by events may create insecurity, anxiety, perturbation and anger, feelings which in their projective movements readily turn social minorities, dissidents or outsiders into scapegoats. In any case, given the pace of change, you may be without the time needed to modify, with any reasonable adequacy, the framework that links up experience and expectation.

There is of course another side to this, and Mannheim clearly points it up. Times of turmoil not only expose to obvious view the basis of an existing framework of experience and expectation, but also give new emphasis to a range of yet to be reached possibilities. These possibilities are, in a sense, always there in everyday life, but do not lie in obvious view, for reasons contingent upon the politics of historical time. In Mannheim's words: 'in every historical event numerous factors are acting upon one another and very often the ostensible triumph by one by no means annihilates the rest, but merely makes them less apparent, on the surface, than those factors the significance of which is more immediately perceptible' (Mannheim 1960, p. 189).

This is to come upon, from a particular angle, the vital distinction between experience which is inclusive and experience which attains a singular intensity of focus, in our social as well as our individual lives. In two different essays, Koselleck cites the same quotation from Count Reinhard in a letter of 1820 to the German poet, Goethe. It is an observation based on the emergence of a different historical temporality arising from events which seem to outstrip all previous experience: 'a completed experience is united into a focus, while that which has yet to be made is spread over minutes, hours, days, years, and centuries; consequently, that which is similar never appears to be so, since in one case one sees the whole, while in the other only the individual parts are visible' (Koselleck 1985, p. 34, p. 272). This is certainly worth the repetition, since it encapsulates one of the central problems in the hermeneutics of historical experience, and to it Koselleck adds that an experience which is completed cannot be fully reconciled with what has yet to come, since a history already awaiting us would deprive us of the ability to experience it, and so close time down.

We can extrapolate further than this by noting that a landmark experience not only punctuates the common stream of experiences in everyday life, but also illuminates what subsequently transpires in everyday life as its historical significance is worked through and integrated into a broader range of expectation. So, with the landmark experience of the Nuremberg trials, we are still assimilating this historically not only in relation to the Holocaust, but also in its many ramifications, extending into what is 'normally' taken as the mundane and familiar, as for example in the light of Arendt's arresting remark about the banality of evil. This has had continuing resonance in every significant war crimes trail, just as its echoes are distinctly present in the contemporary debate following from Goldhagen's (1997) account of Hitler's 'willing executioners' (see, for example, Paris 2001, pp. 312–314). These examples show not only how the space of expectation can be extended, but also how historically significant events result in the expansion, across time and space, of the horizons of experience. This returns us to the value of Count Reinhard's observation. Grasping the sense of possibility beyond expectation or the 'normal' order of significance is the task of reconciling different historical temporalities, and relating the unity of a nodal experience to its various parts as these lead to and from it over the course of historical time.

Conjunctive and communicative experience

Mannheim adds a further dimension to the first of Koselleck's categories through his distinction between conjunctive and communicative experience.[4] Conjunctive experience involves a direct and immediate encounter with a particular form of sociality, in definite situations and contexts, and as such is existentially bound, so that any knowledge deriving from it is fully apprehended only for the social circles they involve and in the communicative forms locally found within a specific experiential space. It is knowledge that has a conjunctive validity, and a range of communicability which is 'restricted to those who participate in the total existential relationship within which and out of which this knowledge arises' (Mannheim 1982, p. 193). A subject's *habitus* is formed primarily in this sphere of experience and operates most effectively within its specific situations and contexts as these are spatially and temporally defined.

The organising structure of conjunctive experience is implicit in the routine patterning of everyday life, and the knowledge associated with it is embedded in the ordinary social world we regularly inhabit. It is a historically configured social experience, related to an objective social location and specifically focused as a result, yet adaptive and able to be reoriented through the improvisations and variations proceeding from the conceptual schemata of the *habitus*. As knowable experience it is associated with the *habitus* in its practical definition, for the concepts and categories which it utilizes do not exist 'for the sake of theoretical contemplation, in order to rest in them, but rather to pursue life in and through them' (Mannheim 1982, p. 199). These concepts and categories are intended to be applicable only for those sharing the same conjunctive experiential space, as in a small gathering, community or network. The experiences that they help to organize are specifically resonant within that social milieu, and the experiential knowledge with which they are associated is not directly transferable to different social contexts or different forms of social life. Their horizonal scope in everyday life is the local and immediate.

Mannheim contrasts this kind of localized, present-centred experience and knowledge with that which is communicable beyond such specific milieux, and applicable in various different contexts. As Friedman has remarked, Mannheim is not terribly clear about all this, and it may at first seem that he simply reproduced in another form the fixed binaries of classical sociology. This is not the case because, as Friedman points out, the conjunctive/communicative distinction is one which refers to different social forms of experience at any particular time, and yet can also be applied to any form of experience since 'any one experience contains both communicative and conjunctive aspects' (Friedman 2001, p. 51–52). This relates to the everyday in that it is phenomenologically lived and yet at the same time incomplete, or in Mannheim's terms having, in potential, various objective tendencies each of which 'could in principle be carried to its logical conclusion if its distinctive direction were pursued' (1982, p. 234). When an objective possibility is realized in the pursuit of its distinctive direction, these specific tendencies are carried over to new horizons of experience, so exceeding a previous space of expectation and calling into question the ostensible triumph of a predominant outlook or perspective in its bearings on the lived formation of everyday life.

In writing of Lefebvre, Peter Osborne similarly marks out the everyday as a sociological category that is at once empirical and utopian: 'empirical in the multiplicity and variety of its concrete forms' and 'utopian in its harbouring of the promise of a concrete universality of relations at the level of society as a whole, in the fullness of its complex sociality'. As Osborne observes, the conceptual power of the everyday lies in the distinction between these two moments or aspects of its experience (Osborne 1995, p. 192). Communicative experience is thus not dependent on the kind of social life involved, but on the realization of a quality and capacity to resonate more broadly beyond the confines of specific milieu. It is this which allows it to become widely felt and imagined, and so communicative as 'an articulation between local sociality and the larger public sphere' (Friedman 2001, p. 60). In this articulation, communicative and conjunctive experience are brought into synthesis or combined in a new synergy. Experience extends its temporal horizon, expectation its existential space.

Accelerating time and historical difference

The acceleration of historical time in modernity has made the articulation of communicative and conjunctive experience notoriously more difficult. One of the key features of modernity to which Koselleck points is the continuing expansion of difference between experience and expectation. One of the consequences of this is a sharp divergence in experience between different historical generations, and an accompanying steep gradation of difference between experience and expectation within and across distinct temporal phases. The Victorian historian, J.A. Froude, noted this as far back as 1864: 'The world moves faster and faster, and the difference will probably be considerably greater. The temper of each new generation is a continual surprise' (Briggs 1965, p. 3). This is another aspect of the historicization of time in modernity as it is has become manifest in distinct and obliquely related temporalities and the fractured connections of experience and expectation. Raymond Williams's concept for the continually surprising new 'temper' of successive generations was 'structure of feeling'. The strength of this concept is not so much in its relations with what the anthropologist Ruth Benedict called patterns of culture, but in its relations with cultural phenomena of emergence.

This is because structures of feeling initially develop between conjunctive experience and its communicative expression, marking the first creative impetus towards a new way of configuring experience. They are, in the moment where they begin to be manifest, emergent or pre-emergent as they arise from a collective response to what seems experientially new for an up-and-coming generation. Structures of feeling derive from the *habitus* of a particular generation or group but begin to coalesce in the space between articulated order and everyday life. There they push at the edges of what is possible, and are realized as disturbance, tension, blockage and trouble because of their challenge to social conventions or settled, dominant perspectives (Williams 1979, pp. 167–168; see also Williams 1977, pp. 128–135). In their break with habitual standpoints and their stretching the limits of what is possible, structures of feeling exemplify collective experience in a process of becoming. As the still-being-shaped experience of experiences, a structure of feeling is generated through the tension felt between experience and expectation, when people strive toward some new possibility, or when they try to achieve communicative value for experience in its conjunctive aspects. That is why, as I have argued elsewhere, the concept's real cutting edge is felt in its application to liminal forms of experience, as a pre-emergent form coming into form, the first distinctive signal of that which is striving to be born from the old but which has not yet become, in any relatively settled way, fully configurative (Pickering 1997, ch. 2).

The value of Williams's concept is that, *inter alia*, we can apply it as a check against the tendency in Koselleck's work to treat the metaphor of the horizon as an abstract idea divorced from people's spatial and temporal experience in everyday life. All the contributing elements of such experience are lived in the flow of events and occurrences, and new structures of feeling develop out of that flow in the effort to articulate the distinctive specificity of generational experience as this comes through in explorations of the differences between expectation and possibility. That said, it is clear enough that new structures of feeling emerge with increasing frequency in modernity because of the acceleration of historical time. This has produced the expectation of an increasing divergence between the conditions and circumstances of the past and those of the future. What used to be called the 'generation gap' is one example of this divergence, but its consequences are much broader because of the ways it attenuates historical understanding in everyday life, and provides a ready ground for plans and prognoses, hopes and dreams, disengaged from the realities of everyday experience in the past. This creates a specifically modern version of living too much in the future.

If in its temporalized application 'horizon' is the extent of our expectations, arising from our spatially configured – yet retroactively altered – accumulated experience, how can we then assess the legibility of the future? How can we know what marks the horizon of expectation as 'that line behind which a new space of experience will open, but which cannot yet be seen' (Koselleck 1985, p. 273). Here again it is productive to shift the terms around so that we avoid the exaggeration of saying that, despite possible prognoses, the expectational horizon 'confronts an absolute limit' (Koselleck 1985, p. 273), for this neglects the crucial quality of mutability in the temporal horizon as we move towards it. The horizon defines a limit, but that limit is never fixed either spatially, or in its metaphorical extension, temporally. The space of expectation is limited only by the rate at which the horizon of our experience expands.

This is in a sense a commonplace as, for example, with the revision of expectations as a way of learning from everyday experience. The limit of experience is marked by the not-yet, the so-far-inexperienced, what is within the present a tendency whose fuller realization remains to be achieved, with a possible ambush from the unexpected always lying up ahead. Yet in the face of normalized expectation, we need to insist that there is nothing absolute about this limit, for the space of expectation is not a fixed space and the horizon of experience is a moving horizon when perception exceeds recognition and conjunctive experience achieves communicative value.

Temporally, everyday life is experienced backwards and forwards in a dual relation: the horizon of the past is brought into the present and the horizon of the future opens out from the present, with neither bearing the warranty of continuity or change. Both horizons are contingent on the configurations of social memory and planned organization, and so on the politics of historical time. In ways that are always changing, historical time is generated through the tension between experience and expectation. Our own historicality is shaped and made intelligible by this tension, but we only move successfully from the space of expectation to the horizon of experience once we have an adequate range of possibilities and adequate criteria of choice.

This is quite different to simply choosing what you will. The subjectivist claim that all options 'are equally worthy, because they are freely chosen, and it is choice that confers worth' contains a basic contradiction, because if all options are equally worthy, how can choices be made between them? As Taylor argues, 'unless some options are more significant than others, the very idea of self-choice falls into triviality and hence incoherence' (1991, p. 37–39). Choice only makes sense within a horizon of expectation that has set up conditions of significance according to which certain things will prove worthwhile, and others will not. There has never been a more vacuous injunction in modern times than simply 'do your own thing'. The injunction ignores not only the horizonal constraints on experience but also the varying temporalities of expectation as these have been outlined.

Koselleck's own engagement with these different temporalities underwrites the importance of his twin concepts as units of analysis. The terms of the concepts need to be open to the interchange argued for so far, as a way of extending their analytical reach, but their value nevertheless lies in the way they provide means for addressing Koselleck's concern with the kinds of experience ushered in by modernity. These are not so much of rapidity of change or excess of the unexpected, but of the increased distance between experience and expectation, and the urgent need continuously to transform existing frameworks of interpretation and understanding, action and aspiration. For some, this leads to the opposite of living too much in the future, since it turns the future into a burden that they bear in the lost prospect of the past. Among other things, this is a characteristic feature of the problem of generational displacement, or of different temporalities coexisting, but not communicating.

That kind of displacement has profound consequences for the relations between lived experience and historical understanding. It is commonplace in modernity to expect our everyday experience to be conditioned by historical pressures and forces removed from experience itself. This expands the distance between experience and history. We learn from experience, but not from history, as historical acceleration becomes the condition of hope. This is never more the case than in times of revolutionary change. When the turmoil of such change has subsided, experience reverts to the space in which we search for points of convergence and threads of continuity across the different temporalities of historical time, yet this process is foreclosed when we understand the present only as 'the actuality of the most recent period', which in turn generates the need to 'recapitulate the break brought about with the past as a continuous renewal':

> Modernity can and will no longer borrow the criteria by which it takes its orientation from models supplied by another epoch; *it has to create its*

normativity out of itself. Modernity sees itself cast back upon itself without any possibility of escape.

(Habermas 1987, p. 7; original emphasis)

The ability to learn from experience is possible only on the basis of a reliable set of interpretations that permit events to be drawn together in some sort of pattern. In modernity, this ability seems to be condensed into the space of individual life, creating the illusion that we are 'masters of our fate', free from tradition and the trammels of precept and past example. If it is as though everything is now possibility – you just 'do your own thing' – what Habermas calls the 'absurd hope of a defiant individualism' is nevertheless the outcome of a loss of hope in any form of redemption within a rationalized, fragmented society (Habermas 2001, p. 140). We may invest in this absurd hope out of disillusionment with the liberal belief in progress, yet we internalize a version of that belief in our heroic substitution of historical time by individual lifetime as the site of advance and improvement. Our salvation also seems to reside in personal life projects because our horizon of expectation does not and cannot extend into the Hereafter as the culmination of what lies beyond the space of our worldly experience.

As Koselleck notes, the advent of the modern belief in progress accompanied an unleashing of previous horizonal limits that had tied the future to the past and ensured the relatively continuous transfer of experience into expectation. The relative absence of this transfer is characteristic of the experience of modernity, leading to a closed past with a diminution of desired social continuities and an open future with no guarantee of progressive social transformation. Habermas criticizes Koselleck here for overlooking the way in which the telos of progress served to close off the future as a *source* of disruption, and so led to 'a degeneration of modernity's consciousness of time open toward the future' (Habermas 1987, p. 12). The end-result nevertheless remains a divergence of experience and expectation as the basis for our apprehension of historical time.

Central to this divergence is the collapse of various temporal and spatial horizons under conditions of time-space compression in modernity and late (or post) modernity (see Harvey 1991). The successive waves of such compression facilitate capital circulation and accumulation at the expense of an increasing fragmentation of social and historical experience. This is accompanied by the feelings of uncertainty and insecurity characteristic of the anomic qualities of modernity and its temporal extensions and intensifications. The radical sense of historicality that results makes it more and more difficult to maintain a meaningful relation to lived experience and a sense of place in time (or even to know how this may be constituted). Under these conditions, the temporal relation between experience and expectation changes sharply though the stages of one's own lifetime and through the succession of historical generations as they come to stand in contrast to each other. The sense of contrast increases as one gets older and each new generation develops its distinctive structure of feeling, so that the different temporal dimensions in which people experience historical time seem more and more discrepant. Inexorable movement forward in time makes more complex and difficult the qualitative assessment of change and continuity within the context of everyday life.

One of the most important legacies of the Enlightenment was belief in social improvement, in progress and an objective of worldly completeness. The hazards of an open future superseded belief in the afterlife, and people came to be seen as making their own history, subject of course to limiting conditions, which included the scope of their psychological, cultural and political horizons. There were all sorts of ways in which this belief was taken, among them the notion of backward or primitive 'races' and the development of social Darwinism, or in contrast, the vision of a communist utopia.[5] In the more general terms of our key themes, the ideology of progress drove a wedge between experience and expectation, with 'expectations that reached out for the future' growing increasingly 'detached from all that previous experience had to offer'. Once the future was seen as different to the past, the past ceased to provide a template for the future: 'the task of progressive advance is not soluble directly on the basis of experience'. History was thus reconceived as specific, contingent and unique, and so distinct from the future. Expectation could no longer 'be satisfactorily deduced from previous experience' (Koselleck 1985, pp. 279–281).

Putting it another way, the loss of certainty in the space of experience has been compensated by the gain of certainty in the horizon of expectation. The modern contrast between existential doubt and scientific truth is just one instance of this shift. The conception of historical singularity and distinction disrupts the sense of continuity and sequence, example and case. Expectation no longer follows experience. It is now the other way round, with each generation facing its own historical conditions uniquely, without benefit from the past, for the past is what has to be overcome, historicized as 'then' in opposition to 'now'. Writing in the late 1980s about the apprehension of historical time which follows from the exhaustion of the rational myth of progress, Mercer expressed this with sardonic accuracy: 'The sixties and seventies are effectively historicized in much the same way as historians treat "the twenties" or "the forties". What happened the day before yesterday now looks like it happened a long time ago, and sometimes it looks as if it never happened at all' (1990, p. 51).

Accordingly, historical time becomes fragmented into distinct, incommensurable temporal phases, each sustaining their own utopian surplus as a result of continual renewal and incessant change, whether in science and technology or in political planning and prognosis. The legacy of a loss of faith in progress is simply acceleration, with the danger that experience becomes focused primarily around the experience of expectation. So Koselleck formulates the temporal structure of modernity in terms of the twin dicta: 'The lesser the experience, the greater the expectation' and 'the greater the experience, the more cautious one is, but also the more open is the future'. The future is then not one of optimizing progress, but of movement towards the realignment of experience and expectation where expectation is based on the 'long-term formal structures in history which allow the repeated accumulation of experience' (Koselleck 1985, p. 288).

Experience and expectation are mutually impoverished by their divergence and separation. It is only when the space of one is brought into alignment with the horizon of the other that experience is properly funded, and expectation properly limited. Hence Koselleck's conclusion: 'History is only able to recognize what continually changes, and what is new, if it has access to the conventions within which lasting structures are concealed' (1985, p. 288). We have still to work through the many implications which this entails beyond our own event horizons and our everyday expectations of the conventions of experience, as we eagerly take up a newspaper, gaze at the TV set or invest in the utopian surplus of cyberspace.

Notes

1   The present article is intended as a companion piece to an earlier article on Gadamer, primarily because of the extent of common ground between Gadamer and Koselleck (Pickering 1999; see also Gadamer 1996). Among other things, what brings Koselleck and Gadamer together is 'the construction of a hermeneutic procedure that places understanding as a historical and experiential act in relation to entities which themselves possess historical force', focusing thus on the interchange between the temporality and historicality of lived experience (*Erlebnis*) in everyday life and forms of historical consciousness and knowledge (Tribe 1985, p. xiii). What is of close interest to them both are the specific conditions of this interchange in modernity.

2   There are critical points to be made about both these accounts, as for example the diffusion of guilt in Guterson's treatment of racism, and its inscription of a revised Orientalism (Meyer 2002). They are cited here simply as concurrent examples of the dialectic of experience and expectation in relation to cultural identity and difference.

3   The existence in English of such words as preconception, presumption, presentiment and foreboding, as well as anticipation, suggest how finely nuanced our ideas about expectation as a general phenomenon can be. Exploration of what these fine distinctions entail would be a worthwhile endeavour.

4   The following section is something of a spin-off from a book on cultural creativity being co-written with Keith Negus, Goldsmith's College, UK. There we try out similar distinctions about forms of experience and the creative attainment of communicative value. Two relevant publications piloting our work are Negus and Pickering (2000, 2002).

5   As these examples suggest, conceptions of historical development and futures past are contingent on one's place in space and time, and against this Koselleck tends to make generalized assertions about experience and expectation and their relation to historical consciousness. We need then to ask whose historical consciousness is being discussed in order to counter a certain Eurocentrism in Koselleck's historiography and theoretical orientation to modernity. The same applies to conceptual uses of 'horizon', as for instance in the relation between ideas about the horizon and histories of imperialism.

References

Bakhtin, M. (1986) *Speech Genres and Other Late Essays*, University of Texas Press, Austin, TX.

Briggs, A. (1959/1965) *The Making of Modern England*, Harper, New York.

Friedman, J. (2001) 'The iron cage of creativity', in *Locating Cultural Creativity*, ed. J. Liep, Pluto Press, London, pp. 46–61.

Gadamer, H. G. (1960/1996) *Truth and Method*, Sheed & Ward, London.

Gale, R. (1967) 'Indexical signs', in *The Encyclopaedia of Philosophy*, vol. 4, Macmillan, New York.

Gibson, W. (1986) *Neuromancer*, Grafton Books, London.

Goldhagen, D. (1997) *Hitler's Willing Executioners*, Abacus, London.

Guterson, D. (1995) *Snow Falling on Cedars*, Bloomsbury, London.

Habermas, J. (1987) *The Philosophical Discourse of Modernity*, Polity, Cambridge.

Habermas, J. (2001) *The Postnational Constellation*, Polity, Cambridge.

Harvey, D. (1991) *The Condition of Postmodernity*, Blackwell, Oxford.

Kogawa, J. (1983) *Obasan*, Penguin, Ontario/London.

Koselleck, R. (1979/1985) *Futures Past: On the Semantics of Historical Time*, The MIT Press, Cambridge, MA & London.

Koselleck, R. (1959/1988) *Critique and Crisis: Enlightenment and the Pathogenesis of Modern Society*, Berg, Oxford/New York/Hamburg.

Lakoff, G. & Johnson, M. (1980) *Metaphors We Live By*, University of Chicago Press, Chicago/London.

Mannheim, K. (1935/1960) *Man and Society in an Age of Reconstruction*, Routledge & Kegan Paul, London.

Mannheim, K. (1982) *Structures of Thinking*, Routledge & Kegan Paul, London/Boston/Henley.

Mercer, K. (1990) 'Welcome to the jungle: identity and diversity in postmodern politics', in *Identity: Community, Culture, Difference*, ed. Jonathan Rutherford, Lawrence and Wishart, London, pp. 43–71.

Meyer, K. M. (2002) '"Tan"talizing others: multicultural anxiety and the new orientalism', in *High-Pop: Making Culture into Popular Entertainment*, ed. Jim Collins, Blackwell, Oxford, pp. 90–113.

Negus, K. & Pickering, M. (2000) 'Creativity and cultural production', *International Journal of Cultural Policy*, vol. 6, no. 2, pp. 259–282.

Negus, K. & Pickering, M. (2002) 'Creativity and musical experience', in *Popular Music Studies*, eds D. Hesmondhalgh & K. Negus, Arnold, London/New York, pp. 178–190.

Osborne, P. (1995) *The Politics of Time: Modernity and Avant-Garde*, Verso, London and New York.

Paris, E. (2001) *Long Shadows: Truth, Lies and History*, Bloomsbury, London.

Pickering, M. (1997) *History, Experience and Cultural Studies*, Macmillan (now Palgrave), Basingstoke/ London.

Pickering, M. (1999) 'History as horizon: Gadamer, tradition and critique', *Rethinking History*, vol. 3, no. 2, pp. 177–195.

Taylor, C. (1991) *The Ethics of Authenticity*, Harvard University Press, Cambridge, MA.

Tribe, K. (1985) 'Translator's introduction', in *Futures Past: On the Semantics of Historical Time*, Reinhart Koselleck, The MIT Press, Cambridge, MA, pp. vii–xvii.

Williams, R. (1977) *Marxism and Literature*, Oxford University Press, Oxford & New York.

Williams, R. (1979) *Politics and Letters*, New Left Books, London.

Patrick ffrench

A DIFFERENT LIFE?
Barthes, Foucault and everyday life

How might the injunction to 'think differently' in the work of French theorists Roland Barthes and Michel Foucault have informed a re-thinking of everyday life? In Barthes' work, a critical analysis of myth and ideology in the contemporary everyday life of the late 1950s gives way to counter-ideological strategies that might seem to move away from the everyday and towards the utopian. However, the utopian imagination at work in Barthes' thought is effective precisely in its insistence on the everyday detail. This is reflected in the later work in the attention given to the incident and the haiku. In his later work, Foucault turns towards antiquity in response to his own assessment of the ubiquitous diffusion of relations of power and the need to 'think differently'. It is, however, in the interviews and specifically in a series of comments on homosexuality that Foucault is most attentive to the 'possibilities for new life' in his own time. It is through the undoing of already established relations and the experimentation with different modes of relation that a locus of difference can be found in everyday life. This is characterized by Foucault as a heterotopia. Foucault's tentative suggestions of different possibilities are oriented towards an intensification of pleasures, counter to the psychoanalytic attention to desire. However, Foucault's account of pleasure is associated with mortality, suggesting the question: is this different life one destined only to posterity and its own transcendence? Deleuze's reading of Foucauldian subjectivation suggests a different strategy of resistance, more attuned to the immanence of a life.

Keywords   Barthes; Foucault; homosexuality; resistance; subjectivation; utopia

In 1984, on the occasion of the ceremony in the courtyard of the Salpetrière mortuary marking the death of Michel Foucault, Gilles Deleuze read the following excerpt from *The Use of Pleasures*:

> There are times in life when the question of knowing if one can think differently than one thinks, and perceive differently than one sees, is absolutely necessary if one is to go on looking and reflecting at all. People will say, perhaps, that these games with oneself would be better left

Cultural Studies Vol. 18, No. 2/3 March/May 2004, pp. 290–305
ISSN 0950-2386 print/ISSN 1466-4348 online   © 2004 Taylor & Francis Ltd
http://www.tandf.co.uk/journals   DOI: 10.1080/0950238042000201527

R Routledge
Taylor & Francis Group

backstage; or, at best, that they might properly form part of those prelimi-
nary exercises that are forgotten once they have served their purpose. But
then, what is philosophy today - philosophical activity, I mean, if it is not the
critical work that thought brings to bear on itself? In what does it consist, if
not in the endeavour to think differently, instead of legitimating what is
already known?

(Foucault 1985, pp. 8–9)

In his panegyric, Deleuze thus emphasized that Foucault's philosophical activity
was mobilized by a desire to think differently, or at least to speculate about the
possibility of doing so. That Deleuze was speaking after Foucault's death
precluded, with tragic irony, the possibility that it was now a question of living
rather than or as well as thinking differently for Foucault himself, but it also
opened out that possibility for others as part of Foucault's legacy. I want in this
article to explore certain elements of post-1968 French critical thought which
articulate the project of critique, speculation and invention with a desire to live
differently. The guiding question is thus: how is the project of critical, theoretical
thought mobilized by a desire to modify the conditions of one's everyday life?
Moreover: what forms of modification of everyday life arise from the project of
critical thought, particularly when this critique is articulated as a critique of
everyday life? Foucault's phrase might be reformulated accordingly: 'There are
moments in life when the question of knowing if one can live differently is
indispensable if one is to go on living at all'.

   Living otherwise can of course take different forms; one could ask: is it a
question of changing the *collective* forms of everyday life? Or are we talking about
a *purely personal* modification of the conditions and the quality of one's own
existence? But are the collective and the personal projects for a different life so
easily distinguishable? Is it not precisely the period of the late 1960s in French
thought, or earlier, with Sartre, that sees the intertwining and the inseparability
of the two projects? Particularly with reference to the period post 1968, if 'the
personal is the political', this is because, on the one hand, 'personal life', outside
the institutionalized spaces of work or education is interpreted, in this period,
as being subject to power through subtle and productive means. If everyday life
outside the sphere of production is as politically subjected as the life within it,
then the project to live differently, personally, is also a political one, which
impinges on the collective. The period of the 1960s sees a change in the contours
of French Marxist-oriented thought: revolutionary changes in the conditions of
life in the sphere of production, in work, are not seen as sufficient to alter the
fundamental conditions of political subjection. The key event of 1968 bears
witness to a crisis of leftist thought, where the project for a different life, for a
revolution of everyday life, comes into conflict with the agenda of change in
working conditions. It is a moment of epistemological change in the forms that
collective and 'personal' imagination and experimentation with different lives

can take. It is also the case that, through writing, and other intellectual engage-
ments, the subject who imagines a different life, however personal, constitutes
him or herself, despite his or her protestations (Barthes, Foucault, Debord) to
the contrary, as a kind of hero, or saint, whose effort to imagine a different life
is exemplary, and forms a legacy or a testament. It is partly through this
testamentary dimension that the space for a different life is made possible.

The project of a revolution, or at least a modification, of everyday life is not,
however, new, or particular to this context. The earlier reference to the critical
writer as a kind of saint establishes a tradition of a kind for this agenda. Barthes'
(1976) work on Loyola, Foucault's insistence on asceticism (1985, p. 9), point
to the relevance of this approach. There is also a lineage particular to French
intellectual history of this mode of articulation of the modification of one's
everyday life with forms of collective utopia: both Surrealism and Existentialism
form a pre-history for the project to critique the stratified forms of everyday life
and imagine, experiment, or practice different ways of living. Two landmark
novels as important events in the tradition of this kind of thinking, Breton's *Nadja*
(1928) and Sartre's *Nausea* (1938) form part of the contour of the literary and
philosophical modernity which the post-war generation will inherit; both offer
accounts of protagonists who, through a series of encounters, radically change
the conditions of their lives. If Breton's narrative tells of the failure of the
narrator to live up to the challenge that the eponymous heroine represents, to
think differently, Sartre's Roquentin strips away, painfully, all the layers of his
appurtenance to social, discursive existence, tapping dangerously into a visceral
'real' to emerge, differently, into redemption through art. The point of contention that will be raised later by Michel Foucault is that existentialism thinks of
its different life as authentic, but a wider chronology of the project for a different
life can evidently be traced. For the moment I want, however, to focus on two
writers whose legacies impose a rethinking of the everyday.

The focus here is on writers in whose work a critical project is linked to the
imaginative postulation of different ways of living, in the present and near future.
In the present, that is, not in a utopia postulated as at the end of the horizon,
realizable only through a collective revolution, and not in the exploration of the
past. Thus, if Foucault's *History of Sexuality* is mobilized, as he confesses, by a
desire to ask if one can think differently from the way one does, the route this
project takes is through the archaeology of forms of relation to self as they are
construed in the sexual and dietary manuals of Greek and Roman antiquity. The
imagining of a different life takes the detour of history in order to unfix thought
from itself and enable difference: 'free thought from what it silently thinks'
(Foucault 1985, p. 9). Though this detour may be entirely necessary, the imagination and, to an extent, the living, of a different life in Foucault's present, is
not to be found here but in Foucault's fragmentary comments, mostly in interviews, about homosexuality. It may be that this offers an immediate link between
Barthes and Foucault; both Barthes and Foucault however seem to me to orient

their different thought and their different lives, their legacies and their testaments indeed, away from this categorization of their *identity*, seeking rather to retain a certain inventiveness, a certain asociality. It is perhaps fitting and ironic then to open a discussion of Barthes and everyday life with the notion of a resistance to the social and a trajectory that leads away from it.

Roland Barthes: everyday utopia

Roland Barthes is an exemplary figure for this enquiry since, as Knight suggests, he 'never stopped hypothesizing and fantasizing how things might be otherwise – otherwise, that is, than in his alienated and class-torn society' (1997, p. 2). Knight's book *Barthes and Utopia* identifies Barthes as an important utopian thinker of the present. Barthes writes in *Roland Barthes par Roland Barthes* of utopia as that which mobilizes the desire of the writer and produces meaning (Barthes 1977, p. 76). Utopia, for Barthes, is that *other place*, *non-place* or *not yet placed place* that unhinges thought and life from themselves. Meaning, or in other words difference, requires this displacement that opens a space of desire. The everyday is thus of interest to Barthes insofar as it is or can be made different from itself. Language both opens up this space of difference and desire, and closes it off, as meaning 'takes' and becomes immobile. The everyday first emerges as an object of concern in the context of a critique of the petrified forms that meaning takes on in the myth. Indeed early French structuralism, it could be argued, is driven precisely by this impetus to disengage everyday life from itself. It coincides with a moment at which everyday life becomes both an object of political and ideological control and of intellectual critique. Barthes' essay 'Myth today' in *Mythologies*, in many ways inaugural of structuralist semiology, is appended to a series of short essays on 'some myths of everyday life in France', or 'the language of so-called mass culture' in the mid- to late 1950s (Barthes 1972a). Barthes says in the preface that he is undertaking to reveal the ideological upholstery that supports the '*what-goes-without-saying*' (1972a, p. 11). If Barthes' subject matter is taken primarily from culture, from the world of leisure (wrestling, adverts, exhibitions, magazines) as opposed to the world of work, this reflects what Ross (1995) has called the 'colonization of everyday life' in France in the 1950s and 1960s, the huge influx of objects and capital devoted to the deployment of the leisure and culture industries. 'Style' was no longer the province of the individual artisan or dictated by tradition; everyday life is 'stylized' in a way that permitted the identification, ordering and control of those to whom it no doubt appeared in the guise of new and exciting opportunities for pleasure. That Barthes's 'ideological critique', in *Mythologies*, is devoted to cultural forms rather than to economic or political forms suggests the existence of this new terrain of exploitation in popular culture, which we may now take for granted.

Around the period of *Mythologies* 'everyday life' had thus become a specific object of critique and analysis. The Soviet invasion of Hungary in 1956 and the widespread disillusionment with the PCF that resulted created new possibilities for leftist critique, which could escape from the straightjacket of orthodox Stalinist economic determinism. The cultural sector – that sphere of life that did not pertain to the world of production – could thus become an object of study for Marxist intellectuals outside the PCF like Henri Lefebvre or Edgar Morin. The almost instantaneous introduction of consumer goods (refrigerators, washing machines, TVs, etc) on a mass scale into France, the promotion of a certain kind of 'lifestyle' in their advertising (as in Perec's novel *Things*), the emergence of an economy of consumption rather than of production co-incide with the emergence of a new leftist-oriented and specifically ideological critique. Groups such as *Socialisme ou barbarie* and *Arguments* (of which Barthes was a founding member), both with their own journals, were the pioneers of this kind of non-affiliated Marxist critique.

To focus more specifically on Barthes' itinerary, one can see in the articles in *Arguments* a microcosm of the development of his work towards the utopian radicalism of *Tel Quel* textuality. In a text on Brecht he points to the necessity of semiology as an aspect of any ideological critique and revolutionary art: 'revolutionary art must admit a certain arbitrary nature of signs, it must acknowledge a certain "formalism" in the sense that it must treat form according to an appropriate method, which is the semiological method' (Barthes 1972b, p. 75). The 'formalist' appearance of semiology, and of theory – the sense that it deviates from a *practice* oriented towards everyday life, is justified as an element of Marxist ideological critique since any non-arbitrary, non-formalized language, which claims its foundation in *essence* or in *nature* derives from the mendacious and exploitative realm of myths. Semiological 'formalism' is thus an element of a 'revolutionary art', a *responsibility of forms*. Strictly *formal* analysis and subversion is a way out, one way out, of the ideological trap of *everyday* language. Later, Barthes will insist on the excessively coded and formalized worlds of Sade, Fourier and Loyola (among others) as utopian strategies for short-circuiting the stranglehold of stereotype-saturated discourse. Significantly, it is the texture of the *everydayness* of these utopias that fascinates Barthes; it is the coded details of utopian lives or the everyday life of utopia which mobilize desire. It is then in the context of his association with the journal *Tel Quel* that Barthes would develop the notion of the *Text*, a radically anti-communicative practice of writing *in process* directed towards the analytic dissolution of stereotypical meaning, in effect of 'meanings' as such. The trajectory thus moves from an analytic perspective on the new economy of consumption and communication, to a greater insistence on the alienated quality of any communication, and the postulation and exploration of utopian strategies to evade such alienation. The celebration and investigation of the Marquis de Sade as a hero of such a textuality *of the limit* can thus make sense in the context of an itinerary which develops from the *critique of everyday life* of the late 1950s. For Barthes, however, it is less Sade's textuality or theory as such which is celebrated, and more the re-organization of everyday life that the Sadean utopia proposes through the text: 'The Sadean utopia – like that of Fourier, for that matter – is measured far less against theoretical statements than against the organization of everyday life, for the mark of utopia is the everyday; or even: everything everyday is utopian: timetables, dietary programmes, plans for clothing, the installation of furnishings, precepts of conversation or communication' (Barthes 1976, p. 17). Barthes reading of Sade thus eschews meditation on pornography, evil, violence, materialist philosophy, to elaborate an 'ethnography of the Sadean village' (1976, p. 17).

The emergence of the semiological project from the leftist critique of everyday life and petty-bourgeois stereotypes might thus be imagined as premised on the following strategic imperatives, which describe Barthes' trajectory:

- Analyse the everyday language of the petty-bourgeoisie in relation to the various figures and objects with which it constructs its universe, or with which its universe is constructed, a universe in which provincial nineteenth-centuryism attempts to come to terms with a new influx of consumer objects, the appeal to Nature remaining the same.
- Insist on a formal analysis of this language to undo the appeal to essence and nature through which this culture renders its world politically innocent.
- In order to counter the appeal to nature and essence which grounds the stereotype as something which goes without saying, affirm alternative systems which highlight the codified, formally arbitrary nature of language as such, of any language.
- To catalyse desire, stultified in the realm of the stereotype, insist on an imaginary domesticity, a utopian construction of the everyday, characterized by an excessive formality, where formality is meant in both senses: systematic and coded, and excessively polite, whence Barthes' insistence on a 'principle of delicacy, against ideological arrogance' (Barthes 1976, author's translation) and his enjoyment of this in Sade's texts.

Barthes' desire for difference, for a different texture of the everyday opens a space of *jouissance*. His writing, in both content (Sade, Fourier, Loyola, Japan, Pleasure) and form – the fragmented mosaic of *S/Z* onwards – is motivated by the enjoyment of a perverse cataloguing and systematizing of everyday life, a different, utopian domesticity that ruins the *what goes without saying* of the everyday stereotype, and imagines a different life. Barthes's re-reading of his own texts in *Roland Barthes by Roland Barthes* charts this development. The consistent enemy is the stereotype or the Doxa, by which life is frozen into *product*. The leftist revolutionary project and the semiological dream are both utopian strategies deriving from a critique of everyday life moulded around the dominance of the stereotype. The theorization of the Text – writing in process, without arriving at product – and the insistence on the utopia of the code in Sade or Fourier are utopian strategies precisely in the offering of alternative imaginary systems to the everyday life of the stereotype. A decisive moment in this trajectory is when the *body* comes onto the scene, the body as that precisely which is absent from the stereotype, the latter being a disembodied discourse, 'where the body is missing' (Barthes 1977, p. 90), as opposed to an invested one, 'a vested discourse' (1977, p. 137). The semiological and textual models are abandoned, or nuanced, when it appears that they risk becoming secondary *Doxa*, systems that threaten to restrict the freedom of the individual of singular mind. They are nuanced precisely through their investment by desire: 'one must introduce into this rational image-repertoire the texture of desire, the claims of the body' (Barthes 1977, p. 71). Thus, from a 1972 text on Bataille, 'Les sorties du texte' ('The sorties of the text'), a linguistics of *value* is postulated, in which the subject writes in his body, according to the singular, individualized values – tastes, pleasures, perversions – particular to that body, the body here being not so much the physical element as whatever pertains to that individual after or beyond the effect of discourse. The body is the individual, insofar as he or she is different, 'my body is not the same as yours' (1997, p. 117). A different consideration of everyday life and utopia emerges from this conception. The individual lives, breathes his or her utopia *in* their everyday life in so far as this life is that of their body. 'Life of the body' here does not mean, necessarily, the physical life as opposed to the life of the mind, intellectual life, a life of exercise, diet, abstinence from stimulants, and so on. It means the life of singular taste, perversion, enjoyments, inasmuch as these are those of the individual at the expense of the Doxa, of the *disembodied* stereotype. The utopian everyday life of the body is then a life in relation to which the body is in desire or in enjoyment, invested.

As soon, however, as this life takes on, through writing, the character of a product, a finished work, as soon as, in Barthes terms, it 'takes', it 'turns', as milk curdles or a sauce thickens, it ceases to have value for the body, it becomes disembodied. Thus, the strategy of the writer, whose desire is in language, whose world of enjoyment is linguistic, is to remain at, or to attain that state of language *before* the crystallization of *meaning*. The writer, Barthes, seeks to avoid any suggestion of heroism, seeks '*la perte de tout héroisme*' (the loss of all heroism) since 'my body is not a hero' (1977, p. 60). The end result, the final utopian strategy of the writer is the *incident,* that which falls, without explanation, without adjectival qualification, the *haiku*. The everyday here has a different sense than the common, the stereotypical. It is the incidental detail of any day, articulated in its singularity and absolute difference, but not as exception to the rule or the commonplace. It is indeed, a different conception of the commonplace – the ordinary not in terms of submission or difference to a law of sameness but the common in so far as it is characterized by the difference of each moment, each infinitely divisible incident from the next. Barthes' trajectory, from *Mythologies* to his last works, moves from the critical analysis of the myths that determine everyday life in France to the utopic recovery of the incidental texture of 'a life'.

So Barthes' fascination with the utopic appears not so much as an idealized flight to an other space, a hysterical reflection of an unsatisfactory real, and rather as an affirmatively perverse indulgence in the quality of the everyday and its micro-textures. This is pursued in Barthes' lectures at the Collège de France in 1976-77 under the heading 'Comment vivre ensemble?' ('How to live together?') (Barthes 2002). The analysis of the figures and dimensions of communal spaces is articulated here as a teaching motivated by the desire of the lecturer, Barthes himself, thus as fantasy. This fantasy is named by the term 'idiorrythmie' – one's own singular rhythm, one's own speed – and the utopian space is one that maintains a distance that allows the singular rhythms of different lives to exist alongside each other. While at first glance Barthes' utopic imaginary may appear to move in a different direction to the increasing critique of opposi-tional or transgressive construals of power-relations in the work of Foucault, with closer attention they may be seen as more allied. There are lines to be drawn and resonances to be brought to light between the later work of Foucault and Barthes' exploration of the figures of 'living together' in the 1976–77 seminar, for example. For reasons of economy, this work will need to be done elsewhere. However, might not Foucault's notion of *heterotopic* spaces, that is 'effectively realized sorts of utopias' (Foucault 2002, p. 1574, author's translation), or localized spaces of difference, be seen in proximity to Barthes' emphasis on the deflection of the incident, the punctual unhinging of an ideologically saturated real? A distinction might nevertheless be introduced: rather than as fantasy and as motivated by desire, in Foucault's account of the heterotopia, it is character-ized as a real and localizable space (in contrast to the unreality of utopia, properly speaking) *from which* (Foucault figures it as a mirror) I am led to realize the unreality of where I am. I am led thus to *reconstitute* myself where I am. Might this not lead to an account of Foucault's later work in which a *locus of difference within* the texture of everyday life gives rise to an opportunity for its reconstitu-tion, or at least its reconfiguration? This is the question towards which I want to direct the second part of this article.

Michel Foucault: the dimension of the testament

In *The Will to Knowledge*, Foucault introduces the vital concept of the biopolitical, according to which power operates in the politics of modernity not primarily through the imposition of the law, having recourse ultimately to death as its force, but through the norm. Power produces and manages life, distributing deviance in relation to a normative life. Life, insofar as it is normal, everyday, in one sense of that word, is produced, managed and organized by, in and through power. One of the techniques of biopolitics is the production of lives, or of subjects – that is of individuals who construct and recognize themselves as subjects. Thus, the next phase of Foucault's project was to analyse the archaeology of the relation to the self, the ways in which the self works upon itself and takes itself as an object. This took him as we know into the exploration of Greek and Roman discourses on the management of the body and of sexual relations with others, in *The Use of Pleasures* and *The Care of the Self*.

If we return to my introductory comments on Foucault's postulation of the question: 'can one think otherwise?' it seems possible to see this project, the deviation via the Greeks and Romans, as something more than simply archaeological, analytic and historical. Given the notion of the biopolitical – 'life' managed and produced by power – can one not see Foucault's project as motivated by a desire to imagine or to think, at least, a different life other than that produced and managed by power? The project takes the long detour of the history of sexuality only in order to unstick thought from the thought and the life produced by power. The detour is only interrupted by death. Nevertheless, in fragmentary, unsystematic and unworked comments in his interviews Foucault takes shortcuts, postulating ways of life that take the individual into unmanaged spaces, spaces of freedom.

Desire, Foucault writes, in *The Will to Knowledge*, submits us to 'the austere monarchy of sex' (1978, p. 159). Psychoanalysis comes under attack specifically for affirming our subjection to the Law – in Lacanian terms, to the Phallus. It is not in terms of desire, desire for sex or for the sex – *le sexe-désir* (sex-desire), that our counter-attack should be made, but in terms of pleasure: 'It is the agency of sex we must break away from, if we aim – through a tactical reversal of the various mechanisms of sexuality – to counter the grips of power with the claims of bodies, pleasures and knowledges, in their multiplicity and their possibility of resistance. The rallying point for the counterattack against the deployment of sexuality ought not to be sex-desire, but bodies and pleasures' (Foucault 1978, p. 157). It is not through desire, then, that we are going to live differently, invent new ways of life, but through *bodies and pleasures*.

Foucault's critique of desire resonates paradoxically both with Barthes and with Lacan's accounts of desire. For Barthes, desire is strangely close to perversion, in that the desire that mobilizes his enjoyment in, say, a text or a photograph, is singularily his *desire*. Moreover, *jouissance* disturbs the satisfaction of the attainment of what you desire. You get what you want, but more. Barthes's desire is always *more than* what satisfies, what comforts, and this *more than* is culturally and subjectively unsettling. Foucault's suggestion that in affirming desire one affirms one's subjection is confirmed by Lacan's dictum: 'Man's desire is the desire of/for the other' ('Le désir de l'homme c'est le désir dé l'Autre', Lacan 1977, p. 58). But what does Foucault mean by saying that the insistence of a counter-attack against the discursive web of sexuality should be on *bodies and pleasures*? The phrase *bodies and pleasures*, not *subjects and desires*, connotes multiplicity, anonymity, passage, flight, the orgy. In the context of *relations among human beings*, it seems to privilege multiple, non-territorial, non-institutional relations. It seems like a critique of the *couple*, of the *family*, in favour of the orgiastic, the fugitive, the cruised encounter. It reads like an imagining of a Sadean dis/utopia, and in this light it resonates with the ex-Situationist Raoul Vaneighem's fantasized solution to social alienation of retiring to a castle with 40 beautiful courtesans and dying of an excess of debauchery, with his proposal of infinite desire: 'The complete unchaining of pleasure is the surest way to the revolution of everyday life' (Vaneighem 1967, author's translation); 'We have not yet guessed to what extent we have been led to desire an end instead of desiring without an end' (Vaneighem 1998, author's translation).

Certain comments by Foucault in interviews in the 1970s confirm this reading – a revolution of everyday life through an intensification of pleasures: 'What we have to work on, it seems to me, is not so much to liberate our desires, but making ourselves infinitely more susceptible to pleasures' (1997, p. 137). The injunction is repeated on a number of occasions, in Foucault's interviews, that 'We have to create new pleasure' (1997, p. 166). The revolution of everyday life through the creation of new pleasures, through the intensification of pleasure leads, in Foucault's writings and that of others, into strange territory. The call for the intensification of pleasure, the creation of new pleasures is not an apology for hedonism, for an art of living well, *le bien vivre*; indeed, it seems to lead away from anything that might be defined as pleasure in the social or cultural spheres. The *other* space that the inventiveness and creativity Foucault calls for is at the same time a move into a zone of relations as yet unidentifiable within the social fabric, and a move into a dimension on the threshold of what is recognizable as 'life'. Whence the question: does Foucault's insistence on *bodies and pleasures*, his call for the intensification and multiplicity of pleasures, lead to death, real or metaphorical? This much is suggested by another interchange in an interview of 1982, shortly after Foucault was hit by a car and hospitalized for a week. The interviewer, Stephen Riggins, insists on the austere quality of Foucault's private life: 'One of the things about you that is very impressive is the sort of monachal austerity in which you live. . . . You do not fit the image of the sophisticated Frenchman who makes an art out of living well' (translated as *l'art de bien vivre*). Foucault answers:

> Actually, I think I have real difficulty in experiencing pleasure. . . . It's not as simple as that to enjoy oneself. . . . I would like and I hope I'll die of an overdose of pleasure of any kind. Because I think it's really difficult, and I always have the feeling that I do not *feel* the pleasure, the complete total pleasure, and, for me, it's related to death. . . . I think that the kind of pleasure that I would consider as *the* real pleasure would be so deep, so intense, so overwhelming that I couldn't survive it. I would die. . . . Once I was struck by a car in the street. . . And for maybe two seconds I had the impression that I was dying and it was really a very, very intense

pleasure. . .. It was, it still is now, one of my best memories (Laughs). It's true that a glass of wine, of good wine, old and so on, may be enjoyable, but it's not for me. A pleasure must be something incredibly intense . . . I'm not able to give myself and others those middle-range pleasures that make up everyday life (trans. *la vie de tous les jours*). . . . That's the reason why I'm not a social being, why I'm not really a cultural being, why I'm so boring in my everyday life.

(1997, p. 129)

Even granting a distinction between what Foucault says in what he writes and his *everyday life*, as he puts it, it is clear here that the pleasure Foucault postulates is oriented towards death. It resonates with Vaneighem's dream of dying through an excess of debauchery, and with remarks by Foucault throughout his work on Sade, that the subjectivity of the libertine, Juliette, is dissolved, disappears in the affirmation of pleasure that she articulates and enacts. This pleasure towards death brings Foucault closer to Barthes' *jouissance*, and to Lacanian desire – the ethics of psychoanalysis being premised on the injunction to act in conformity with your desire, not to give way on your desire, in any circumstance. On the one hand, the call for a counter-attack affirming bodies and pleasures, repeated insistence on the intensification of pleasures, the exploration of new pleasures; on the other, an austere way of life and a denial of the pleasures of everyday life in favour of pleasures so intense you die from them. Foucault's imagining of a different life flirts with death and disappearance. The pleasures imagined or explored have the flavour of annihilation.

This prompts a re-reading of comments about S&M and drugs in which Foucault affirms them as possible avenues for experimentation with greater and more mobile pleasures; Foucault's statements about these practices foreground the *delocalization*, the *desexualization* of pleasure, rather than the expansion of sex, hinting that it is a question of developing new possibilities for pleasure, new relations between bodies outside and beyond the framework of sexuality, 'le dispositif de la sexualité', as he terms it (1976). In particular, Foucault notoriously desexualizes homosexuality, which for him is primarily the possibility of developing and inventing a new way of life, 'une mode de vie homosexuel' (a homosexual way of life) (1997, p. 158), which can enable a liberation, even for heterosexuals, from the matrix of sexuality by and through which power exercises itself. If heterosexuality, as Foucault argues, is oriented towards an accomplishment or the goal of sex, courtly love being a paradigm here, in contemporary homosexual relations (in the 1970s) sex is realized immediately. Sex comes first, life comes after, a reversal of the heterosexual structure which locates life, relations within the teleological narrative of sex (indeed one could speculate that narrative as such might be premised on such a heterosexual teleology). With homosexuality then, individuals have the possibility, so to speak *after heterosexuality*, of inventing new kinds of *ways of life*, new forms of relation outside the limiting, power-suffused teleology of sex. Friendship as a way of life, *l'amitié comme mode de vie* (the title of one of Foucault's interviews), designates the non-sexual but erotic relation that Foucault sees as desirable, but not as an object of desire.

> Another thing to distrust is the tendency to relate the question of homo-sexuality to the problem of 'Who am I' and 'What is the secret of my desire?' Perhaps it would be better to ask oneself, 'What relations, through homo-sexuality, can be established, invented, multiplied and modulated?' The problem is not to discover in oneself the truth of sex but rather to use sexuality henceforth to arrive at a multiplicity of relationships. And no doubt that's the real reason why homosexuality is not a form of desire but some-thing desirable. Therefore we have to work at becoming homosexuals and not be obstinate in recognizing that we are. The development towards which the problem of sexuality tends is the one of friendship.
>
> (1997, pp. 135–136)

A different life is to be invented in the post-sexual unidentifiability and strange-ness of relations. So, Foucault asks, what is it to be naked amongst men? We can read nakedness here as meaning both the lack of tension in the sexual dynamic (the teleology of striptease is disenabled, ruining narrative, and desire), but also a lack of tools with which to construct a relation, a lack of ready-made formulas with which to be with the other. The necessity of inventing a new way of relating. Foucault's *bodies and pleasures* appears for a moment to be a Sadean vision of orgiastic anonymous pleasures in bathhouses – San Franciscan, Greek or Roman. But this is a deviated reading of only part of a more general imagining of as yet uninvented forms of relation outside the *dispositif* (the apparatus) of sexuality. Pleasures that are more than simply sexual are at stake. The inventiveness Foucault has in mind is a diffusion of pleasure over the whole body and beyond it into the whole fabric of the relations one has with others:

> two men of noticeably different ages – what code would allow them to communicate? They face each other without terms or convenient words, with nothing to assure them about the meaning of the movement that carries them towards each other. They have to invent, from A to Z, a relationship that is still formless, which is friendship, the sum of everything through which they can give each other pleasure.
>
> (1997, p. 136)

Butler's account of subjectivation in Foucault, in *The Psychic Life of Power* (1995), suggests that, since there is no power without resistance and no resistance without power, resistance to power as it is mediated through the net of sexuality can come in the form of an excess. An excess of subjectivation, above and beyond what power needs to produce subjects, is re-articulated as resistance.

Homosexuality in this instance is re-articulated not as the truth and secret of one's desire but as the possibility at least of new and strange relations after and beyond sex. One could imagine it voiced in this statement: You identify me as homosexual, I identify myself as homosexual (or why not, *as heterosexual*) but I am going to claim that identity not as my truth, as the truth of my desire, but as a local and strategic means of inventing different relations with others, of *realizing* virtual relations:

> Homosexuality is a historic occasion to re-open affective and relational virtualities, not so much through the intrinsic qualities of the homosexual but due to the biases against the position he occupies; in a certain sense diagonal lines that he can trace in the social fabric permit him to make these virtualities visible.
>
> (1997, p. 138)

'*Bodies and pleasures*' (1978, p. 157) should thus be understood and translated not in the narrow restrictive frame of sexuality as truth, Foucault's 'perverse' desire, but as *affective and relational virtualities*. From this perspective the renewal of life, the possibility of a different life arises only on the other side of everyday life, life inasmuch as it is produced and subjected to power or ruled by the economy of pleasure. The life that remains when one subtracts subjection, the matter of the body that matters, is a zone of abjection, or risked unrecognizability, which is proximate to death, intimate with death. It is worth asking again, does Foucault's different life, the one of bodies and pleasures, pleasures so intense that you might die, only live in proximity to death or within its domain?

In both of the theoretical corpuses I have been considering everyday *life* appears as that which is captured in the trap of ideologically saturated meaning (meaning as such) or in the apparatus of power. However, beyond the space of this analysis, after its epistemological dissolution of the structures it considers, the goal, as Foucault proposes, is to liberate thought and life from the modes to which they are contingently attached, so as to enable different ways of thinking and different ways of life. Everyday life becomes the space of the potential emergence of 'new relations, new virtualities', or of the utopic *in the everyday*, the space for potentially new kinds of pleasure outside the *dispositif* of desire and sex. This dynamic of difference seems premised on a structure of transgression: one steps *over* or outside the limit of a present epistemology in order to experiment with new and different, as yet unexplored areas. It is for this reason that, in relation to life, the *new life* or the *other life* may appear to be *on the other side* of the limit of death as a legacy left to those who will come after: French thought of this mould would be testamentary in its essence.

Might a different way of thinking the critical or resistant line *in* the everyday suggest itself if we pay closer attention to the inflection given to Foucault's later work by Deleuze? To return to the scene of the obituary address given by Deleuze at the Salpetrière would also suggest the relevance of Deleuze's obituary writings on Foucault, in *Foucault* (1986) and in *Negotiations* (1995).[1] Deleuze locates in the final period of Foucault's work the discovery of *subjectivation* as a way out of the potential impasse for difference, for thinking and living otherwise, which results from the analysis of power. Furthermore, in the remarkable text 'Desire and Pleasure' (1996) Deleuze elaborates a critique of Foucault's notion of pleasure (as in 'bodies and pleasures') which figures it not as resistance but as a re-territorialization. It would seem that pleasure in Foucault's sense is still, for Deleuze, too linked to a transcendental notion of subjectivity. To counter this, Deleuze offers 'life' (the 'a life' of his final article [1997]) as a plane of immanence. In this light, we should note Deleuze's qualification of subjectivation as a concept in Foucault's work which offers a line of flight or an escape route out from under the ubiquitous net of power thrown in *Surveiller et punir* and *La volonté de savoir*. In *Negotiations* Deleuze specifies what he means by the term: 'Subjectification [sic.] was not for Foucault a theoretical return to the subject but a practical search for another way of life, a new style' (1995, p. 106), and 'Nothing excites so many stupid reactions as this simple, precise, and grand theme in Nietzsche and Foucault. The third common point, finally, has to do with processes of subjectification: once again, this is nothing to do with constituting a subject, its about creating ways of existing, what Nietzsche called inventing new possibilities of life' (1995, p. 118). Subjectivation, as Deleuze notes, has little to do with subjectivity, it does not designate a 'return' or the recognition of anything like an authentic 'self' or a truth of oneself. Truth in this sense always serves power. The doubling of subjectivation is rather a disengagement from lines of power and from games of truth, and the invention of 'facultative' (rather than essential) criteria for living, rules recognized as relative and to be abandoned as soon as they become subject to knowledge and to power. Subjectivation is localized and punctual; it does not operate according to the matrix of transgression which would see a different life *on the other side* of a line, but straddles the line and follows it, acknowledging the risks of such a position:

> The time comes once we've worked through knowledge and power; it's that work forces us to frame the new question, it couldn't have been framed before. Subjectivity is in no sense a knowledge formation or power function that Foucault hadn't previously recognized; subjectification is an artistic activity distinct from, and lying outside, knowledge and power. In this respect Foucault's a Nietzschean, discovering an artistic will out on the final line. Subjectification, that's to say the process of folding the line outside, mustn't be seen as just a way of protecting one's self, taking shelter. It's rather the only way of confronting the line, riding it: you may be heading for death, suicide, but as Foucault says in a strange conversation with Schroeter, suicide then becomes an art it takes a lifetime to learn.
>
> (Deleuze 1995, p. 114)

In this account, subjectivation becomes something like a pragmatics of difference within the everyday, rather than a utopian strategy of orientation towards the other place. It designates a strange kind of turning inside out, an alignment of 'oneself' with the dimension of the outside, as suggested in the final words of Deleuze's *Foucault*:

> The most distant point becomes interior, by being converted into the nearest: *life within the folds*. This is the central chamber, which one need no longer feel is empty since one fills it with oneself. Here one becomes a master of one's speed and, relatively speaking, a master of one's molecules and particular features, in this zone of subjectivation: the boat as interior of the exterior.
>
> (1988, p. 123)

In this Baconesque involution (cf. Deleuze 2003), becoming a 'master of one's speeds' resonates for me with the Barthesian notion of the singular rhythm I pointed to earlier, with an *idiorrythmics*. Is this to say that Barthes' *desire* for an everyday, domestic utopia and Foucault's heterotopias first in terms of *pleasure* then as annihilation, then, as read by Deleuze, subjectivation, finally resolve their internal differences in the figure of *singularity*? The task would then be to re-think the community of singularities, the everyday sociality of the singular.

Notes

1   I have written more extensively on Deleuze's take on Foucault, specifically on the notion of 'Life as a work of art' in an article with that title in Gratton and Sheringham's *The Art of the Project* (Berghahn, forthcoming).

References

Barthes, R. (1972a) *Mythologies*, trans. Annette Lavers, Cape, London.

Barthes, R. (1972b) *Critical Essays*, trans. Richard Howard, Northwestern University Press, Evanston.

Barthes, R. (1976) *Sade, Fourier, Loyola*, trans. Richard Miller, Hill and Wang, New York.

Barthes, R. (1977) *Roland Barthes by Roland Barthes,* trans. Richard Howard, Macmillan, London.

Barthes, R. (2002) *Comment Vivre Ensemble: Cours et Séminaires au Collège de France (1976–77)*, Seuil/IMEC, Paris.

Butler, J. (1997) *The Psychic Life of Power*, Stanford University Press, Stanford.

Deleuze, G. (1988) *Foucault*, trans. Sean Hand, London, Athlone.

Deleuze, G. (1995) *Negotiations*, Columbia University Press, New York.

Deleuze, G. (1996) 'Desire and pleasure', in *Foucault and His Interlocutors*, ed. A. Davidson, University of Chicago Press, Chicago, pp. 183–189.

Deleuze, G. (1997) 'Immanence: a life', *Theory, Culture & Society*, vol. 14, no. 2, pp. 3–8.

Deleuze, G. (2003) *Francis Bacon: The Logic of Sensation*, trans. Daniel W. Smith, University of Minnesota Press, Minneapolis.

Foucault, M. (1978) *The History of Sexuality: an Introduction (The Will to Knowledge)*, trans. Robert Hurley, Vintage, New York.

Foucault, M. (1985) *The Use of Pleasure; The History of Sexuality Volume 2*, trans. Robert Hurley, Penguin, Harmondsworth.

Foucault, M. (1997) *Ethics: The Essential Works I*, trans. Robert Hurley and others, ed. Paul Rabinow, Penguin, London.

Foucault, M. (2002) 'Des espaces autres', in *Dits et Ecrits*, Gallimard, Paris, pp. 1571–1581.

Knight, D. (1997) *Barthes and Utopia: Space, Travel, Writing*, Oxford University Press, Oxford.

Lacan, J. (1977) *Ecrits: A Selection*, trans. Alan Sheridan, Tavistock, London.

Ross, K. (1995) *Fast Cars, Clean Bodies*, MIT, Cambridge, MA.

Vaneighem, R. (1967) *Traité se avoir-vivre à l'usage des jeunes générations*, Champ Libre, Paris.

Vaneighem, R. (1998) *Nous qui désirons sans fin*, Gallimard, Paris.

Ben Highmore

HOMEWORK
Routine, social aesthetics and the
ambiguity of everyday life

Routine is a central feature of everyday life, yet its peculiar rhythms, and the range of experiences associated with it, are often neglected within cultural studies and sociology. Simmel's attempt to provide a sociological aesthetics is seen as a project that needs reanimating for the study of everyday life routines. This does not mean, however, that Simmel is the only, or the best, guide to the aesthetic dimensions of everyday routine life. In an attempt to provide some co-ordinates for instigating a socio-aesthetic approach to routine, this paper discusses a number of writers who couple aesthetics and the everyday, and who might provide frameworks for the study of experiential aspects of routine life. It also suggests that an inverted reading of John Dewey could provide socio-aesthetic study with the 'formless' forms required to bring everyday background routines into the foreground. The socio-aesthetic study of cooking undertaken by Luce Giard provides an example of the complexity of such an approach. Lastly the article looks briefly at new directions for 'everyday life aesthetics', more specifically at Henri Lefebvre's unfinished project of rhythmanalysis.

Keywords everyday life; routine; aesthetics; John Dewey; Luce Giard; Henri Lefebvre

What else could I do – besides go home to walk the dogs, make dinner, go to bed? Sometimes routine is soothing, but at other times it's a burden.

(Paretsky 2001, p. 376)

My characteristic reaction to emotional turmoil is to clean the kitchen sink scrub the work tops and tidy away the mess, of which there is always plenty cluttering draining board, sink, dresser and so on. And then I cook – order first, then nurture.

(Martin 1984, p. 23)

Ambiguity is a category of everyday life, and perhaps an essential category.

(Lefebvre 1991, p. 18)

Cultural Studies Vol. 18, No. 2/3 March/May 2004, pp. 306–327
ISSN 0950-2386 print/ISSN 1466-4348 online   © 2004 Taylor & Francis Ltd
http://www.tandf.co.uk/journals   DOI: 10.1080/0950238042000201536

R Routledge
Taylor & Francis Group

How do the routines of everyday life feel to you? Do you wear them lightly or do they press down on you like a dull weight? Do the routines and habits of daily life comfort you with their worn and tender familiarity, or do they pull irritably at you, rubbing your face in their lack of spontaneity and event? When cleaning or cooking does time ricochet past in the half-light of the daydream or stutter and collapse in the stupor of drudgery? Can domestic routines become precious moments snatched from more thoroughly exhaustive work practices, or do their rhythms constantly signal their lack of value? And how, supposing we wanted to, would we call attention to such 'non-events', without betraying them, without disloyalty to the particularity of their experience, without simply turning them into 'events'?

There is something ambiguous and problematic about routine. Modernity, it would seem, needs to be characterized by the increased routinization of everyday life: the scientific management of the workplace, attempts to extend this into the household realm and forms of bureaucratization pervasively establishing their routines throughout the social realm. Yet, what routine feels like, how it is experienced, is by no means clear. Partly, I think, because routine is not only a form dictated from above. We establish our own daily routines to give our lives rhythm and predictability. We use routine to bring order and control to lives that may otherwise seem entirely determined by the contingencies of context, or as Martin describes it, routines are 'the mundane process by which meaning is created and maintained even in the face of the chronic flux and disturbance of experience' (1984, p. 23). Yet, routines are also foisted on us, like a straightjacket of dull repetition. To start to inquire into the experiential aspects of routine, to get some idea of the effects and affects of this regular and regulated rhythmicity, it is necessary, I think, for social and cultural studies to rekindle what Simmel (1968) once called a 'sociological aesthetics'.

Simmel was interested in analysing modern life from the perspective of social forms by investigating the patterning of social and cultural life. He was also interested in the sensory-mental effects and affects that modern life produced in the bodies and consciousness of individuals. Aesthetics, pressed into the service of sociology and cultural studies, would similarly mean foregrounding form and privileging the patterning of experience. It would also mean scouring artworks (films, novels, visual art and so on) to find productively expressive forms for bringing everyday social experiences, often relegated to the background, into the foreground (see for example the artworks discussed in Molesworth 2000). It would mean, in other words, that we treat artworks as forms of social and cultural research that are particularly suited to the description of experience. However, here, it seems to me, routine is problematic. It sits ambiguously on the borders of form and formlessness. Used to mark the rhythms of the day, certain routines provide a form for framing experience (for instance, the routines of getting out of bed, getting dressed, washing and the like). Yet, when routines saturate and subsume temporal experience, instead of marking time they unmark it by dedifferentiating it, leaving us temporally adrift (for instance, the difficulty we have in assessing the passing of time in thoroughly standardized work routines). Similarly, while everyday life has been a vivid subject for the modern artwork in general (from impressionism to the *nouvelle vague* and beyond (see Ross 2000 and Gumpert 1997 for visual art's connection to the everyday)), the structures of routine do not seem to easily provide aesthetic forms. Indeed, the artworks most attentive to routine might well be those that signal a crisis in form (for instance, the inevitable difficulty of narrative forms to accommodate routine).

There are many issues at stake here and this essay is only an initial attempt to sketch out the problems and possibilities for a socio-aesthetic inquiry into routine. Although I will begin by looking at the routines of industrialized work, it is the domestic realm that most insistently, I think, registers the central ambiguity of routine, its characteristically dual nature of comfort and constraint. In providing a grounding for a social aesthetics, I want to suggest that the work of John Dewey can provide a worthwhile resource, even if it does mean offering an inverted reading of Dewey. Cooking will serve as an example for the possibilities of social aesthetics, particularly as it has been deployed in the work of Luce Giard in the second volume of *The Practice of Everyday Life* (de Certeau *et al.* 1998). Lastly, I will give a brief glimpse of the possibilities of Lefebvre and Régulier's project of rhythmanalysis for extending the scope of socio-aesthetic approaches to everyday routines.

From work to home

The massive routinization of work practices that we associate with modernity has helped to characterize routine as an experience of deadening repetition. While routinization can be evidenced in most occupations, it has been the Fordist assembly line that has given us the most familiar image of repetitious physical activities that are enslaved to the rhythm of the machine (Doray 1988). Charlie Chaplin's classic evocation of an assembly line worker in his 1936 film *Modern Times* sees Chaplin's character trying to keep up with the punishing rhythm of the line, and in the process physically adopting the regular but jerky movements of industrial machinery. The work environment in the early scenes of *Modern Times* is one of almost complete mechanization; in a time-and-motion project, for instance, Chaplin undergoes mechanized feeding while continuing his assembly line work. It is the way that the factory routines push the body into new patterns of behaviour that is most vividly displayed, and offers a critical image of industrial work routine. When Chaplin is finally ejected from the factory, he has become machinic, both in his physical gait and in his automated response to what he sees as objects in need of tightening (buttons for instance).

When Chaplin's character is working on the assembly line he is perceptively attuned to the machine; his is an intense attention, alert and concentrated. Yet, often as not, it will be something closer to inattention and distraction that will characterize the experience of routine. Indeed it would be precisely when an activity *becomes routine* for someone, that levels of concentration can be relaxed, allowing room for attention to be diverted to other things; radio listening, wishful daydreaming, imaginative drifting, anxious accounting, nervous obsessing and so on. Chaplin's figuring of assembly line work, though, does allow for a truth to be told, a truth perhaps as telling as one that empiricist realism might provide. It is a truth that Lefebvre, a great admirer of Chaplin, calls a 'reverse image'. For Lefebvre, an authentic reverse image performs a critique of everyday life by providing 'an image of everyday reality, taken in its totality or as a fragment, reflecting that reality in all its depth *through* people, ideas and things which are apparently quite different from everyday experience, and therefore exceptional, deviant, abnormal' (Lefebvre 1991b, p. 12). The idea of a 'reverse image' is something that we will need to come back to. It suggests that one response to the aesthetic problem generated by everyday routine might productively be to explore forms of exaggeration and imaginative extrapolation, like those that Chaplin's film evidences. It is through the exaggeration of machinic behaviour that Chaplin sheds light on an actual critical truth of assembly line living, a truth about the relationships between humans and machines, one that wouldn't be available from forms of participant observation, for instance.

However, discussions of aesthetic sociology don't need to decide in advance on the merits and demerits of the forms of aesthetic investigation, and we should not give up on social and sociological realism just because more experimental forms also have their productivity. Linhart, a Maoist activist working in a large Renault car factory on the outskirts of Paris in the 1970s, provides a more descriptively realist version of assembly line work:

> The first impression [. . .] is one of a slow but continuous movement by all the cars. The operations themselves seem to be carried out with a kind of resigned monotony, but without the speed I expected. It's like a long, gray-green, gliding movement, and after a time it gives off a feeling of somnolence, interrupted by sounds, bumps, flashes of light, all repeated one after the other, but with regularity. The formless music of the line, the gliding movement of the unclad gray steel bodies, the routine movements: I can feel myself gradually enveloped and anesthetized. Time stands still.
>
> (Linhart 1981, pp. 13–14)

Linhart's anticipation of fast moving assembly lines is, presumably, due partly to comic representations such as those by Chaplin. Instead, Linhart emphasizes the slow monotony of the assembly line; he also suggests very different effects and affects. It is the dreamlike experience of industrial routine that comes to the fore here, the hypnotic rhythms that induce reverie as much as manic concentration. Other accounts of assembly line work (for instance, Hamper 1992) concur with Linhart and point out how debilitating such reverie can be; making the working day seem actually much longer than it would be if there were something to tax concentration. We might also note how Linhart describes the form of the assembly line as contradictory, as both the regularity of movement and the 'formless music of the line'.

The ambiguity of routine and the sense that it is often accompanied by inattention or simply concentration directed elsewhere, can be seen in other routine activities. The daily commute to work is perhaps one of the most distinctive of modern routines. Commuters often describe their lack of attention to the actuality of these journeys, undertaken, it would seem, as if on autopilot. Yet discussion of commuting is also accompanied by routine descriptions of the frustration and impotence experienced as traffic jams and poorly resourced infrastructures make the commute increasingly lengthy. As rightly understood by both Le Corbusier and the Situationists (one of the few things I would imagine they could agree on) the commute was an extension of the working day. It is time handed over to employers without any recompense: 'commuting time, as Le Corbusier rightly pointed out, is a surplus labor which correspondingly reduces the amount of "free" time' (Debord 1959, p. 57). In her study of French quotidien culture in the late 1950s and early 1960s, Ross points out that along-side this critical assessment of the commute exists another experience that recognizes the commute as a limited freedom within a culture of constraint. Ross quotes from the autobiography of novelist (and driving enthusiast) Françoise Sagan:

> These days, solitude is a luxury too. People are rarely alone; they're either at the office or at home with the family. I've heard friends, both married men and women, say: 'Traffic jams? You don't know what you're talking about. They're very peaceful. It's the only time you're alone' . . . They're alone and free for an hour, bumper to bumper.
>
> (Sagan, quoted in Ross 1995, p. 55)

The image of a frustrated, enraged and edgy driver, crawling through traffic (and it is Michael Douglas' sweaty irritation at being stuck in traffic at the start of the 1992 film *Falling Down* that springs to mind) is here met with an image of commuting as an almost meditative and reclusive time and space.

Another example of the ambiguity of routine might be found in childcare. To pick up any of the numerous childcare advice books directed at parents, is to be told about the importance of routine. The success of childcare, it would seem, is dependant in some crucial ways on routine. To not offer consistent routines is to encourage biological anarchy: 'if your child does not have reasonable consistency in her daily routines, her system does not know when she should be asleep and when she should be awake' (Ferber 1986, pp. 98–100). In the literature, the maintenance of everyday routines is necessary to accommodate and tame the circadian rhythms that regulate temperature and energy. However, aside from the purely biological argument, parents are continually told that routine also provides stability, predictability and, most important of all, security. Establishing routines is thus the key to happiness: 'chaos makes us all feel as if we've got no control over the situation. Children are happiest when they have a structured routine' (Green 2000, p. 2). Of course, it is also these routines that are often likely to become the emotionally draining occasions where children and parents struggle over power, independence and control.

Childcare routines are not of course just routines for children but for parents as well. Exhausted from a full day's work, the nighttime routines of washing and preparing children for bed can seem like a burdensome routine: one more obligation to fulfil before the day is finally yours. Weary, routinized and clearly in a different circadian phase than my children, my tendency is to try and marshal them through the various stages efficiently and without too many tears (mine and theirs). When tired, I tend towards Fordism. However, even when most tired and fractious, and even when the children seem most recalcitrant to my management, these routines are peppered with moments of tenderness and affection. It is the *simultaneity* of this that strikes me as both interesting and centrally important to the study of daily life, the way that routine can be experienced simultaneously as joyous and tedious, tender and frustrating.

The habits and routines of everyday life suggest an arena marked by tenacity; routines and habits hold on to us and we hold on to them, oftentimes unwittingly and sometimes unwillingly. Routines and habits can be hard to acquire and harder still to break. In this sense everyday life is often experienced as something deeply ambiguous, as simultaneously comforting and frustrating. I tell myself that I will use my time more productively, that I will start a new fitness routine, I will use my evenings to pursue new hobbies, but old routines hang on insistently and I find myself slumped in front of the TV, glass in hand, relaxed, happy and slightly ashamed. Everyday life often drifts, sometimes in fits and starts. Distraction and inattention often characterizes a routine consciousness that might be described as diffuse. I wash, clean and cook, while also dreaming, reminiscing and worrying. Such coupling of 'state of minds' and 'states of action' suggests a need for a form of registering everyday life that can accommodate the simultaneity of contradiction. That need is aesthetic.

Aesthetics and the everyday

It is worth taking a quick audit of some of the influential ways that the connections between aesthetics and everyday life have been figured, partly in order to be clear about what kind of aesthetic approach I am suggesting here. Aesthetics has been a feature of many approaches to everyday life studies: indeed any attempt to seriously describe the living aspects of social and cultural life might rightly be thought of as having an aesthetic remit. Aesthetics is constantly negotiating between its origins as a philosophical project directed at those sensual, creaturely aspects of life that are not subsumed by rationalist thought (see Eagleton 1990), and a concern with the assessment and production of artworks. It is the slippage between the project of describing sensate, emotional life (a project that the artwork is seen as peculiarly adept at addressing) and the *evaluation* of artworks *and* experience that might characterize both the problem and potential of aesthetics for the study of everyday life.

The ethnographic work of Willis offers a useful entry into this slippery arena. The terms 'imagination', 'creativity', and 'symbolism' are employed extensively in Willis' work, but rather than being oriented to the consideration of artworks (where they might seem to be more 'at home'), they are employed to describe the everyday culture of young people. Willis' work attends to the materially lived culture of working class youth to reveal the creativity at work in the way they adopt and adapt cultural materials; for instance, in the various ways that members of subcultures use clothing (Willis 1990). Recently Willis has offered an account of his personal academic trajectory as a way of explaining his 'grounded aesthetics' approach to everyday life (Willis 2000). Like many of those involved in cultural studies, Willis' initial academic study was in literature. In 1968, he embarked on a programme of doctoral study on the lived culture of hippies and bikers, while at the same time teaching the study of literature. Willis' literary studies had prepared him to look at the figurative details of high-cultural texts, and it was this 'close-reading' that he now applied 'to try and understand the bike culture in the city centre of Birmingham', where he finds a rich symbolic imagination at work. 'Almost on autopilot, by chance or unconsciously', he writes, 'there I was trying to use the categories of art to understand an example of lived culture'. This application of close 'textual' analysing to living culture 'seemed to grant significance where condescension had ruled' and resulted in an aesthetic attention that:

> Reconnected [with] what had been slowly drained out of literary studies at Cambridge – in a word the *social connection*, the connection with real life in all its tumbling profusion and messiness. At the same time, however, these same approaches and techniques, violently relocated to the social, *also* offered an immediate inoculation, so to speak in the other direction, against the flattening reductions of social science.
>
> (Willis 2000, p. ix, p. x)

Here then, aesthetics is not shorn from its relation to complex figuration and values of beauty, rather, such an approach is used to revalue the cultural *work* that had previously ranked as decidedly non-aesthetic. Such revaluation performs a 'reverse-image': seen from this perspective the potential of ordinary creativity is revealed as profound and extensive. Seen from the perspective of sociological realism such a revaluation must seem, in contrast, decidedly over-optimistic, purposefully downplaying aspects of cultural impoverishment, boredom and cultural subjugation. In as much as Willis locates aesthetic values in everyday life, his work might be seen as inheriting something from humanist Marxism, namely the critique of art as a symptom of alienation and elitism. Yet where humanist Marxism cast the supersession of aesthetic elitism into the future, Willis demands we recognize it in the present. The 'reverse image' of endless ordinary creativity then, would work as a partial truth, an image of potentiality, exaggerated and made concrete.

The revolutionary aesthetics of humanist Marxism is given a substantial role in Henri Lefebvre's multi-volume *Critique of Everyday Life*. In 1961, in the second volume of the critique, Lefebvre claims that the radical alterations of everyday life that critical attention will demand (the revolutionary transformation of everyday life), will include the end of art as a specialized realm: 'at one and the same time, art must fulfill itself, and then supersede itself. Ultimately it must disappear' (Lefebvre 2002, pp. 36–37). But if art disappears, aesthetics will not. Art will not be superseded by everyone becoming musicians and sculptors, or by the wide availability and appreciation of 'quality' culture and 'quality' goods. For Lefebvre, Marx suggested a much more profound aesthetic dis-alienation:

> He imagines a society in which everyone would rediscover the spontaneity of natural life and its initial creative drive, and perceive the world through the eyes of an artist, enjoy the sensuous through the eyes of a painter, the ears of a musician and the language of a poet. Once superseded, art would be reabsorbed into an everyday which had been metamorphosed by its fusion with what had hitherto been kept external to it.
>
> (Lefebvre 2002, p. 37)

However appealing such a vision is, both Lefebvre and Willis ultimately provide little with which to recover *routine* for aesthetic attention. And that is because for both of them aesthetics is already a term of value. As such, the ambiguous and devalued experience of routine would fit awkwardly into such an approach. However far they both want to extend the remit of aesthetics, their understanding of aesthetics is governed in advance by already established categories of art (and art appreciation).

In a similar way, the extension of 'aesthetics' to include representation more generally and 'style' more particularly, is also, for my purposes at least, limited. For instance, in his wide-ranging essay 'Postmodernism and the aestheticization of everyday life', Featherstone (1992) suggests three significant domains for recognizing the aestheticization of the everyday. First off, he suggests that the 'historic avant-gardes' (by this he mainly refers to Dada, surrealism and the

Soviet avant-gardes of the 1910s and 1920s) sought 'to efface the boundary between art and everyday life' (Featherstone 1992, p. 268). Such a project continues into more recent history, for example, in the work of Pop Art. Such avant-garde subcultures refused to inhabit the specialized and transcendent realm of the institution of 'fine art': the museum, the academy, the connoisseurship of an elite, its striving for beauty and sophistication. Such an account of avant-gardism is also the overriding argument that Bürger (1984) provides in his *Theory of the Avant-Garde*. Featherstone's second example of the aestheticization of everyday life is the life lived aesthetically. His example is, of course, Oscar Wilde, but any number of artists or celebrities would do. The precariousness of this category is marked by its extension into the present with the notion of 'life style'. As such the aestheticization of daily life in terms of fashion, design, food, music, etc. must be seen as at the heart of the modern everyday. As soon as we make choices about clothes or the colour of a room, we are part of an aestheticization of daily life. Elizabeth Wilson in her recent study of bohemianism (Wilson 2000) provides an excellent resource for critically extending this argument: in many ways the very aestheticizing practices of Bohemianism bring with them a practical criticism that challenges the ideological normalcy of everyday life (its regulation of sexuality, regimes of work and leisure, and so on). For Featherstone, 'the third sense of the aestheticization of everyday life refers to the rapid flow of signs and images which saturate the fabric of everyday life in contemporary society' (1992, p. 270). Clearly, this points to the intensification of mass-media forms and would include everything from newspapers to cinema, from billboards to road signs.

Featherstone's essay is a diagnosis of modernity and postmodernity, his project is to trace some of the ways that 'stylization' has penetrated everyday life. Indeed if one were to swap the word 'style' for 'aesthetics' in his essay's title nothing much would be lost. It is the way that social life invests in the outward garb of representation, stylized into a variety of looks that is the central topic. The experience of routine is of course an element against which much of this aestheticizing is aimed. Indeed, the first two categories might explicitly be seen, both essentially and historically, as fundamentally constituted antagonistically to routine. Yet aesthetics as it was initially conceived was concerned with areas of experience that were, precisely, difficult to make sense of. As Eagleton reminds us, aesthetics as formulated in the eighteenth century by Baumgarten refers 'to the whole region of human perception and sensation, in contrast to the more rarefied domain of conceptual thought' (Eagleton 1990, p. 13). That routine would be exempt from such reference would seem unthinkable. That it has been is due no doubt to the successful colonization of aesthetics by the artwork and the institutional structures of value that surround it. The initial project of aesthetics, and the one that Simmel seems to favour, has yet to be fulfilled, at least in the academic realm of aesthetics. To rekindle it might mean that we have to act perversely, to fashion 'reverse-images' out of aesthetic theories that are anchored in regimes of valorized art and beauty, but can be redirected in reverse to accommodate the ambiguity of routine. It will also mean that the first task of aesthetics (or perhaps more inclusively, *aisthesis*) will not be judgment but description; the description of what Eagleton refers to as 'our creaturely life' (1990, p. 17).

Art, experience and everyday life

John Dewey's 1934 book on aesthetics, *Art as Experience*, might on the face of it seem an unlikely resource for thinking through some of the issues that I have been outlining. Dewey is ultimately interested in the artwork, and partly because of this he ends up jettisoning precisely the kind of experience that I think will be most useful for a socio-aesthetic approach to everyday routines. Therefore, my reading of Dewey will necessarily have to work in reverse, resuscitating as aesthetic precisely that which cannot finally be included in his category of aesthetic experience.

In his approach to art, Dewey recognizes a vital connectivity between art and ordinary experience. It is here that Dewey carves out a space *prior* to the artwork for thinking about ordinary experience in aesthetic terms. Arguing that the separation of the work of art from its 'origin and operation in experience' militates against aesthetic insight, Dewey states that:

> A primary task is thus imposed upon one who undertakes to write upon the philosophy of the fine arts. This task is to restore continuity between the refined and intensified forms of experience that are works of art and the everyday events, doings, and sufferings that are universally recognized to constitute experience.
>
> (Dewey 1934, p. 3)

Everyday experience is thus figured as the material basis of aesthetics for Dewey. But Dewey is not suggesting that all experience is equally open to aesthetic attention, or to being designated as aesthetic. What Dewey sets up is a distinction between a ceaseless flow of experiences and what might best be thought of as experience-events; particular experiences that are separated from this flow due to their finitude and consummation. In this Dewey is an inheritor of German *Lebensphilosophie*, particularly the understanding of experience put forward by Wilhelm Dilthey in the late nineteenth century (Dilthey 1976). Both Dilthey and Dewey distinguish between experience in general (the condition of being sensate) and *an* experience: an experience that raises itself out of the mere continuum of the everyday to take on a specific shape, specific form. For Dewey 'we have an experience when the material experienced runs its course to fulfilment' (1934, p. 35).

The examples he gives make clear that while this relates to the everyday, it relates to it precisely when it transcends the routine-ness of experience:

> There is that meal in a Paris restaurant of which one says 'that was an experience'. It stands out as an enduring memorial to what food may be. Then there is that storm one went through in crossing the Atlantic – the storm that seemed in its fury, as it was experienced, to sum up in itself all that a storm can be, complete in itself, standing out because marked out from what went before and what came after.
>
> (Dewey 1934, p. 36)

While weather and eating clearly belong to the everyday, routine world, the experiential significance of them only emerges for Dewey when the possibilities of food and weather are played out to fulfilment. The aesthetic realm may be made up of everyday-like material, but the everyday needs to be resolved so that art can function 'to shape it into a satisfyingly integrated whole' (Shusterman 1992, p. 53).

Against this, the routines of everyday life operate as a morass of only partial significance and incompleteness. In as much as routine experience is often unresolved, open to contingency and peculiarly formless, it simply counts itself out of full aesthetic consideration:

> Things happen, but they are neither definitely included nor decisively excluded; we drift. We yield according to external pressure, or evade and comprise. There are beginnings and cessations, but no genuine initiations and concludings. One thing replaces another, but does not absorb it and carry it on. There is experience, but so slack and discursive that it is not *an* experience. Needless to say, such experiences are anesthetic.
>
> (Dewey 1934, p. 40)

And yet here, precisely at the moment when Dewey is busy excluding the kind of experiences that seem characteristically routine, just at the moment when he demands that we reserve aesthetics for those experiences that are more fully formed, he himself seems to find a way of producing an aesthetics of routine. I cannot think of many better descriptions of the experience of everyday routine-ness than those offered by Dewey. The idea of slack experience seems eminently suited to the diffuse consciousness of routine. Similarly the idea of 'drift', the picking up and letting go of concentration, works to point to the strange character of routine. Dewey beautifully articulates the impossibility of finding an origin to routine: the way routine and habit creep up on you, the way you can never locate the moment when an activity became routine. It should also be noted that 'slackness' and 'drift' are themselves descriptions of forms, albeit more formless forms than those more self-contained entities that Dewey wants to privilege.

What Dewey offers us is an aesthetics of routine experience that centres on the notion of inchoate experience:

> Oftentimes, however, the experience had is inchoate. Things are experienced but not in such a way that they are composed into an experience. There is distraction and dispersion; what we observe and what we think, what we desire and what we get, are at odds with each other. We put our hands to the plow and turn back; we start and then we stop, not because the experience has reached the end for the sake of which it was initiated but because of extraneous interruptions or of inner lethargy.
>
> (Dewey 1934, p. 35)

Of course, inner lethargy and extraneous interruptions are no strangers to routine, as anyone routinely cooking for children will know. Inchoate experience is unfinished experience, experience in its 'tumbling profusion and messiness' (as Willis might say), it is experience that is constantly beginning again, full of repetitions, red herrings, distractions, unfulfilled wishes, and so on. It is as, Dewey notes, where 'what we observe and what we think, what we desire and we get' are in contradiction. Such contradiction is where we begun, it is the ambiguity of routine.

Doing cooking

Dewey's description of routine experience is of course fairly abstract, and while 'slackness', 'inchoateness' and 'drift' seem absolutely essential to achieving aesthetic forms that might bring the experience of routines into focus (however blurrily), we need to pack them out with live content. Giard's study of cooking is, to my mind, exemplary in its ability to pour content into the kind of slack and drifting aesthetic forms that Dewey wants to hold at a distance. Giard's work was part of a project directed by de Certeau in France in the 1970s (Highmore 2002, pp. 146–156). The goal of the project for de Certeau 'will be achieved if everyday practices, 'ways of operating' or doing things, no longer appear as merely the obscure background of social activity, and if a body of theoretical questions, methods, categories, and perspectives, by penetrating this obscurity, make it possible to articulate them' (de Certeau 1984, p. xi). Needless to say, then, that both de Certeau's work and the work of Giard are understood here as socio-aesthetic research practices.

Giard's foregrounding of cooking, and more particularly of women cooking, was a specific attempt to bring a range of feminist issues to the investigation of everyday life. Giard negotiates a pathway between the desire to condemn patriarchal inequality (the burden of routine cooking falling inexorably on women, for example), and the wish to celebrate the invisible skill and achievement of women's routine work. It is the way this ambiguity is threaded through her descriptions of cooking that makes it such a fitting vehicle for describing aspects of routine. For instance, towards the end of a section that is spent mainly elaborating on women's 'creative ingenuity', the register suddenly shifts and Giard reminds us that 'this women's work' is without remuneration, and its success without duration: 'yes, women's work is slow and interminable' (1980, p. 159). This shifting of perspective is neither woven into an explicit dialectic, nor resolved by argument. The two images simply exist simultaneously. If she does pursue the image of women's creativity with more tenacity, then this works as a tactical 'reverse image', counterbalancing the lack of attention to the productivity of women's work.

Cooking, in Giard's work, spills out from being a set of discrete activities to being a sensual realm that continually drifts. Within this realm, 'feminine savoir faire', all the tricks-of-the-trade of routine cookery, are passed on, not via explicit communication, but through a bodily, sensual osmosis, as if being close to continual cooking is enough to know its operations. After a childhood spent resisting her mother's entreaty to learn how to cook, Giard recognizes that she too 'had been provided with a woman's knowledge and that it had crept into me, slipping past my mind's surveillance' (1980, p. 153). This is a know-how communicated via smells and gestures, where bodily techniques count for more than the instructions of written recipes. It is no wonder, given this address to the non-cognitive senses, that cooking and eating is fertile ground for Proustian *mémoire involontaire* (involuntary memory). Remembering and reminiscence are simultaneous with the practicalities of cooking and eating. Flavours and smells conjure the textures of an intimately experienced past: joy and unhappiness, love and anxiety are the secret cargo of cooking.

The skill of cooking, for Giard, is multiple and diffuse, and it 'unfurls in a complex montage' (1980, p. 158). The basics of nutrition, the practices of care and affection, are coupled with intricate planning and timing. As a routine practice, Giard's understanding of cooking relates to the 'cosmology of shopping' that, for Miller, is often guided by love, but a love that is 'compatible with feelings of obligation and responsibility' and is, at times, 'accompanied by hatred and resentment' (1998, p. 19). Such multiple calls on the attention, and such an ambiguous address to the emotions, suggests that the inattention that we might associate with routine is better described as a peculiar layering of attention that can simultaneously dream of the past and worry about the future, while conducting precision timed manoeuvres.

Giard's work points to an issue that will be crucial to social aesthetics, as it has been for aesthetics more generally, namely the question of the relationship between experience and expression. For an approach to everyday life that specifically wants to foreground the sensual realm of smells, gestures, and tastes, the question of expression will not resolve itself through recourse to already established forms of sociological presentation. Clearly, Giard has in mind some more intimate authorities than those of the academy. Addressing herself to the women of her past, Giard writes: 'I would like the slow remembrance of your gestures in the kitchen to prompt me with words that will remain faithful to you; I would like the poetry of words to translate that of gestures; I would like a writing of words and letters to correspond to your writing of recipes and tastes' (1980, p. 154). Translation, correspondence and faithfulness point to an issue of socio-aesthetic inquiry (the adequacy of expression to register experience) that will never, to my mind, be fully resolved – there are no perfect forms of correspondence. But this does not mean that it is not of crucial importance: in many ways a project like Giard's stands or falls on how you respond to her mode of expression, whether its evocative phrasing feels appropriate to the experiences she addresses. The proof of socio-aesthetic expression is, to coin a phrase, in the pudding (and given that Giard is expressly describing women's experience of routine life my judgment will count for little).

But if there is one place where expression and experience seem to find a 'naturally' productive correspondence it is in the sheer variety of modes, genres, and resources that are called upon to articulate 'doing cooking'. Ranging across academic modes (anthropology, historiography, sociology) literary modes (autobiography, novels) and empiricism (the intricate inclusion of 'women's voices' gathered from interviews), the very writing of Giard's project seems to 'unfurl in a complex montage'. Such polyvocal textual cookery has much to offer the study of routine, and is itself far from a routine practice within academic writing.

If everyday life suffers from neglect, such neglect should point us to a living 'politics' of social life. Such a politics, here at least, starts by giving voice to the dense and often invisible routine worlds of the everyday. Such a practice involves finding that voice, those voices, and generating expressive forms for their communication. To claim such a project as socio-aesthetics is not to forget that in the process it marks a debt of honour, an ethics of remembering:

There have been women ceaselessly doomed to both housework and the creation of life, women excluded from public life and the communication of knowledge, and women educated at the time of my grandmother's generation, of whom I would like to retain the living and true memory. Following in their footsteps, I have dreamed of practicing an impoverished writing, that of a *public writer* who has no claim to words, whose name is erased. Such writing targets its own destruction and repeats, in its own way, the humble service to others for whom these non-illustrious women (no one knows their names, strength, or courage anymore) represented for generations basic gestures always strung together and necessitated by the interminable repetition of household tasks performed in the succession of meals and days, with attention given to the body of others.

(Giard 1980, pp. 153–154)

An ethics of remembering, of making a textual space for those who have been denied a public voice, is predicated on an aesthetics that can 'do justice' to the complex bodily, social and temporal experience of the routine care of others.

Giard prioritizes the body and its gestures in her study of routine cooking. Her method of socio-aesthetic attention is more implicit than explicit: it starts with the body, with bodies skilfully manipulating food. Out of this, Giard weaves a polyvocal tapestry or montage that can accommodate multiple and contradictory attitudes (critiques of patriarchy, celebrations of women's know-how) and is capable of describing the varied temporalities of cooking (the minute-by-minute, second-by-second event-ness of cooking, alongside the temporal drift of imagination; the memories that cooking continually evoke). We might find, though, a more explicit methodological framework for Giard's approach in Lefebvre and Régulier's project of rhythmanalysis. But before this, it is worth briefly noting a powerful argument that urges a rethink of the priority given to theorists such as Lefebvre and de Certeau.

Situating aesthetics

The recent interest in everyday life within cultural studies has brought into sharp relief the contradictory ways that it has been conceptualized, described, analysed and valued. Felski, for instance, charges cultural studies with overburdening everyday life: 'within cultural studies, everyday life is often made to carry enormous symbolic weight. Either it is rhapsodically affirmed and painted in glowing colours or it is excoriated as the realm of ultimate alienation and dehumanization' (Felski 1999, p. 31). Her argument is aimed, for the most part, at a tradition of thought that has characterized the everydayness of everyday life as a repressive sphere, but one that holds within it the possibilities of creative subversions, which are occasionally realized when festive-like forces break through the tedium of habit. In this account of everyday life, everydayness (habit, routine, the work-a-day world), marked indelibly with the stamp of capitalist reason, has to be transcended and estranged in a bid to recover some sense of everyday life as authentic and valuable. Interestingly, she recognizes that such a tradition privileges an aesthetic dimension:

> The conviction that the everyday can only be redeemed by its aesthetic transfiguration will become the leitmotif of a French intellectual and political tradition most prominently represented by Henri Lefebvre and by the Situationists. Here aesthetics refers not to a pristine sanctum of high art, but a loose ensemble of techniques, performances, and intensities of experience that can revive and even revolutionize the everyday by registering its rich and mysterious particularities.
>
> (Felski 2002, pp. 608–609)

Here aesthetics, for all its loosening from high art, is still anchored to the premise that creativity is accorded primary value. This is aesthetics as prescription (this is how to live) and not aesthetics as description (how do people live?). Quite rightly, Felski notes that such a position 'often looses sight of the mundane, taken-for-granted, routine qualities which seem so central to its definition – the very everydayness of the everyday' (1999, p. 18). Recognizing that Lefebvre and the Situationists – and, in a different way, de Certeau – are 'beholden to an avant-gardist framework', she asks rhetorically: 'why are routine and habit the object of such scorching and unremitting disdain' (2002, p. 612, p. 610)? The answer is partly aesthetic: an aesthetic attitude that insistently valorizes invention, creativity and subversion will be hard pressed to accord much value to the habits and routines of everyday life. If, as Felski suggests, 'the temporality of the everyday [. . .] is that of repetition, the spatial ordering of the everyday is anchored in a sense of home and the characteristic mode of experiencing the everyday is that of habit' (1999, p. 18) then a different sense of aesthetics is needed.

Like Felski, I am keen to shift attention away from a tendency that oscillates between damning the everydayness of the everyday while it ekes out a list of minor subversions that can be found there. The antidote, for Felski, is to rehabilitate the social phenomenologist perspective that characterizes everyday life as the world of the self-evident and the taken-for-granted. No doubt such a tradition offers a wealth of insights into *aspects* of those habitual activities that 'we cannot pause to question' (Felski 1999, p. 29), but it does not get close to being able to describe and unpick the complex and ambiguous montage of feelings, memories, and attitudes that Luce Giard finds in cooking. More pertinent to my project is the search for aesthetic forms and approaches that are not stymied by the need to make categorical judgments as to the worth or otherwise of routine. If routine is often simultaneously frustrating and comforting, alienating and homely, and if a routine consciousness can be distracted and concentrated at the same time, and if the temporal experience of routine is both drawn-out and compressed, then the necessary aesthetic forms are going to have to be able to express a high degree of complexity and ambiguity.

For Giard, the aesthetic form most able to articulate this complexity is montage, and Giard's work, as I have already said, can best be described as a polyvocal montage. It is worth though, finally, mentioning the possibility of another, related approach to everyday life routines, partly because it reveals another side to the work of Lefebvre that is too easily overlooked. For all his gruff certainty about the extent to which everyday life is characterized by alienation and for all his avant-gardist promotion of the festive, Lefebvre is expressly concerned with finding ways of describing the ambiguous complexity of everyday life (a point that Felski significantly underplays in her account of Lefebvre and mostly misses in her rendition of de Certeau). Towards the end of his life, but, I would argue, implicit throughout his work on everyday life, he promotes the project of rhythmanalysis. Rhythmanalysis is premised on the understanding that everyday life is a polyrhythmic ensemble of competing and overlapping rhythms. The most central conflict and imbrication is between the linear rhythms of rationalized modernization and the cyclical rhythms of nature. While any mention of nature for some might smack of misty-eyed romanticism, for Lefebvre it is the very condition for a social understanding of our material, biological existence.

Rhythms and routines

In an essay that unveils the project of rhythmanalysis, Lefebvre and his co-llaborator Régulier note the victory of linear 'clock' time ('homogenous and desacralized time') over previous, more cyclical temporal experiences:

> From that historic moment, it [clock time] became the time of the everyday, subordinating other aspects of daily life to the spatial organization of work: times for sleep and waking, times for meals and private life, relationships between adults and children, entertainment and leisure, relationships in the home. However, everyday life is shot through and cut across by the larger rhythms of life and the cosmos: days and nights, months and seasons, and more specifically still, biological rhythms. In everyday life, this results in constant interaction between these rhythms and repetitive processes linked with homogenous time.
>
> (Lefebvre & Régulier 1985, p. 190)

Lefebvre and Régulier suggest that the contemporary experiences of routine life (mealtime, bedtime, the school run, the commute and so on) are the outcome of processes of modernization. Crucially however they insist that rather than this heralding the simple subjugation of material biology by social forces, only an understanding that can recognize how biological rhythms are orchestrated by linear rhythms and how biology also exceeds this orchestration, is going to be up to the job of comprehending everyday life. Take, for example, hunger. Routines of cooking, feeding and eating, may well be set by a number of other forces besides hunger: the school day, work shifts, nutritional advice, TV sched-ules, tiredness, convenience, advertising and so on. Often as not in our house the process will involve some intimate contact with technology: the whir and ping of the microwave, for instance, or the guesswork involved in using an oven with a broken thermostat. Modernity impacts at every level, but, and here is the rub, it constantly runs up against the finite limits of human bodies. While modern forms of eating govern our bodies (to a certain degree), our bodies also orches-trate our eating. We might live in a time of increasing prosthetic expansion, but the point is precisely that this expansion is prosthetic and that limbs and organs remain *relatively* unchanged. Lefebvre and Régulier describe, for instance, how work routines affect sleep patterns: 'someone who wakes at six in the morning because his work has given him this rhythm may perhaps still be tired and in need of sleep' (1985, p. 192). Here the needs of the body are the remainder that exceeds the rhythm of technical modernity. Stress, excessive tiredness, digestive problems, etc., are the rhythmic protest of what some science fiction writers call our 'wetware'. Of course, as the theorists of modernity will remind us, technological modernity does affect our bodies, our human sensorium, but the question is to what degree. We might be more agile in crossing busy roads due to the complex training of modernity, but we are also vulnerable, fleshy creatures when speeding motor vehicles impact against us.

In one of his first explicit references to the project of rhythmanalysis, Lefebvre mysteriously suggests that rhythmanalysis 'might eventually displace psychoanalysis' (1991a, p. 205). It is hard to know precisely what he might have meant by this, and no doubt we shouldn't make too much of such a passing reference. There is, though, one aspect of contemporaneous psychoanalytic theory that does allow for a productive analogy. Laplanche, in his 1970 book *Life and Death in Psychoanalysis*, discusses the vexed question of how, in Freud's writing on sexuality, instincts (bodily, biological) relate to drives (psychical). Laplanche, reading Freud in his zealously careful manner, concentrates on discussing how the sexual drive 'finds support' in 'vital somatic instincts' (Freud, quoted in Laplanche 1985, p. 15). Laplanche is particularly interested in this supporting relationship and how sexually charged zones (the mouth, for instance) can simultaneously be organs for eating, and so on. The crucial question for Laplanche is how to describe the relationship of 'finding support'. Laplanche discusses how the process of an emerging sexual drive is related to somatic instincts by *anaclisis* (attachment, leaning, support, propping, etc.). The sexual drive is thus 'propped up' by, and is 'leaning on' the instincts of self-preservation: 'emergent sexuality attaches itself to and is propped upon another process that is both similar and profoundly divergent: the sexual function is propped upon a nonsexual, vital function [. . .] a "bodily function essential to life"' (Laplanche 1985, p. 16). Here is not the place to go into the details of Laplanche's work, but the term anaclisis and its cognates might very well be used to describe the kinds of imbrications between the linear rhythms of modernity and the cyclical, age-old, and primary rhythms of the body.

Modern routines (public and private), with their linear time patterns, are grafted onto the rhythms of the body. For Lefebvre and Régulier, 'it takes about ten years to train the body to these rhythms, and it is not unusual for children to reject social rhythms' (1985, pp. 191–192). The point here is that the grafting (the leaning and propping) does not erase the rhythms of the body. What modernity does is to redirect and exploit the rhythmic capacities of the body, sometimes to the point of exhaustion. Technological modernization then is limited to the finite capacities of the body: to go beyond these capacities is to break bodies (which, of course, is sometimes the case). Although wedded to increasing throughput the architects of assembly line work routines recognized the need for a remorselessly sluggish but regular rhythm, rather than one that would quickly incapacitate a work force. Crucially, technological modernization is only interested in the bodily capacities that it can profitably exploit, leaving other capacities and rhythms frustrated (which is why, to adapt the title of well known book, Lefebvre might well claim 'We have never been human' – the exploitation of our full *human* potential, our species-being, has yet to come).

Now a number of crucial points would emerge at this juncture that would need much further elaboration than is possible here. It is worth, though, itemizing a couple of them. Firstly, rhythmanalysis refigures a relationship between modern social life and the body. Instead of modern capitalism autogenously determining (in the strongest sense of the term) modern bodily experience, modernity 'finds support' (it has to or it won't succeed) in human bodies and their sensuous activities: similarly, bodies exert their 'limits and pressures' on modernity (which is all too seldom acknowledged in theory, or listened to in the larger social world). This means that rather than opting for a social constructionist position, we would need to take a more measured social-accentuationist (or social-anaclitic) position (especially when it comes to such routine practices as eating, cooking, etc.). Secondly, the non-synchronicity between the cyclical rhythms of the body and the linear rhythms of some routines produce a number of symptoms. On the one hand, it produces stress, illness and frustration, but it also seems to produce reminiscence. Perhaps then this dissonance reminds the body of other, subterranean rhythms that though present are submerged by the dominance of linear routines. These primary rhythms are the ones we inherit from childhood, rhythms that speak of the body's unused potentiality. In this way, reminiscence and stress are linked because they both perform implied critiques of modern linear rhythms simply by reminding the body of other possible rhythms (not that this will provide much comfort for the sufferer). That which exceeds linear rhythmicity is the rhythm that connects us to childhood and to childhood possibilities. Such a return works on both an individual level and a more cultural, social one as well. Perhaps one of the sentiments most often associated with everyday life (and disparaged no doubt because of this) is nostalgia. Seremetakis shows how nostalgia can join together the individual and the social by grounding everyday life in a loosely historical recognition that how we live now is neither inevitable, nor necessary. Like Giard her example is food: a specific type of peach to be precise (Seremetakis 1996a, 1996b). There is in this coupling of routine and food an insistence on the body that refutes any simple judgment about the virtue or vice of routine life.

Giard's interweaving of technical virtuosity, nostalgic reminiscence, and critical frustration, is theoretically related to a schema suggested by Lefebvre and Régulier:

The living body can and should be seen in terms of the interaction of the organs within it, each one having their rhythms but subject to a spatio-temporal whole. Furthermore, this human body is the locus and seat of interaction between the biological, the physiological (nature) and the social (often called the 'cultural') and each of these areas, each of these dimensions, has its own specificity, and thus its space-time: its rhythm. Hence the inevitable shocks (stresses), disorders and disturbances within this whole, whose stability is never absolutely guaranteed.

(Lefebvre & Régulier 1985, p. 196)

Stress, frustration and involuntary memory poke holes in the smooth surface of the present; they do so by insistently invoking history (a history of the body) and disturbing the fake continuity of the present.

So while expertly chopping vegetables, synchronizing the cooking times of different foods, remembering childhood flavours and smells, marshalling children to the table; while feeling undervalued or content, tired and agitated or happy – the multiple rhythms of everyday routines harmonize and clash. Rhythmanalysis is a socio-aesthetic approach because it suggests forms for grasping the experiential actuality of the everyday in all its complexity, and because it prioritizes the material and biological body that is doing the experiencing. This is of course a very different notion of the aesthetic than the one Felski finds so problematic in the work of Lefebvre and de Certeau. This is an aesthetic dedicated to description. It is the other side of Lefebvre's heuristically productive 'reverse-image' (the reverse of the reverse, so to say). And if we read Lefebvre through Giard's work on cooking it allows us to recognize that, close up, the formless forms that Dewey invokes are really dense entanglements of attitudes and responses, feelings and practices: a complex orchestration of the contradictions of being so archaically modern.

References

Bürger, P. (1984) *Theory of the Avant-Garde*, trans. M. Shaw, Manchester University Press, Manchester.

de Certeau, M. (1984) *The Practice of Everyday Life*, trans. S. Rendall, University of California Press, Berkeley, CA.

de Certeau, M., Giard, L. & Mayol, P. (1998) *The Practice of Everyday Life, Volume 2: Living and Cooking*, trans. T. J. Tomasik, Minnesota University Press, Minneapolis.

Debord, G. (1959) 'Situationist theses on traffic', in *Situationist International Anthology*, ed. & trans. K. Knabb, Bureau of Public Secrets, Berkeley, CA, pp. 56–58.

Dewey, J. (1934) *Art as Experience*, Minton, Balch and Company, New York.

Dilthey, W. (1976) *Selected Writings*, ed. & trans. H. P. Rickman, Cambridge University Press, Cambridge.

Doray, B. (1988) *From Taylorism to Fordism: A Rational Madness*, trans. D. Macey, Free Association Press, London.

Eagleton, T. (1990) *The Ideology of the Aesthetic*, Blackwell, Oxford.

Featherstone, M. (1992) 'Postmodernism and the aestheticization of everyday life', in *Modernity and Identity*, eds S. Lash & J. Friedman, Blackwell, Oxford, pp. 265–290.

Featherstone, M. (1995) 'The heroic life and everyday life', in *Undoing Culture: Globalization, Postmodernism and Identity*, Sage, London, pp. 54–71.

Felski, R. (1999) 'The invention of everyday life', *New Formations*, vol. 39, pp. 15–31.

Felski, R. (2002) 'Introduction', *New Literary History*, vol. 33, no. 4, pp. 607–622.

Ferber, R. (1986) *Solve Your Child's Sleep Problems: The Complete Practical Guide for Parents*, Dorling Kindersley, London, New York, Sydney & Moscow.

Giard, L. (1980) 'Doing-cooking', in *The Practice of Everyday Life, Volume 2: Living and Cooking*, M. de Certeau, L. Giard and P. Mayol, trans. T. J. Tomasik, Minnesota University Press, Minneapolis, pp. 149–247.

Green, C. (2000) *Beyond Toddlerdom: Keeping Five- to Twelve-Year-Olds On the Rails*, Vermillion, London.

Gumpert, L. (ed.) (1997) *The Art of the Everyday: The Quotidian in Postwar French Culture*, New York University Press, New York.

Hamper, B. (1992) *Rivethead: Tales from the Assembly Line*, Fourth Estate, London.

Highmore, B. (2002) *Everyday Life and Cultural Theory: An Introduction*, Routledge, London and New York.

Laplanche, J. (1985) *Life and Death in Psychoanalysis*, trans. J. Mehlman, Johns Hopkins University Press, Baltimore and London [first published in France 1970].

Lefebvre, H. (1991a) *The Production of Space*, trans. D. Nicholson-Smith, Blackwell, Oxford [first published in France 1974].

Lefebvre, H. (1991b) *Critique of Everyday Life: Volume One*, trans. J. Moore, Verso, London and New York [first published in France 1947].

Lefebvre, H. (1992) *Éléments de rythmanalyse: Introduction à la connaissance des rythmes*, Éditions Syllepse, Paris.

Lefebvre, H. (1996) *Writing on Cities*, ed. & trans. E. Kofman & E. Lebas, Blackwell, Oxford.

Lefebvre, H. (2002) *Critique of Everyday Life: Volume Two, Foundations for a Sociology of the Everyday*, trans. J. Moore, Verso, London and New York [first published in France 1961].

Lefebvre, H. & Régulier, C. (1985) 'The rhythmanalytical project', in *Henri Lefebvre: Key Writings*, eds S. Elden, E. Lebas & E. Kofman, Continuum, New York and London, pp. 190–198.

Linhart, R. (1981) *The Assembly Line*, trans. M. Crosland, John Calder, London.

Martin, B. (1984) '"Mother wouldn't like it": housework as magic', *Theory, Culture and Society*, vol. 2, no. 2, pp. 19–36.

Miller, D. (1998) *A Theory of Shopping*, Cornell University Press, Ithaca, NY.

Molesworth, H. (2000) 'House work and art work', *October*, vol. 92, pp. 71–97.

Paretsky, S. (2001) *Total Recall*, Penguin, London.

Ross, D. A. (ed.) (2000) *Quotidiana: The Continuity of the Everyday*, Charta, Milan.

Ross, K. (1995) *Fast Cars, Clean Bodies: Decolonization and the Reordering of French Culture*, MIT Press, Cambridge, MA.

Seremetakis, C. N. (1996a) 'The memory of the senses, part I: marks of the transitory', in *The Senses Still: Perception and Memory as Material Culture in Modernity*, ed. C. N. Seremetakis, University of Chicago Press, Chicago, IL and London, pp. 1–18.

Seremetakis, C. N. (1996b) 'The memory of the senses, part II: still acts', in *The Senses Still: Perception and Memory as Material Culture in Modernity*, ed. C. N. Seremetakis, University of Chicago Press, Chicago, IL and London, pp. 23–43.

Shusterman, R. (1992) *Pragmatist Aesthetics: Living Beauty, Rethinking Art*, Blackwell, Oxford.

Simmel, G. (1968) 'Sociological aesthetics', in *The Conflict in Modern Culture and Other Essays*, trans. K. Peter Etzkorn, Teachers College Press, New York, pp. 68–80.

Willis, P. (1990) *Common Culture*, with S. Jones, J. Canaan & G. Hurd, Open University Press, Milton Keynes.

Willis, P. (2000) *The Ethnographic Imagination*, Polity, Oxford.

Wilson, E. (2000) *Bohemians: The Glamorous Outcasts*, I. B. Tauris, London.

Elspeth Probyn

EVERYDAY SHAME

This article explores aspects of the everyday through a consideration of shame. Drawing on and extending Bourdieu's notion of the habitus, notably in relationship to Silvan Tomkins' affect theory, and to Bourdieu's predecessor Marcel Mauss, the paper argues for the positivity of everyday shame. The very different although complementary privileging of the physiological in Tomkins and in Mauss allows for a radical rearticulation and understanding of the habitus and of everyday life. In this article, their understandings serve to provide a model that more fully comprehends the productive nature of shame within postcolonial societies.

Keywords   affect; Bourdieu; everyday life; habitus; Mauss; out-of-place; shame; Tomkins

I have moved around a lot in my life, and my body hates it. It loves the rituals of everyday life, and hates the thought of disruption. When I immigrated to Australia, it went into somatic spasms as I ripped it from its accustomed everyday routines. This is not a tale of woe, nor even very unusual, but the experience does provide me with ample evidence of a strange little strain of shame: the body's feeling of being out-of-place in the everyday. It is a shame born of the body's desire to fit in, just as it knows that it cannot. 'You're not from here': the slip of tongue, the flash of ignorance faced with an entirely different arrangement of the everyday. It is no big deal, compared to the experiences of others violently uprooted. It is just a little shaming from within fed by the desire to be unnoticed, to be at home in the everyday of someone else's culture.

In this article, I argue that shame compels a rethinking of how we conceptualize the everyday as it is lived. Shame, as we will see, dramatically questions taken-for-granted distinctions between affect, emotion, biography, and the places in which we live our daily lives. Moreover, in its insistence on the located and embodied nature of shame as a response to others, it may undo the moral normativity that underpins habitual concepts of guilt. Shame rips the everyday out of its habitual stasis: its sentencing within the present. If in common sense the everyday is privatized, personalized as 'my life', shame makes apparent the ways in which the everyday experiences of radically differently positioned selves are contagious – as Gatens argues, 'the contagiousness of "collective" affects' exposes 'the breaches in the borders between self and other' (1999, p. 14).

Cultural Studies Vol. 18, No. 2/3 March/May 2004, pp. 328–349
ISSN 0950-2386 print/ISSN 1466-4348 online   © 2004 Taylor & Francis Ltd
http://www.tandf.co.uk/journals   DOI: 10.1080/0950238042000201545

Routledge
Taylor & Francis Group

Affect theory, in particular approaches indebted to Tomkins, promises a different gestalt of the everyday, wherein it becomes impossible to maintain 'culturally constructed "feelings" and "emotions" [as] substantially divorced from the materiality of the body' (Gibbs 2002, p. 337). Tomkins, a clinical psychologist working in the 1950s and 1960s, argued for a model of radical interconnectedness premised on the idea that humans have innate affects. The affect system serves to amplify at a physiological level the stimuli of everyday life. Tomkins' (1995/1963) list of paired affects included interest–excitement, enjoyment–joy, surprise–startlement, distress–anguish, contempt–disgust, anger–rage and shame–humiliation. Far from delimiting the possibilities of affective life, the distinct nature of affects provides an optic into the complex combinations that characterize the everyday. They are also both intensely individual and social; more importantly, and as I argue, they undo any opposition that relies on alignments of private/public.

Of the affects, it is shame that most interests me, in part because it spectacularly shows the self in its essential vulnerability – its everyday dependence on the proximities of others, of place, of routine, of biography and history.[1] If shame is felt as 'a sickness of the self' (Tomkins), it is also the affect most clearly based in the positivity of interest. As Tomkins clearly argues, without interest there cannot be shame. Shame is the body's way of registering that it has been interested, and that it seeks to re-establish interest. Interest is to be understood widely: the bodily and physiological continually alert us to the interest of everyday life. Elsewhere (Probyn forthcoming) I argue that this focus on interest is desperately needed within cultural studies' analyses. Here I explore shame and interest as resources in rethinking concepts such as the everyday habitus. In the context in which I write, shame also provides a way of navigating the complexity of everyday life in a postcolonial milieu, and demonstrates both the singularity of Aboriginal and non-Aboriginal cultures and their deep interconnection.

Most experiences of shame make you want to disappear, to hide away and to cover yourself. However, the disjuncture of place, the everyday, self and interest can produce a particularly visceral sensation of shame. It is felt in the rupture when bodies cannot or will not fit the place – when, seemingly, there is no place to hide. Here I mine my own physical reactions and those of others to think through the types of unacknowledged knowledge that are buried in the everyday, and that scramble notions of ordinary and extraordinary.[2] As part of a larger project on shame, I am particularly interested in finding new descriptions of what bodies do and say as they inhabit everyday places. Although commonly understood as negative – both in the strict sense of being a negative affect and in the more usual one of being bad or wrong – I want to argue that shame is immensely productive politically and conceptually in advancing a project of everyday ethics.[3] In political climates such as Australia – dealing (badly) with issues around Aboriginal and non-Aboriginal reconciliation – this conceptual project takes on the edge of urgently needed political rethinking as we become ever more mired in guilt, on the one hand, and moral denunciations on the other.[4]

At the level of theories, descriptions of shame tend to be differentiated according to whether shame is seen as an affect or as an emotion. In general, descriptions of shame understood as an emotion tend to privilege cognition and even sometimes disparage what the feeling body does in shame. Conversely it seems that those who use affect to describe shame are more interested or open to considerations of what happens in the body (and its components such as the brain and the nervous system). While I am most interested in descriptions that allow us to comprehend the physicality of the body – those more wedded to the vocabulary of affect – here I pursue a more social scientific explanation of this phenomenon. In particular, I am interested in shame's role in reworking the possibilities of the body and its habitus. The term is, of course, most associated with Pierre Bourdieu who uses it to designate how social structures are embodied in everyday practice. Investigating the physiological aspect of shame, I will also enlist ideas developed by his predecessor, Marcel Mauss. Their ideas may reanimate a sociological comprehension of what we feel when we feel shame, of how the physiological experience of shame intersects with the physicality of place. The colour, the place, the everyday histories of bodies all come alive in shame.

Sociologically speaking, it is hard to find ways of describing the body's movement, and feeling: its affects and how the body changes in proximity to other bodies, or in different places. As a strategy, I turn to telling stories and to retelling those of others. Deep down all I ever want to do is to tell stories of the everyday. However, this can cause problems, especially when they are seen as a recounting of the personal. Shameful stories exacerbate the understanding of narrative as merely referencing personal idiosyncrasies. In academic writing, this coalescing around the personal, compounded by shame's seemingly personal quality, renders telling tales difficult, causing painful misunderstandings. Personally, I think it's high time that we got beyond such social scientific unease, but let me cite Benjamin in defence.

> 'It was as if the shame of it was to outlive him.' With these words *The Trial* ends. Corresponding as it does to his 'elemental purity of feeling,' shame is Kafka's strongest gesture. It has a dual aspect, however. Shame is an intimate human reaction, but at the same time it has social pretensions. Shame is not only shame in the presence of others, but can also be shame one feels for them. Kafka's shame, then, is no more personal than the life and thought which govern it.
>
> (1992, p. 125)

Benjamin puts it perfectly. There is something pure about shame as a feeling, even as it publicly twists the very sense of self. Yet, shame always plays on that doubledness of the public and the private, the extraordinary and the mundane. It is perhaps the most intimate of feelings but seemingly must be brought into being by an intimate proximity to others. Shame makes our selves intimate to our selves, and equally it is social and impersonal; or at least, as Benjamin puts it, no more personal than the life and thought that carry it. In the face of much criticism about 'the subjective', which is then further debased (in some minds) by the labelling of a genre of academic writing as 'the personal', I use Benjamin's thoughts not as an alibi but as inspiration. In this sense, everyday stories of shame may allow us to develop a wider notion of the everyday – of what is personal and what is social.

The body is key here: it generates and carries much more meaning that we have tended to see. That said, using and describing how one's body or those of others react in different contexts can sometimes be exemplary, and sometimes not. It is a bit of an experiment. As Massumi writes, 'exemplification activates detail', and the success of examples hinges on their detail (2002, p. 18).[5] Personally, I do not think that stories can have too much detail, although perhaps theories can. But enough prevaricating, let's get on the road.

Getting to Uluru

As many will know, at the heart of Australia there is a big rock. It is really big, and sort of red, or many shades of red. It is, debatably, the world's biggest monolith and made of arkosic sandstone. To give some idea of its stature, it is 9.4 km in circumference, 345 metres high, 3.6 km long and 2 km wide. Walking at a good pace, it takes several hours to circumnavigate. It is thought to extend downwards several kilometres, like an iceberg in the desert. Known still by some as 'Ayers Rock', its Aboriginal name Uluru has become increasingly common usage. It is symbolically central to many groups. Most legitimately, it is at the heart of Anangu belief, the Aboriginal people who have lived in the vicinity of Uluru for some 22,000 years, or more. It is also at the heart of white Australia's imagining of itself, although many Australians have not been – it is an expensive enterprise to get to the centre from the east coast where much of the population lives. This does not stop the masses of foreign tourists for whom 'Ayers Rock' is also a central destination. They pique our envy, and perhaps incite shame as they flash around our cut-price dollar.

The rock works differently for tourists than for either the Anangu or for white Australians. For the latter, Uluru is part of the everyday mythology of living in this vast continent. For the Anangu, now the legally recognized cus- todians of the rock and the park, it is where the everyday is most clearly inhabited by the spiritual and the historical. For the Anangu, Uluru is the site of the energy called Tjukurpa, a Pitjantjatjara word that encompasses their history, religion and law. In the words of Yami Lester, the chair of the Uluru-Katajuta Board of

Management: 'In the past some people have laughed and called it dreaming but that Tjukurpa is real, it's our law, our language and family together'.[6] The Tjukurpa can be said to map the relationships and the travels and activities of the ancestral beings who inhabit the land. Uluru is a busy place, with dozens of sacred sites both for women and men. Next to the grandeur of their tales, any other story is mundane. Certainly mine is:

In the very dead of winter, we made our way to Uluru.[7] Eliot's phrase – pinched from the epic journey of the Magi – made us smile as we descended down from Darwin. We were on holiday and allowed to be corny. The really hot days were behind us, and the sun would now be on our backs until we turned west at Alice Springs, 1,600 kilometres south of Darwin. The rhythm of time changed slightly as we hit the Stuart Highway. In the back, against the bags, my feet out the window, my body slowed and became all eyes to take in the subtly changing landscape. Nature stops and tea breaks gear-shifted the smooth flow of time and space. I wondered again and again at the marvel of a billy boiling in minutes, perched on a nest of twigs. It is all so new, in such an ancient land. The dryness is pervasive; the land yields up a sigh when I squat to pee. At night we sleep on foamies – a luxurious version of the swag, little rectangles under the stars.

We turned right at Alice and after stopping in the seemingly ghost-drenched former Lutheran mission of Hermannsburg, continued onto a rough track through the Finke Gorge. The riverbed was as dry as could be, but debris from the last time it flooded was left high in the branches of the great river gums. The four-wheel drive clambered up and down sand dunes and rocks. Sometimes you could walk faster but I didn't want to leave the vehicle and my companions – it had subtly become home, a snug encapsulation of another quotidian. It's easy to explain how such a radically different configuration could feel like home: a secure human and nonhuman capsule upon which my life depended. It's harder to know why it so displaced my real home. I caught those whiffs of feeling before thought sets in, when the reference of home would not compute. My body had moulded to the interior, my senses fixated on the outside registering new information.

On the road to Uluru we found a track into the mulga and made camp far away from the noise of the big tourist buses. It was crepuscule, or as one of companions said in Australian, 'crepuscular'. He climbed a dune and came back to say that we could see the rock. Dark had fallen and by the light of the gas lamp I read my novel. The rock could wait.

The next day we broke camp faster than usual. We had a destination. We had plans. For all that the image of the rock burned in my sense of Australia, I was less excited than my companions who had seen it many times before. Vague feelings of discomfort lingered as I sat in the back. Maybe I wouldn't like it, or worse, maybe I wouldn't have the right feeling.

After the undulations of the previous country, the land was undeniably flat. A wide-open flatness that does the heart good. And it is red, well more than red can convey. We drove with no sign of change to the land. How could something that big disappear, or fail to appear?

Then there it was. Awe-inspiring, mind-bogglingly there. Wow – a useless word; but Wow. Complying with a request from their daughter, my companions played her favourite song for the sighting of the rock: 'Beds are Burning' from Midnight Oil's *Diesel and Dust* (1985). As we got closer – movement in slowed time – I breathed in an elation that seemed to be the result of a million things resonating. Then as I breathed out the quiverings were transposed into sobs – great, big, ugly ones. Peter Garrett and the boys sang over them. The anthem of good white Australia dissipated out the window and into the red dust:

> The time has come to say fair's fair
> To pay the rent, to pay our share
> The time has come, a fact's fact
> It belongs to them, let's give it back.

Like a child, I cried myself out and felt that sleepy, empty calm. In a daze, I walked around the rock, registering somewhere its magnificence. We drove to Yulara, the Ayers Rock Resort. Our travels continued but I'll leave us there, filling the water tanks and picking up supplies.

The place of emotion

As many are beginning to argue, the past is carried somatically into everyday life. Young, a somatic psychologist, writes, 'bodies are passed down in families . . . The body is the flesh of memory' (2002, p. 25, p. 47). If somatic psychology is a recent development, the ways in which the body is marked by large social forces has been a key point in much sociology. In an attempt to figure out where and how shame erupts, connects with the inhabited body, and its histories of place, I turn now to the work of Bourdieu, who has done much to promote an analysis of how and why the social enters into our bodies and selves.

Elaborated in the 1960s and 1970s, Bourdieu's set of concepts, such as cultural, social and symbolic capital, the field, hexis and the habitus promised a more grounded study of distinction and difference than was the norm. These concepts were designed to speak across the great divides within the social science and the humanities and an intellectual situation where the cultural cannot be mentioned in the same breath as the biological, the social as the economic. Crude divisions, elaborated in ever increasingly sophisticated ways, still operate to separate the objective and the subjective, the inside and the outside, cognition and non-cognition, the body and the social. As he recounts in a 1985 interview, subsequently published in French with the provocative English title, 'Fieldwork in Philosophy', Bourdieu wanted to elaborate a 'genetic structuralism'.

> The analysis of objective structures – those of different *fields* – is inseparable from the analysis of the genesis at the heart of biological individuals of mental structures which are in one instance the product of the incorporation of social structures themselves: social space and the groups which are distributed across it, are the product of historical struggles (in which agents are engaged by function of their position in social space and the mental structures through which they comprehend this space).
>
> (1987, p. 24)

As will be well known, Bourdieu conceived of individuals as agents formed by and through mental structures: the ideas, the representations, the abstractions such as class and gender, etc. As such, agents incorporate these structures or representations in the ways they inhabit social spaces. These mental representations delimit how they can move and in which spaces they can move. Bourdieu's description complexly represents what we all may have felt – our bodies seem to know when they are at ease in a situation, when they know the rules and expectations, and conversely they also tell us loudly when we are out of our leagues, fishes out of water. The field is then a way of describing how all social spaces are inscribed by rules that are, by and large, unstated because as agents we have incorporated them. This 'genetic' knowledge is what allows us access to certain spheres, and enables us to operate, or not, within them. It is the mechanism that turns the extraordinary into daily life. It produces the feeling of the everyday. Conversely, when that knowledge fails us or is not up to the demands of the field, we are alerted acutely by what I've called the feeling of out-of-placeness, what happens when a body knows it does not belong within a certain space: in Bourdieu's terms, there is a schism between the habitus and the field, and this makes us feel, quite literally, out of it.

In this regulation of feeling '*bien dans sa peau*', or conversely out of it, the habitus is crucial. Again, it is the space of incorporation – a favourite Bourdieusian term – where the force of history gets played out in our ways of positioning ourselves and our ways of being in the world. While the body and the social come together in much of his work, Bourdieu is, however, rather vague about the place of emotion or of affect within the habitus – is how the body feels in feeling important, or is the 'feeling body' a side issue compared to the big questions about class and social capital? His attention to the physicality of the embodied habitus does promise a way of thinking about emotion and affect as simultaneously social and physical. This attention to the feeling body, as I will discuss shortly, is more clearly foregrounded by Marcel Mauss.

Habitus is a good point of departure in trying to get at the body's everyday operations. As a concept it can be a little clumsy, but it also provides a useful framing of how the structures of education, social position, class, gender etc., become embedded in our ways of inhabiting the world. Habitus, for Bourdieu, also focused on 'the *generative* capacities of dispositions' (1990, p. 53fn). More precisely, for Bourdieu the concept also seems to have had the wider function within the epistemology of an engaged sociology of the everyday: the Francophone tradition of *la sociologie engagée* where the point of sociology is to intervene in what it elsewhere only purports to study. At another level, habitus was to correct the two tendencies within the social sciences that Bourdieu spent much of his life fighting: objectivism, and more pointedly subjectivism. On this point, here is what he had to say in *The Logic of Practice*:

> [T]he concept of the habitus, which is predisposed by its range of historical uses to designate a system of acquired, permanent, generative dispositions, is justified above all by the false problems that it eliminates, the questions it enables one to formulate better or to resolve, and the specific scientific difficulties it gives rise to.
>
> (1990, p. 53fn)

Here the concept provides a way out of the perils of objectivism which 'universalizes the theorist's relation to the object of science', and of subjectivism which 'universalizes the experience that the subject of theoretical discourse has of himself as subject' (1990, pp. 45–56). In French sociology, this has often been taken as a way of warding against that nasty Anglo habit that some of us have of playing fast and loose with the subjective. But, in fact, I do not think that this is warranted by Bourdieu's thoughts. At another level, as in much sociological and anthropological research, Bourdieu relied heavily on the subjective accounts of his informants.

How else are we to enter other people's everyday lives? This was, of course, precisely Bourdieu's interest: how to account for practical knowledge – the stuff which people gather and deploy in their everyday lives and which constitutes for Bourdieu the real reason that one does sociology. Hear, for instance, in the following quotation the way in which habitus, as a warning to the researcher, shifts into habitus as generative of interest:

> One has to situate oneself *within* 'real activity' as such, that is in the practical relation to the world, the preoccupied, active presence in the world through which the world imposes its presence, with its urgencies, its things to be said and done, things made to be said, which directly govern words and deeds without ever unfolding as spectacle.
>
> (1990, p. 52)

Generative is an important term in Bourdieu's argument about what the habitus does (although all concepts are, or should be, by their nature generative). The habitus as a description of everyday lived realities is that which generates practices, frames for positioning oneself in the world, and indeed ways of inhabiting the world. Analytically it acts as an optic into that world. These two sides come together in his description of the habitus as 'a metaphor of the world of object, which is itself an endless circle of metaphors that mirror each other ad infinitum' (1990, p. 76).

The way in which Bourdieu makes the habitus both an object of study and an analytic is repeated throughout his work. The search for a hinge, or for different hinges, that will render evident the coinciding of the objective and subjective worlds of sociality is at the heart of Bourdieu's project. In one of the many lovely phrases that tend to get lost in his prose, Bourdieu states that 'the habitus – embodied history, internalized as second nature and so forgotten as history – is the active presence of the whole past of which it is the product' (1990, p. 56). Elaborating on this, he argues that

> The habitus, a product of history produces individual and collective practices – more history – in accordance with the schemes generated by history . . . [the habitus] ensures the active presence of past experiences, which, deposited in each organism in the form of schemes of perception, thought and action, tend to guarantee the 'correctness' of practices . . . more reliably than all formal rules and explicit norms.
>
> (1990, p. 54)

In this way, institutions and privileges 'produce quite real effects, durably inscribed in belief' (1990, p. 57). There is, I think, something quite poignant about Bourdieu's insistence and his persistence in following through on this crucial insight. This is encapsulated by the way the habitus delivers a history that is 'both original and inevitable' (1990, p. 57).

Poignant though this may be, Bourdieu does not wax lyrical about emotions. On one reading, he seems almost dismissive:

> Emotion . . . is a (hallucinatory) 'presenting' of the impending future, which, as bodily reactions identical to those of the real situation bear witness, leads a person to live a still suspended future as already present, or even already past, and therefore necessary and inevitable – 'I'm a dead man', 'I'm done for'.
>
> (1990, p. 292fn)

Here emotion projects the habitus' tendency to continually frame and adjust between the unlikely (possibility) and the likely (probability). This can be clearly heard in Bourdieu's description of how 'agents cut their coats according to their cloth and so to become the accomplices of the processes that tend to make the probable a reality' (1990, p. 65). In this rather dour depiction of the workings of the habitus, emotion seems to presage the fact that aspirations are always severely tailored by the reality of daily life. Either hallucinatory or fatalistic, emotion seems to be the body's way of registering its return to 'the present of the presumed world, the only one it can ever know' (1990, p. 65). There are no flights of fancy possible here; emotion in this understanding acts like the miner's canary as hope is snuffed out.

Which emotion produces the statement, 'I'm done for'? At once, it is the cry of fear. It might also express the realization that there is nothing left to fear but fear itself. The sense of emotion as anticipation/resignation is supported with a discussion of the physical behaviour of bodies: 'lowering or bending of the head or forehead as sign of confusion or timidity, and also shame and modesty'. Bourdieu concludes that 'Male, upward movements and female, downward movements . . . the will to be on top, to overcome, versus submission. . . . [it is] *as if* the body language of sexual domination and submission had provided the fundamental principles of both the body language and the verbal language of social domination and submission' (1990, p. 71, emphasis added).[8]

In this manner, the body's expressions – including that classic one of shame, the hanging of the head – become a trope to describe the wider structures of social domination. Within this schema, emotions seem to act as synecdoche for the body. The body, these 'acts of bodily gymnastics', root 'the most fundamental structures of the group in the primary expressions of the body . . . as is clearly seen in emotion' (1990, p. 71).

The role of emotion becomes more pronounced in Bourdieu's exposition of belief and the body. 'Practical belief', he argues, 'is a state of the body' (1990, p. 68); 'Enacted belief [is] instilled by the childhood learning that treats the body as a living memory pad'. This learning ensures that values are 'made body', and instils a 'whole cosmology'. Belief – what he calls 'the almost miraculous encounter between the habitus and the field' – is then crucially linked to emotion's role in animating the body. Emotion and bodily gymnastics are central to the fact that 'it is because agents never know completely what they are doing that what they do has more sense than they know'. It is the simple act of 're-placing the body in an overall posture which recalls the associated thoughts and feelings' (1990, p. 69). These acts of the body in emotion then are key to the work of symbolic capital, arguably the most valued of the forms of capital in Bourdieu's well-known theory of distinction.[9]

> Symbolic power works partly through the control of other people's bodies and belief that is given by the collectively recognized capacity to act in various ways on deep-rooted linguistic and muscular patterns of behaviour, either by neutralizing them or reactivating them to function mimetically.
>
> (1990, p. 69)

From this encapsulated picture, we can say that emotion is part of the body's knowledge. It seems to work to amplify or reduce instilled tendencies, and as such it sounds more like affect. As in Massumi's argument, affect is distinguished as 'irreducibly bodily and autonomic' from emotion as 'subjective content, the sociolinguistic fixing of a quality of experience' (2002, p. 28). This is important in clarifying the type of knowledge emotion plays in Bourdieu's understanding of the body. In Bourdieu's description, emotion is not directly cognitive although its effects may initiate cognition:

> The body believes in what it plays at: it weeps if it mimes grief. It does not represent what it performs, it does not memorize the past, it *enacts* the past, bringing it back to life. What is 'learned by the body' is not something that one has, like knowledge that can be brandished, but something that one is.
>
> (1990, p. 73)

This idea of the body as what 'is' sits uneasily with Bourdieu's argument about the 'hallucinatory' role of emotion. As we saw, emotion '"presents" an impending future'; it causes the body to adjust to the inevitability of the future as past. Bourdieu's phrasing of this is: 'I'm a dead man', 'I'm done for'. Earlier I queried the resignation that this expresses – a sort of sociological equivalent of 'sod's law' where things will go bad if they can. In this description, emotion presages and confirms the finality of the habitus. In line with this, as exemplified in the above quotation, the body can only re-enact the past. Listening carefully to the sequence of events described, the body feels, enacts an emotion, and then brings into being the past. It is therefore the feeling body that has the consequence of summoning the past – a spectral past as future.

This describes the ways in which through class, or at times gender, or just by familial instruction, life can seem to dead-end itself. But what of the body's range of affective expressions? Sometimes we weep and are caught within grief and joy. The role of the habitus may well be to sort out that confusion, to reproduce the feeling of inevitability. However, there may also be times when feeling shakes up the habitus; when the body outruns the cognitive capture of the habitus.

In sum, Bourdieu's use of emotion seems to close down the possibilities for the body that his own theory authorizes. The separation of the feeling body and emotion, and the implicit role of the latter as a cognitive adjustment mechanism, conceptually means that the body is captured in and by the social. While Bourdieu admits the physicality of the body, he clumsily contains this within a dour and vague evocation of emotion. It is a thin way of describing what elsewhere Bourdieu so richly evokes. The exciting ideas about the body, or about agents being active within the making of their worlds, are undercut if the body that '*is*' just constitutes a container for what it has been. This may be Bourdieu's reworked Marxism speaking, or perhaps his misapprehension of the emotions as a nefarious form of false consciousness (a term that he would not use, but that seems apt in this situation). Whatever the source of his curtailing of emotion's role, it is a dead-end vision that can only make sense if ultimately Bourdieu evacuates evidence of the physiological expressions of the affective body.

A sociology of humanity

It is disappointing to find glimpses of an exciting vision only to find that at the crucial point it has been withdrawn. However, I will now step back in time and consider Bourdieu's predecessor, Marcel Mauss. Mauss, I hope, lets us appreciate the physiological nature of the habitus and the feeling body, beyond it being always and already social, or inversely impossible.[10]

According to James, Mauss was the first to coin habitus as a sociological concept. She also mentions that originally the term was used medically to describe the outward appearance of the face and the body in relation to its internal state of health or sickness (1998, p. 20). Habitus is an important tenet in Mauss' striving to comprehend 'l'homme total', a vision of a sociological accounting for totality that joins 'the local connectedness of form and content, . . . the tangible aspect of human life . . . in relation to the body and its material experience, the techniques of work, and the rhythmic enactment of ritual and symbolic performance' (James 1998, p. 15). Schlanger describes Mauss' work as 'a fieldwork of modernity' (1998, p. 193), in which we can hear an early supplement to Bourdieu's 'fieldwork in philosophy'. In Karsenti's description, Mauss' project concerned nothing less than 'an enquiry into the principles on which the human being is "assembled" . . . a reorientation of the conceptualization of the social' (1998, p. 76).

As Mauss candidly put it, 'after having of necessity divided things up too much, sociologists must strive to reconstitute the whole . . . The study of the concrete, which is the study of completeness is possible' (1990, p. 80). Mauss' challenge included the detailed analysis of the parts as well as the task of figuring how to make them re-connect. In some ways, it is totality from below, one that works through example and detail. For Mauss, it is through the triple analysis of the physiological, psychological, and the societal that one might arrive at an understanding of the total man. In this, the practical, living everyday body was key: through the body's physiology: 'the co-ordination of articulated motions by which it functions and by which it embodies and conveys meaning . . . these efficacious bodily acts [education, fashion, prestige] confirm the social nature of the *habitus*' (Schlanger 1998, pp. 198–199).

Along with the sheer breadth of Mauss' project, there is also something very appealing about the man. In ways that must have been quite shocking at the time, and that remain refreshing, Mauss allowed for everyday human foibles within his sociology of humanity. That humans habitually do things wrong or clumsily, that our actions and techniques attest to trial and error, mistakes and sometimes plain stupidity was not only accepted by Mauss but also often corroborated by examples from his own experience. In his exposition of body techniques, he recounts, for example, how his swimming technique was a product of a time when 'swimmers thought of themselves as a kind of steamboat' (1979, p. 99). He then depicts himself pushing though the water spouting great streams of water. And what to say of a thinker who on presenting his work – and his challenge – to the Société de Psychologie, remarks that he was inspired in his thoughts about swimming when he came into contact with someone 'whose initials I still know, but whose name I can no longer remember'. Apparently, the article was excellent, but says Mauss, 'I have been too lazy to look it up' (1979, p. 98).

Mauss' ideas about the body and its techniques were infused with his experiences within the trenches of WWI. As is detailed in Fournier's (1994) biography: 'Besides his grief at the loss of friends and colleagues, Mauss also discussed the sentiments of fear and panic he had to endure, and his recognition of the physical and moral force of instinct, which animates or on the contrary discourages and isolates the individual during extreme moments' (in Schlanger 1998, p. 209fn).[11] While he was rather scathing about a theory of the emotions *per se*, Mauss was not shy about using his own emotional experiences – which for me is a huge point in his favour. For instance, in regards to the war he recalls how 'I have also experienced fear, and how it is reinforced by panic to the point that not only the group, but also the individual will itself, even the brute instinct of self-preservation, dissolve all at once' (1979, p. 14). In response to psycho-logical theories of *sthenia* and *asthenia* (courage and weakness towards life), Mauss refers again to the tripartite integration of the physiological-psychological-sociological. Within this complex, instinct is a driving force that, in some regards, exceeds man's symbolic capacities. Humans might communicate with symbols, but the only reason that we have symbols and can communicate with them is that we have instincts: 'The exaltations and ecstasies which create symbols are proliferations of instinct' (1979, p. 16). As Karsenti argues, Mauss' conception of the connection between the corporeal and the psychic was 'not a causal relationship that keeps one outside the other' (1998, p. 76). In relation to this body-psychic linkage, the social cannot be seen as merely that which is imposed or internalized. In the search to grasp the collective totality of our being, the social needs to be understood as 'truly internal, natural in the strong sense of the word' (Karsenti, 1998, p. 77).

The striking thing about Mauss' model, along with its combination of strangeness and commonsense, is the way in which totality is understood through the intersection of quite distinctive elements. In other words, totality is not totalizing. Humanity is not, in this sense, an abstraction but a real call to study all the things that make us. Hear, for example, the number of things going on in Mauss' description of totality:

[W]e converge with physiology, the phenomena of bodily life, for it seems that between the social and the bodily the layer of individual consciousness is very thin: laughter, tears, funerary laments, ritual ejaculations, are physiological reactions just as much as they are obligatory or necessary or suggested or employed by collectivities to a precise end, with a view to a kind of physical and moral discharge of its expectations, which are physical and moral too.

(1979, p. 10)

Compared to Bourdieu's equivocation about the body and emotion, Mauss goes straight to the pervasiveness of physiological convergences. In contrast to the way that the social seems to close down the body in the Bourdieusian habitus, Mauss is careful to highlight the very thin layer that exists between the physiological and the social. That layer is inhabited and disturbed by the feeling body – its tears, laughter and ejaculations. Unlike Bourdieu, these do not have to be contained as emotion, which as we have seen plays a crucial role in closing down the habitus. While Mauss also links the body's feelings to 'a precise end', his emphasis is on the very physiology that animates the social. This gives a very different picture of embodiment and of sociality where the body does not fall away before the social. The social here is charged by physicality and human physiology: the wants, needs and desires of the body revelling in its affects. The embodied everyday social becomes, to repeat Karsenti's phrase, 'natural in the strongest sense of the word'.

Mauss' mind passionately ranged widely over very different domains. These days we do not often see such passion. The rare places where passion, excitement and interest show up is in arguments that grapple with what the scientific passions might mean if translated into the humanities. For instance, Connolly's recent work engages with current neurological theories in order to advance or renew thinking within the humanities. For Connolly, work such as LeDoux's *The Emotional Brain* can be made to reverberate with Deleuzian philosophy. Connolly finds much of interest, enjoyment and awe in the everyday: the possibility that there might be 'something mute in the world that has not yet been translated into the register of thought'. Connolly uses the interest provided by these very different domains of research to argue for an alternative and quotidian ethical sensibility: 'a constellation of thought-imbued intensities and feeling', the 'stuff of new techniques of thinking' (Deleuze, in Connolly 1999, p. 23, p. 27).

At first glance, it might seem that shame is hardly a subject associated with passion, and if it is a sensibility then surely it is only a painful and uneasy one. Shame is undoubtedly painful, as well as interesting because it activates so many sensations. But shame does more than sensibilize us to the vast variety of sensations that inform daily life; it also proposes a sensibility at once practical, ethical and needed: 'the appropriate reaction to one's own shame is a type of self-transformation', as Redding summarizes Nietzsche's view (1999).

Let us get back to that sense of out-of-placeness in the everyday and shame. Here shame cannot be understood outside of its sheer bodily intensity. As I have indicated in the examples of Bourdieu and especially Mauss, there are traditions of thought within the social sciences that have attended to the physiological, and have seen in it a necessary component to understand the total human (a sociology of humanity that is perhaps a conceptual forebear to Gilroy's (2000) planetary humanism). At a fundamental level, one thing we all share is a biological body. Its somatic effects may be experienced differently, but the body *is*. We are human because of the physiological, and the somatic – how could it be otherwise? Without that basic level, all our theories about embodiment and the everyday fall flat.

Of bodies in other places

What of that example of my moment of affect left so rudely all these pages ago? Now that it has faded, how to get back into that body sitting in the back of a Land Cruiser, choked on the sight of a huge rock? Where did that affect come from? Was it a reaction to the divorcing of my life and another's? Did that moment of affect mark a shame produced in the schism between my habitus and the field? Or did that space (the rock, the music, my home in the Land Cruiser, the weeks of camping rough) all allow for a radical rearticulation of the everyday? Was I infected by my own past, or that of a completely other culture? Affect theorists respond to such questions with assertions about the biological basis for affect. In this way, we begin to see two interconnected levels: we feel the physiology of being affected, and then emotionally respond through the resources of our habituses. Emotion then 'represents the assemblage of any affect with our previous experience of that affect' (Nathanson 1996, p. 13); 'Affect is biology, while emotion is biography' (Basch, in Nathanson 1996, p. 13). Nathanson, a practicing psychologist and follower of Tomkins, argues that 'so much is going on in the brain that nothing gains attention unless it triggers an affect'. Like Tomkins, he is clear that we are born with innate affects. These are, according to Nathanson, the palette each of us gets; it is in our experience-affect combinations that we differentially experience both individual and collective emotions.

These ideas help in understanding where affect and emotion fit together within the habitus. They begin to sketch out a wider understanding of the role of affect in the everyday. The terms – biography vs. biology – are, however, rather clumsy. But in the search to understand the connections between levels, we're not constrained to one particular language. Mahood, an Australian writer experimenting across the genres of memoir and novel, demonstrates a more nuanced way of describing how and where the physiological and biographical converge. Her book, *Craft for a Dry Lake* (2000), is an extended meditation on bodies out-of-place. She beautifully conveys how bodies move, change and adapt to place, or refuse to – how the physiology of the everyday body meets the physicality of place.

> Crossing the border back into the Territory, my childhood rushes to meet me. The colours begin to intensify, the light sharpens. I begin to feel something in my bones and nerves and viscera. I would not describe it as an emotion. It is more like a chemical reaction, as if a certain light and temperature and dryness triggers a series of physical and nervous realignments . . . My pulse is up, everything takes on a hallucinatory clarity.
>
> (Mahood 2000, p. 35)

Later Mahood describes her affective reaction to the land as more than an ensemble of mental images: 'it is something else too, a set of visceral alignments over which the intellect has no jurisdiction' (2000, p. 174). Mahood's book is ostensibly in honor of her father's memory and her voyage back to her family's station in the Tanami, a vast track of land between the Simpson Desert and Western Australia. It is also an account of her affective experiences, told in the terms of her physiological realignments to the land, and deeply relational. She writes from one plane to another, scrambling any neat and hard distinction – such as that between biological affect and biographical emotion, or between body and social. Her emotion is biological, and her biography is affectively written on the land. The description of her journey is, in Mauss' sense, total. The full range and reach of the everyday habitus is glimpsed in its continual relation to land, time and place.

Mahood's habitus is deeply informed by being a white woman in relation to the land that was her family's and is now Aboriginal land. When she is invited to a big women's business ceremony, she finds herself automatically, biologically, following the Aboriginal tradition of setting camp in the direction of that land: 'that country that my father turned into a cattle station' (2000, p. 124).[12] As the women's bodies turn in the direction of their country, we feel the way that humans act in accord with tropism too. Like flowers our bodies react to such different stimuli, innately turning this way and that. The relations of relation seemingly multiply indefinitely. As a child, she was given a skin name by the local Aboriginal women on the station, 'a formality which places [whites] in a category of relationships and behaviour'. She now acknowledges the ambivalence: 'It's as if I have come by a secret password by dishonest means and have hoarded it against the moment when it might open a magic door' (2000, p. 125).[13]

To map all the relationships that compose Mahood's habitus would take a long time. At once, she is shy, embarrassed, proud – but is she ashamed? Not in the usual sense, and she pushes back the obvious emotional expression of white shame that she associates with urban romanticism about Aboriginal culture.

> The primordial landscape is scattered with the evidence of ancestral acts of rape, copulation, dismembering. It is about a physical encounter with the land itself, a wounding, a letting of blood, a taking of the country into oneself, of taking oneself into the country.
>
> (2000, p. 195)

The recognition of an Aboriginal singularity is crucial, even as her relationship to it is profoundly implicated in her habitus. In contrast to the unfathomably deep relationship to the land that is part and parcel of Aboriginal daily life, the non-Indigenous seem to flounder. 'Whites who live here struggle to articulate an attachment over which they have no control' (2000, p. 195).[14] 'They leave and return, resentfully, full of anger and indigestible griefs'. These white experiences are 'scratches on the land' that cannot be understood without an appreciation of 'the price the homage this country extracts'. 'Acceptance' is possible, 'predicated on limited ambition: a moment by moment focus on the job to be done, the life to be lived'. It seems unendurable, just as it seems amazing that whites keep at it, rearing livestock in ridiculous conditions. Mahood wants us to acknowledge that keeping at the impossibility of being in this place is predicated on 'a narrow and deeply grounded wisdom' (p. 195).

Everyday shame

Mahood's account points to a different sense of shame, which illuminates a richer and complex understanding of the everyday. Her shame, seemingly part of her daily experience, cannot be collapsed into white guilt. There is, in fact, no guilt to be found in her landscape. And in this, there is also no morality.[15] The shame I sense in Mahood's account is predicated on interest – the type of interest that's hard to come by unless it's deep within your habitus. In her description of her father and those who stayed on as managers of now Aboriginal-owned land, there is a sense of the affective complex of anger–rage, terror–fear and shame–humiliation. The clinical description of anger-rage – the frown, clenched jaw, red face – uncannily captures the image of the tough, laconic, white Australian on the land. To live, to continually return to live a life circumscribed with 'limited ambition' is to be placed within the ambit of interest interrupted – of shame. It also eerily recalls Bourdieu's example: 'I'm a dead man, I'm done for'. We hear again that awful finality that the habitus seems to guarantee. However, in a more telling way, Mahood also depicts how bodies continually try to escape that finality. They act out and alongside the sentencing of 'I'm done for'.

As a cipher for a larger history of everyday white shame, Mahood's physiological reactions repeatedly speak of interest, and interest foiled. This cannot be understood outside of her habitus. Here the physiological is the psychological and the social. The body *is*. And the body is its reactions to the dryness, the light, the history which are enfolded fully within that particular habitus.

Neither heroic, nor scandalous, this shame is deeply interested and interesting in ways that cannot be easily described. It is not purely social (that would make it easier to eradicate). Nor can it be written into some general account of a white psychology. The physical and visceral acting of affect disturbs such pigeon-holing. It does recall strongly Mauss' assemblage – the physiological-psychological-sociological intersection – and maybe that language can begin to shed light on the delicacy of white shame, experienced not as monumental but as mundane. If, as the affect theorists put it, we are born with a basic palette of affects, how, where, and when they move us also needs to be understood in different shades of terms. If the social is natural, physical and physiological, we need to make our descriptive language as muted as the colours of the land.

Again, what of my own little example? The constant deferral already speaks of shame. The moment that I described of seeming pure affect certainly did translate into shame; or more precisely two different kinds of shame coincided. It's hard to describe the differences but Tomkins' precise terms may help. The exaltation before and in the sight of Uluru can be precisely described as interest-excitement, and enjoyment-joy. There may also have been some of the neutral affect Tomkins calls surprise-startle. The eyebrows up, eyes wide open and blinking, smiling and looking and listening: I couldn't quite believe I was there. Then the near simultaneous movement to sobbing, head down, fingers covering my face. Well, yes these are the classic facial displays of shame. At this level, I felt the heat of shame – it ripped into me physiologically, and was beyond my cognitive control.

Equally at that moment, in that tensing together of sensation, there was a splitting of shame. As Massumi has argued, the difference between emotion and affect can also be described as a bifurcation in response, where 'language functions differentially to intensity' (2002, p. 25). At another level than the affective, I became aware of my shame. I became cognizant of my shame, which referred itself back onto more shame. The fact that Midnight Oil was playing cannot be forgotten. Their words cannot be ignored. 'How do we sleep while our beds are burning?' 'The time has come to say fair's fair'.

This emotional, or what we might even call cognitive shame exists with that other little shame that whispers in the habitus: the body calling out its hopes and discomfort because it feels out-of-place. This shame is the body saying that it cannot fit in although it desperately wants to. One of the important thoughts to take from Bourdieu's notion of the habitus, or Mauss' description of the total man, is that our bodies and their everyday biographies may be more complicated than we've given them credit for. Conceptually, they challenge any neat division of biological affect and biographical emotion, the social and the physiological. Memory is a strange thing, and it is placed in hard to find areas of the body and the brain. The point is clumsily put, but it does remind us that our bodies and histories are constituted by so much more than we usually allow for.

Across a number of different theories, descriptions and stories, I have tried to argue for a reconsideration of everyday shame. I am driven by the interest and possibilities of what shame might do – to our bodies, our concepts and ideas, and how we inhabit everyday life. Not all uses of shame are good. Why should they be? But shame is an everyday fact of human bodies and life. Sometimes it leads to reactionary acts, sometimes it compels close inspection of how we live, and becomes the necessary force to catalyse an ethics of the everyday: 'a visceral . . . commitment to more generous identities, responsibilities and connections might be cultivated' (Connolly 1999, p. 21). Let us be shameless in this project.

Notes

1   In relation to how shame can highlight the construction of the ordinary and the everyday, see Ferrell's (2003) lovely essay on shame, and indigenous and non-indigenous peoples in the context of a town 'that prided itself on the ordinary'.

2   The experiential aspects of the interplay of the ordinary and the extraordinary has had a profound influence in my work (e.g. Probyn 1997), and has been theoretically supported and inspired by Morris' writing.

3   While Tomkins pursues with fervor exactly how affects work in the body, he is equally passionate about what affects do to the self and society. This can be heard over and again in statements like, 'the nature of the experience of shame guarantees a perpetual sensitivity to any violation of the dignity of man' (1995, p. 136). This also animates the need for analyses where 'the biopsychological mechanisms and the social products be integrated into a science of man and not polarized' (1965, p. 72). For a more comprehensive discussion of what this entails for cultural studies, see Probyn (forthcoming). I have been hugely influenced in this project by Sedgwick and Frank (1995).

4   The interventions into the debate about reconciliation in Australia (a formal and government evoked, although neglected, term) are too numerous to mention. However, for arguments based in a Deleuzian framing of the social, see Gatens and Lloyd (1999) and Probyn (2000, 2001).

5   See also Probyn (1996) for an extended deployment of 'examples', indebted to Agamben's arguments.

6   As cited on http://www.thesalmons.org (accessed 12 September 2002).

7   My thanks to Robyn and Jack Durack for taking me on a wonderful voyage that profoundly disturbed my everyday by introducing me to new land and ideas.

8   Elsewhere (Probyn forthcoming) I elaborate on the gendered dynamics of this description. See also feminist uses (Skeggs) and evaluations of Bourdieu (Lovell, Felski).

9   Bourdieu distinguishes between cultural capital, which is the 'incorporation' (the making body) of objective markers of social distinction from symbolic capital that is the 'world-making and changing' ability he states is the possession of artists and writers (see Bourdieu 1986/1984, pp. 241–258). See also Hage (1998) for an interesting application of Bourdieu's ideas.

10 There are connections between Bourdieu and Mauss, although there's little acknowledgement of any debt Bourdieu might have owed to Mauss. There is a vague sense that Mauss got Bourdieu wrong – which is totally illogical of course. It seems to me that Mauss got 'straightened out' in Bourdieu's thought. He never really took Mauss' ideas on, although he was cognizant of Mauss' place in the field of French sociology. How could he not be? Mauss was Emile Durkheim's nephew and did much to propagate Durkheim's influence in French sociology. In 1930, Mauss also held the Chair of Sociology in the Collège de France which Bourdieu was to later occupy. He published three volumes of Mauss' work in his series, *Le sens commun*. Marcel Fournier – Mauss' preeminent bibliographer – comments that Bourdieu seemed to find Mauss less rigid than his uncle. He adds that there are several profound links between Mauss and Bourdieu especially in terms of their attention to the logic of practice and their understanding of the discipline and the role of the sociologist as politically engaged through sociological practice. My thanks to Marcel Fournier for these comments. For the most complete positioning of Mauss' work, see Fournier (1994).

11 Mauss' experience of WWII was perhaps even more traumatic, although by then he was writing much less. Pickering (1998) remarks that Mauss, who did not hide the Jewishness clearly marked in his second name of Israël, may have stepped down in 1940 from his position of director of Ecole Pratique des Hautes Etudes (5th section) because of Nazi pressures.

12 Aboriginal law dictates that there are separate women's and men's spiritual roles and duties.

13 From the perspective of an anthropologist, Biddle (1997) describes – in an embodied, and therefore grounding breaking, approach – other aspects of these forms of relation.

14 I am well aware that this sounds romanticized, and of course there are pressing realities that also inform Aboriginal life. For a compelling and convincing argument about an Aboriginal epistemology in connection to country, see Moreton-Robinson's (2000) groundbreaking argument about 'incommensurability'.

15 There are large arguments about the relation of guilt to shame, and about the more productive nature of guilt. In particular, Nussbaum's (2001) recent opus on the emotions posits guilt over what she calls the primitive nature of shame. Her argument about guilt's more positive role is based on the equation of guilt and reparation, whereas shame refers back to primal scenes in childhood. I find this argument flawed on two levels: first, the equation of guilt and reparation flows from her model of neo-liberalism and the project of

'reforming' individuals and their societies. This turns on a traditional notion of morality, and normativity. This recalls the familiar Foucauldian and Deleuzian formulations of morality as opposed to ethics. Secondly, and central to my argument, Nussbaum goes to great lengths to erase the physiology of the body in her account of the emotions. While too broad to enter into here, elsewhere I explore the erasure of the bodily and the experiential in Nussbuam's project (Probyn 2004). While less surprising in Nussbaum, a recent turn to evacuate the experiential body can also be seen in the work of feminist who one would have thought to be more sympathetic to the body's knowledges. See, for instance, the critique of Berlant's argument against sentimentality (Probyn forthcoming) and the unease exhibited in Brown and Weigman's respective accounts of the problems of teaching women's studies (Probyn 2004).

References

Benjamin, W. (1992) *Illuminations*, trans. H. Zohn, Fontana Press, London.
Biddle, J. (1997) 'Shame', *Australian Feminist Studies*, vol. 12, no. 26, pp. 227–239.
Bourdieu, P. (1987) 'Fieldwork in philosophy', in *Choses Dites* (trans. as *In Other Words: Essays in Reflexive Sociology*), Minuit, Paris; Polity, Cambridge (1990).
Bourdieu, P. (1990/1980) *The Logic of Practice*, Polity, Oxford.
Connolly, W. (1999) 'Brain waves, transcendental fields, and techniques of thought', *Radical Philosophy*, March/April, pp. 19–28.
Felski, R. (2000) 'Nothing to declare: identity, shame and the lower classes', in *Doing Time: Feminist Theory and Postmodern Culture*, New York University Press, New York.
Ferrell, R. (2003) 'Pinjarra, 1970: shame and the country town', *Cultural Studies Review*, vol. 9, no. 1, pp. 23–34.
Fournier, M. (1994) *Marcel Mauss*, Minuit, Paris.
Gatens, M. (2000) 'Privacy and the body: the publicity of affect', *ASCA Yearbook*, ASCA, Amsterdam.
Gatens, M. & Lloyd, G. (1999) *Collective Imaginings: Spinoza, Past and Present*, Routledge, London.
Gibbs, A. (2002) 'Disaffected', *Continuum: Journal of Media and Cultural Studies*, vol. 16, no. 3, pp. 335–341.
Gilroy, P. (2000) *Against Race: Imaging Political Culture Beyond the Color Line*, Harvard University Press, Cambridge, MA.
James, W. (1998) '"One of Us": Marcel Mauss and "English" anthropology', in *Marcel Mauss: A Centenary Tribute*, eds W. James & N. J. Allen, Berghahn Books, New York.
Karsenti, B. (1998) 'The Maussian shift', in *Marcel Mauss: A Centenary Tribute*, eds W. James & N. J. Allen, Berghahn Books, New York.
Lovell, T. (2000) 'Thinking feminism with and against Bourdieu', *Feminist Theory*, vol. 1, no. 1, pp. 11–32.

Mahood, K. (2000) *Craft for a Dry Lake*, Anchor/Random House, Sydney.

Massumi, B. (1996) 'The autonomy of affect', in *Deleuze: A Critical Reader*, ed. P. Patton, Blackwell, Oxford.

Massumi, B. (2002) *Parables for the Virtual: Movement, Affect, Sensation*, Duke University Press, Durham.

Mauss, M. (1979) *Sociology and Psychology*, trans. B. Brewster, Routledge & Kegan Paul, London.

Moreton-Robinson, A. (2000) *Talkin' Up to the White Woman: Indigenous Women and Feminism*, University of Queensland Press, St. Lucia, QLD.

Nathanson, D. L. (ed.) (1996) *Knowing Feeling: Affect, Script and Psychotherapy*, Norton, New York.

Nussbaum, M. C. (2001) *Upheavals of Thought: The Intelligence of the Emotions*, Cambridge University Press, Cambridge.

Pickering, W. S. F. (1998) 'Mauss' Jewish background: a biographical essay', in *Marcel Mauss: A Centenary Tribute*, eds W. James & N. J. Allen, Berghahn Books, New York.

Probyn, E. (1996) *Outside Belongings*, Routledge, New York and London.

Probyn, E. (1997) 'The extraordinary ordinary: an interview with Elspeth Probyn', in *Foreign Dialogues*, Mary Zournazi, Pluto, Sydney.

Probyn, E. (2000) 'Shaming theory, thinking dis-connections: feminism and reconciliation', in *Political Transformations*, eds S. Ahmed, C. Lury & B. Skeggs, Routledge, New York and London.

Probyn, E. (2001) 'Eating skin', in *Thinking Through the Skin*, eds S. Ahmed & J. Stacey, Routledge, London.

Probyn, E. (2004) 'Teaching bodies: affects in the classroom', *Body & Society*, in press.

Probyn, E. (forthcoming) *Blush: Faces of Shame*, University of Minnesota Press, Minneapolis.

Redding, P. (1999) *The Logic of Affect*, Melbourne University Press, Melbourne.

Sedgwick, E. K. & Frank, A. (1995) 'Shame in the cybernetic fold: reading Silvan Tomkins', in *Shame and it Sisters: A Silvan Tomkins Reader*, eds E. K. Sedgwick & A. Frank, Duke University Press, Durham.

Skeggs, B. (1997) *Formations of Class and Gender*, Sage, London.

Tomkins, S. (1963) *Affect, Imagery, Consciousness Vol 2: The Negative Affects*, Springer, New York; Tavistock, London.

Tomkins, S. (1995) In *Shame and it Sisters: A Silvan Tomkins Reader*, eds E. K. Sedgwick & A. Frank, Duke University Press, Durham.

Andrew Metcalfe & Ann Game

EVERYDAY PRESENCES

The everyday is often seen as the time when nothing happens. This is a view that follows from a sense of chronological time, Euclidean space and Hegelian identity-play. The everyday can also be experienced as the time of eternity, the space of infinitude and the ontological condition of love. This epiphanic experience of the sacred is not of a release from the everyday but a return to it. The sacred is not the exception to the everyday but the ground of our everyday belonging to the universe.

Keywords   everyday; infinity; I-Thou; presence; love; face

Introduction

This article signals a shift from the desire-based post-structuralism of our book *Passionate Sociology* to a more inclusive love-based understanding of sociality in our recent book *The Mystery of Everyday Life*. The problem we found was that despite all our attempts to refigure desire, the primacy of separate terms remained: self, identity and linearity are unavoidable where there is desire. The basic formulation of desire – self and other – refers to two terms that interact with each other, rather than a relational logic. In this article, we provide an account of the time-space and being involved in a relational logic.

This conceptual shift has implications for the significance of a sociology of the everyday. This relates, for example, to understandings of the unknown and the unknowable. In desire-based logics, the Other is elsewhere, eluding the self in an endless deferral: an excess that is unknown. A relational logic, on the other hand, presumes the possibility of a meeting with the unknowable, a meeting that takes place in the here and now of the everyday. Within this logic, then, contra Derrida, 'the present' and 'presence' have a mysterious quality that can be 'known' through our participation in the world.

The everyday and the exceptional

The everyday is normally aligned with the mundane and profane, as the opposite of the sacred. Accordingly, for Buber, in his early years, religious experience was 'the exception . . . the experience of an otherness which did not fit into the

Cultural Studies Vol. 18, No. 2/3 March/May 2004, pp. 350–362
ISSN 0950-2386 print/ISSN 1466-4348 online   © 2004 Taylor & Francis Ltd
http://www.tandf.co.uk/journals   DOI: 10.1080/0950238042000201554

context of life' (1966, p. 17). However, Buber's understanding and experience of the everyday changed:

> Since then I have given up the 'religious' which is nothing but the exception, extraction, exaltation, ecstasy; or it has given me up. I possess nothing but the everyday out of which I am never taken. . . . I do not know much more. If that is religion then it is just everything, simply everything that is lived in its possibility of dialogue.
>
> (1966, p. 18)

'Each of us', said Buber,

> is encased in an armour which we soon, out of habit, no longer notice. . . . [Only when] a moment has imposed itself on us [do we] . . . take notice and ask ourselves, 'Has anything particular taken place? Was it not of the kind I meet everyday?' then we may reply to ourselves, 'Nothing particular, indeed, it is like this everyday, only we are not there everyday.' The signs of address are not something extraordinary . . . The waves of the aether roar on always, but for most of time we have turned off our receivers.
>
> (2002, pp. 12–13)

This article explores the implications of this different understanding and experience of the everyday, offering an account of an everyday experience, and then surveying the range of conceptual issues raised by the example.

Love at first sight

It is the second week of the school year, and my younger son, Max, is in his first year at kindergarten. In the afternoons, he tells me that his days have been 'all wonderful', but in the mornings his nerve is still occasionally failing him. Three days ago, still unable to console him long after the other parents had left the classroom, I had to pull him from me and abandon him to the teacher's care. As I walked away, I could see him huddled wretchedly under a low table, crying.

This morning Leo and Max were to make the trip to school with their uncle and cousin, but at the last moment Max panicked. He would not go to school unless I took him. Then, when we parked near the school, he said he would not leave the car. His refusal only lasted a moment, but it triggered in me a spasm of cold fear, to which I reacted with anxiety and irritation. This was still my condition as we stood outside the car and the boys put on the school backpacks that always seem too big for them.

Then, leaning over to help Max, I noticed from the corner of my eye that we were being watched. About ten steps from us, an office worker entering her building had been stopped in her tracks by the sight of Leo and Max struggling to put their arms through the right straps. She was slim and quite tall; she was too young, probably, to have children of her own; I sense she held a takeaway cup of coffee in one hand and a workbag on the other arm. I cannot tell you anything more about her appearance, and I would not recognize her if I passed her in the street, but at that moment I had an overpowering sense of the bright and lively look in her eyes. It wasn't as if she had stopped to stare: it looked instead as if the sight she had come upon had captivated her, incapacitated her, opened the most tender feelings. The woman and I caught each other's looks for a moment, and we smiled in recognition, unguarded smiles of what I clearly felt was love. Then the spell broke, and we all went about our business.

So is this, I wondered later, what happens when people fall in love at first sight? When this woman became lost in this detail of the morning, lost in the vision of my children, her eyes showed that she no longer knew who or where or when she was, so am I also right in feeling, I wondered, that this everyday occurrence raises profound questions about time, space, ways of being and ways of knowing?

When did this happen?

Abba Justus, a Coptic monk, had just one question for the people he encountered: 'What time is it now?' Had I been asked that question on this morning, I would have been able, in one sense, to give a very precise answer. It is 7:50, and the boys have not yet dressed for school; it is 8:20 and these traffic lights are going to make us late. Yet, the more precise this sense of time, the more incapable I was of answering the monk's question. 7:50 is never *now*.

7:50 is an experience of clock time, its specific qualities based on quantification and measurement in minutes, hours, days, years. Clock time is a line of distinct, separate, identical units, and it is this line of past, present and future units that allows us to live nostalgically in the past or future, alienated from where we presently are. When everyday life becomes a matter of achievements and points of arrival – getting to school on time, raising the children successfully – you are no longer *experiencing* life. The everyday becomes either an endless repetition of the past or a desirous rush to arrive at some other time when, you fantasize, life will really begin.

Now let us think about my meeting with love. In such moments, we do not think about time as a repetition of the past or the means for arriving in the future; we are not fighting time or saving it, not trapped in it, not measuring it according to the vibration of quartz atoms. The experience is invigorating and creative because we are living the time of life's flux and flow, a time, indistinguishable from cycles of living and dying, in which everything moves and changes.

Yet it is in this now, when our receptors are open to the roaring waves of life, that we feel held in moments of timelessness, awe-filled moments 'out of time' which we experience through a sense of infinitely tender compassion. There is space here for everything. *Time stood still*, we say, when describing experiences of belonging with whatever changes occur. It is in the moment that we find eternity.

Eternity, on this understanding, is not an exception to the everyday. It is not a long time period and it is not a *forever after* that stretches beyond the end of the measurable line of time. Eternity *is* the everyday. It is experienced as a return to and not an escape from ordinary life. When we are rushing about purposefully, aware of the smallest movements of the hands of our clocks, we are absent from *here* and from *now*. Eternity is the return of these humble life truths.

As Berger notes, no matter how elaborated our measurements and understandings of clock time, there remains hidden within them this sense of the local and cyclical:

> The calculation returns from the astronomic to the local, like a prodigal son. This weakness of the mind, this homesickness which cannot or will not altogether abandon the here-and-now, can be interpreted in two ways. It can be seen as the revealing weakness which proves how lost and impotent man is in the universe; or it can be seen as the vestige . . . of the original truth.
> (1991, p. 37)

Like Berger, we think that the here and now are indispensable truths about the nature of life everyday, but Berger's notion of 'the vestige' cedes too much to the chronological. Eternity is not a survival of an origin but the presence of the origin. It remains the original time without which chronology is inconceivable.

Rather than being the impossibly thin sliver of life designated by a clock time, *now* holds all temporal possibilities. There is room here for all time, but the past is not here a discrete flashback and the future is not a discrete glimpse of what is yet to come. The past and future exist in the eternal as phenomena of the present. In chronological time, the past *was*, but in eternity it *is*. Eternity has no need for vestiges because times are not alienated on an abstract line.

I saw this experience of eternity on the face of the office worker. Although my children were apparently strangers to her, her fond expression showed that she saw in them a deep familiarity that she had forgotten she knew. Perhaps what she saw touched her own first days at school, perhaps it touched her own eagerness and vulnerability, but it did not simply *refer* to these personal experiences. She was not simply *remembering* something from the past, and my children were not simply *symbolizing* something located elsewhere, for even though her look was soft, it was bright and vital and not faraway or nostalgic. There was archaic recognition in her look, but also new and ongoing amazement. Whatever amazed her was present to her, and through her, but also went beyond her and included my children.

Awe, which Durkheim put at the heart of religious experience (1976, p. 416ff), is central to this experience of nowness. The officeworker had been walking along, distracted from the roaring waves of (her) life, when there suddenly swept over her a sense of *this very moment*. In this revitalization of significance, this revelation of the *Ah!* of life, she felt at once a moment of newness and a sense of *I know this already*; *I've always known this*.

Here then we have an experience of repetition – of the *every*day – that differs from the blasé and enervating sense of daily repetition. The eternal feels so alive not because it is an escape from the everyday routines, but because it is *present* to these repetitions! We can think here of Eliade's account of the significance of the eternal return in primitive cultures (and while doing so we should note that 'the primitive' loses its chronological and vestigial sense when understood within Eliade's terms). Citing several examples of rituals celebrating origin myths, Eliade discerns

> the same 'primitive' ontological conception: an object or an act becomes real only insofar as it imitates or repeats an archetype. Thus, reality is acquired solely through repetition or participation: everything that lacks an exemplary model is 'meaningless', i.e. it lacks reality. Men would thus have a tendency to become archetypal and paradigmatic. This tendency may well appear paradoxical, in the sense that the man of a traditional culture sees himself as real only to the extent that he ceases to be himself (for a modern observer) and is satisfied with imitating and repeating the gestures of another. In other words, he sees himself as real, i.e. as 'truly himself', only, and precisely, insofar as he ceases to be so.
>
> (1971, p. 34)

The experience of eternal repetition is creative – original, originary – because it is accompanied by a sense of 'newness': the original takes us back to origins by giving us the sense of 'for the first time'. This is the temporality of love at first sight. This is the original originary eternal love.

Where did this happen?

This discussion of time has already implied that there is a spatial sense that accompanies eternity. The woman looked at my children and felt life revitalize. This implies an undoing of the distance that guarantees the separate existences of the subjects and objects of knowledge in the familiar Hegelian scenario.

To highlight this point, let us take a contrasting example of an everyday encounter, as described in Hegelian terms. 'Hell is other people', Sartre famously claimed, and in *Being and Nothingness,* he locates hell in a public park. He imagines sitting there, in the park, grass and trees at measurable distances around him. Then another man passes:

[I]nstead of a grouping *toward me* of the objects, there is now an orientation *which flees from me* . . . [T]here is a total space which is grouped around the Other, and this space is made with *my space*; there is a regrouping in which I take part but which escapes me, a regrouping of all the objects which people my universe . . . [T]he very quality of the object, [the grass's] deep, raw green is in direct relation to this man. This green turns toward the Other a face which escapes me. I apprehend the relation of the green to the Other as an objective relation, but I can not apprehend the green *as* it appears to the Other. Thus suddenly an object has appeared which has stolen the world from me . . . [I]t appears that the world has a kind of drain hole in the middle of its being and that it is perpetually flowing off through this hole.

(1992, pp. 342–343)

In this account, the world is an array of objects set out in an abstract empty homogenous Euclidean space that is centred on the subject. The other is a thief who steals my world by threatening to turn me into an object of *his* world. In other words, the world is stolen because I cannot be where the other is without losing where I am. The world is his or it is mine: we do not bring the world alive for each other but steal it from one another. Social life is a matter of him *or* me, even though we cannot do without each other. I am here *or* there. I look at him and, rather than revitalization, feel life drain from me.

This is a good description of how I was when terrified that Max's tantrums would steal away my identity as a parent who is capable and lovingly protective, would steal away my program for the day and the week, would steal away my sense of the world as a stage for my projects. There was a distance between Max and me, but it was an empty space that registered opposition rather than difference. Because it threatened me in ways I did not dare admit, even to myself, it was a distance that I would have to appropriate by a masterful display of effective parenting. No wonder there was a self-righteous urgency in my determination: I was indeed out to save the world, *my* world!

Let us compare the Sartrean situation with that set out by Merleau-Ponty. The latter uses the term 'flesh of the world' to remind us of the primal fact that we are made of the same stuff as the world, and that this, for phenomenologists, is how we know: 'Immersed in the visible by his body . . . the see-er does not appropriate what he sees . . . he opens himself to the world . . . [M]y body is caught in the fabric of the world' (1964, pp. 162–163). We know the world with and through our bodies: 'Things arouse in me a carnal formula of their presence' (1964, p. 164). We are in the world, and the world is in us: relational logic reversibly entwines inside and outside:

Since things and my body are made of the same stuff, vision must somehow take place in them . . . 'Nature is on the inside,' says Cezanne. Quality, light, colour, depth, which are there before us, are there only because they awaken an echo in our body and because the body welcomes them.

(1964, p. 164)

The spatial logic set out by Merleau-Ponty was at play this morning for the office worker. What did she see in my children? Nothing! Everything! Where was she positioned, here *or* there? Both! Nowhere! *Who* is she? No *one*! Everyone!

Whatever she recognized, it was not a finite external thing that could be grasped or known once and for all. She recognized no-thing-ness, without being able to define the limits of what she recognized. Feeling part of the world she saw, she *felt* what she saw: the tenderness she felt was a tenderness *of* as well as a tenderness *about*. These are all ways of saying that in this moment of captivation, the woman was no longer an observer of an external world but a mystical participant in vision. In an inner-city street, a busy young woman on her way to work was astonished by a radiant vision of the blooming of life itself.

This discussion implies that the infinite space that is characteristic of eternity arises from the primacy of participation. This is a point also made by the physicists Bohm and Peat:

there is indeed a meaning to a reality that lies outside ourselves but . . . it is necessary that we, too, should be included in an essential way as partici-pators in this reality. Our knowledge of the universe is derived from this act of participation which involves ourselves, our senses, the instruments used in experiments, and the ways we communicate and choose to describe nature.

(2000, p. 55)

The universe is not infinite because it is bigger than anyone can measure. It is infinite because we who would know are part of the 'it' we would know. Infinity, then, is not just endless counting but an inability to even begin counting. Not an immeasurably long way away, infinitude is always *here*, just as it is always *now*, the condition of our belonging to the universe and each other. Infinitude is the fundamental quality of all relations.

Who looked and what was seen?

I have described this everyday incident as an experience of love, and yet I cannot describe the office worker, even though I was looking at her with such interest. I suspect that she would be equally unable to identify Leo, Max and me. What does this tell us? Why do I have such a keen sense of the keen fascination in her look but no sense of her eyes' colour or shape, no sense of what her face looked like? The answer is that my sight had no destination. It did not conclude, in a knowledge claim, when arriving at the objective characteristics of the woman's face. It is not so much that I saw her, as I might see some *thing*, but that I saw *with* her, with her aid, with her eyes.

Levinas puts this well in his account of face-to-face relations:

> You turn yourself toward the Other as toward an object when you see a nose, eyes, a forehead, a chin, and you can describe them. When one observes the colour of the eyes one is not in social relationship with the Other. The relation with the face can surely be dominated by perception, but what is specifically the face is what cannot be reduced to that.
>
> There is first the very uprightness of the face, its upright exposure, without defence. The skin of the face is that which stays most naked, most destitute. It is most naked, though with a decent nudity. It is the most destitute also: there is an essential poverty in the face. . . .
>
> The face is . . . signification without context. I mean that the Other, in the rectitude of his face, is not a character within a context . . . a professor at the Sorbonne, a Supreme Court justice, son of so-and-so . . . Here, to the contrary, the face is meaning all by itself. You are you. In this sense one can say that the face is not 'seen.' It is what cannot become a content, which your thought would embrace; it is uncontainable, it leads you beyond.
>
> (1985, pp. 85–87)

When Levinas says 'you are you', he is not associating you-ness with a self-contained identity. The word *you* is like the words *now* and *here*: it indicates a presence that can be experienced as a whole but never known as a totality, never defined, contained, represented *in absentia*. I can only use the word *you* to you, with you, in the course of a meeting with you. It is a participatory word that emerges from meeting, as part of a relationship. Whereas I am master of what I discern as the objective characteristics of the other, and probably prefer to list these characteristics without the other being present (for their presence would bias my objectivity), it is your presence that puts the word *you* in my mouth.

Within the sort of relation that Levinas is discussing, the other is at once different to me and the same as me, and there is a mysterious incapacity to say where the boundaries of this sameness and difference fall. The other fills me with wonder, yet this wonder teaches me about the strangeness I find in myself. In relation, the boundaries between inside and outside are suspended, making it impossible to clearly distinguish entities, showing how everything belongs together, is implicated in everything else.

This is the point of Buber's discussion of the difference between I-It and I-Thou, which, Buber says, are the two primary words, pertaining to different forms of relation:

> If *Thou* is said, the *I* of the combination *I-Thou* is said along with it.
> If *It* is said, the *I* of the combination *I-It* is said along with it. . . .

The life of human beings is not passed in the sphere of transitive verbs alone. It does not exist in virtue of activities alone which have some *thing* for their object.

I perceive something. I am sensible of something. . . . This and the like together establish the realm of *It*.

But the realm of the *Thou* has a different basis.

When *Thou* is spoken, the speaker has no thing for his object. . . . *Thou* has no bounds. . . .

The relation to the *Thou* is direct. No system of ideas, no foreknowledge, and no fancy intervene between *I* and *Thou*. . . . No aim, no lust, and no anticipation intervene between *I* and *Thou*. . . .

(1958, pp. 3–12)

These accounts by Levinas and Buber of presence – of nothingness, nakedness, destitution, primitiveness – are of great conceptual significance, for they remind us of a relational domain that cannot be discussed in the familiar concepts of Hegelian thought: viz. subject, object, identity, negation, desire, mastery, movement, self-certainty, representation. In the meeting, there are no identifiable subjects, objects and desires. It is not that these are transcended or negated: there is room for all these possibilities but at the same time it is clear that no identification can be adequate, that no identities stand alone, that none can serve as a conclusion of knowing. What I know in the eternity of the meeting is infinite, which is not a huge amount of or even an endless amount of knowledge but a knowledge of the mystery, the no-thing-ness, of the whole.

Levinas' account of face-to-face relations can also be located within contemporary discussions of vision. In contrast with Jay's (1993, pp. 556–560) reading of Levinas, we take him to be saying that there are different ways of looking. Whereas the Sartrean look, for example, is a powerful, objectifying gaze, a face-to-face encounter implies a dialogic way of looking. In other words, Levinas' meeting has a similar logic to that of Merleau-Ponty's entwinement of vision and the visible (1964, pp. 162–164).

How do I know?

Knowledge of relations is only available through participation. It is not an alienated knowledge *about* but a knowledge *with* and *through*. As Buber notes, 'I [cannot] . . . describe the form which meets me, but only body it forth. And yet I behold it, splendid in the radiance of what confronts me' (1958, p. 10). It is the logic that the Persian poet Rumi had in mind when he tried to explain how you learn of the silent person's hidden nature:

I sit in front of him in silence,
and set up a ladder made of patience,

and if in his presence a language from beyond joy
and beyond grief begins to pour from my chest,
I know that his soul is as deep and bright
as the star Canopus rising over Yemen.
And so when I start speaking a powerful right arm
of words sweeping down, I know him from what I say
and how I say it, because there's a window open
between us, mixing the night air of our beings.

(1995, p. 30)

This is how I know the office worker, and how she knows my sons and me. We know because we met, because her look captivated me just as the sight of my children transfixed her.

Such knowledge is not masterful. When the naked vulnerability she accepted from Max and Leo was given to me, it returned me to a presence that is deeper than the finite and deeper than any things or names or identities that I might describe. For an amazed moment of recognition, I experienced a direct understanding of mystery and infinity: I knew the mysterious infinity of this woman, these children, this world, and therefore, because these encounters kept showing me more about myself, of me. We are often afraid of poverty and destitution, thinking of them as conditions of weakness and incapacity, yet such humility is the only way to know the mystery of the life in which we participate. This primitive poverty brings riches. These riches are not ours, but we share in them.

This discussion changes the way we might think about love. While Hegelian terms work well in discussions of desire (see Game & Metcalfe 1996), they are not able to talk of love without reducing it to a mirror-play of identities. This everyday experience of love at first sight suggests that love is not a personal matter. I do not love someone because of who they are: because of the total set of their attributes. I love them *just because*, regardless of who they are. I love not their personal qualities and accomplishments but their tender vulnerability, their nothingness, with which and through which I experience the wholeness that accompanies the infinite. Love is never exclusive but always infinitely inclusive.

These are not easy issues to discuss in academic discourse. As Steiner observes in *Real Presences*, a book on art as annunciation:

To try and tell of what happens inside oneself as one affords vital welcome and habitation to the presences in art, music and literature is to risk the whole gamut of muddle and embarrassment. . . . Structuralist semiotics and deconstruction are expressions of a culture and society which 'play it cool'.

(1989, p. 178)

So let us not play it cool. We are saying that the principle of love is angelic, that the nothingness we encounter in the meeting that is love is annunciatory, an announcement and manifestation of our primitive infinitude (see Serres 1995, Metcalfe & Game 2002). Love is what connects us with, allows us to belong to, the universe. Without love, we are alienated and only capable of alienated knowledge. Without love, we are trapped outside the vitality of life. Without love, the everyday is a time and space we must get through to arrive at the otherworld: the fantasy time and space where life really happens. With love, we return to the everyday and find there – here, now – the wonders of life. As Buber puts it: 'man dwells in his love. That is no metaphor, but the actual truth' (1958, p. 14).

A vision of the street

In *Preludes*, T. S. Eliot talks of having 'a vision of the street as the street hardly understands'. In commuter traffic of tramping feet and evening newspapers and short square fingers stuffing pipes, Eliot feels something else, though the word 'something' is not quite right:

> I am moved by fancies that are curled
> Around these images, and cling:
> The notion of some infinitely gentle
> Infinitely suffering thing.

Through giving himself over to the details of particular moments in the street, Eliot senses the endless compassion of the eternal and infinite: the universal acceptance that holds together and holds apart this newspaper reader, these tramping feet, this pipe-smoker. In a similar way, the fleeting detail of two little boys struggling with shoulder straps gave an office worker a vision of eternity and infinity.

Theoretically, these 'details' can be understood in the relational way that Deleuze and Guattari speak of a specific body or form:

> There is a mode of individuation very different from that of a person, subject, or substance. We reserve the name *haecceity* for it. A season, a winter, an hour, a date have a perfect individuality lacking nothing, even though this individuality is different from that of a thing or a subject.
>
> (1987, p. 261)

Deleuze and Guattari make the important point that it is not a matter of either/ or: a relational logic insists that any 'individuality' is simultaneously thing *and* no-thing, finite *and* infinite (1987, p. 262)

Two children putting on schoolbags may seem scarcely worth attention, but, in a way that was both mundane and inspired, this moment changed my world. I had not seen these children when I had been busy looking for trouble from Max; I had not seen them in their particularity, but only as objective reflections of my subjecthood. However, the beautiful lively vulnerable fearless openness of this woman's look swept away my irritations and purposes and self-consciousness, and gave me a vision of the heartbreaking beauty of children struggling with their schooling (the heartbreaking beauty of this woman, of these passers-by, of me, struggling to be good people). These boys, so nervous, so open, so keen, with their match-stick legs and with, at this age, no self-conscious swagger in the constant dishevelment of their uniforms, these boys seemed to *bloom* with the tender freshness of life. We talk of the bloom of a rose or a peach, referring to the down on the skin that affirms the swelling life inside the flower or fruit, but we also see this blooming when, with soft eyes, we're amazed by the impossibly tender hair on the skin of children, by the vulnerable eagerness of their softly freckled faces.

Of course, I could not see my children like this without seeing the world afresh. When my perspective was lowered by my fear of a tantrum, I had not noticed the glorious open blueness of the sky or the vital greenness of the street trees. This was the first sunny morning after days of rain, and the world was clean and full of promise. As Max and Leo and I walked to school, hand in hand, I could feel the world smiling at us, with us, through us.

References

Berger, J. (1991) *And Our Faces, My Heart, Brief as Photos*, Vintage, New York.

Bohm, D. & Peat, F. D. (2000) *Science, Order and Creativity*, Routledge, London.

Buber, M. (1958) *I and Thou*, Scribner, New York.

Buber, M. (1966) *The Way of Response*, Schocken Books, New York.

Buber, M. (2002) *Between Man and Man*, Routledge, London.

Deleuze, G. & Guattari, F. (1987) *A Thousand Plateaus*, University of Minnesota Press, Minneapolis and London.

Durkheim, E. (1976) *Elementary Forms of the Religious Life*, Allen & Unwin, London.

Eliade, M. (1971) *The Myth of Eternal Return*, Princeton University Press, Princeton, NJ.

Game, A. & Metcalfe, A. (1996) *Passionate Sociology*, Sage, London.

Jay, M. (1993) *Downcast Eyes: The Denigration of Vision in Twentieth-Century French Thought*, University of California Press, Berkeley, CA.

Levinas, E. (1985) *Ethics and Infinity*, Duquesne University Press, Pittsburgh.

Merleau-Ponty, M. (1964) *The Primacy of Perception*, Northwestern University Press, Evanston.

Metcalfe, A. & Game, A. (2002) *The Mystery of Everyday Life*, Federation Press, Sydney.

Rumi (1995) 'The night air', in *The Essential Rumi*, ed. Coleman Barks, Penguin, Ringwood.

Sartre, J.-P. (1992) *Being and Nothingness*, Washington Square Press, New York.

Serres, M. (1995) *Angels*, Flammarion, Paris.

Steiner, G. (1989) *Real Presences*, Faber, London.

Melissa Gregg

A MUNDANE VOICE

This essay offers strategies of speaking and studying 'the mundane' as a means to inaugurate an interventionist politics in cultural studies. Using Meaghan Morris's example of anecdotal and colloquial address, a mundane voice is shown to situate and contextualize our understanding of major concepts circulating in international theory, and broaden the audience for academic debate. Studies of 'everyday life' have been hampered by a too-close affinity with hegemonic structures of knowledge production, requiring further gestures of parochialism to hasten a speaking position aware of its own partiality and limitations. Attention to the singularity or 'this-ness' of a cultural site humbles the tasks cultural studies can perform, introducing some curiosity to what we think we know about the cultures from which we speak. Reflecting on the fate of Michel de Certeau's work in the boom period of cultural studies' expansion, the paper suggests that cultural studies' radical potential can be expanded if we are not inflected by preconceptions about what defines politics, especially against the fashions of intellectual commodification. Morris creates affective connections between past, present and future political concerns: a different temporality for political investment than the cycles of electoral models, or the dictates of commodity culture, afford, and one that cultural studies might still learn to adopt.

Keywords   mundane; Meaghan Morris; speaking position; anecdote; cultural studies; politics

Prologue: bleeding sail (to no avail)

It goes like this: walking to my office, the anti-war outcries on noticeboards, pavements and lampposts multiply in synchronicity with the advancing front line. After a seminar, I wait forever for a bus home, but the latest peace rally has the CBD grid-locked. Flicking on the TV news, the Sydney Opera House screams 'NO WAR' from its highest sail (in a 'terrorist'-wary western capital city, two nobodies scale the national landmark to make their point in blood-red paint). I am feeling useless. With a deadline looming, I have got to work. The protests cannot beckon any more. I am trapped, for the moment, in the mundane.

Isn't everybody? Here I want to contemplate the usefulness of speaking and studying 'the mundane', on the one hand, as a preferable alternative to the

Cultural Studies Vol. 18, No. 2/3 March/May 2004, pp. 363–383
ISSN 0950-2386 print/ISSN 1466-4348 online   © 2004 Taylor & Francis Ltd
http://www.tandf.co.uk/journals   DOI: 10.1080/0950238042000201563

R Routledge
Taylor & Francis Group

way 'the everyday' gets figured in dominant models of cultural studies practice; on the other, as a means to materialize the potential Massumi (2002, p. 256) lately encourages, from a 'proudly, loudly' political cultural studies. Voicing the mundane is a means to puncture some of the posturing that haunts academic work, a contextualizing measure that can enhance the modest tasks cultural studies performs. I do not want to reject 'the everyday' as a valuable conceptual device (as this issue testifies, it stimulates such a strong body of thought as to survive any such attack), rather my aim is to draw to light some problems with the way theories circulate in an international academic milieux. It is my hope that a consideration of our, and others' mundane dispositions might bring back a kind of parochialism to intellectual debate, and in so doing introduce some curiosity about what we think we know as theorists (Sedgwick & Frank 1995).

My anxiety at writing through a period of international turmoil is a condition so familiar to cultural studies as to be mundane itself – something that Morris, following Tony Bennett, calls the temptation of a 'spiral' form of political engagement: 'always swinging between activist desire and angst about its own effects, it has the form of precisely the doomed circularity that is known in everyday language as running round like a headless chook' (1992a, p. 466). Countering this dilemma in her own work, Morris introduces a different temporality for cultural studies' political goals, and as I will argue here, provides an exemplary method to speak and study the mundane. Her style of intervention invests in a longer time frame for social change than cycles of electoral politics typically afford. At the same time, it remains wary of the use-by-dates and limited spheres of applicability of intellectual fashions. Morris's idiosyncratic techniques – the use of anecdote, an affective tone, a colloquial focus – remind critics of their own place in the culture under investigation, and challenge still prevalent assumptions which extol detached intellectual discourse. It is a speaking position convinced of the unique role cultural studies can play in a democratic society if it takes the task of 'what counts as politics, to whom' as the basis of *its* everyday. At moments like these, when the intensity of political activity around us seems overbearing, and the monopoly on what counts *as* political is claimed by both Left and Right, this very specific undertaking assumes heightened importance.

Attention to the mundane humbles the tasks cultural studies can perform. It reminds writers to consider questions of audience (who does this work address? who does it leave out? what are the effects?) and reveals the decisions behind sites chosen for study. With the mundane as the origin and subject of analysis, we can recognize when writers neglect bits of culture that seem less interesting, less radical or ill-fitting their preferred interpretive models. Beginning with the aim of rendering legible new political performances – what I claim is part of cultural studies' epistemological and political value (see Gregg 2004) – inverts the practice of applying political theory *to* everyday life. It creates a means to expand what constitutes politics if we are not inflected by preconceptions. Focused as it is on the places where abstractions (meaning here, imposed ideas of politics) must eventually land, the mundane lends an honesty and concreteness to intellectual work.

Underpinning my concerns here is a belief that structures for intellectual practice must respond to and ameliorate the effects of economic change. In terms of cultural studies' relationship to globalization, I want the idea of the mundane to inject some much needed parochialism into academic work. Now, parochialism has some bad press, especially the kind Morris herself describes as characterizing conceptual debate. 'One consequence of the mundane globalization immediately affecting intellectuals', she writes, is 'the indignant parochialism of assuming that you always already *know* the political import of this or that product or practice' (Morris 1993a, p. 42). I agree with Morris that this kind of assumed knowledge 'will not be very helpful in the future' (1993a, p. 42), and that one of the best ways to counter it is to use the limitations of our situated speaking positions more productively. It is precisely because we seem destined to share a theoretical vocabulary internationally (which is not to say globally) that we need to work harder to explain how particular concepts work in the contexts from which we write and speak. In an internet-wired, international conference-attending, US-led publishing network of interaction, pivotal terms and theories are too often taken for granted in cultural studies' everyday. We need means to habitualize self-reflexivity in our theoretical assumptions and investigative practices, especially if our goal is to widen the audience for these concerns in the future.

Speaking the mundane

In *The Pirate's Fiancée*, Morris (1988, p. 7) describes the matter of creating a speaking position as 'a problem of rhetoric, of developing enunciative strategies . . . precisely in relation to the cultural and social conventions that make speaking difficult or impossible for *women*'. Histories of academic practice, which naturalize particular forms of speech in priority over others, create a legacy that is hard to combat: by definition, disciplinarity renders impotent other forms of speaking and knowing. In de Certeau's (1984, pp. 138–139) estimation, the power of this 'scriptural economy' is its capacity to treat language as 'a disorderly nature that has to be cultivated':

> The mastery of language guarantees and isolates a new power, a 'bourgeois' power, that of making history and fabricating languages. This power, which is essentially scriptural . . . defines the code governing socio-economic promotion and dominates, regulates, or selects according to its norms all those who do not possess this mastery of language.

Attuned to this selective discourse, *The Pirate's Fiancée* grapples with, although ultimately rejects, the legacy of European philosophy implicit in Certeau's description, to the extent that it cannot recognize the new framework for knowledge feminism demands.[1] Morris is not content with accommodating gestures:

> there is little to be gained from projects to disrupt the discourse of philosophy by inscribing difference if and when such a project comes down to reiterating a single, fundamental thesis held to be always usefully true of all philosophy ('it's phallogocentric . . .') – and to countering philosophical discourse by maintaining, from place to place and text to text, the rigidity of a 'different' *style*.
>
> (1988a, p. 102)

Merely 'allowing' women to contribute to philosophical discourse is not enough. According to this perspective, obeisance to disciplinary convention entails an 'immediate loss of political (and rhetorical) flexibility for feminist interventions in different institutional and discursive contexts' (1988a, p. 102).

With its comparatively loose disciplinary demands, Morris's work in cultural studies explores just these possibilities for feminist intervention. Her chosen methodology renders transparent the assumptions behind her speaking position, cognisant of the conventional ways these factors are elided in the scriptural economy of academic address. Trained in French, and practiced in a number of writing applications, Morris brings a certain formalism to her brand of cultural studies.[2] Explaining her use of anecdotes, what I am claiming is her principal device to voice the mundane, she claims they offer unique properties for argumentation:

> They are oriented futuristically towards the construction of a precise, local, and *social* discursive context, of which the anecdote then functions as a *mise en abyme*. That is to say, anecdotes for me are not expressions of personal experience, but allegorical expositions of a model of the way the world can be said to be working. So anecdotes need not be true stories, but they must be functional in a given exchange.
>
> (Morris 1988/1996, p. 150)

Anecdotes offer a discursive space in which a singular idea can be positioned, offered and demonstrated. As an 'image within an image', the *mise en abyme* corresponds with what Margaret Morse (1998), following Greimas, calls 'the enunciative fallacy'. This is the understanding that a fictitious certainty governs any speech act between an 'I', 'here and now' and a 'you'. In recognition of this fallacy, Morris employs a genre that patently avoids claims to authenticity, but creates 'first-order *simulations* of the speaking subject, and the time and place of enunciation' (Morse 1998, p. 12). The failure of any attempt to communicate pure intention through discourse is therefore acknowledged, alongside the admission that simulations of such a relationship can be, and are functional.

A common literary device, in philosophy the allegorical mode is generated by conditions in the objective world, rather than the subjective intention of the writer (Buck-Morss 1989, p. 229).[3] In Morris's use, there's a little of both: from a literary point of view multi-layering affords an oblique means to mount an argument. It is a way of creatively figuring what would otherwise appear as a dense and prosaic discussion, to make the complexities of cultural debates more attractive to a broader audience. Yet, the implications of Buck-Morss' assessment, that allegory conveys something of the status of the objective world, suggests Morris's preference for anecdote might respond to the way our experience is shaped in postmodern times. Certainly anecdotes afford a refining mechanism for Morris, they bring down to a manageable level the complexity of culture, so that a specific point can be forwarded. They offer a way out of what troubles her about cultural studies' '"fraught space" of ethical grandiloquence': 'in which massive, world-historical problems are debated on such a level of generality that they cannot possibly be solved, and posed in ways which do not, will not and cannot ever connect to agencies by which actual social futures may be given a "definite shape"' (Morris 1992a, p. 466). Anecdotes only pretend to speak from a clearly delimited context. In Morris's case, 'oriented futuristically', they try to create affective connections between those in the past, present and future.

Uncle Billy's television

A neat example of this speaking position comes in the brief article, 'Uncle Billy, Tina Turner and Me' (1998a). In this piece, Morris relates a succession of anecdotes about watching television. This is one:

> TV for me came gently into a way of life that (I now realize) had barely changed since the Depression. By the 1960s, I was living with my other Nanna in East Maitland. She chopped wood to warm the bath, stoked coal to heat the stove, hauled washing through the wringer and fed the chooks before breakfast. Most of our neighbours did. At some stage, my Great-Uncle Billy bought a TV, and Nanna and I would go over the road to watch it.
>
> My main memory of this, however, is not the set or a show but a *smell*. Like our own, Uncle Billy's house was old (my great-grandfather had owned it), dark (blinds were never opened), musty in parts (front rooms where people had died), and it smelt faintly of the flood-mud caked into our ceilings by the 1955 Flood. Uncle Billy sometimes smelt, too – of old age, and ancient singlets. Nanna perfumed her hankie in self-defence and wore

flowery talcum powder. It all mixed in with the sweet scent of coal that drifted in on the breeze every evening.

(1998a, p. 116)

A sense of warmth guides this description. Safety and contentment seem to underwrite the scene, conveying the knowing satisfaction of a childhood world just big enough to comprehend. This is a rural culture of self-reliance. Nothing here is touched by an 'outside', whether it's Nanna's routines, Uncle Billy's singlets or the cloistered house. The words used have particular impressions. TV came 'gently' into this space, as if one is caressed by experience, time is of such a negotiable pace. Note the different ways events are individualized: the enumeration of tasks, the various smells. Morris notices the different ways they each watch TV: 'Nanna and I were into narrative: we hated missing the dialogue, and shared a passion for analysing character even on spectacle shows like "Bandstand". Uncle Billy was a raging formalist. All he cared about was "snow", and he'd lumber up every five minutes to play with the reception' (1998a, p. 116). Details offer recognition of so many micro-histories: the length of time the house has stayed in the family, the passing of ancestors, the legacy of natural disasters (major moments in local history) and the Depression (significant to broad-scale history). Combined with this is the smell of coal wafting in, a signifier for a representative kind of working-class town and a culture soon to be surpassed with the kind of technological advances television represents. These densely packaged recollections provide a way of figuring a commentary on the increased temporalities of the present. True to her claim, Morris's anecdotes are oriented futuristically – returning to the moment of television's introduction highlights the disrupted, multiple times and stimuli currently surrounding us.

To this end, Morris's anecdotes accord with Massumi's challenge to cultural studies, of moving away from abstract assumptions to do with an aspiring collectivity (the 'constituency' on which conventional political theories rely) towards the potential offered in writing 'singularity'. It is what Massumi (2002, p. 222) calls 'this-ness': 'an unreproducible being-only-itself'. In the more approachable terms Morris herself offers, it is 'a historical analysis attuned both to socio-economic contexts and to the individuating local intensities' (Morris 1992a, p. 4). These 'local intensities' come out when we attend to the mundane. Anecdotes figure a singular instance of how 'this' happens *here*, which does not preclude other experiences, but acts as an example of 'how the world can be said to be working' in this context. It is a voice that does not pretend to speak for others, conscious of its status as a simulated enunciative act.

Morris presents a difficult argument in the 'Uncle Billy' essay. Against dominant theories of communication – that see viewers either as 'passive, uncritical sponges', or instead claim 'that no one is ever mesmerized, fooled or drugged by watching television' (1998a, p. 118) – Morris shows the insufficiency of blanket condemnations or celebrations of television. People come to the medium with different histories, hopes and agendas, she claims: 'Watching TV is a volatile business, insignificant at times and intensely emotional at others' (1998a, p. 118). A later anecdote sees Morris driving down a local street on Grand Final Day: listening to Australian sports satirists Roy Slaven and HG Nelson call the Rugby League Grand Final on radio, she recollects the code's latest TV advertising campaign, in which American singer Tina Turner appears as the new face promoting football for a more diverse audience.[4] Despite an early love of the game, until this point TV football's dominant discourse had seemed 'too White and Male and Ugly' (1998a, p. 118) for Morris to enjoy – its dominant imaginary 'an ocker in an armchair with a sixpack'. But with Tina Turner as mascot, what can be imagined for the code is re-articulated: coupled with Roy and HG's tongue-in-cheek commentary, TV football now seems keen to incorporate and encourage more histories and interests than one, overly masculine target market. This snapshot of a moment, related by anecdote, gives Morris an overwhelming 'desire for other people's stories': she wants to hear other narratives, of people's pasts, their families, their lounge rooms – how all these lives have been impacted by social change. Morris craves histories that brush against the ones that mainstream accounts allow (accounts of television's penetration give her a 'sense of a vaguely faulty memory' (1998a, p. 115) – as if her experience should somehow be different to what it was). This is a an urge to hear how cultural changes land in the context of people's everyday, what I am calling a desire for the mundane. As a 'set of events mediating relationships between people in particular situations', television here figures a different approach to narrating history: an approach that speaks and studies the banal ways people negotiate their lives in meaningful ways. Hearing the football commentary drifting from other people's car stereos that day makes Morris wonder 'why passages of joy and humour between diverse strangers can't also be creative of "history"'. Roy and HG remind Morris of Tina Turner on TV and, in turn, that initial moment when television 'gently' entered her life. For the first time since those nights in the lounge room at Great Uncle Billy's, Morris concludes the essay wondering 'what *he* saw' (1998a, p. 119).

Anecdotes allow Morris to create a subtle analysis of the multiple temporalities and different histories people bring to their uses of culture. Morris argues that we need to hear the mundane stories behind people's approaches to media, to counter the celebratory rhetoric that often inflects broad-scale histories of cultural change. Cultural studies provides a way to find these counter-histories, to make theoretical appraisals more inclusive and reflective of reality. Mixing personal, anecdotal and colloquial material, Morris brings us in contact with people, making us curious about their different experiences. Her ability to mobilize an affective connection between strangers, families, the present and the past is a key part of her interventionist style.

'Exemplification activates detail', Massumi writes, 'The success of the example hinges on the details. Every little one matters . . . Each detail is like another example embedded in it' (Massumi 2002, p. 18). In the Uncle Billy essay, each successive anecdote unveils another instance of how the world is working. When a 'cognitive map' (Jameson 1991) for orientation is increasingly elusive, each simulated recollection contributes to a greater project in sense making. The essay brings to mind Benjamin's sense of allegory, identified by Buck-Morss 'as the activity of the ponderer, whose reflective attitude is one of recollection':

> The memory of the ponderer holds sway over the disordered mass of dead knowledge. Human knowledge is piecework to it in a particularly pregnant sense: namely as the heaping up of arbitrarily cut up pieces, out of which one puts together a puzzle . . . The allegoricist reaches now here, now there, into the chaotic depths that his knowledge places at his disposal, grabs an item out, holds it next to another, and sees whether they fit.
>
> (Buck-Morss 1989, p. 241)

In the contemporary intellectual climate, however, this appealing project is more difficult to manifest. There is simply no time for pondering in an academic job; sound bite demands and e-mail overload thwart the possibility of a reflective attitude. Morris takes seriously the difficulty and responsibility of producing cultural theory under these conditions. In this vein, and against Massumi's (2002, p. 18) encouragement of 'inattention as a writing tool', Morris's anecdotes are concerted responses to the difficulty of creating a speaking position in today's intellectual environment. Inattention might be a fruitful option when wedded to a book contract, but Morris's work remains mindful of the many ways others are still struggling for a space from which to speak.

It is this mindfulness that contrasts more celebratory models of cultural studies politics evident in the 'boom' period of the 1980s and 1990s (Morris 1992a). Here I want to clarify Morris's mode of speaking and studying the mundane as an alternative to the way theories of everyday life land *in* cultural studies of this period rather than emanating *from* the culture being studied. As Morris's 'Banality in cultural studies' (1988/1996) shows, incorporating a few terms from a writer's broader concerns enacts a further metonymical shift when what is assumed of the theory is then used to make arguments about whole societies. Employed in the service of long-term projects, I will venture that Morris's own theoretical forays survive the publishing boom due to their recognition of the shortcomings of any number of selective discourses when positioned in a mundane context. Taking the fate of de Certeau's work as an example, I then want to highlight the still pressing problem of reification in cultural theory: the way that 'commonsense' interpretations of major concepts come to substitute for an entire *oeuvre*. To me this remains a fundamental issue in the international dissemination of theory, not the least because of the exorbitant market for 'readers' in themed areas and 'introductions' to key thinkers.

These trends in marketing and dissemination require strategic methods of response to counter the now evident trend towards commodification even in intellectual work.

Postmodern problems

In her widely cited essay 'Banality in cultural studies', Morris critiques post-modern theory and cultural studies' absorption of its political tenets for silencing other versions of political performance which might threaten the hegemony of postmodern diagnoses. Neither project 'leaves much place for an unequivocally pained, unambivalently discontented, or *aggressive* theorizing subject' Morris writes:

> It isn't just negligence. There is an active process going on in both of dis-crediting – by direct dismissal (Baudrillard), or covert inscription as Other (cultural studies) – the voices of grumpy feminists and cranky leftists ('Frankfurt School' can do duty for both). To discredit such voices is, as I understand it, one of the immediate political functions of the current boom in cultural studies (as distinct from the intentionality of projects invested by it). To discredit a voice is something very different from displacing an analysis which has become outdated, or revising a strategy which no longer serves its purpose.
>
> (1988/1996, p. 160)

Morris's affective address brings an urgency to her complaint. She intervenes to pinpoint a moment when feminism, as one instance of an alternative politics, gets written out of the picture. The trouble postmodernism poses for Morris is that it can exist as an intellectual debate without reference to feminism, a political intrusion that might question its assumptions. The sheer ease with which such a radical and important historical movement can be forgotten reveals the manner in which intellectual histories are constantly subject to contestation.[5] For Morris, feminism in 1980s cultural studies is not an unfortu-nate casualty of history so much as a threat written out of a jealously guarded academic conversation. The political practices postmodern theories do recog-nize and celebrate – 'resistance' and 'subversion' in the face of a monolithic, globalized system of capital – are therefore argued to have gained inflated precedence in cultural studies. As such, the discourse gaining legitimacy with cultural studies' publishing success contributes to the process of disregarding feminist approaches. Taking the work of Chambers and Fiske as representative, Morris questions the way that these writers reinscribe the distinction between 'participant' and 'observer' that feminist cultural studies previously helped dissolve. In Chambers' and Fiske's models, she argues, the writers immerse themselves within a culture in the spirit of ethnography, and apply cultural studies theories (often formulated in a foreign context) to make sense of the practices they observe. However, Morris detects a sense of mastery attending the use of maxims like 'pleasure through resistance', the political ambivalence of youth and the subversive consumption practices of urban subcultures. What is problematic is the way the critic here ends up the conduit for some pure and relatable intention of the subjects being studied – in Chambers' case, metropolitan youth; in Fiske's, the wider public of whatever country he happens to be in during his 'intercontinental wanderings' – as if the writer is somehow able to distance himself from the culture he is describing.[6]

The critical significance of Morris's allegorical mode here becomes evident. In her words, allegory is a 'convenient way' to 'frame a critique of a narrowly *metonymic* argument quite prevalent in cultural studies today, whereby a singular form in the built environment ("*the*" tower) is taken, by a process of inflation and conflation, to be emblematic not only of a general condition of culture . . . but also of a historic intellectual "place" of enunciation' (1992b, p. 3). It is the self-consciousness lacking in these studies of space that is objectionable: the subject of analysis, coupled with the form of address that authorizes its epistemological value, cannot recognize the selectivity at the heart of each project. Both naturalize a detached and exclusionary means of speaking and studying culture while claiming to relate others' practices as subversive. This playfulness, which changes nothing in either the academic or 'everyday' culture being studied, is for Morris inadequate 'to the problems of committed intellectual practice in the places that I, at least, inhabit' (1992b, p. 3).

For Morris, the 'consumption-as-resistance' line of thought is a poor substitute for the intellectual richness of immersing oneself within a study. This is the significant difference cultural studies brings to the academy, the realization that acknowledging one's own partiality and attraction to the culture being studied can bring new insights to cultural thought (see CCCS 1978, McRobbie 1980, Frow & Morris 1993). However, 'the choice of the term "ethnography"' in Chambers' and Fiske's models 'emphasizes a possible "ethnic" gap between the cultural student and the culture studied' – suggesting the observer is somehow not implicated in the same processes as the study's participants. 'The "understanding" and "encouraging" [writing] subject may share some aspects of that culture,' argues Morris, 'but *in the process of interrogation and analysis* is momentarily located outside it' (1988/1996, p. 157). Such a perspective brings paternalism to cultural studies' assumptions. It reinforces a hierarchy of the academic-as-expert, and the punk youth, the beach goer or the housewife as the subject in need of explanation. The adamant distancing Chambers and Fiske bring to the task of relating others' everyday pleasure serves to discount the value of feminist studies, which demonstrably benefit from situating one's 'self' squarely within the analysis (Probyn 1993, 2004; see also Steedman 1986, 1997).

The fate of de Certeau

Yet the tendencies manifest in Chambers' and Fiske's work are only symptomatic of a broader problem Morris identifies in cultural studies of the same period, which is the way European theory is used to denote 'signs of theoretical-ness' and 'signs of audience' rather than contributing to the epistemological usefulness of a study (see Morris 1992a, p. 477).[7] The concepts of 'resistance' and 'subversion' significantly impacted cultural theory as de Certeau's work became available during the 1980s. They offered radical critics the means to read ordinary citizens' use of public space as filled with implicit political potential against the rigid grid of experience imposed by dominant discourses. De Certeau emphasized the many coping strategies, the empowering art of timing behind people's efforts at practicing place. However, by the end of the 1980s, certain sentences from *The Practice of Everyday Life* were increasingly invoked towards uncritical, politically ambivalent ends, shorn of the sensitivity and breadth of cultural examples evident in his own writing.

Morris is not alone in her suspicion of a cultural studies politics heavily dependent on European theory. Bennett also sees 'the limitations of rummaging through the past for aspects of carnival whose mutated echoes can be made to be heard in the present' (cited in Barcan 1995, p. 83). More recently, Barcan claims that 'if the detection of subversive moments became a frequent analytical endpoint, especially in analyses of "the popular", it also eventually begged the question of the ends or purposes of such subversions, and indeed of cultural analysis itself' (1995, p. 83). De Certeau's broader methodology was disregarded by those willing to sustain a burgeoning publishing market for cultural studies.[8] One element of his project became overly inflated, so that the idea of 'consumption as resistance' became a principal signifier for the field of cultural studies itself.

This is a pivotal moment in which the definition of politics becomes dangerously tied to the symbolic power of one concept. 'The everyday' is seen as *the* definition of the political, which not only barbarizes de Certeau – not to mention Lefebvre – but it also closes down cultural studies' potential to include so much more than this. Furthermore, and this is where Massumi's latest work is instructive, 'Where has the potential for change gone? How does a body perform its way out of a definitional framework that is not only responsible for its very "construction", but seems to prescript every possible signifying and countersignifying move as a selection from a repertoire of possible permutations on a limited set of predetermined terms? How can the grid itself change?' (Massumi 2002, p. 3). Contentment with 'the everyday' as the necessarily subversive limits the possibility of more radical demands from cultural theory. Thinking back to Morris's use of anecdotes to orient a project futuristically, projects that relate theory *to* culture do little to intervene in its reproduction. This particular use of de Certeau's 'praxis as enunciation' appears to be 'a sign of ethical consent to the political *status quo*' (Morris 1992a, p. 466).

In the repetitive studies of the boom period, cultural sites and subversive practices are invoked without the broader intention of seeking to change culture for the better:[9]

> To me there's something unpleasant about the picture of safe, happy, beaming academics spotting signs of subversiveness here and there, and patting 'the people' on the head. *Myths of Oz*, by Fiske, Bob Hodge and Graeme Turner is a local book that seems to me to partake of this kind of normalizing paternalism, in part because the direct transportation of the critique of 'high culture' from Britain (where it matters a lot) to Australia (where I don't think high culture matters much at all) skews the rhetoric of the text towards a defence of, indeed an apologia for, the kind of mainstream white male culture . . . I've always experienced as massively dominant, and sometimes oppressive.
>
> (Morris 1990, p. 475)

The assuredness of the male academic speaking position assumed in the work of Chambers, Fiske, Turner and others of the period is troubling because it can't adequately recognize its own complicity with the hegemonic culture under investigation. While their sites for analysis may reflect local experience (such as the pub, the beach or the home in *Myths of Oz*), what is equally important to analyse are unacknowledged factors such as the gendered and racialized relations these same locations yield. It is the extent to which the experiences of women differ in these sites, precisely the factors leading to women's exclusion or exceptional treatment, that warrants interrogation for Morris. Her argument asks whether an elegy for these sites constitutes the most necessary task for cultural studies at this point in history. A project centred on those places most implicated in perpetuating the male dominance of so many leisure practices serves to silence feminist insights (a criticism that, unfortunately, Graeme Turner's response to Morris still does not appreciate, when he reads her critique as anti-populist).[10] The popularity of leisure practices does not make them, or discussions of them, egalitarian. Morris's interventions make considerations of audience a matter of due process when speaking and studying everyday life, so that in multicultural and post-colonial societies like Australia, cultural studies avoids the trap of speaking on others' behalf (see Morris 1990, p. 479).

As an alternative to the way everyday life is appraised in these (admittedly select) examples, Morris's example of speaking and studying the mundane deploys a colloquial voice that tries to respect the reader by not talking down or censoring ideas that might be too hard. Following Foucault, she offers a 'specific' intellectual function for the varied demands of intellectual work in Australia (Foucault 1980; see also Hall 1992, p. 291).[11] For Morris, it's 'no good talking *about* the local, the specific, the different and the heterogeneous if we do not know how to *address* constituencies other than or merely beyond our own professional and academic milieux' (Morris 2000, p. 229). 'It is when we presume to speak publicly *as* critics and theorists of other people's fears and anxieties', that, in her view, 'we need to be able to find the words and the levels that work' (2000, p. 229). It should be clear that I am in favour of 'the mundane' as an exceptionally productive level from which our studies might arise. It is a grounding mechanism, a gesture of honest and humble beginnings, from which our speech might depart and, necessarily, land. As an example of such a strategy, and against the sense of mastery or abstraction hindering other models of studying everyday life, Morris situates herself squarely within the site for analysis. In each case, she begins with what she calls 'a pressing, wordless feeling that I must work to render sociable – by writing out of it a cultural history that may *serve* a political struggle' (1992c, p. 79). Rather than acceding to the fashions of intellectual disciplines, Morris's work always starts as 'a way of answering questions that arise for me insistently in the course of my everyday life' (1992c, p. 78). This, to my mind, is the key strength of studying the mundane: it is focused on the new experiences emanating *from* the everyday, rather than imposing upon it a second-order, and often foreign, hermeneutic.

New heights

As an example of Morris's practice, and against the ways de Certeau is deployed in other cultural studies models to gain popularity, 'Great moments in social climbing: King Kong and the human fly' is a key interventionist text in the quest to overturn discourses governing everyday experience. In the essay – one of a number that investigate the spatial economy of notable sites in the Australian mundane (Morris 1988b, 1993b) – Morris reveals the gendered assumptions of a particular tourism economy that, like the cultural theory that attends it, discounts 'this-ness' in favour of overarching master narratives of consumption/resistance. Morris seeks new paradigms to recognize the agency and critical reflection in people whose actions are otherwise considered subject to proscriptive spatial formulations. Her means of countering the inadequacies of postmodern theory is 'to study instead the everyday, the so-called banal, the supposedly un- or non-experimental' (1988b, p. 202) – what I am calling 'the mundane'. Morris asks how dominant theories 'fall short of women's modernity' (1988b, p. 202), and in doing so writes from a place where the lives studied are often untouched by the privileges theoretical distinctions, like postmodernism, harbour.

Acknowledging the importance of de Certeau's work in expanding cultural theory's reckoning with popular uses of space, the essay reads Chris Hilton's unprecedented scaling of Sydney's Centrepoint Tower to draw out a more complex consideration of de Certeau's theories than celebrants afford. Morris approaches the aura of a tell-all theory with great scepticism, attuned to the derivation that begins once a theory leaves its singular enunciative context. If de Certeau's *Practice of Everyday Life* offers evidence of the political agency denied by other postmodern theories, his influential 'Walking in the city' chapter still relies on a hierarchical view (a God-like eye) to read New York as an open narrative full of tactical uses of space. 'In fact', Morris writes in this essay,

> de Certeau's visit to the World Trade Center is a way of mapping all over again the 'grid' of binary oppositions within which so much of the debate *about* structuralism was conducted . . . 'The tower' here serves as an allegory of the structural necessity for a politics of resistance based on a bipolar model of power to maintain the imaginary position of mastery it must then endlessly disclaim.
>
> (Morris 1992c, p. 13)

In one sense, de Certeau redresses our critical outlook from the oppressive model of contemporary power in American (Jameson) and French (Baudrillard) postmodern theory to one in which spaces and openings for unrest and conditional adaptation are possible. Still, 'blockages' in the theory appear (Foucault & Deleuze 1977): as my previous section describes, the very means by which resistant practices can be observed through de Certeau's model relies on a certain mastery or separation which necessarily takes the observer outside (above and beyond) the culture being studied. Nonetheless, Morris seems to take to heart Daryl Slack's motto, whereby '[s]uccessful theorizing is not measured by exact theoretical fit but by the ability to work with our always inadequate theories to help us move understanding "a little further on down the road"' (Daryl Slack 1996, p. 113). Using strains from Certeau's work underutilized by others, in combination with what is observable in popular culture, Morris takes productive 'tools' from the theory to create an even more intricate model of political participation (Foucault & Deleuze 1977).

The Australian ABC documentary *A Spire* is the source material used for Morris' analysis.[12] The programme captures a day in the life of ordinary bloke Hilton who decides to climb the tallest tower in Sydney's CBD. In her reading, Morris claims the act unhinges so many problematic assumptions in the theories of space and politics dominating cultural studies: the still detectable distinctions between elite and popular practices, the (masculine) voyage and the (feminine) home, notions of public opposed to private space, and simplistic formulations of the difference between radical and reformist politics. Against these tendencies, Hilton's climb is shown to enact an exemplary performance for feminist cultural studies to hold dear; a valuable 'case' and model for future use.[13] As part of a decade-long investigation into property development's gendered interests (collected in *Too Soon Too Late*), the piece begins by describing Centrepoint Tower as a site almost insurmountably oriented towards consumption. The manoeuvrings of real estate speculation, the capitalist motives behind the shopping arcade development, the exploitative mindset of the tourism industry are all revealed as the historical conditions now limiting people's prospects for movement and experience within this building. But rather than producing an orthodox Left critique, painting the patriarchal and money-hungry investors as backing the building for the benefit of their own hip-pockets, Morris depicts Hilton's climb as a literal uprising that deconstructs traditional ways of figuring space through performance in cultural theory. 'What happens in *A Spire* is more like a polemical expansion of the public space of the street to include the top of the Tower, and an extension of the temporality of "home" to incorporate the voyage', writes Morris. So already two fundamental components of feminist cultural theory are inaugurated in Hilton's act: dismantling the public and private distinction and, with it, the separation between home and voyage in matters of politics. In terms of movement, he 'follows a "smooth" trajectory' through space:

> into a bus, up the Tower, down the stairs, into a taxi – that, far from defining a *break* from the setting everyday life, extends the hours of labor inventing and testing homemade tools, talking with friends, practicing in the back-yards, the cliffs, and the car-parks available around the city. The logical consequence is that since the concept of 'home' now subsumes 'adventure' (dynamism, change, thus time as well as space), it is no longer interiority and closure alone, but also exteriority and surface . . . 'Home' in this sense does not mean a state of 'domesticity,' nor does it signify 'ownership.' It is a version of the active principle that de Certeau calls 'practicing place'.
>
> (Morris 1992b, p. 48)

While the act of climbing the Tower is on its own (on the face of it) an act of transgression against notions of private property, Morris sees in the very concep-tualization of the act evidence of a more fluid popular understanding of space than current discursive descriptions allow or suggest. Pointing out the number of traditional distinctions to be made (the private backyard, the public terrain of the cliff face, the shared space of the bus, but the not-quite private safety of the taxi on escape, and, fascinatingly, the open stairwell where Hilton expected to be arrested after executing the climb, but was not), Morris shows how this amazing physical feat rearranges accepted notions of what and where concepts central to radical politics apply. Hilton confuses our sense of where a protest should take place, indeed what constitutes protest: what aims and objectives should be served, and who should be at the receiving end of our demands. Morris sees the performance as sympathetic with feminist objectives, for the way that all of these concepts crucial for male-dominated political diagnoses are irrevo-cably messed up.

The essay conveys how Hilton's act is a political intervention directed towards those it speaks for: the people rendered silent by the discourses that decide politics and govern our experience of space. This kind of performance has more significance for Morris than complaints that serve only to reinscribe the phallic power of the site attacked:

> Chris Hilton made a spectacle of himself, and then helped make a film about it. He produced a social analysis with an act of exhibitionism and then exhibited his analysis in public. In practicing this mode of (very athletic) effeteness, he brought down the Tower not by renouncing the heights, but by reaching them instead. In this way, he invented a form of vernacular criticism which does *not* miss the point about the kind of wealth and power invested in urban towers – but rather, makes a spectacle about that very point.
>
> (Morris 1992b, p. 51)

Morris conveys here the spirit of de Certeau's project, the 'vernacular criticism' he tried to trace following the footsteps of 'the ordinary man' (de Certeau 1984). Thinking through the significance of Hilton's achievement, Morris reads the climb as truly 'popular' in the sense Certeau adduced: 'a way of doing things characterized by an art of *timing*, rather than by a topological relation to some other "zone" (whether "high", or "elite", of "mass") of cultural space' (1992b, p. 2). But Morris's use of popular evidence in the more colloquial sense, as the actions *of the people*, avoids the trap of importing whole models of cultural theory to foreign contexts. It is in the analysis of a singular 'event' that she sees cultural studies as most effective, those moments that freeze 'diverse temporal and social trajectories' just long enough for us to see something new is happening (Frow & Morris 1993, p. xv).

Conclusion

In this, and other investigations of the Australian mundane, Morris's ambivalence to the orthodoxy of cultural studies practice fuels a determination to expand the scope of, and participation in, the field itself. Her approach considers people's actions and involvement in events as significant historical exercises in themselves, a democratic political vision with the openness to recognize how people act in dissonance with theoretical models. By beginning with a context that warrants its own attention, Morris's initial parochialism strives outward from the mundane to find connections with other sites and experiences elsewhere. It is a step that identifies the limitations of its partiality from the outset, nonetheless hopeful that a new condition might be significant enough to risk being shared.

When competing emphases for political engagement dictate the terms on which intellectual debates take place, this project of studying the mundane can at times seem irrelevant and far from glamorous. However, if our goals as cultural critics resemble 'whole-field modulation' and '"radical" intervention', as Massumi baits, this more humble and protracted critical task is, I think, necessary. Reflecting on her work, Morris writes that it is

> always open to the unanswerable charge of doing nothing to stop the Antarctic melting or to mend the hole in the ozone layer. True. I none the less feel that I am more usefully employed in using as much imagination as I possibly can to change the cultural climate in which ideas for doing so are formulated and in which they circulate than I would be in elaborating 'whole new' futures with – at least in my case – rather dubious practical value.
>
> (Morris 1993a, p. 34)

In our current context, as plans unveil for the destiny of a 'whole new' Iraq for instance, the kind of modest and prolonged political project Morris engages seems preferable to the dangers of imposing our own common-sense cultural ideologies. While there may be 'a certain commodity boredom' amongst cultural critics 'with the slow, incremental temporality endured by any struggle with serious designs on the future' (1993a, p. 34), I think we need to recognize that this is the terrain of cultural studies' *becoming* (Massumi 2002). As Morris writes:

> Cultural critics work primarily as mediators – we are writers, readers, image producers, teachers – in a socially as well as theoretically obscure zone of values, opinion, belief, ideology and emotion. This is slow work, and whatever political effectivity we might claim for it can only be registered, most of the time, by gradual shifts in what people take to be thinkable and doable, desirable and liveable, acceptable and unbearable, in their particular historical circumstances. In more peaceful or settled times, this can be cast by its enthusiasts as an intrinsically splendid endeavor. In fearful or turbulent times, it is easily denounced as trivial.
>
> (1992c, p. 79)

It is at the level of the mundane that political interests ultimately land. Situating the mundane as the site for analysis forces us to grapple with the concrete ways political discourses shape experience. The particular focus Morris initiates for cultural studies – the gendered and consumerist interests of political and economic imperatives – remain key places in need of cultural studies' attention, given that these discourses patently influence people's experience of space, their land, and especially now, their country. A cultural studies that invokes 'the everyday' without intervening in its reproduction is not enough: seen in the Foucauldian perspective Morris adopts, it puts limits on 'the undefined work of freedom' (Foucault 1984, p. 46). Cultural studies should take confidence in its own objects and methods of enquiry to work through the times of fear and turbulence that surround us. Following Morris, it has mechanisms to recognize the subtle and determined ways people forge responses to social change.

Noticing these, and relating them, we might broaden the reach of our mundane work, continuing to spark a 'desire for other people's stories'.

Notes

1   This is why Morris finds the philosophy of Michèle Le Doeff such an exception in the context of feminist practices available in the 1980s: 'Le Doeuff's practice *as* a woman writing philosophy is one which precludes the ventriloquy of the dutiful daughter, since it demands a different articulation of philosophy's relations to women (thus, a different philosophy)' (Morris 1988a, p. 76).

2   As a freelance writer, Morris's fluency in a number of disciplinary knowledges and writing styles during the 1980s and 1990s is important to recognize in contrast to other cultural studies figures in Australia, the USA, the UK and Canada at the time, whose training typically fell in the disciplinary fields of English literature, history, sociology or communications.

3   Reading Benjamin's *Passagen-Werk*, for instance, Buck-Morss describes his allegorical style as 'imposed upon the subject as a cognitive imperative, rather than the artist's choosing it arbitrarily as an aesthetic device'. The subjectivity modernism encourages impels Benjamin to allegory, in this formulation, making 'visibly palpable the experience of a world in fragments' (1989, p. 18).

4   Australia has a number of distinct football codes. Rugby League (played predominantly in Queensland and New South Wales) differs from Rugby Union, although both privilege passing the ball by throwing to team mates who surge forward in lines to score a 'try' (a touchdown). Both of these codes differ again from 'Australian Rules' (played in other states), which uses the same-shaped oval ball but is premised on running with, bouncing and kicking the ball, eventually through goal posts. All of these are separate again from 'soccer', which is the term for European football. That my editors did not know these distinctions is exciting and encouraging for my argument that an outreaching, rather than inward-looking parochialism might breed curiosity amongst intellectuals and the cultures from which they speak.

5   Elsewhere I argue that progressivist histories of cultural studies contribute to a similar forgetfulness of the radical potential the field offers (Gregg 2004).

6   The term 'international wanderings' is Fiske's own, from the preface to *Reading the Popular*, where he writes: 'One of the advantages of being an academic is that theories travel well, with only a touch of jet lag . . . These essays . . . are a bricolage of frozen moments in my thinking about popular culture, a series of snapshots taken by an academic on his intercontinental wanderings in the 1980s' (1989, p. ix). It is precisely this mode of address, which flaunts the privilege and value of detached reflection on local specificities, that Morris's project seeks to unhinge.

7   Seigworth and Macgregor Wise (2000) call this 'window dressing', when cultural studies deploys philosophy in an attempt to add theoretical weight to

an argument – see their introduction to the *Cultural Studies* special issue on Deleuze and Guattari. To my mind, such practices often seem to stem from an inadequate knowledge of, or confidence in, cultural studies' own unique objects and modes of enquiry, which is an absence this paper tries to fill.

8   The sales figures for subculture studies led some commentators to suggest cultural studies could attribute its 'international dissemination – if not the whole of its existence – to a successful publishing strategy' (Bourdieu & Wacquant, in Striphas 2002, p. 440).

9   The repetitiveness captured in Morris's biting speculation: 'I get the feeling that somewhere in some English publisher's vault there is a master-disk from which thousands of versions of the same article about pleasure, resistance, and the politics of consumption are being run off under different names with minor variations' (1988/1996, p. 156).

10   Turner misses the broader point, that the white male academic voice is rarely modified in any way other than in an effort to sell more books. Morris further clarifies her argument, in response to his response: 'whatever the determinants of the book's wider reception, my own criticism of *Myths of Oz* are, rightly or wrongly, *feminist* criticism. They are not attacks on its popular status, or its playful approach, *per se*. It is true that more "serious" versions of the method of analysis used by *Myths of Oz* are available in academic Cultural Studies. I don't agree with those, either'. So one general issue I want to raise is whether it is always useful to assume that criticism of a 'popular' work necessarily involves an assertion of 'academic' territorial imperatives (Morris 1991, p. 33).

11   For an extensive discussion of the way the specific intellectual differs from Gramsci's model of the organic intellectual, see Lewis (2000). I would like to acknowledge the importance of Lewis's work in stimulating my own thinking about Morris.

12   The choice of film review is symptomatic of Morris' broader belief in the need for cultural critics to make use of the skills and disciplines in which they are trained. As a writer competent in a number of applications – film critic, translator, publisher, editor, freelance writer and teacher – Morris is especially aware of the ways different genres can be employed to better or worse effect.

13   In her opening chapter to *Too Soon, Too Late*, Morris articulates the relationship she sees between cultural studies and history in this way: 'My preference is to turn to history for a context prolonging the life of the ephemeral item or "case": saturating with detail an articulated place and point in time, a critical reading can extract from its objects a parable of practice that converts them into *models* with a past and a potential for reuse, thus aspiring to invest them with a future' (1998b, p. 3).

References

Barcan, R. (1995) 'A symphony of farts: Saul Alinsky, social activism and carnivalesque transgression', *The UTS Review*, vol. 1, no. 1, 83–92.

Buck-Morss, S. (1989) *The Dialectics of Seeing:Walter Benjamin and the Arcades Project*. MIT Press, Cambridge, MA and London.

Centre for Contemporary Cultural Studies Women's Studies Group (1978) *Women Take Issue:Aspects of Women's Subordination*, Hutchinson and CCCS Birmingham, London.

Daryl Slack, J. (1996) 'The theory and method of articulation in cultural studies', in *Stuart Hall: Critical Dialogues in Cultural Studies*, eds D. Morley & K.-H. Chen, Routledge, London and New York.

De Certeau, M. (1984) *The Practice of Everyday Life*, trans. S. Rendall, University of California Press, Berkley and Los Angeles.

Fiske, J. (1989) *Reading the Popular*, Unwin Hyman, Boston.

Fiske, J., Hodge, B. & Turner, G. (1987) *Myths of Oz: Reading Australian Popular Culture*, Allen & Unwin, Sydney.

Foucault, M. (1980) *Power/Knowledge: Selected Interviews and Other Writings, 1972–1977*, trans. & ed. C. Gordon, Harvester Press, Sussex.

Foucault, M. (1984) 'What is enlightenment?', in *The Foucault Reader*, ed. P. Rabinow, Pantheon Books, New York.

Foucault, M. & Deleuze, G. (1977) 'Intellectuals and power', in *Language, Counter-Memory, Practice*, ed. D Bouchard, Cornell University Press, Ithaca, NY.

Frow, J. & Morris, M. (eds.) (1993) 'Introduction' to *Australian Cultural Studies: A Reader*, Allen & Unwin, Sydney.

Gregg, M. (2004) 'Scholarly affect: voices of intervention in cultural studies', PhD thesis, Department of Gender Studies, The University of Sydney.

Hall, S. (1992) 'Cultural studies and its theoretical legacies', in *Cultural Studies*, eds L. Grossberg, C. Nelson & P. A. Treichler, Routledge, London.

Jameson, F. (1991) *Postmodernism, Or, The Cultural Logic of Late Capitalism*, Duke University Press, Durham.

Lewis, T. (2000) 'Critical habitations: cultural studies and the politics of intellectual location', PhD thesis, Department of English with Cultural Studies, The University of Melbourne.

Massumi, B. (2002) *Parables for the Virtual: Movement, Affect, Sensation*, Duke University Press, Durham and London.

McRobbie, A. (1980) 'Settling accounts with subcultures: a feminist critique', *Screen Education*, vol. 34, spring, pp. 37–49.

Morris, M. (1988/1996) 'Banality in cultural studies', in *What is Cultural Studies?*, ed. J. Storey, Arnold, London (originally published 1988).

Morris, M. (1988a) *The Pirate's Fiancée: Feminism, Reading, Postmodernism*, Verso, London and New York.

Morris, M. (1988b) 'Things to do with shopping centres', in *Grafts: Feminist Cultural Criticism*, ed. S. Sheridan, Verso, London.

Morris, M. (1990) 'A small serve of spaghetti: the future of Australian studies', *Meanjin*, vol. 49, no. 3, pp. 470–480.

Morris, M. (1991) 'Response to Graeme Turner', *Meanjin*, vol. 50, no. 1, pp. 32–34.

Morris, Meaghan (1992a) 'On the beach', in *Cultural Studies*, eds L. Grossberg, C. Nelson & P. A. Treichler, Routledge, New York, pp. 450–478.

Morris, M. (1992b) 'Great moments in social climbing: King Kong and the human fly', in *Sexuality and Space*, ed. B. Colomina, Princeton Architectural Press, New York.

Morris, M. (1992c) 'Critical reflections', *Artforum International*, vol. 30, no. 8, pp. 78–79.

Morris, M. (1993a) 'Future fear', in *Mapping the Futures: Local Cultures, Global Change*, eds B. Curtis, J. Bird, T. Putnam, G. Robertson & L. Tickner, Routledge, London.

Morris, M. (1993b) 'At Henry Parkes Motel', in *Australian Cultural Studies: A Reader*, eds J. Frow & M. Morris, Allen & Unwin, Sydney, pp. 241–275 (originally published 1988).

Morris, M. (1998a) 'Uncle Billy, Tina Turner and Me', in *The Space Between: Australian Women Writing Fictocriticism*, eds H. Kerr & A. Nettelbeck, University of Western Australia Press, Perth.

Morris, M. (1998b) *Too Soon, Too Late: History in Popular Culture*, Indiana University Press, Bloomington, IN.

Morris, M. (2000) '"Please explain?" Ignorance, poverty and the past', *Inter-Asia Cultural Studies*, vol. 1, no. 2, pp. 219–232.

Morse, M. (1998) *Virtualities: Television, Media Art, and Cyberculture*, Indiana University Press, Bloomington and Indianapolis.

Probyn, E. (1993) *Sexing the Self: Gendered Positions in Cultural Studies*, Routledge, London.

Probyn, E. (2004) *Blush: Faces of Shame*, University of Minnesota Press, Minneapolis.

Sedgwick, E. K. & Frank, A. (1995) 'Shame in the cybernietic fold: reading Silvan Tomkins', in *Shame and its Sisters*, Duke University Press, Durham.

Seigworth, G. J. & Macgregor Wise, J. (2000) 'Introduction: Deleuze and Guattari in cultural studies', *Cultural Studies*, vol. 14, no. 2, pp. 139–146.

Steedman, C. (1986) *Landscape For a Good Woman*, Virago, London.

Steedman, C. (1997) 'Writing the self: the end of the scholarship girl', in *Cultural Methodologies*, ed. J. McGuigan, Sage, London.

Striphas, T. (2002) 'Banality, book publishing and the everyday life of cultural studies', *International Journal Of Cultural Studies*, vol. 5, no. 4, pp. 438–460.

Anne Galloway

INTIMATIONS OF EVERYDAY LIFE
Ubiquitous computing and the city

Ubiquitous computing seeks to embed computers into our everyday lives in such ways as to render them invisible and allow them to be taken for granted, while social and cultural theories of everyday life have always been interested in rendering the invisible visible and exposing the mundane. Despite these related concerns, social and cultural studies have been almost entirely absent in discussions of the design of ubiquitous technologies. This essay seeks to introduce researchers in both fields to each other, and begin to explore the ways in which collaboration might proceed. By exploring mobile and ubiquitous technologies currently being used to augment our experiences of the city, this paper investigates notions of sociality, spatialization and temporalization as central to our experiences of everyday life, and therefore of interest to the design of ubiquitous computing.

Keywords   control society; embodiment flow; spatialization; temporalization; ubiquitous computing

[E]veryday life consists of a multiplicity of rhythms. Everyday life thus entails a range of flows, each with their own 'proper time' (e.g., duration, pace, frequency). Likewise, we could argue that everyday life consists of a multiplicity of spatializations, including forms of embodiment. If we were to use 'space of places', we would have to bear in mind the inherently dynamic, volatile, contested, unstable, and *multiplicitous* (rather than duplicitous) nature of 'place'.

(van Loon 2002, p. 93)

The most profound technologies are those that disappear. They weave themselves into the fabric of everyday life until they are indistinguishable from it.

(Weiser 1991, p. 1)

Introduction

Ubiquitous computing seeks to embed computers into our everyday lives in such ways as to render them invisible and allow them to be taken for granted, while

Cultural Studies Vol. 18, No. 2/3 March/May 2004, pp. 384–408
ISSN 0950-2386 print/ISSN 1466-4348 online   © 2004 Taylor & Francis Ltd
http://www.tandf.co.uk/journals   DOI: 10.1080/0950238042000201572

Routledge
Taylor & Francis Group

social and cultural theories of everyday life have always been interested in rendering the invisible visible and exposing the mundane. Despite these related concerns, social and cultural studies remain in the background of discussions of ubiquitous technology design. This essay seeks to bring together researchers in both fields, and begin to explore the ways in which collaboration might proceed. Of course, this is a large project, and this essay is only a first and tentative step in that direction. My strategy involves asking more questions than posing answers so that other researchers may begin to locate their own interests and make their own connections.

For the purpose of this special issue, and in the interests of critiques of everyday life, this essay explores ubiquitous computing in terms of sociality, spatialization and temporalization. The first part looks at the origins of ubiquitous computing and its concern with social and cultural practices. The second part of the essay addresses current ubiquitous computing, context-aware technologies, and particular projects explicitly using notions of space, time and embodiment to augment our experiences of the city.

The third and final part of the essay examines the centrality of spatialization, temporalization and embodiment in the performativity of everyday life, and further connects these concerns to ubiquitous computing. The primary goal of this essay is to draw out ways in which social and cultural theories of everyday life may begin to contribute to discussions of the design of ubiquitous computing, and how critiques of everyday life will increasingly need to account for emerging ubiquitous technologies.

The social origins of ubiquitous computing

In 1991, *Scientific American* published Weiser's article 'The computer for the 21st century' and planted the seed for a new paradigm in computing that is arguably set to dominate the coming decades. In the late 1980s, researchers at Xerox Palo Alto Research Center (PARC) moved away from personal computing – which they understood as forcing computers to the centre of our attention – and towards what they called ubiquitous computing, or Ubicomp, which 'takes into account the natural human environment and allows the computers themselves to vanish into the background' (Weiser 1991, p. 1). In other words, they were interested in 'invisible' computers that would allow us to focus on life beyond computational devices. According to Weiser, not only would ubiquitous computing liberate us from the constraints of desktop computing, it would free us from equally isolating immersive and simulated virtual reality environments. From the perspective of design, ubiquitous computing was also novel because Weiser's inspiration came from the social and cultural realms more than from the technological (Weiser 1993a).

Weiser began with an explicit interest in the role of computers in everyday life, and a desire to build computers that did not interfere with our everyday activities:

> A good tool is an invisible tool. By invisible, I mean that the tool does not intrude on your consciousness; you focus on the task, not the tool. Eyeglasses are a good tool – you look at the world, not the eyeglasses. The blind man tapping the cane feels the street, not the cane.
>
> (Weiser 1993b, p. 7)

Rheingold visited PARC for an article he was writing for *Wired Magazine*, and interviewed Weiser:

> The lab's new direction, Weiser says, 'recognizes even more that people are social creatures'. He referred to his ideas as a form of 'postmodern computing', in that he wants to 'return to letting things in the world be what they are, instead of reducing them' to data or virtualizing them into illusions. 'Ubicomp honors the complexity of human relationships, the fact that we have bodies, are mobile', he said.
>
> (Rheingold 1994a, p. 3)

The degree to which Weiser was able to convince fellow computer scientists of the importance of social and cultural issues in the development of ubiquitous computing varied. In 1999, Weiser was diagnosed with cancer and given 18 months to live; he died after six weeks. An obituary from the Department of Electrical Engineering and Computer Sciences, University of California, Berkeley (1999) recalled that,

> When he was diagnosed with cancer, he decided to spend his remaining time writing a book clearing up some of the confusion around ubiquitous computing. Weiser wanted to sit by the seaside and write the book on the real essence of ubiquitous computing. 'They've completely missed the non-technical part of what ubiquitous computing is all about', he told Xerox's chief scientist and PARC's director, John Seely Brown.

Unfortunately, Weiser died before he could write his book and now, four years later, while many Ubicomp research projects conduct ethnographic evaluations of technology in use, we could still make the case that the 'non-technical' or broader social and cultural aspects of ubiquitous computing remain insufficiently explored and represented in the design process.

Ubiquitous computing vs. virtual reality

From the beginning, Weiser was concerned not only with describing what Ubicomp was, but also what it was *not*. Most importantly, ubiquitous computing was seen to be fundamentally different from the virtual reality technologies that dominated the popular consciousness of the time.

> [V]irtual reality is only a map, not a territory. It . . . focuses an enormous apparatus on simulating the world rather than on invisibly enhancing the world that already exists. Indeed, the opposition between the notion of virtual reality and ubiquitous, invisible computing is so strong that some of us use the term 'embodied virtuality' to refer to the process of drawing computers out of their electronic shells. The 'virtuality' of computer-readable data – all the different ways in which it can be altered, processed and analysed – is brought into the physical world . . . By pushing computers into the background, embodied virtuality will make individuals more aware of the people on the other ends of their computer links.
>
> (Weiser 1991, p. 2)

The corporate Xerox PARC researchers had positioned themselves against virtual reality, when VR represented a unique mix of military, university and counter-culture values (Rheingold 1994b, Hillis 1999). Against the seemingly boundless freedom promised by proponents of virtual reality, Ubicomp did not seek to transcend the flesh and privilege the technological. Instead, ubiquitous comput-ing was meant to go beyond the machine – render *it* invisible – and privilege the social and material worlds. In this sense, ubiquitous computing was positioned to bring computers to 'our world' (domesticating *them*), rather than us having to adapt to the 'computer world' (domesticating *us*). As Norman (1998, p. 261) later wrote 'today, it is the individual who must conform to the needs of technology. It is time to make technology conform to the needs of people'.

Ubiquitous computing as calm technology

By 1996, Weiser and Seely Brown were predicting the 'coming age of calm technology'. Despite the rather mundane contexts projected for ubiquitous computing – computers in everyday objects and places – it was also presented as exceptional technology:

> The most potentially interesting, challenging, and profound change implied by the ubiquitous computing era is a focus on *calm*. If computers are everywhere they better stay out of the way, and that means designing them so that the people being shared by the computers remain serene and in control . . . [W]hen computers are all around, so that we want to compute while doing something else and have more time to be more fully human, we must radically rethink the goals, context and technology of the computer and all the other technology crowding into our lives. Calmness is a funda-mental challenge for all technological design of the next fifty years.
>
> (Weiser & Seely Brown 1996, p. 3)

But what exactly did they mean by 'calm technology?' They described technology that moves between the *periphery* and *centre* of our attention, outside of conscious awareness (but not completely absent) until we actively focus on it. In this way, they argued, the 'result of calm technology is to put us at home, in a familiar place' (Weiser & Seely Brown 1996, pp. 4–5). Put otherwise, calm technology could be distinguished as technology that would be so embedded, so pervasive, that it could be *taken for granted*. It would be informative without being over-whelming or distracting. They suggested that ubiquitous computing would become 'so commonplace, so unremarkable' that we would forget its enormous impact, just as we have with writing and electricity, two other ubiquitous technologies (Weiser & Seely Brown 1996, p. 2).

Weiser believed that the design of ubiquitous computing would greatly benefit from research in the humanities and social sciences. Social and cultural studies of everyday life are uniquely suited to question the implications of 'invisible' and context-aware technologies, and we may begin to ask how critiques of everyday life can contribute to the design of ubiquitous computing. To continue this larger project, the second part of this essay looks at current Ubicomp, context-aware technologies, and particular projects that bring the space and time of social interaction to the foreground.

Current ubiquitous computing

In its broadest sense, ubiquitous computing is currently seen to comprise any number of mobile, wearable, distributed and context-aware computing applications. In this way, Ubicomp may consist of research into 'how information technology can be diffused into everyday objects and settings, and to see how this can lead to new ways of supporting and enhancing people's lives', as examined by *The Disappearing Computer* Initiative (http://www.disappearing-computer.net), as well as the 'integration of physical and digital interaction', explored by the *EQUATOR Interdisciplinary Research Collaboration* (http://www.equator.ac.uk). A wide variety of scientific research labs around the world are currently studying the many types of hardware and software components necessary for ubiquitous computing. In addition to research in engineering, computer and hard sciences, continuing investigations in human-computer interaction and computer supported cooperative work draw on psychology, anthropology and sociology (see for example Nardi and O'Day 1999, Dourish 2001, Brown *et al.* 2002).

Context-aware computing

Central to ubiquitous or pervasive technologies is the ability of computers to be perceptive, interpretive and reactive. In other words, information infrastructures must be able to shift from periphery to centre, and to recognize and respond to actual contexts of use. Context-aware computing therefore relies primarily on two types of information: physical location and user identity, both requiring extensive data acquisition, storage and delivery mechanisms.

The global positioning system (GPS) is a now familiar location-awareness technology. An increasingly common technology enabling broader context-awareness is radio frequency identification (RFID) tags. Put simply, individually programmed RFID tags, or transponders, use radio signals to capture and share data between mobile and fixed computing devices, allowing automatic data capture and object identification. For example, since the 1980s, very small RFID tags have been inserted under the skin to track livestock, and built into new automobiles to allow for automated vehicle identification (AVI). They may be invisibly embedded into virtually any object, and global industry and business are currently working towards implementing RFID tags throughout the entire supply chain (http://www.aimglobal.org/technologies/rfid/).

Of concern here are the implications of context-aware computing for privacy in everyday life. Such comprehensive monitoring or surveillance is not contained by either space or time, as these technologies may cross both physical and social boundaries (Langheinrich 2002). For example, consumer profiles could expand to include not only what people have purchased, but where, when and by whom these items are used. Not only might consumers automatically receive individualized information, but they might also be denied access to information not deemed part of their data profile. In addition, ephemeral or transitory activities may be captured, stored and redistributed in perpetuity. The questions of where data will be stored, and who owns or has access to these data, become paramount issues in the development of ubiquitous computing that respects social and democratic expectations around everyday privacy (Lederer *et al.* 2002). The question of 'invisibility' also raises concerns over privacy, as it may be impossible for people to recognize, let alone control, their interaction with ubiquitous computing applications (Nguyen & Mynatt 2002). Partly in response to such concerns, and despite the current focus on 'seamless' applications, Ubicomp researchers are now suggesting more 'visibility' and recalling Weiser's notion of 'seamful' interaction, with 'beautiful seams' (see for example MacColl *et al.* 2002).

Hybrid worlds: between physical and virtual spaces

The types of ubiquitous computing of interest here are those that most openly seek to create unique forms of inhabitable space and means of habitation, and therefore raise issues not only of spatialization, but also of temporalization and embodiment. So-called mixed reality technologies are explicitly concerned with questions that have long been in the arena of social and cultural discussions of everyday life.

Mixed reality environments refer to spaces that combine elements of the physical and virtual worlds. According to Milgram *et al.* (1994, p. 1), 'rather than regarding the two concepts simply as antitheses, however, it is more convenient to view them as lying at opposite ends of a *continuum*, which we refer to as the *Reality-Virtuality (RV) continuum*'. At one end of the continuum are seen to be 'real' objects that can be observed directly or 'sampled and then resynthesized via some display device', while at the other end are 'virtual' objects that are 'simulated' through 'some sort of a description, or *model*, of the object' (Milgram and Kishino 1994, p. 1). Similarly, a '*real image* [is] any image which has some luminosity at the location at which it appears to be located . . . [whereas] a virtual image of an object [is] one which appears *transparent*, that is, which does not occlude other objects located behind it' (Milgram & Kishino 1994, p. 2). Put otherwise, the 'real' is defined as material fixed in place, whereas the 'virtual' is defined as immaterial, outside of time, both distant and close.

Mixed-reality comprises anything between the two extremes of the spectrum, and combines aspects of both to create a *hybrid* environment. The two most common types of mixed reality technologies are 'augmented reality' and 'augmented virtuality'. Augmented reality seeks to enhance physical spaces and objects with virtual reality; augmented virtuality seeks to enhance virtual reality with real-world data and objects. Of interest here is augmented reality, which attempts to overlay physical objects with virtual objects in real-time and allows people to experience the virtual as if it were real (Azuma 1997). In some ways, augmented reality has the same ultimate goal as virtual reality: to create new interactive spaces through computation. Where they differ is in how they see this best accomplished, which, in part, involves their assumptions about space, time and the body.

While augmented reality is much closer to Weiser's vision for Ubicomp than is augmented virtuality, Falk *et al.* (1999, p. 3) refine the concept by introducing the term 'amplified reality'.

> While augmented reality is about enhancing our impressions of everyday objects in our surrounding, *amplified reality* is about enhancing the *expressions* of objects and people in the world . . .
>
> An amplified object is self-contained in regards to its properties. In practice, this means that that the properties are *embedded* parts of the object. In contrast, augmented reality superimposes virtual properties on an object, which in effect does not change the actual object, but rather how we perceive or experience it. Augmented properties are not persistent outside the augmented reality. The important difference between these two approaches lies in the proprietary rights to the information. An amplified object controls the flow of information, while in an augmented reality system the perceiver is in control of the information . . . In other words, an

augmented reality systems alters the impressions of its user, without there being any corresponding properties in the *expression* of the object she is perceiving. This is quite different from ordinary life.

Most notable in this description is the introduction of computation as a *material* for designing not only the digital realm but also the physical world (see also Orth 2001, Redström 2001), and a shift from concerns with the functional *use* of computers to the *presence*, expressions and aesthetics of computational arte-facts in everyday life (Hallnäs & Redström 2001). I think Weiser would have been interested in this more existential design approach to embedded comput-ing, and cultural studies of everyday life offer further critical insights into discussions of 'reality' and 'virtuality' (see for example Massumi 2002; Shields 2003).

To continue my exploration of the connections between ubiquitous comput-ing and theories of everyday life, I would like to introduce several projects that focus on augmenting and amplifying physical spaces and experiences through a variety of mobile and context-aware technologies. The projects, presented in alphabetical order, are in various stages of development, prototyping or testing. All information has been culled from whatever online project descriptions and research progress reports were available at the time of writing.

Amplified and annotated city spaces

All of the following projects use wireless and ubiquitous technologies to explore our everyday experience of the city. Their shared interests in moving through the city as integral to its experience bring to mind Lefebvre's (1991) production of space and de Certeau's (1984) spatial practices. Theorists of everyday life will also recognize Benjamin's (1969, 1999) *flâneur* and the ability of technology to make the invisible visible, as well as Situationist *derivé* and *detournément*. Their visions also conjure Lynch's (1960) city as our experiences with districts, edges, paths, nodes and landmarks, and their relational properties (Lynch 1984). All of these projects raise issues of spatialization, temporalization and the social; issues which allow us the opportunity to reexamine our assumptions about the city and everyday life (cf. Borden *et al.* 2001). If virtual reality technologies may be understood as visual, and spatial, technologies (Hillis 1999), these wireless and ubiquitous technologies firmly add the dimensions of sound, and time, to our everyday experiences.

Amble Time

A project by Media Lab Europe's Everyday Learning research group, *Amble Time* overlays a digital map of the city with context-aware spatial and temporal information:

A shortcoming of standard maps is their inability to convey a sense of temporal scale. Can I stroll to the park for lunch, or would it take me all day? *Amble Time* adds an element of time to a PDA-based tourist map. By using a GPS system and your average walking speed, it creates a bubble that indicates everywhere you could walk in an hour. Alternatively, given a final destination, it can show where you could roam along the way and still arrive on time. In the second situation, as your position changes and time ticks by, the bubble slowly shrinks and morphs until eventually it highlights the shortest path to your destination.

> (http://www.medialabeurope.org/el/Projects/Amble_Time.htm)

In an interview with the BBC (2003), lead researcher Brendan Donovan explains further:

> Say that you have to be at the train station at 3 o'clock. The software draws a bubble around you showing everywhere that you could walk to and still get to your destination on time . . . You could click on various locations on the map and see what times the trains were running or see information about restaurants etc.

Amble Time provides a means to augment physical spaces by providing context-specific information to mobile users walking through the city. The city emerges as a spatial, temporal and embodied experience, as the traditional map is visually overlaid with information on particular places physically accessible within particular frames of time. *Amble Time* also associates everyday life in the city with consumerism, where ubiquitous computing may bring mobile users closer to sites of consumption. If projects like *Amble Time* were to be commercialized, what might be the impact on practices of consumption and everyday life? If we recall the metaphor of domestication used above, could we claim that Ubicomp may still be used to indirectly domesticate consumers by leading them to commodified experiences?

Sonic City

Sonic City is a joint project between the Play Research Studio of the Interactive Institute and the Future Applications Lab of the Viktoria Institute, Sweden, in which the city is seen to act as a musical instrument.

> In the project *Sonic City*, we are developing an application that enables people to create music by walking through a city. From wearable and context-aware computing, perception of place, time, situation, and activity is applied to real-time, personal audio creation. We are exploring and prototyping new experiences and interactions with audio content, considering mobile

behaviors and urban conditions as parameters in music composition . . . Implementation involves a portable laptop, biometric and environmental sensors. Sensor data is processed, transmitted as MIDI signals and mapped to musical parameters in a program created in the interactive environment PD. Ultimately, we intend the program to run on a PDA or as a wearable device.

(http://www.playresearch.com/projects/soniccity/)

Essentially, *Sonic City* conjures city spaces in terms of sound and music, that is, as the ability to create sound and experience musical compositions. Since sound and music necessarily comprise the passage of time, space is also defined in terms of time. Furthermore, music is expressive and 'where it presents a world, a world one could be in, there only a person can go' (Evens 2002, p. 173). Again, the city is explored in terms of spatialization, temporalization and embodiment. Perhaps more importantly, we may ask what role sound plays in these processes. How do sound and music affect the performance and experience of space and time? What are the expressive qualities at play here? How does sound interpolate bodies in motion?

Sonic City expands the reach of technology by making it mobile, while simultaneously limiting its reach by playing the music to individually carried devices. The project raises interesting connections as music is performed not only through movement in space and time, creating mobile musical 'soundscapes' (Westerkamp 1999), but is also connected to the body through wearable computers which may be seen to create musical human-machine hybrids, or embodied music (see, for example, Hayles 1999, Grenville 2002).

> For illustration, consider the following scenario: a person is taking a walk through the busy streets of her town without any particular destination in mind. She puts on a pair of headphones and switches on her music creation device. Progressively, she begins to hear an evolving musical rhythm of concrete urban sounds, a tempo which follows her steps. The tempo keeps an acceptable pulse even when she stops for a red light, and catches up when she starts walking again. The structure of the music composition is non-linear, such that it changes each time her path does: switching to a bridge as she turns left after the bookshop on the corner, and back to the motif as she crosses the street. She decides to walk through a park: the music adapts to this different, quieter environment, shifting to a more basic rhythm pattern consisting of a few ground sounds. A more complex pattern emerges when she leaves the park and heads for a busy street. At some point, she cannot help but to try a little dance step: this disturbs the system that was expecting roughly binary steps. After brief structural chaos, the device stabilizes to a newly syncopated rhythm pattern as she walks on.
>
> (Gaye *et al.* 2003, p. 2)

Sonic City also conjures Situationist *derivé*, or playful 'nomadic' wanderings through the city, as it creates mobile musical ambiences and 'rewrites' the urban experiences of the user. Here we may also ask what roles sound and mobility play in our experiences of the city. Do notions of embodiment better capture a sense of mobility than do notions of the body? How may the body be understood as a wearable device, or perform as a musical instrument? How can Ubicomp be used to resist, or 'write against', totalizing concepts of the city?

Tejp

Also a joint project between the Play Research Studio and the Future Applications Lab, *Tejp* (Swedish for 'tape') consists of sound-based prototypes inspired by 'situationism, graffiti and other forms of street art'.

> This project explores various possibilities for overlaying personal traces and information on public spaces through different mediums and behavior patterns. It is our hope that *Tejp* will transform spectators into players and encourage playful ways to personalize territory in the public realm. We also hope to connect local communities by providing a space and sounding board for existing social relationships.
>
> (http://civ.idc.cs.chalmers.se/projects/pps/tejp/)

The first of two prototypes consists of audio tags, 'left at hidden places in public spaces [where] personal messages that have been previously recorded are whispered to by-passers as they lean towards [the tag]':

> Someone who wants to share personal messages anonymously (or not) records it into the small box by talking, singing, playing music etc. to it while holding a button. He/she sticks [the audio tag] on a wall somewhere . . . Passers-by notice/recognize the sticker because of its particular yet discrete design, leans/reaches towards it and hears the content of the tag. Others happen to pass by the device without seeing it, and hear its content by accident.
>
> (http://civ.idc.cs.chalmers.se/projects/pps/tejp/prototype1.html)

The audio tags create a means for people to interact with their physical and social surroundings in novel ways, annotating spaces and creating particular places, again performing the city through practices of spatialization, temporalization and embodiment.

The second prototype is called *Glitch*:

> An array of speakers are [*sic*] hidden in public places. The speakers loudly broadcasts interference glitches caused when passersby receive incoming

messages and phone calls. The prototype draws attention to the amount of personal communication taking place in a given space and will be used to analyze behaviors in response to its presence in the public realm . . .

The nature and origin of the noises are familiar and easily identifiable but the speakers are hidden. Because of the linear disposition of the speaker array along a usual pedestrian path, the glitches stalk the person during the whole phase of mobile communication initiation.

(http://civ.idc.cs.chalmers.se/projects/pps/tejp/prototype2.html)

While *Tejp* draws on *derivé*, *Glitch* appears to be inspired more by Situationist tactics of *détournement*. As a disruptive, or interruptive, technology *Glitch* makes tangible what may otherwise be intangible: the volume of mobile phone communication in a given space. *Glitch* also has the ability to render strange that which has become common-place, and create the technology anew. Transforming familiar meanings around mobile technologies draws attention to the place of these technologies in our everyday lives. How might other wireless technologies be used to defamiliarize particular technological practices and offer critiques of everyday life? How might ubiquitous technologies offer people a means to resist totalizing concepts of the city or of technology in general? Relatedly, how might wireless and ubiquitous technologies be used to limit social agency? What are the privacy implications of such technologies?

Texting glances: ambient interludes from the Dublin cityscape

Texting Glances is a joint project of the Story Networks Group at Media Lab Europe and the Networks and Telecommunications Research Group (NTRG), University of Dublin, Trinity College. Instead of using audio annotation and mobility, it focuses on waiting-place annotation through text and image:

> The system proposes to introduce a personal yet sociable and visual activity into urban 'waiting' spaces. Personal, because the input device is a cell phone; sociable and visual, because people can work together to co-construct a visual narrative. As people wait, they text to the system; the system responds to their texting by providing an image; as more people text the sequence of visuals plus text forms a multi-authored narrative. *Texting glances* is an ambient 'waiting' game in which transient audience participants use SMS texting to evolve a visual story on a large display which is installed in a public space such as a bus or train station.

> We imagine *Texting Glances* has a network of sites in the City. The moving audience interacts with the sites as they go about their daily lives. Audience can become author by adding to the image content of the system. Images 'live' in the system and are triggered into making an appearance, at any time and at any place by other users. An image can go undiscovered for months

unless exposed by the audience. Audience can also become collector and download passing images. The city becomes a hiding place for images to be uncovered and collected. *Texting Glances* could affect changes in behavior as people move to different city spaces to find new images and stories.

(Vaucelle *et al.* 2003, pp. 1–2)

In addition to raising issues of collective memory, *Texting Glances* conjures cultural studies of *in-between* spaces. For example, Clifford (1997) examines the hotel lobby as a metaphor for being away from home, in movement, in ambiguity. Morris (1988, p. 3) explains that motels 'memorialize only movement, speed and perpetual circulation;' the motel then represents 'neither arrival not departure, but the "pause"'. Braidotti (1994, pp. 18–19) also focuses on the 'places of transit that go with travelling: stations and airport lounges, trams, shuttle buses and check-in areas. In between zones where all ties are suspended and time stretched to a sort of continuous present'. What might ubiquitous technologies add to these discussions of non-space or in-between spaces? What might constitute the temporality of waiting? What sorts of rituals occur in these liminal spaces?

Urban tapestries

Sonic Geographies is a set of technological experiments being developed by Proboscis' Social Matrices research programme, which:

> takes sound as the entry point for excavating and mapping urban experience and invisible infrastructures of the city. A series of experiments and scenarios are being developed that operate as maps and journeys but also as highly personal renderings of sonic experience – sounds of the personal world in conversation with sounds of the city . . .
>
> The excavation is designed to open up a new space of enquiry into the experience of the city, and how sound functions as a kind of infrastructure for understandings of place and geography particular to contemporary conditions in the city.
>
> (Proboscis 2003, p. 2)

Of particular note is the *Urban Tapestries* project:

> *Urban Tapestries* allows users to annotate their own virtual city, enabling a community's collective memory to grow organically, allowing ordinary citizens to embed social knowledge in the new wireless landscape of the city. Users will be able to add new locations, location content and the 'threads' which link individual locations to local contexts, which are accessed via handheld user devices such as PDAs and mobile phones.
>
> (http://www.proboscis.org.uk/urbantapestries/index.html)

> Users of *Urban Tapestries* will be able to select threads to follow (such as
> historical or social threads linking individual places), or drift across all the
> threads. Having selected a thread, the user will receive a map of the locations
> in the area associated with it. They can either follow it as a trail, or set the
> system to give a proximity alert when they pass a location.
>
> (http://www.proboscis.org.uk/urbantapestries/scenarios_2.html)

The *Urban Tapestries* project, and *Sonic Geographies* in general, raise issues of the
lived city, 'invisibility', storytelling and the performance of collective memory
(see, for example, Calvino 2002, Boyer 2003). How are space and time in the
city negotiated by wireless technologies? What might constitute a sense of 'place'
in such scenarios? How might ubiquitous technologies map mobile experiences
of everyday life? How might such technologies rearticulate what it means to
'write' the city? How are individual and collective memory reconfigured by
these and similar Ubicomp applications?

All of the above ubiquitous computing projects can be seen to problematize
our understandings of spatialization, temporalization and, to varying extents,
embodiment. The final part of this paper will more closely examine these
categories of everyday life, and their connections to ubiquitous technologies.

Beyond structure: spatialization, temporalization and everyday life

Cultural studies may be seen to privilege ethnography and historiography in its
accounts of everyday life, while it also remains indebted to a variety of philosophical approaches within phenomenology and existentialism to explain our
being-in-the-world (Highmore 2001). As such, critiques of everyday life have
offered unique perspectives to help social and cultural theorists manoeuvre the
space between purely objectivist and subjectivist accounts (Gardiner 2000). In
many ways, theories of everyday life are exactly what Weiser referred to when
he wrote that the humanities and social sciences are good at making visible what
is invisible, and exposing the taken-for-granted aspects of lived experience that
form our common ground. However, we risk falling back into interior/exterior
dichotomies if we use theories of everyday life to account for what is *really* going
on under the surface of things. As van Loon (2002, p. 94) reminds us, 'We will
not understand anything about everyday life as long as we seek to reduce it to
epiphenomena of hidden and secret "structures"'.

Post-structural thought in the humanities and social sciences, and especially
that of Deleuze and Guattari, shifted the ground of study from interior/exterior
dichotomies toward what might be called the 'relational' and notions of decen-
tred subjectivity. This move focuses attention on the space *in-between* subjects and
therefore not on any particular subject; in other words, the space of subjectless

subjectivities where 'the product is the process' (Bains 2002, p. 112) and full accounting, or representation, becomes impossible.

This shifts analysis away from totalizing explanations or representations and towards decentralized performativity, which 'forces one to consider the space that would otherwise simply be glossed over as void. Suddenly, what happens between matters most' (van Loon 2002, p. 90). However, the 'void' of relational space is not empty at all; it is where everyday life happens. Theorists such as Bakhtin, Debord, Vaneigem, Lefebvre and de Certeau explored these relational spaces in terms of dialogic and material practices of everyday life. And rather than desiring and searching for the 'unification between representation and authenticity', we may instead look to performances of spatialization and temporalization in *shadows* and *resonances*:

> The shadows, however, no longer represent 'objects' but have become flows; they entail variations and differentiations only in intensity, not essence. Without having to resort to any other authentic being than the shadow flow itself, we do not have to make up stories about origins of being. Instead, the matter at hand is pure performativity . . .
>
> What the shadow does to vision and spatiality, resonance does to hearing and temporality. The resonance is sound that comes after; it is a trace that marks the vanishing event, the presence that never sustains . . .
>
> [W]hereas the relationship between the object and its shadow is relatively immediate and mimetic, the relationship between a sound and its resonance is always necessarily delayed. We need both figures if we are to make sense out of spatialization in cultural analyses and do justice to its im/ materiality.
>
> (van Loon 2002, pp. 91–92)

In this way, the performativity of everyday life involves spatialization, temporalization, embodiment and identification at play – those processes that perform space, time, bodies and identities so essential to being-in-the-world. Rather than looking at shadows and resonances as *representing something else*, we may understand them as spatially and temporally variable flows and intensities of the same 'things'. We are after all, as Weiser tried to convince fellow engineers and computer scientists, *mobile* creatures.

Shadows and resonances allow us to engage relations and *in-betweeness*, and drawing on the notion of flow from the work of Deleuze and Irigaray, Shields (1997, p. 2) explains that fluid relations are spatial, temporal and also material:

> The significance of the material quality of flows is that they have content, beyond merely being processes . . . Flows signal pure movement, without suggesting a point of origin or a destination, only a certain character of

movement, fluidity and direction . . . It is not that they are relational between objects or fixed points – which are taken as immutable mobiles – but they are the being of relation.

Flows may also be understood in terms of embodiment and becoming. As suggested above, the performative in the everyday has often been overlooked as studies tend to focus on structures, bodies and subjects. But as Harrison (2000, p. 497) claims, it is 'the performative, collective, and material nature of embodiment' that may lead us to conclude that 'everyday life should be understood in terms of enaction and immanence'.

So we may turn to the flows of everyday life and ask what spaces and times – what *places* – are being performed in ubiquitous computing, or more precisely, what are the spatializing and temporalizing roles of these sociotechnical assemblages? We may also begin to ask more questions about Ubicomp, materiality, embodiment and sociality.

Technology as everyday transductions and flows

Despite broader shifts from representation to performativity, theories of technological innovation, like theories of everyday life alluded to above, seem to maintain an almost contradictory sense of consistency and coherency. Part of this stems from the tendency to discuss new technologies as (representational) objects or artefacts, rather than as (performative) 'practices, arrangements and ensembles . . . which permit certain objects to materialize or solidify and not others' (Mackenzie 2003, p. 3).

Technical innovation as cultural practice has been explored within social studies of science and technology (see, for example, Latour 1999, Stengers 2000) but there remains the problem of applying relational ways of thinking to theories of technology and everyday life. As information technologies become more pervasive in everyday life, the analytical usefulness of such concepts becomes evident, and the concept of *transduction* provides a means to refocus our investigations towards non-representational understandings of technological practice:

> Transduction provides a way of thinking about technologies processually, that is, as events rather than objects, as contingent the whole way down, rather than covering over or reducing contingency . . . It proposes that both normalizing and generative capacities of technologies can be understood as a process of individuation, as an ontogenetic process which results in individuated things and which involves both ordinary and singular events. Much of what is represented as 'new' is in fact the capture and containment of the processual mode of existence in technology.
>
> (Mackenzie 2003, pp. 4–5)

Applied to Ubicomp, the concept of transduction allows us to shift our focus from ubiquitous computers as networked objects or artefacts, to ubiquitous computing as diverse procedures or performances in which socio-technical assemblages take shape. The primary benefit of this sort of approach is the ability to identify precise moments and locations in which we may possibly intervene and alter the course of events, thereby reasserting the role of social and cultural agency – and the potential for critiques of everyday life – in the development and use of ubiquitous computing.

Mackenzie (2002) also suggests that *technicity* is a transductive way of understanding technology in terms of flow and movements between abstraction and concreteness, or virtuality and actuality. These and other ontological categories – the virtual, concrete, abstract and probable – have also been explored in terms of intensities and flows by Shields (2003). The idea here is that by focussing our attention on these relations and flows, we may better understand the role of technologies in the spatialization, temporalization and embodiment of everyday life.

> Beyond technical objects, technicity inheres with the relationality of the ensembles or assemblages composed of bodies, institutions, conventions, representations, methods and practices. Read transductively, technical objects evolve over time by articulating diverse realities with each other. Technicity is a transcontextual linkage which can be objectified in context-limited ways, but also exceeds its objectification, stabilization or immutabilization.
>
> (Mackenzie 2003, p. 18)

Put differently, any given ubiquitous technology may be understood to comprise its contexts of research, development, manufacture, sale, implementation, use and eventual disposal. Shifting socio-technical arrangements are negotiated in particular space-times, and it becomes impossible to reduce Ubicomp to discrete (stable) objects of computation. And so, in order to begin to understand ubiquitous technologies transductively, we must seek out their intimations – their shadows and resonances – and begin to ask about their flows.

Ubiquitous computing, power and everyday life

Research into human-computer interaction and ubiquitous technologies has begun in earnest to examine the value of embodiment and presence from a broadly phenomenological perspective (see, for example, Dourish 2001, Hallnäs & Redström 2002, MacColl *et al.* 2002), but has largely taken for granted related matters of spatialization and temporalization. The very desire of Ubicomp to become embedded or pervasive technology serves to render space and time invisible; it quite simply seeks to go anywhere and be everywhere. One of the consequences of this approach is that relations of power and control are rendered similarly invisible.

Deleuze (1997) makes the case that although there remain disciplinary social institutions, we have moved away from a disciplinary society (following Foucault) and towards a more pervasive and intrusive society of control. This control manifests itself in multitudes of interconnected networks, where people, objects, activities and ideas are deeply intertwined, and dichotomies between public and private, or global and local, become untenable. If the disciplinary society may be understood to *mould* individual and collective behaviour through categorical segregation and fixing, societies of control instead *modulate* interactions by integrating and organizing difference. Control societies comprise hybrid and mobile forms of interaction, rather than structures that follow predictable rules. At issue here are not objects or subjects, but relations between bodies, and processes of embodiment; performed in these processes are relations of power and control in everyday life.

Easily envisioned as part of Latour's (1999) 'proliferation of hybrids', ubiquitous computing is the archetypal hybrid and mobile technology at work within a society of control. Latour (1999, p. 214) claims that we live and act as a 'collective of humans and non-humans' in which

> an increasingly large number of humans are mixed with an increasingly large number of nonhumans, to the point that, today, the whole planet is engaged in the making of politics, law, and soon, I suspect, morality . . . The nasty problem we now have to deal with is that, unfortunately, we do *not* have a definition of politics that can answer the specifications of this nonmodern history.

The techno-political implications of Ubicomp have a broad reach largely beyond the scope of this paper, but it is important to articulate a few basic questions and concerns around pervasive computing, power and control in everyday life.

If we indeed live and act as a collective of humans and non-humans, as I believe we do, then our connections and relations to our technologies need to be evaluated by means which recognize this multiplicity. Despite the appearance of novelty, ubiquitous computing draws on a long and complex history of relations between materials and ideas, industry and business, government and law, individuals and groups, to name but a few. All of these processes have been mobilized – and will continue to be mobilized - to shape Ubicomp as we know it. To separate ubiquitous computing from these contexts is to deny that it is always already embedded in practices of everyday life. It is precisely this blurring of boundaries, this hybridization, that challenges traditional practices of autonomy and social control, and makes responsibility and accountability increasingly difficult to locate. Just as context shapes Ubicomp, so too ubiquitous computing shapes contexts of interaction. Recalling Latour, I believe we are not politically ready to engage Ubicomp as long as we continue to assume that ubiquitous computing merely comprises new tools, neutral in and of themselves, and independent of broader networks of relation.

To begin, we need to be clear on, and be able to justify, what it is about the mundane nature of everyday life that can be 'improved' through augmentation, amplification or attempts to merge the physical and the virtual – especially if the technologies themselves are expected to become ordinary and pervasive aspects of everyday life. We need to become more careful about contrasting interaction as it occurs in everyday life with the types of interaction that are possible because of this 'novel' medium we call computation, and recognize the ways in which the virtual is not separate from the real. The 'mixed-reality' enabled by ubiquitous computing may be better understood as shifting intensities or flows of the virtual and the actual, rather than as points on a continuum between the virtual and the real. Through technicity and transduction, Ubicomp may be seen as assemblages and procedures that actualize virtualities in particular ways, and enact particular spaces, times, bodies and relations of power. Without necessarily advocating a Marxist approach, it is still important to ask how ubiquitous technologies may bring together and organize unequal local and global populations.

For example, the technology that allows someone on the street to record their thoughts at a particular location and share it with others – as in the *Urban Tapestries* or *Texting Glances* projects discussed above – also mobilizes local and global procedures and policies surrounding the use of city architecture and public space, the manufacture, implementation and ownership of computer hardware, and socio-technical assemblages for the acquisition and administration of data. If similar types of ubiquitous computing processes are embedded in our everyday urban environments, we need to understand which relations may be privileged and which may be prohibited, again, both locally and globally. What sorts of politics and ethics will we need to ensure accountability in these global ensembles in which we are embroiled? At which points in our processes and procedures may we successfully intervene and affect change, and at which points are particular changes especially difficult or not even possible?

The matter of surveillance in context-aware computing has already emerged as the single greatest social concern surrounding Ubicomp. Public awareness and protest of now familiar video surveillance and data tracking technologies is expanding to address the types of public and private monitoring, as well as citizen interventions, enabled by hundreds of thousands of invisible, mobile computers, including RFID tags (see, for example, Rheingold 2002). Engineer Steve Mann suggests that a possible response to surveillance technologies is to turn them back on the powers-that-be through what he refers to as *sousveillance* (Mann & Niedzviecki 2002). Aware of the potential privacy violations made possible by mobile, context-aware computing, Mann argues that citizens may resist institutional control by using the same technology to gather data on the institutions themselves. For example, by attempting to digitally mediate and record our interactions in 'public' spaces like shopping malls or airports, we may find ourselves stopped by security guards and forbidden to proceed. In these procedures, we are made aware of the private control of these locations; through the customs of protecting property or national security, regulation of these spaces allows only one-way monitoring. Presumably, this awareness allows for a more informed citizenship, while also calling for greater institutional transparency. However, in a society of control it remains unclear how the perpetuation of surveillance, even if bottom-up rather than top-down, may be a successful act of resistance and actually affect change.

We also need to ask how ubiquitous technologies like those used in the *Amble Time* project may be commercialized and not only track the movements of people and objects, but also lead people directly to places of consumption. In the design of these types of technology, maps of the city need to be programmed and, presumably, businesses will be able to pay to have themselves included as points on the map. As such, the maps include and exclude particular aspects of the city, and just as new empowering relations may be enabled, so too may certain unequal power relations be perpetuated and new limitations or restrictions emerge. Without accounting for these possibilities, the design of ubiquitous technologies may set us on paths for which we are not socially and culturally prepared, and at the same time limit chances for creativity, serendipity and innovation. We need to continually ask about the risks and stakes involved in ubiquitous applications, as our everyday lives will be increasingly intertwined with 'invisible' technologies.

Moving through the city, and through public spaces, has always been a performative practice where the citizen is relatively able to use the material world for her own purposes and enjoyment, and engage in critiques of everyday life (see, for example, de Certeau 1984, Lefebvre 1991, Borden *et al.* 2001). Where ubiquitous technologies might fail is if they prevent or inhibit the ability of a person to experience the city on his own terms; if they start from a premise of what the city *is* rather than allowing it to emerge through the movements of its people. The ability for users to comment on a map, to delete meaningless places, add meaningful places, and to share those comments and places with others, may provide means of putting practices of spatialization and temporalization in the hands of users – allowing them to manipulate, or shape, their city – instead of limiting the potential of everyday life and controlling the flow through abstracted technological objects and models of information. Individuals and collectives need to feel safe and secure in the midst of all these computers, and we need to devise ways of balancing those possibly conflicting needs and desires.

By recalling *Sonic City* and *Tejp*, we may ask how ubiquitous technologies may act as critiques of everyday life. These types of critiques may guide decision-making at local and global scales, and we need to better understand how

Ubicomp may be used to resist and sustain networks of control, and how people may be able to engage with pervasive computing on their own terms (see, for example, Rheingold 2002). With the variable sounds and rhythms of *Sonic City*, the city is spatialized and temporalized through embodied movement and material practices. The shifts and delays in real-time sound and musical composition as the walker passes through particular environments draw our attention to *resonances* of everyday life, as sound implicates the spaces in-between (Evens 2002). Perhaps most importantly, technology demonstrably slows down in these moments, allowing not only space and time for reflection, but creating space and time for becoming and tracing our being-in-the-world. We need to understand exactly what happens during delays and 'crashes', instead of hiding, ignoring or naturalizing them.

A similar critique of everyday life is taken in the *Tejp* sound prototypes. The audio tags created by random passersby and 'whispered' at other passersby immediately conjure *resonances* of everyday life as physical and social boundaries are breached. The potential for both individual and collective action and experience is limited only by the location and governance of tags, and users are offered glimpses of different experiences in the process of making their own expanding the sense of inter-connection. The *Glitch* prototype more obviously disrupts our understandings and expectations of mobile technologies in public spaces by rendering audible what is usually inaudible, and making publicly visible our reactions to these technologies. In these ways, particular 'invisible' ubiquitous technologies may be used to render other material and social processes 'visible', and we may ask how certain relations are enacted in certain contexts, and how those relations create and flow into new contexts. This may enable us to articulate exact processes and events that mobilize specific relations between people, objects and ideas, which, in turn, offer us means to support or resist.

The relations between Ubicomp, power and everyday life are complex and in flux, and yet we need to ensure the responsible development, implementation and use of ubiquitous technologies. Without an understanding of the local and global stakes at hand, we risk the control of people in everyday life and decreased quality of life for everyone.

Conclusions

Visions for ubiquitous computing originated with the social and cultural, and have the ultimate goal of embedding computational devices in everyday objects and places. However, the contribution of social and cultural studies to Ubicomp has been mostly restricted to ethnographic evaluations of technologies and human-computer interaction. This essay, as part of a larger project, points to another place of possible articulation: theories and practices of everyday life.

When everyday life is understood in terms of spatialization, temporalization and embodiment, ubiquitous computing offers a unique opportunity to evaluate the 'relational' as flows, intensities and transductions that mobilize sociotechnical assemblages. In this way, neither technologies nor familiar categories of everyday life are allowed to slip back into oppositional relationships of interiority and exteriority, and theories of everyday are also better able to account for the increasing pervasiveness of communications technologies in everyday life.

Weiser wanted ubiquitous computing to become *invisible,* but he also called on the humanities and social sciences to make visible to engineers and computer scientists what is often invisible so that they could better design for context-awareness. Theories of everyday life are dedicated to that very task, and provide a means by which to explore augmented and amplified reality applications, and understand the ways in which they spatialize, temporalize and embody everyday life. Conversely, ubiquitous technologies will become more active in the performance of everyday life, and social and cultural studies will benefit from an awareness of their design principles and particular applications. It is my hope that social and cultural theorists, as well as designers of ubiquitous computing, will find new ways of looking at the roles of technology in everyday life. This essay is an attempt to move us in that direction by asking questions and suggesting possibilities, and it will be left to researchers in both fields to take up the challenge of future collaboration.

References

Azuma, R. (1997) 'A survey of augmented reality', *Presence: Teleoperators and Virtual Environments*, vol. 6, no. 4, pp. 355–385.

Baines, P. (2002) 'Subjectless subjectivities', in *Shock to Thought: Expression after Deluze and Guattari*, ed. B. Massumi, Routledge, London, pp. 101–116.

Bakhtin, M. (1981) *The Dialogical Imagination: Four Essays by M.M. Bakhtin*, ed. M. Holquist, University of Texas Press, Austin, TX.

BBC (2003) 'Digital maps tell the time', 9 May 2003, [online] Available at http://news.bbc.co.uk/1/hi/technology/2986655.stm

Benjamin, W. (1969) *Illuminations*, Schocken, New York.

Benjamin, W. (1999) *The Arcades Project*, Harvard University Press, Cambridge, MA.

Borden, I., Kerr, J., Rendell, J. & Pivaro, A. (eds) (2001) *The Unknown City: Contesting Architecture and Social Space*, MIT Press, Cambridge, MA.

Boyer, C. (2003) *City of Collective Memory: Its Historical Imagery and Architectural Entertainments*, MIT Press, Cambridge, MA.

Braidotti, R. (1994) *Nomadic Subjects*, Columbia University Press, New York.

Brown, B., Green, N. & Harper, R. (eds) (2002) *Wireless World: Social and Interactional Aspects of the Mobile Age*, Springer, London.

Calvino, I. (2002) *Invisible Cities*, Vintage, New York.

Clifford, J. (1997) *Routes*, Harvard University Press, Cambridge, MA.

de Certeau, M. (1984) *The Practice of Everyday Life*, University of California Press, Berkeley, CA.

Debord, G. (2003) *The Society of the Spectacle*, Zone Books, New York.

Deleuze, G. (1997) *Negotiations: 1972–1990*, Columbia University Press, New York.

Department of Electrical Engineering and Computer Sciences, University of California, Berkeley (1999) 'Mark Weiser dies at 46', [online] Available at http://www.cs.berkeley.edu/Weiser/bio.shtml

Dourish, P. (2001) *Where the Action Is: The Foundations of Embodied Interaction*, MIT Press, Cambridge, MA.

Evens, A. (2002) 'Sound ideas', in *Shock to Thought: Expression after Deleuze and Guattari*, ed. B. Massumi, Routledge, London, pp. 171–187.

Falk, J., Redström, J. & Björk, S. (1999) 'Amplifying reality', *Proceedings of the First International Symposium on Handheld and Ubiquitous Computing (HUC) '99*, Springer Verlag, London, [online] Available at http://civ.idc.cs.chalmers.se/publications/1999/AmpReality.pdf

Gardiner, M. (2000) *Critiques of Everyday Life*, Routledge, London and New York.

Gaye, L., Holmquist, L. E. & Mazé, R. (2003) 'Sonic city: the urban environment as a musical interface', *Proceedings of NIME '03*, [online] Available at http://www.viktoria.se/fal/projects/soniccity/pdf/soniccity.pdf

Grenville, B. (2002) *The Uncanny: Experiments in Cyborg Culture*, Vancouver Art Gallery, Vancouver.

Hallnäs, L. & Redström, J. (2002) 'From use to presence: on the expressions and aesthetics of everyday computational things', submitted for publication, [online] Available at http://www.math.chalmers.se/~redstrom/thesis/hi/use2presence.pdf

Harrison, P. (2000) 'Making sense: embodiment and the sensibilities of the everyday', *Environment and Planning D: Society and Space*, vol. 18, no. 4, pp. 497–517.

Hayles, N. K. (1999) *How We Became Posthuman: Virtual Bodies in Cybernetics, Literature, and Informatics*, University of Chicago Press, Chicago, IL.

Highmore, B. (2002) *Everyday Life and Cultural Theory: An Introduction*, Routledge, London.

Hillis, K. (1999) *Digital Sensations: Space, Identity and Embodiment in Virtual Reality*, University of Minnesota Press, Minneapolis.

Langheinrich, M. (2002) 'Privacy invasions in ubiquitous computing', paper presented at Ubicomp 2002 Privacy Workshop, Göteborg, Sweden, [online] Available at http://guir.berkeley.edu/pubs/ubicomp2002/privacyworkshop/papers/uc2002-pws.pdf

Latour, B. (1999) *Pandora's Hope: Essays on the Reality of Science Studies*, Harvard University Press, Cambridge, MA.

Lederer, S., Dey, A. K. & Mankoff, J. (2002) 'Everyday privacy in ubiquitous computing environments', paper presented at Ubicomp 2002 Privacy Workshop, Gothenburg, Sweden, [online] Available at http://guir.berkeley.edu/pubs/ubicomp2002/privacyworkshop/papers/lederer-ubicomp02-workshop.pdf

Lefebvre, H. (1991) *The Production of Space*, Blackwell, London.

Lynch, K. (1960) *The Image of the City*, MIT Press, Cambridge, MA.

Lynch, K. (1984) 'Reconsidering the image of the city', in *Cities of the Mind: Images and Themes of the City in the Social Sciences*, eds L. Rodwin & R. M. Hollister, Plenum Press, New York, pp. 151–161.

MacColl, I., Chalmers, M., Rogers, Y. & Smith, H. (2002) 'Seamful ubiquity: beyond seamless integration', Technical Report Equator-02-020, Equator, September 2002, [online] Available at http://www.dcs.gla.ac.uk/scripts/global/equator/moin.cgi/SeamfulUbiquity

Mackenzie, A. (2002) *Transductions: Bodies and Machines at Speed*, Continuum, London.

Mackenzie, A. (2003) 'Transduction: invention, innovation and collective life', draft, [online] Available at http://www.lancs.ac.uk/staff/mackenza/papers/transduction.pdf

Mann, S. & Niedzviecki, H. (2002) *Cyborg: Digital Destiny and Human Possibility in the Age of the Wearable Computer*, DoubleDay Canada, Toronto.

Massumi, B. (2002) *Parables for the Virtual: Movement, Affect, Sensation*, Duke University Press, Durham, NC.

Milgram, P. & Kishino, F. (1994) 'A taxonomy of mixed reality visual displays', IEICE (Institute of Electronics, Information and Communication Engineers) Transactions on Information and Systems, Special Issue on Networked Reality, E77D (12), pp. 1321–1329.

Milgram, P., Takemura, H., Utsumi, A. & Kishino, F. (1994) 'Augmented reality: a class of displays on the reality-virtuality continuum', *Proceedings of Telemanipulator and Telepresence Technologies*, SPIE vol. 2351, pp. 282–292.

Morris, M. (1988) 'At Henry Parkes Motel', *Cultural Studies*, vol. 2, pp. 1–47.

Nardi, B. & O'Day, V. (1999) *Information Ecologies: Using Technology with Heart*, MIT Press, Cambridge, MA.

Nguyen, D. H. & Mynatt, E. D. (2002) 'Privacy mirrors: understanding and shaping socio-technical ubiquitous computing systems', unpublished manuscript, [online] Available at http://quixotic.cc.gt.atl.ga.us/~dnguyen/writings/PrivacyMirrors.pdf

Norman, D. (1998) *The Invisible Computer*, MIT Press, Cambridge, MA.

Orth, M. (2001) 'Sculpted computational objects with smart and active computing materials', doctoral dissertation, Massachusetts Institute of Technology, Cambridge, MA, [online] Available at http://web.media.mit.edu/~morth/thesis/thesis.html

Proboscis (2003) Urban Tapestries Postcard, [online] Available at http://www.proboscis.org.uk/urbantapestries/UT_postcard_2003.pdf

Redström, J. (2001) 'Designing everyday computational things', PhD thesis, Dept of Informatics, Göteborg University, [online] Available at http://www.math.chalmers.se/~redstrom/thesis/

Rheingold, H. (1994a) 'PARC is back', *Wired 2.02*, [online] Available http://www.wired.com/wired/archive/2.02/parc.html

Rheingold, H. (1994b) *Virtual Reality*, Simon and Schuster, New York.

Rheingold, H. (2002) *Smart Mobs: The Next Social Revolution*, Perseus, Cambridge, MA.

Shields, R. (1997) 'Flow as a new paradigm', *Space and Culture*, vol. 1, pp. 1-8.

Shields, R. (2003) *The Virtual*, Routledge, London.

Stengers, I. (2000) *The Invention of Modern Science*, University of Minnesota Press, Minneapolis.

Van Loon, J. (2002) 'Social spatialization and everyday life', *Space and Culture*, vol. 5, no. 2, pp. 88–95.

Vaneigem, R. (2001) *The Revolution of Everyday Life*, AK Press, New York.

Weiser, M. (1991) 'The computer for the 21st century', *Scientific American*, vol. 265, no. 3, pp. 94–104, [online] Available at http://www.ubiq.com/hypertext/weiser/SciAmDraft3.html

Weiser, M. (1993a) 'Some computer science issues in ubiquitous computing', *Communications of the ACM,* July 1993, [online] Available at http://www.ubiq.com/hypertext/weiser/UbiCACM.html

Weiser, M. (1993b) 'The world is not a desktop', *ACM Interactions*, January 1994, pp. 7–8, [online] Available at http://www.ubiq.com/hypertext/weiser/ACMInteractions2.html

Weiser, M. & Brown, J. S. (1996) 'The coming age of calm technology', [online] Available at http://www.ubiq.com/hypertext/weiser/acmfuture2endnote.htm

Westerkamp, H. (1999) 'Soundscape composition: linking inner and outer worlds', lecture held at Soundscape voor 2000, Amsterdam, Holland, 19–26 November 1999, [online] Available at http://www.sfu.ca/~westerka/writings/soundscapecomp.html

Mark Poster

CONSUMPTION AND DIGITAL
COMMODITIES IN THE EVERYDAY

The category of the everyday has designated in social theory the remainder, what is left over after the important regions of politics and production. This left consumption in the under-theorized domain of the everyday. Since Veblen — and more recently Baudrillard and de Certeau — consumption has been reconfigured as significant in its own right, as a complex, articulated area related directly to culture. Liberal thinkers have also claimed consumer activity as central to society, as the domain where the individual is realized. This paper will review these positions and attempt to develop an understanding of consumption in daily life in relation to digital cultural objects. It will also argue that these mediated commodities, in the practices of appropriation connected with them, configure subjects in ways that are difficult to reconcile with existing structures of domination.

Keywords digital commodities; postmodernity; agency; media; combinatory; cultural object

Everywhere a consumer

In the USA and in most industrialized countries, individuals in their everyday lives are bombarded continuously by advertisements. Walking in the street or driving through it, one's eyes are assaulted by billboards, store signs, huge electronic monitors, brand names on the clothing of others, promotional information on buses, benches and company cars. The visual space of contemporary urbanity is a mosaic of images and texts all selling something, all competing for the attention of the passers-by with bright colours, tempting imagery and large size. Entry inside buildings is no respite from the assault. Department stores feature monitors urging the shopper to buy the products on the screen (McCarthy 2001). The purchase itself is no mere acquisition but a submission to the publicity departments of untold corporations of one's preferences as the information flits at electronic speeds from one's credit card through the computers networked around the globe and finally into the omnivorous databases of the insatiable transnational behemoths. In the space of the city, the individual is labelled and branded into the category of the consumer with a consistency that would be admirable were it not so deplorable.

Cultural Studies Vol. 18, No. 2/3 March/May 2004, pp. 409–423
ISSN 0950-2386 print/ISSN 1466-4348 online   © 2004 Taylor & Francis Ltd
http://www.tandf.co.uk/journals   DOI: 10.1080/0950238042000201581

Imagine my surprise then when I visited Ljubljana, Slovenia in June 1987, a couple of years before everything collapsed in degrees of chaos on the other side of the Cold War's Iron Curtain. Hollywood programmed my mind to expect a depressing urban landscape dominated by a monotony of greys. Nothing could be farther from the truth. A hiatus in the conference I was attending afforded me a chance to stroll in the city. Even in my jet-lagged state of mind, I was truly astonished, upon perambulating through some main streets, to find an almost complete absence of billboards, signs, images, the repertoire of the marketer's imagination. So bereft of advertising were the streets that the only way to discover what a retail shop was selling was for the visitor to the city to walk right up to the shop window and peer inside. The relief from advertising, for this New Yorker cum Southern Californian, was in turn disconcerting, arresting and fascinating. I was charmed by the lack of information as my eyes relished the buildings, trees, shrubs and, yes, people. How different was an urban experience of the everyday without the relentless appeals of the market! Ljubljana taught me to look differently at the visual spectacle of Los Angeles, with strip mall sandwiched next to strip mall in an appalling homage to free enterprise in its postmodern mode.

The alternative to the street as the space of everyday life is the home. Here one is no more secure than when outside from the constant hawking of wares and services. An array of media facilitates the intrusion of marketers into the home. Least annoying for most of us are the ads that arrive every morning with the daily newspaper. Soft pornography strewn across the pages of the most respected dailies is a privilege of the marketing department of corporations that somehow eludes the moralists who decry its presence in other media such as the World Wide Web or cable television. Erotic images are acceptable, for this logic, when they are part of a commercial. Radio and television commercials are bothersome too, but by now they merge almost into invisibility and inaudibility inside the shows themselves as our minds filter out their blaring solicitations. Videotaped movies and DVDs enjoyed in living rooms and dens increasingly feature promotional material at the beginning of the media, forcing one to fast forward to avoid them. Most objectionable perhaps are the calls from telemarketers, interrupting us at dinner or whenever their statistical predictions of our availability indicate they are most likely to reach us. Even FAX machines attached to private telephone lines are not immune to wiles of the solicitor, at least not until some recent rulings by the US courts may impose a modicum of restraint. Advertisers offer free Internet service providers, free e-mail accounts, even free computers, if only the individual would act like a consumer and permit the tracking of purchasing activity. In every room of the home except the toilet, the private individual is hailed, by dint of the media, as a consumer. In public and in private, publicity finds us and renders us — consciously or not, willingly or not, and above all else — as consumers.

Without media, the activity of consumption and the figure of the consumer do not take on their current status as major aspects of social life. A very different inflection characterized consumption before the advent of contemporary media. Notwithstanding my nostalgic descriptions of the streets of Ljubljana and the Berlin Winterfeldt Markt, I do not argue that the earlier conditions were somehow better, more moral or closer to democracy. Far from it. Rather consumption in the era of mechanical reproduction was a different regime of practice, a different technology of power to use Foucault's (1980) term, from what currently prevails. The analysis of consumption in the recent period must take into account the role of the media in supporting this difference. For each type of media, the analysis also must determine the specific relation to activities of consumption, and with the concomitant construction of the consumer subject. Before turning to the question of media regimes and consumption, I shall consider the understanding of this question by prominent theorists of consumption, in particular Michel de Certeau, testing the extent to which their contribution to the analysis of consumption includes recognition of the place of the media.

Consumer theory and the media

Social and cultural theory in the modern era was preoccupied with two main questions: the democratic nation state and the industrial economy. The values of freedom and equality were calibrated to the understanding of politics and economics. Issues of family life, gender relations, sexual preference, consumer patterns and emotional dynamics were clearly subordinate to the world-historical concerns of determining the most appropriate institutional forms for the realization of human freedom. With great subtlety, intellectuals and scholars investigated the variations of state formation, industrial development, and market cycles. In these areas, the essence of human nature was actualized. A promethean vision of human progress accompanied arguments over the organiz-ation of modern life. In this theoretical context, the consumer was decidedly a secondary figure. Consumption was considered necessary for the reproduction of labour and the satisfaction of needs. Yet, it was not connected directly to the great drama of human betterment. A domain of 'passivity', consumption was outside history, a sideshow to the main event of political economy. Firat and Dholakia put it well when they write, 'the "passivation" of consumption came to be the prevalent mode of consumption in modernity' (1998, p. 65). The free citizen and the free labourer were modernity's achievements, not the free consumer. What could not be thought during the heyday of modernity was consumption as a regime of practice, one that varied significantly from period to period, that was intelligible as an activity, which was central to the cultural process of constructing a symbolic order.

A salient feature of *post*modernity is the recognition of the complexity and importance of consumption. Michel de Certeau is a leading theorist of this change. His works, especially *The Practice of Everyday Life* (1984), *Heterologies* (1986) and *Culture in the Plural* (1997), constitute a thorough rethinking of the question of consumption in everyday life. Of course, he is not alone in this endeavour, as many of the important discussions of daily life attest (Gardiner 2000). I shall review de Certeau's discussion of consumption with an eye to the question of the media. While recognizing the invaluable contribution de Certeau makes to a reconceptualization of consumption, I raise the question of its incompleteness or inadequacies with regard to the role of media, a problem that plagues much of the social and cultural theory of everyday life.[1] I also take de Certeau as typical of a group of thinkers who work in a similar direction, from Georg Simmel and Henri Lefebvre to Pierre Bourdieu. The following critical evaluation is intended not as a dismissal of the work of these thinkers but as a plea for recognition of the question of information machines.

De Certeau is certainly cognizant of the way commercial capitalism transforms the visual landscape of urban daily life. Much like my impression of the difference between communist Ljubljana and capitalist Los Angeles, de Certeau notes,

> The modern city is becoming a labyrinth of images. It is endowed with a graphics of its own, by day and by night that devises a vocabulary of images on a new space of writing. A landscape of posters and billboards organizes our reality. It is a *mural landscape* with the repertory of its immediate objects of happiness. It conceals the buildings in which labor is confined; it covers over the closed universe of everyday life; it sets in place artificial forms that follow the paths of labor in order to juxtapose their passageways to the successive moments of pleasure. A city that is a real 'imaginary museum' forms the counterpoint of the city at work.
>
> (1997, p. 34)

Advertising for de Certeau mars the city, pollutes the urban panorama, but, we must ask, how are these images to be understood in the context of the fully array of media visuality, including film, television and the Internet? Does de Certeau's highly influential theory of the everyday account for the relation of media to consumption?

An irony characterizes de Certeau's intervention in the theory of consumption. He turns to language theory in order to theorize consumption as an active practice. For historians and social scientists, especially of the period of the 1970s in which de Certeau wrote, social agency was an attribute of action. Language theory, especially structuralist linguistics, was considered by these scholars as a threat to agency, as a deterministic system that eviscerated the freedom of the individual and group. Their view is a modernist one as outlined above. Action here concerns political and economic practices. De Certeau, on the contrary, revalues consumption as an active practice by turning to the very register of analysis regarded by modernists as forestalling such recognition. De Certeau complains that the quantifying methods of social science reduce the understanding of consumption. They see cultural products 'merely as data on the basis of which statistical tabulations of their circulation can be drawn up'. They do not recognize them 'also as parts of the repertory with which users carry out operations of their own' (1984, p. 31). Statistics, he protests, is limited to grasping 'the material used by consumer practices', but 'consumers produce . . . indeterminate trajectories'. There is a '*formality* proper to these practices, their surreptitious and guileful "movement"' (1984, p. 34). De Certeau discovers this 'form' through a poststructuralist theory of language.

De Certeau explores the implications of the modernist study of consumption. He finds that this approach not only misses the 'form' of consumption but also denigrates the position of the consumer. In the hands of modernist social science, 'Consumers are transformed into immigrants' (1984, p. 40). 'The practices of consumption are the ghosts of the society that carries their name' (1984, p. 35) More generally, de Certeau discloses the problem with modernist analyses: 'A society is . . . composed of certain foregrounded practices organizing its normative institutions *and* of innumerable other practices that remain "minor." . . . It is in this multifarious and silent "reserve" of procedures that we should look for "consumer" practices having the double characteristic . . . of being able to organize both spaces and languages, whether on a minute or a vast scale' (1984, p. 48). This is the crux of the matter for de Certeau: the 'form' of consumption missed by the 'technocratic rationality' of social science is its construction of 'spaces and languages'. With this argument goes a sea change in the understanding of consumption. From the passive, quantifiable action of individuals, consumption becomes a cultural creation, a poeisis, as he terms it, a making and a using, a signifying constellation. Here is the sense in which de Certeau deploys a language theory: consumption is a type of 'enunciation', a production of meaning, a sort of speech act. Consumption is not simply a purchase of an object fixed in its meaning but a resignification of that object. Commodities move from factories to stores to homes. The last move includes a remaking of the object, not physically, but culturally. In the practices of food preparation, in the decoration of appliances like refrigerators with children's artwork, notices and memoranda, in every one of the acts of consumption, meanings are constructed and life is thereby organized and configured. Those who find social agency in work and politics systematically ignore the creativity of consumption.

Upgrading the value of the practice of consumption, de Certeau also presented a reconsideration of everyday life. His influential discussion of the rhetoric of walking in the city is only one aspect of his complete rethinking of the everyday. Significantly, he introduced terms of warfare (strategies and tactics)

to theorize the productive side of everyday practices. Strategies are the instrumental actions of large institutions; tactics are the resisting practices of individuals and groups. The difficulty with these categories for the current discussion is
that they occlude the mediation of information machines. They do not allow for
a differential understanding of the material constraints and openings afforded by
each medium. Instead, de Certeau introduces a binary of determinist, institutional strategies and creative, countervailing tactics. But let us look first at what
de Certeau writes about the media.

Explicit discussion of the media is few in de Certeau's chief theoretical
works. *The Practice of Everyday Life* barely mentions media. Here in a rare exception de Certeau speculates on the impact of computers: today, he writes, 'the
scriptural system moves forward on its own; it is becoming self-moving and
technocratic; it transforms the subjects that controlled it into operators of the
writing machine that orders and uses them. A cybernetic society' (1984, p. 136).
These words were written in the late 1970s before IBM's personal computer
appeared so it is understandable that de Certeau thinks of the machine as little
different from mechanical technologies. For him, the computer will control the
user just as machines in the factory dictate the movements of workers. In a
slightly earlier work, de Certeau discerns a salient problem with other information machines, broadcast media. 'Information', he writes, 'especially the press,
television, video, etc., reserves to a smaller and smaller circle of producers the
possession or use of increasingly expensive equipment' (1997, p. 109). He failed
to see that computers would vastly expand positions of speech and counter the
centralization of points of enunciation inherent in earlier electronic media. In
the end, de Certeau worries about the fate of speech in daily life as a consequence
of the spread of broadcast media. His prognosis is not good: 'the press and the
radio deceive or satisfy this "solitary crowd" with celestial magic, the exoticism
of easy love or the terrors of drugs. What spreads is the feeling of fatality.
Humans are *spoken* by the language of socioeconomic determinism long before
they can speak it. . . . Will it be possible for humans to create spaces for
themselves in which their own speech can be proffered?' (1997, p. 111). In this
analysis, the advantages of 'tactics' appear insufficient to combat the alienations
of mediated consumption.

Even with this brief and overly schematic review of de Certeau's theory of
the everyday, it is clear that we need to move on to a framework that addresses
more directly the relation of media to everyday consumption.

Varieties of consumers and media

Before turning to the media in daily consumption, we must first explore further
the issue of consumption. Various theorists have deconstructed the binary
production/consumption to indicate the importance of the latter (Lefebvre

1971, Baudrillard 1998). These efforts succeed in decoupling consumption from production and demonstrate the way consumption brings forth its unique type of human action. Consumption, in the hands of these theorists, has its own semiotics and its own logic of practice. However, consumption here remains too singular, monolithic and ahistorical. If we are to connect consumption with media, it is necessary first to understand the varieties of consumption, the expanse of practices that characterize consumption in different times and places. Certainly different groups consume differently: age, sex, class, gender, ethnicity, race and region – each of these variables affect significantly the patterns of consumption. I am not, however, interested in a totalizing taxonomy of consumption or a comprehensive matrix that would locate each act of consumption. To open the question of media and consumption at the most general level, it is necessary only to outline the broad, historical configurations of consumption. One must ask how consumption has changed over the centuries and look for links with media.

In order to define these historical configurations, one must develop a sort of combinatory in the manner of Louis Althusser (Althusser and Balibar 1970) or a technology of power as in Foucault (1980). One must suggest the common features of consumption that may vary over time in the combination, inflection, and emphasis. The analyst would then be able to comprehend consumption as a cultural construction and each pattern of consumption as a delimited practice. Recently Fuat Firat and Nikhilesh Dholakia offered a combinatory with four variables: the social relationships entailed in consumption, the degree of the public nature of the act and the object consumed, the participation of the consumer in the development or production of the product, and the intensity of activity in consumption (Firat and Dholakia 1998). These criteria afford a complex understanding of consumption patterns, as they show, in early modern, modern and postmodern contexts. They enable and encourage the analysis of many of the aspects of consumption.[2] Although their categories are rich at the social level of consumption, they are limited with respect to cultural issues. They do not adequately point to language, identity and desire as aspects of consumption. When examining the relation of media to consumption, these cultural issues will be particularly exigent.

Nonetheless, Firat and Dholakia present a historical picture of consumption patterns that exposes many of the important issues. They indicate how consumption has become in the modern period of industrial capitalism and representative democracy more and more individual, private, passive, and alienated from production. This classic view of the modern consumer as couch potato contrasts sharply with that of the period antecedent to modernity and to the recent years they are happy to designate as postmodern. In quantitative terms, modern consumer activity increased dramatically with the invention of so many appliances, small and large, and the advance of fashion to promote rapid changes in clothing. Yet in qualitative terms the consumer was increasingly marginalized as a social actor, increasingly denigrated as passive, frivolous, boring, unimportant, and 'feminine' (Huyssen 1986). These characteristics apply most fully to the USA, and to a lesser extent other industrialized societies in Western Europe and Asia; they are least adequate in reference to societies less affected by urban, industrial patterns.

When they move on to consider the consumer pattern of postmodern society, Firat and Dholakia prove the worth of their combinatory. As they show, each of the characteristics of the modern consumer begin to diminish in the closing decades of the twentieth century. A shift in the pattern consumption occurs away from the privacy, individualism, passivity and alienation from work toward other directions. Yet the main feature of postmodern consumption, in their account, is not the collapse of modern traits but the emergence of multiplicity in consuming patterns. What held together as a stable, hierarchy of patterns of consumption in modern society has simply dispersed into heterogeneity. In order 'to keep up with the Jones''one had to have a clear idea of what and how the Jones' consumed. A fixed idea of consumption for wealthy, middle class and poorer folk was generally known and accepted. The only problem was what one could afford, how much money one had to scurry after the lifestyle of the Jones'. Postmodernity, by contrast, entails the vast expansion or fragmentation of consumer patterns. One sees this clearly in the burgeoning of clothing styles that originated among the young, the poor, and the minority groups. These patterns shift first to wealthier youth in majority ethnicities and then, surprisingly, to adults. Consumer culture no longer trickles down from the leisure class but climbs up from society's lower reaches. Cultural capital (Bourdieu 1984) emanates from the lifestyle, language, and self-presentation of benighted groups.

Everyday consumption in postmodernity also differs from the modern in the relation of individual identity to the object consumed. 'In modernity, the subject (the consumer being) encounters the objects (products) as distinct and distanced from her/himself. In postmodern consumption, the consumer renders products part of her/himself, becoming part of the experience of being with products' (Firat & Dholakia 1998, pp. 96–97). In modern society, consumer objects represented social status; in postmodernity, they express one's identity. Along with this change emerges the sense that consumption is part of self-construction. Identity becomes more mobile and fractured, subject to alterations in what and how one feels at the moment. Further complicating the pattern of consumption is globalization. In the modern condition, consumption patterns were defined nationally. Increasingly consumer products flow across national boundaries, grafting onto the local cultures in patterns of hybridity (Bhabha 1993). In Southern California in the early 1990s, I witnessed an exhibition of African art that depicted black African hairstyles as imitations of Afro-American styles. These in turn originated in Afro-American communities as imitations of African practices, part of the return to roots phenomenon. In the postmodern condition, consumption patterns mirror and transform one another across the globe.

Much can be said about the political implications of postmodern consumer patterns. One can question the complicity of capitalism in furthering or benefiting from the new consumption combinatory. Critics like Evan Watkins make strong arguments that the dispersed, multiple, flexible self of postmodernity is highly desirable for the market and production conditions of late capitalism (Watkins 1993). The attractions and promises of postmodern consumption are here little more than alibis for the exploitation and alienation of labour. When the consequences of consumption are examined in a global perspective, the results are more discouraging in terms of widespread poverty, pandemic dislocation, and endemic warfare (Castells 1993, Hardt & Negri 2000). However, for my purposes in this essay, it is necessary to defer such discussion and to turn our attention in the concluding sections to the media. What role do digital media play in the emergence of post-postmodern consumer culture?

General argument: media and meaning

Media play a decisive role in the consumption of cultural objects. Narratives, songs, drawings, dramatic performances, rituals – these cultural objects that date from the distant past, well before the development of technical means of cultural reproduction, required the mediation of language, sound, image and other material methods of objectifying culture. In the millennia before industrial society, the theatre was perhaps the most elaborate of these technical systems (Weber 2002). As we discuss the impressive technical feats of new media and their bearing upon consumption, it is important to bear in mind that media are as old as culture, influencing, constraining, enhancing and generally making possible from the beginnings of human society the practice of culture. Media are neither new nor supplementary but essential to human culture, profoundly influencing what and how symbols, sounds and images are produced, distributed and received.

Digital media and consumption

Digital media radically transform both the cultural object and the subject position of the consumer. When cultural objects are digitized, they take on certain characteristics of spoken language. Like an oral sentence or a song, digitized voice is easily and with little cost reproduced by the networked computer user. We do not say of someone who repeats a sentence out loud, that he or she is a consumer of that sentence. The model of consumption does not fit practices of speech or singing. Similarly, players of digitized sound are not consumers but, in accepted parlance, users. Both the cultural object and the 'consumer' switch registers with digitization into that of speech on the one hand and that of user on the other hand.

Digitized cultural objects, however, also take on characteristics of analogue or mechanical reproduction. In the case of sound, digital reproduction affords an exact replica of the original song or spoken words. Even better than analogue media, digital media clone aural and other cultural objects. In addition, digital sounds, like long-playing records and audio tape and even more efficiently than them, permit massive reproduction and worldwide distribution of copies. Digital cultural objects conform to the protocols of the Internet and course through it as fish in water. 'Consumers' become 'producers' as the functions of reproduction and distribution are structured in the Internet as automatic operations.

Unlike either oral speech or analogue/graphic media of reproduction, digital cultural objects add new operations that obliterate the conditions of the position of consumer. Digital cultural objects may be transformed by the 'consumer' in their reception. Segments may easily be added or subtracted from the cultural object. Bits and pieces of *any other* cultural object may be inserted into or blended with the one in question. The cultural object loses thereby its fixity and the 'consumer' becomes not a user but a creator. It is true that voice performance alters music at each iteration. It is also true that ingenious methods have been devised to mix sounds from several sources in media like audio tape, as in hip hop music. Film too is essentially a montage medium that encourages the rearranging of moving images from the original shooting. However, these operations require learned skills and are difficult to accomplish. Digital objects, by contrast, are *inherently* open to transformation.

The proof of the power of these changes may be seen in the challenge digital media pose to the Levantine corporate structures that control cultural objects: the media industries. In the past decade each major industry has faced a threat to its existence from the digitization of cultural objects and the transformation of consumer into creator/user. At the same time, these corporations have responded by attempting to strip the 'consumer' from the rights it had in the period of analogue cultural objects. The culture industry has attempted to prevent copying of music, print and films, a practice that is most ineffective in the digital domain. The history of copy-protected software indicates the failure of this project. The culture industry has further attempted to restrict the use of the cultural object; with video by introducing regional limits, with audio by crippling playback on computers, embedding watermarks in the digital data to discourage copying, bringing legal action against file-sharing programs, and so forth. In the eyes of the culture industry, the only way to maintain power is to dissolve completely the materiality of the cultural object, eliminating all use practices of consumers with books, long playing records, video and audio tapes, digital video disks and the rest. Instead, the culture industry hopes to make cultural object accessible to consumers only on a pay per use basis. Consumers will have, in this view, no object at all, only access. What this desperate gesture by the culture industry forgets is that the cultural object, at some point, must become accessible to the consumer and at that point it becomes available for recording in digital formats.

Some examples from the history of the struggle between the culture industry and 'consumers' over that past decade will suffice to convince the reader that digital cultural objects are a new breed, one whose implementation offers a wide range of political choices with great consequences for the future of society.

In the 1980s, the music industry trumpeted the coming of digital long-playing records and later compact discs as 'perfect music forever'. They were eager to sell albums at vastly inflated prices in the new formats and to encourage music lovers to replace their 'obsolete' collections of analogue records with 'jewel'-cased, shiny CDs. The greed of the music industry was as unrestrained as their enthusiasm for the 'digital' domain. In addition to highly exploitative, exceptional labour contract conditions that stripped ordinary workers' rights from musicians, the music industry squeezed the retail outlets to hike prices, threatening them with severe retributions for failure of compliance. We know the rest of the story. In the mid-1990s, young people with computers started converting.cda files on CDs into mp3 files and trading, sharing and even selling them in IRC sites and through programs like Scour. Napster, coming along in the late 1990s, was simply the best program that facilitated these exchanges. After the music industry successfully sued Napster, peer-to-peer programs like Gnutella picked up the slack and even amplified the base of user/creators upwards of fifty million (by 2002) world-wide. Enjoying wide bandwidth connections of DSL and cable modems, user/creators exchanged not only mp3 files but entire digitally-encoded movies. Jack Valenti, President of the Motion Picture Association of America, saw this coming and called an extraordinary meeting in 2000 of corporate leaders of all media to combat 'piracy', in other words legally protected control of culture by a motley and decidedly un-artistic coterie of capitalists. Let's be clear about this: no other sector of USA capitalist enterprise has been so challenged since the labour strikes of the 1930s.

If the economic base of the music and film industries is threatened by the humble file-transfer protocols of digital cultural objects as practiced by consumers cum user/creators, the heart of postmodern capitalist culture, television advertising, faces the same fate with the advent of new digital recording technologies for televised programmes. Scholars in television studies have given some attention to the relation of this cultural medium to everyday life. Generally, however, the focus of these studies has been on the patterns of use of TV watchers in the context of the home and family relations. Researchers typically employ qualitative methods (ethnographies) to discover how television watching is integrated into daily life.[3] They have not yet adopted the perspective that

emerges after the introduction of new media (i.e. globally networked computing) in which television might be understood as an information machine.

For example, Ang (2000) discusses most informatively the efforts of the
advertising industry to maintain its economic interest in television as changing
technologies enable the consumer progressively to bypass commercials. Ang
reformulates de Certeau's theory of tactics, resistive consumer practices, for the
media domain. 'The very corporate foundation of commercial television', she
argues, 'rests on the idea of "delivering audiences to advertisers"; that is,
economically speaking, television programming is first and foremost a vehicle to
attract audiences for the "real" messages transmitted by television: the advertising spots inserted within and between the programs. The television business, in
other words, is basically a "consumer delivery enterprise" for advertisers' (Ang
2000, p. 184). Television executives even assert that there is an implicit 'contract'
between advertisers and viewers that the programme may only be viewed so long
as the commercials are received.[4]

As de Certeau might have predicted and as Ang demonstrates, television
watchers have always resisted the intrusion of commercials. Zapping, changing
channels during ads, muting the sound, with the introduction of remote
controls, and zipping, fast-forwarding through ads after time-shifting the
programme onto tape are time-honoured methods whereby consumers use
techno-tactics to circumvent advertising. (The introduction of cable and satellite
technologies, vastly expanding available programming, also deeply upset the
Network control of television.) Thus, consumer society was always fraught with
strife against imposed forms of control. Ang continues, 'The development of the
consumer society has implied the hypothetical construction of an ideal consuming subject through a whole range of strategic and ideological practices, resulting
in very specific constraints, structural and cultural, within which people can
indulge in the pleasures of leisurely consumption' (2000, p. 185). The evidence
of zapping, muting and zipping controverts the happy ideology of consumer
capitalism. Not only is the TV watcher far from a passive couch potato but
consumption, especially in its mediated forms, is a domain of major social and
economic conflict, perhaps of greater significance in the postmodern era than
the classic regions of strife: politics and economics.

The latest round of the struggle over television commercials began with the
introduction of digital television recorders in 2000 (Harmon 2002). These
devices (TiVo and ReplayTV) record programmes on a hard disk and, among
their many features, allow the viewer *automatically* to skip commercials. Clicking
a simple menu option eliminates all commercials, delivering the pre-recorded
programme without interruption. Although little more than 3 million of these
devices were in place by mid-2002, their potential to alter future of television
reception incited worried outcries from television producers and advertisers
alike. Repeating the scenario of the music and film industries, television finds
itself fundamentally at risk simply because the cultural object has been digitized

and the 'consumer' has chosen to deploy the new medium to ends other than those of capitalism.

However, if the new technologies offer consumers the means to mitigate or even bypass the commodification of cultural objects through advertising, capitalism retains numerous techniques to sustain market culture in general and their products in particular. It is enough in this context to mention briefly but one of these: the brand. Consumer objects under capitalism appear in the market with iconic designations known as brands. Names, images, colours, designs and packaging styles are all produced to associate the object (a loaf of bread, a pair of shoes or a toaster) in the purchaser's mind with a manufacturer. As Lury observes, the design effort is to constitute the brand as 'the objective properties of things' (1999, p. 499). Brands function to fix in our minds that commodities come from companies. In the domain of cultural objects, brands have not worked well. Consumers identify cultural objects not with corporations (Universal, Warner Brothers, Random House) but with stars/directors, musicians, and authors. If brands are the basis of the intellectual property of material consumer objects, celebrity creators play that role in the cultural domain. With the changes I have outlined in the nature of the digital cultural object and the consumer/ user/creator, what must now be put in question is precisely the intellectual property of authors.

The functions of the producer and consumer remain relatively stable in markets for non-cultural objects. While new technologies do enable producers to modify commodities to particular consumer preferences in what is termed a postmodern economy, no one argues that consumers are thereby producers, distributors, or reproducers of the commodity. The world of material commodities adheres to the brand and divides agents accordingly into producers and consumers. Not so in the domain of culture. Here the older legal and economic structures that insure commodification on the basis of authorship are disintegrating before our eyes. Copyright law, designed for an age when cultural objects were material commodities like cars and cereals, is now an obstacle to the development of a post postmodern culture, one no longer characterized by fixed cultural objects and positions of creator and consumer, but by fluid text, sounds and images, costless reproduction and distribution, and potentially collective creation.

Notes

1   See Highmore (2002): of the 36 selections in this book, only one can be included in the category of media – an excerpt from Spigel (1992).

2   For an interesting collection on ethnicity, daily life and technology, see the edited volume *Technicolor: Race, Technology, and Everyday Life* by Nelson and Tu (2001).

3   See for example Ang (1985), Silverstone (1994) and Gauntlett and Hill
      (1999).
4   'The free television that we've all enjoyed for so many years is based on us
      watching these commercials', said Jamie C. Kellner, chief executive of Turner
      Broadcasting: 'There's no Santa Claus. If you don't watch the commercials,
      someone's going to have to pay for television and it's going to be you' (cited
      in Harmon 2002).

References

Althusser, L. & Balibar, E. (1970) *Reading Capital*, New Left Books, London.
Ang, I. (1985) *Watching Dallas: Soap Opera and the Melodramatic Imagination*, Methuen,
      London.
Ang, I. (2000) 'New technologies, audience measurement, and the tactics of televi-
      sion consumption', in *Electronic Media and Technoculture*, ed. J. T. Caldwell,
      Routledge, New York, pp. 183–196.
Baudrillard, J. (1998) *The Consumer Society: Myths and Structures*, Sage, London &
      Thousand Oaks, CA.
Bhabha, H. (1993) *Local Cultures*, Routledge, New York.
Bourdieu, P. (1984) *Distinction: A Social Critique of the Judgment of Taste*, Harvard
      University Press, Cambridge.
Castells, M. (1993) 'The informational economy and the new international division
      of labor', in *The New Global Economy*, ed. M. Carnoy, Pennsylvania State
      University Press, University Park, PA, pp. 15–43.
de Certeau, M. (1984) *The Practice of Everyday Life*, University of California Press,
      Berkeley, CA.
de Certeau, M. (1986) *Heterologies: Discourse on the Other*, University of Minnesota
      Press, Minneapolis.
de Certeau, M. (1997) *Culture in the Plural*, University of Minnesota Press, Minne-
      apolis.
Firat, A. F. & Dholakia, N. (1998) *Consuming People: From Political Economy to Theaters
      of Consumption*, Routledge, New York.
Foucault, M. (1980) *Power/Knowledge: Selected Interviews and Other Writings,
      1972–1977*, ed. C. Gordon, Pantheon Books, New York.
Gardiner, M. E. (2000) *Critiques of Everyday Life*, Routledge, New York.
Gauntlett, D. & Hill, A. (1999) *TV Living: Television, Culture and Everyday Life*,
      Routledge, New York.
Hardt, M. & Negri, A. (2000) *Empire*, Harvard University Press, Cambridge, MA.
Harmon, A. (2002) 'Digital video recorders give advertisers pause', *New York Times*,
      23 May.
Highmore, B. (ed.) (2002) *The Everyday Life Reader*, Routledge, New York.
Huyssen, A. (1986) 'Mass culture as woman: modernism's other', in *Studies in
      Entertainment: Critical Approaches to Mass Culture*, ed. T. Modleski, Indiana
      University Press, Bloomington, IN, pp. 188–208.

Lefebvre, H. (1971) *Everyday Life in the Modern World*, Harper Torchbook, New York.
Lury, C. (1999) 'Marking time with Nike: the illusion of the durable', *Public Culture*, vol. 11, no. 3, pp. 499–526.
McCarthy, A. (2001) *Ambient Television: Visual Culture and Public Space*, Duke University Press, Durham.
Nelson, A. & Tu, T. L. N. (eds) (2001) *Technicolor: Race, Technology, and Everyday Life*, New York University Press, New York.
Silverstone, R. (1994) *Television and Everyday Life*, Routledge, London.
Spigel, L. (1992) *Make Room for TV: Television and the Family Ideal in Postwar America*, University of Chicago Press, Chicago.
Watkins, E. (1993) *Throwaways: Work Culture and Consumer Education*, Stanford University Press, Stanford.
Weber, S. (2002) *Theatricality as Medium*, Stanford University Press, Stanford.

J. Macgregor Wise

AN IMMENSE AND UNEXPECTED FIELD
OF ACTION
Webcams, surveillance and everyday life

The essay uses a quotation from Walter Benjamin to ask what 'immense and unexpected field of action' is revealed through the numerous web-cameras connected to the internet. The essay considers the subject of the webcam gaze to be that of everyday life in a society of surveillance and control. Drawing on Mark Andrejevic's concept of digital enclosures and Michael H. Goldhaber's argument that the Internet is an attention economy, the essay considers webcams and other means of online expression in the context of Gilles Deleuze's notion of a society of control. In the end, the essay considers the webcam to reveal aspects of everyday life through senses of thisness, durée, awareness, embodiment and care, as everyday life is caught up in and constituted by intertwined networks of care and control.

Keywords   control; everyday life; surveillance; webcams

Walter Benjamin once wrote that 'the enlargement of a snapshot does not simply render more precise what in any case was visible, though unclear: it reveals entirely new structural formations of the subject' (1969, p. 236). The camera 'manages to assure us of an immense and unexpected field of action'. There are at least two different ways of reading the term 'subject' in this quotation. On the one hand, the subject is the subject of the photograph, that which is photographed. Therefore, the photograph reveals new levels of detail, new structures, to that being photographed. Things look different as the image is frozen, and one zooms in, revealing what could not be seen before (Bachelard once wrote: 'The destiny of every image is enlargement'; quoted in Virilio 2000, p. 13). Early photography contributed to a modern regime of truth: the camera could reveal the world in a new way. Benjamin points out elsewhere that the world poses for the camera in a different way than for the photographer: 'For it is another nature that speaks to the camera than to the eye: other in the sense that a space informed by human consciousness gives way to a space informed by the unconscious' (Benjamin 1979, p. 243). The camera captures that which we are unaware of (for example, how we step out when we walk). Benjamin terms this the 'optical unconscious':

Cultural Studies Vol. 18, No. 2/3 March/May 2004, pp. 424–442
ISSN 0950-2386 print/ISSN 1466-4348 online   © 2004 Taylor & Francis Ltd
http://www.tandf.co.uk/journals   DOI: 10.1080/0950238042000201590

R Routledge
Taylor & Francis Group

Details of structure, cellular tissue, with which technology and medicine are normally concerned–all this is in its origins more native to the camera than the atmospheric landscape or the soulful portrait. Yet at the same time photography reveals in this material the physiognomic aspects of visual worlds which dwell in the smallest things, meaningful yet covert enough to find a hiding place in waking dreams, but which, enlarged and capable of formulation, make the difference between technology and magic visible as a thoroughly historical variable.

(1979, pp. 243–244)

On the other hand, we can read 'subject' as referring to subjectivity, and 'structural formations' as mechanisms of subjectivity and subjectification. The capture of images of people, places and things can be read through the disciplinary project of that same regime of truth; as Foucault (1977) has shown of the panopticon: reveal, document, discipline. The camera's gaze not only reveals the world in a new way and reveals aspects of us that we are unaware of (habits, expressions), but contributes to new social formations.

In a postphotographic era – when images are electronic and not chemical, digital and not analogue (Tomas 1996) – what are the new structural formations of the subject? In the age of the webcam, what is the immense and unexpected field of action? The field of action, I am arguing in this essay, is everyday life in a society of surveillance and control.

Subject

Web cameras (or webcams or simply cams) are small digital cameras of varying quality that are connected to the internet, uploading either intermittent or constant (streaming) images of whatever is in front of the camera to a webpage for public viewing. In 1991, the first camera of this type transmitted live images of a coffee pot in the Trojan Room of Cambridge University to an intranetwork of computer scientists (Stafford-Fraser 1995). Since then, cameras have been connected to the World Wide Web, transmitting images of offices, landscapes and homes to the world (sometimes for a fee). Some people live most of their lives in front of such cameras (e.g. nerdman.com, jennicam.com) and some have even tried to make a living doing so (dotcomguy; see Andrejevic 2004). With the rapidly declining costs of both high-speed Internet access and the cameras themselves, webcams are becoming a common sight on new personal computers and on the web.

The subject matter captured and transmitted by webcams is varied and vast. Webcams capture public spaces (streets, parks, mountains, nature preserves) and personal spaces (offices, living rooms and bedrooms); they range from African safari parks to amateur porn; they are broadcast to potential tourists and to a small circle of close friends or family. Given the numbers and diversity of webcams available on the Internet, there is a tendency to want to totalize their gaze, to argue that everything can now be seen somewhere online via a webcam.[1] For example, Virilio, with typical hyperbole, writes of webcams:

> The Earth, *that phantom limb*, no longer extends *as far as the eye can see*; it presents all aspects of itself for inspection in the strange little window. The sudden multiplication of 'points of view' merely heralds the latest globalization: the globalization of the gaze, of the single eye of the *cyclops* who governs the cave, that 'black box' which increasingly poorly conceals the great culminating moment of history, a history fallen victim to the syndrome of total accomplishment.
>
> (2000, p. 18)

This has parallels with what Baudrillard once referred to as obscenity ('The most intimate operation of your life becomes the potential grazing ground of the media. . . . The entire universe also unfolds unnecessarily on your home screen', 1988, pp. 20–21). The geography of the webcam is a specific one, shaped by access to computers, telephone connections and the Internet, as well as by the banality or exoticness of the subject matter, and its regimes are far too specific to submit to totalizing.

The bulk of the images broadcast by webcam are not the clear, carefully composed, well-lit snapshots of the tourist office or even the family photo album. Indeed, there is an overwhelming presence of the *in-between*, like all those photos with your eyes shut or in mid-sneeze, or where someone moved, blurring their features, or moved partially out of frame. These are the photos that never make it into the album, the ones discarded or deleted almost immediately. Yet, these are the images that we tend to be met with when we pull up a webcam. One of the most famous (or infamous) webcam sites is by Jennifer Ringley (jennicam.com), a young woman who broadcast her life to the Internet from 1996 to 2003. However, as Burgin (2000) has pointed out in an essay on jennicam, most of the day Jenni was not home and one was left watching her empty couch or occasionally her cats. Galleries of earlier images and image archives are often supplied to make up for these absences on webcam sites.

In a way, all of these in-between moments allow for a certain scrutiny of the everyday, because in-betweenness is the essence of the everyday. However, this scrutiny is not at the level of the close-up or enlargement (such as in film or photography), or a result of an increase in detail (because of the limitations of the medium, there is sufficient loss of detail), but a product of time. On the one hand, we have the momentary, the moment caught on camera, or a succession of such moments (a certain this-ness, this moment and then this moment). Benjamin writes:

No matter how artful the photographer, no matter how carefully posed his subject, the beholder feels an irresistible urge to search such a picture for the tiny spark of contingency, of the Here and Now, with which reality has so to speak seared the subject, to find the inconspicuous spot where in the immediacy of that long-forgotten moment the future subsists so eloquently that we, looking back, may rediscover it.

(1979, p. 243)

The difference with the webcam is that we are not necessarily 'looking back' but looking at a Here and Now that is Now (though perhaps not Here in any direct sense).

On the other hand we have the long stretches of time where we can watch a room or street or landscape for hours.[2] It is in this *longue durée* (in terms of rhythm, perhaps, if we are to follow Lefebvre's (1996) rhythmanalysis) as well as the momentariness that webcams reveal aspects of everyday life.

The *longue durée* of the webcam is easily derided as being really, really boring. Indeed, as a direct commentary on the lack of eventfullness of the average cam, there is a live webcam pointed at a wall of peeling paint.[3] The images and the technology do not verge on the magic that Benjamin described with photography, but retain a certain fascination nonetheless. If they are not the sublime, they are a step down from that – the 'cool' perhaps. They also hold other fascinations, which we will consider below. One way of dealing with this boredom is to consider these images as ones to be surfed, to be clicked past, not studied at length. Senft has argued that one views the webcam image not with the gaze of the film audience or the glance of the television audience, but as a grab (in McLemee 2001). Palmer (2000) puts the situation this way:

Like TV, Webcams are especially interested in everyday rhythmic routines at the heart of workplaces, homes, streets, or offices. But unlike TV, at most live Internet camera sites precisely *nothing* happens most of the time. Pointing your browser to a Webcam will more often than not result in the peeling back of an image of an empty (and often dark) bedroom, street, or cityscape. Aside from reminding us of our longitudinal anchoring [Palmer is in Australia], there's often only the very faint sense that something might happen.

If we are not so quick to dismiss the *longue durée*, we can learn something new about the subject; indeed, we can watch the subject transform as we continue to scrutinize it and watch the slow progress of time and light rework the subject over the day(s). This is one of the effects of Andy Warhol's 1964 eight-hour film *Empire*, which consists of a static shot of the Empire State Building over the course of an evening. Our impatience over the speed and eventfulness of webcam images reveals as much about our own cultural presuppositions and habits, as well as the historical construction of attention itself (Crary 1999), than about the subject itself. For example, video shot by aboriginals in Australia exhibit an aesthetic of time, composition and storytelling, favouring long shots of what some would describe as empty landscapes, that would also be considered boring by Western audiences (Michaels 1994).

However, as a means of studying everyday life, webcams can provide only a quite attenuated version of it. Despite what it can deliver (momentariness and *longue durée*), it cannot come close to presenting the thick description, if you will, the level of detail, density and embodiedness of everyday life usually sought by the myriad projects on everyday life since the turn of the last century (see Gardiner 2000, Highmore 2002). Though some webcams provide sound, and a few allow for camera movement, many sensory and spatial dimensions are lost. They lack a sense of presence.

The dream of telepresence has been alive for a long time. Different from the broader idea of teleactivity (being able to be active at a distance, that is, remote control), the idea of telepresence essentially is the idea of being in two places at once – to be where you are, but to feel like you are someplace else. With the telegraph and telephone, and their sense of instanteneity and simultaneity, we began to move closer to this idea.

However, we have never come close to meeting any of the definitions of telepresence, such as the feeling that one is completely immersed in a scene (feeling, touching, tasting, smelling, and so forth). Campanella (2000), following Thomas Sheridan, lists three dimensions for determining true telepresence: the level of sensory information received, the ability to change one's viewpoint in the virtual environment, and the ability to modify the virtual environment. Campanella suggests that with webcams we have at best something that might be called 'low telepresence' or 'popular telepresence' (2000, p. 30). For Campanella, the fact that webcams can show such a multitude of scenes globally makes up somewhat for their grainy, intermittent images. Nevertheless, it is extremely doubtful that anything we will come up with in the near future will even begin to address full telepresence, no matter how cool the latest immersive gear and environments are.

Despite this, there are more connections between the attenuated webcam images and the thickness of everyday life. However, we have to get at these through the second reading of the Benjamin quotation.

Subjectivity

This is a modern panopticon, wherein the cell of privacy is open to an impersonal gaze, and the sense that someone is always watching, potentially at least, is part of the structure of feeling of modern life.

(Carey 1998, p. 129)

In terms of the 'structural formations' of subjectivity, what is revealed by webcams (that is, what is revealed by having live images of oneself captured and broadcast on the Internet even without one's knowledge) is that these structural formations are shaped within a society of surveillance. Though the processes of subjectivation exceed any particular formation (Deleuze 1988, p. 89), we need to consider the gaze of surveillance as part of these formations. The structure of feeling of modern life is that we are being watched.

> All societies that are dependent on communication and information technologies for administrative and control processes are surveillance societies. The effects of this are felt in ordinary everyday life, which is closely monitored as never before in history. . . . Today, routine, mundane surveillance, usually mounted by agencies and organizations that are geographically remote from us is embedded in every aspect of life.
>
> (Lyon 2001, p. 1)

Cameras in public spaces can become flash points for protests over diverse encroachments on civil liberties. For example, 2002 saw protests and debates about the number of cameras being placed not only around monuments and public buildings in Washington, DC, but public spaces more generally (see www.observingsurveillance.org). The number and type of cameras aimed at public spaces is quite diverse, from Closed Circuit Television (CCTV) used by police and security guards to cameras on ATMs, and even webcams aimed out of apartment windows. The city of Tempe, Arizona, even sports a couple of live webcams (entitled Sneaky Peak) on its municipal webpage (www.tempe.gov/millcam/default.asp). The cameras are aimed at popular intersections of the college town.

For the most part, as the obvious cameras work their way into the familiar landscape of our lives, they can be ignored. Indeed, Jennifer Ringley claims that she ignores the cameras in her home (Snyder 2000), that they are just there and what we see on her website is virtually everything that goes on in the house unedited and uncut. However, there is only a certain extent that we can ignore the cameras; we are aware of their presence at some level (again, there is a felt quality of being watched). Despite having at least six live cameras in the house, Jennicam provides only one feed at a time to the website. The switching of the cameras is not automatic, and so the fact that Ringley has to change the feed manually throughout the day belies her claim. The conceit of behaving as if the cameras were not there is one that underlies the current boom in 'reality television', especially shows such as the *Big Brother* series. In an exit interview after being voted off the show, a contestant on the first season of the US *Big Brother* (2000) stated that it was difficult to ignore the cameras, especially since they made noise when they panned or tilted.[4] The conceit is undergirded by the qualities of what Bolter and Grusin

(1999) term 'immediate media', media that tend to erase their own presence, offering windows on the world.

Perhaps it is not a question of whether or not we can ignore the cameras, but rather a question of caring about or minding the cameras. As Ringley writes in her discussion of the concept of her website, 'I keep JenniCam alive not because I want to be watched, but because I simply don't mind being watched. It is more than a bit fascinating to me as an experiment, even (especially?) after five years' (jennicam.com). There are those who do not mind being watched – so long as they are compensated in some way for being watched – and there are those who do mind being watched. Let us take the first group first.

Kellner (1999) writes that these new communication technologies create the possibility for democracy, once everyone has their own channel to broadcast on, their own show and means of expression. However, Andrejevic (2004) has argued that this move towards encouraging personal expression has a darker side in that people are being encouraged to put much of their everyday life on a medium that is easily surveilled, tracked and logged. He argues that capitalism has always worked by means of enclosures: fields, the factory floor and now what he calls digital enclosures. The new digital enclosures include leisure spaces that become work spaces as well, where one's leisure time and activity becomes a means of work. One gets paid for doing what they do everyday, but now they let people watch them and log their movements, purchases and habits: Will live *live* for food.

One perhaps extreme version of this is the site Icepick.com, which connects webcams to household events so that when an event occurs a picture is taken and notation made of time and duration. Events include the front doorbell ringing, the microwave opening, the refrigerator opening, the treadmill working, the toilet flushing (no camera), the cat eating, the cat entering the litterbox and more. A database of images, events and frequency of events is available on the site so that, for example, one can access a graph of the frequency of doorbell rings over the last week by time of day. A barcode scanner has also been installed on the kitchen trashcan to record every item thrown away.

Payment for one's work on such sites comes in many forms: subscriptions to your site, ads on your site, and 'click throughs' (icepick.com is a free site). But it also comes in the much less direct – but no less powerful – forms of convenience (the fruits of direct marketing) and attention. With regards to the latter, in 1997 Goldhaber argued that the economy of the Internet needs to be understood as an 'attention economy', where attention and stardom become the currency and the goal. The term attention economy has recently been used to explain in part the seeming explosion of diaries posted to the web (called weblogs or just blogs). Such diary sites often come in conjunction with a webcam. A competitive economy is established where bloggers seek to out-do each other in some way to increase their fan base. A 2001 article in Salon.com describes the competitive environment of a subset of bloggers with webcams who are young teenage girls, some of whom post wish lists of products they would like (Mieszkowski 2001) – and admirers do send them gifts. Even without the explicit nudity that would make such sites illegal (most of the girls are under 18), the prurience and morality of such sites has been the subject of intense debate, some viewing the sites as harmless fun and others arguing that they present a version of prostitution (some are rumoured to exchange explicit photos of themselves for gifts). Burgin (2000), in his essay on jennicam, argues that her webcam is a 'transitional object' designed to ease Ringley's transition from girlhood to adulthood. Ringley established Jennicam in her college dorm room. From Ringley's perspective, Burgin's argument goes, her webcam is a mirror and not a window and, like all good Lacanian mirrors, brings up questions of identity. Following Winnicott's re-reading of Lacan, Burgin emphasizes the look *from* the mirror as a form of recognition, and therefore the webcam as a bid for attention. The camera itself is a confidante in the absence of parents. One could argue that since these young women are presenting their own images of themselves that this practice has the potential to empower them to be more active agents in the formation of their sexual subjectivity.[5] Whether they actually follow through on this potential is something that deserves careful study.[6] But given the sorts of images used to advertise sites on the major webcam portals, as a group they do not. Such activities may simply reinforce young women's roles as subjects under a patriarchal gaze despite the presumption that they are empowering themselves by doing so. This is much like the assumption that consumers are empowered as they choose amongst the products of capitalism.

Another way of approaching the analysis of digital enclosures and attention economies is through Deleuze's (1995) notion of control societies. Take, for example, a comment from Deleuze on communication: 'Repressive forces don't stop people expressing themselves but rather force them to express themselves. What a relief to have nothing to say, the right to say nothing, because only then is there a chance of framing the rare, and ever rarer, thing that might be worth saying'; and earlier: 'we're riddled with pointless talk, insane quantities of words and images' (Deleuze 1995, p. 129). Given the fact that some populations do not even get the choice of whether to express themselves or not, this comment is problematic, save that it begins to get at the boom in self-expression on the Internet (as well as on television and talk radio): personal web pages, blogs, webcams, etc. When one is forced to talk incessantly, to have an opinion on everything, to always express oneself, there remains little room for thoughtful consideration of what one is saying (not to mention time to listen to others). In addition, 'everyone' expresses themselves but things matter less and less – the control of communication through the proliferation of communication, the compulsion to express more and more. For Rose (1999) this incessant push towards individual autonomy and freedom within the culture of control makes the individual seem empowered. Consumption technologies thus allow consumers to 'narrativize their lives [and provide] new ethics and techniques for living'

(Rose 1999, p. 86). Enter the new web technologies. Writing on first-person video technologies, Dovey writes that

> these expressions of subjectivity are to be found across a range of media (print journalism, literature, the Web) and are not exclusive to the technologies of video, film or the medium of TV. It is rather that the regime of truth generated by and for contemporary western culture *requires* subjective, intimate, exposing expression as dominant form. The camcorder has technical characteristics that lend themselves to this work . . .
>
> (Dovey 2000, p. 57)

Webcams as well lend themselves to this work, and can be viewed as a particular instance of a cultural form produced within a society of control.

However, not everyone wishes to participate in this new economy. The Surveillance Camera Players in New York City provide walking tours of some of the 2400 surveillance cameras found in Manhattan. The tour focuses on Times Square, but the Players also provide a map (www.notbored.org/scp-maps.html) of all these cameras. The group Applied Autonomy has connected a similar map up to a program they call iSee (www.appliedautonomy.com/isee/). By clicking on one's location on the map, and then clicking on where one wishes to go, the software will generate a path that will take you by the least number of cameras possible (sometimes taking you miles out of your way).

Some of those who wish not to participate in this new attention economy come from groups who are overrepresented in surveillance images: minorities, women, and youth.[7] For youth, the space of the street is an especially important cultural space. The coming of CCTV in Britain meant that youth on the streets were even more heavily surveilled, forcing the youth to adapt (Toon 2001). They find the camera's blind spots, and map their own routes through city centres; they know how to blend into the background so as to not cause notice when they are surveilled. These are the tactics of the everyday for these youth.

The awareness of everyday life

Modern subjectivity is not simply about being watched, but also of *watching*. Most studies of surveillance ask the question of why we watch, and many turn to theories of the voyeur (see, for example, Calvert 2000), but I want to ask not why we watch but what is it that is being seen. It is not the real, nor the hyperreal, and what we are seeing through webcams is not everyday life, as we discussed above, since webcams can only present an attenuated version of everyday life. Perhaps it is not a question of whether everyday life is being represented accurately or not. Rather what is being produced through webcams is an *awareness* of everyday life. Lefebvre, discussing the novel *Ulysses* as a 'momentous eruption of everyday life into literature', goes on to say that '[i]t might, however, be more exact to say that readers were suddenly made aware of everyday life through the medium of literature or the written word' (Lefebvre 1971, p. 2). One could argue that television, at first, also made audiences suddenly aware of everyday life through its 'liveness'. Perhaps this is what is happening with webcams.

Webcams provide views of the exotic or the domestic (personal cams) where we are treated to views of houses or spaces. There is a parallel here with reality television and the distinction between the exoticism of *Survivor* and its ilk and the domestic banality of *Big Brother* or *Loft Story*. These cams provide a break from everyday life, and take us into Lefebvre's discussion of leisure in the modern world: 'Leisure must break with the everyday (or at least appear to do so) and not only as far as work is concerned, but also for day-to-day family life' (Lefebvre 1991, p. 33). Hence, the exotic locales and popular focus on sexuality: 'Displays of sexuality and nudity break with everyday life, and provide the sense of a break which people look for in leisure: readings, shows, etc.' (1991, p. 35). However, as noted by Andrejevic, the sphere of leisure is becoming a sphere of work; it does not provide a break in and of itself. Still, webcam images, while being a part of and apart from everyday life, contain their own critique of everyday life.

To represent everyday life one must be a part of it and apart from it; one cannot leave it, but one must break with it. The formation of the modern world for Lefebvre contains 'a complex of activities and passivities, of forms of sociability and communication' (Lefebvre 1991, p. 40), which connect everyday life with the escape from it (the world of leisure and illusion to which we turn). For Lefebvre, this complex of activities is able to be studied by the sociologist: 'Although he cannot describe or analyse them without criticizing them as being (partially) illusory, he must nevertheless start from the fact that they contain within themselves their own spontaneous critique of the everyday. They *are* that critique in so far as they are *other* than everyday life, and yet they are *in everyday life*, they are *alienation*' (Lefebvre 1991, p. 40).

Everyday life of the webcam is part of a transfiguration of everyday life that Virilio (2000) discusses:

> As with *stereoscopy* and *stereophony*, which distinguish left from right . . . to make it easier to perceive audiovisual relief, it is essential today to effect a split in primary reality by developing a *stereo-reality*, made up on the one hand of *the actual reality* of immediate appearances and, on the other, of the *virtual reality* of media trans-appearances.
>
> (Virilio 2000, p. 15, original emphasis)

Virilio's notion of stereo-reality avoids the postmodern trap of thinking that reality has become fully virtual (through TV or the internet), yet acknowledges that the experience of media is part of everyday life. Everyday life becomes a combination of the dual perspectives (one looks out one's window *and* at one's TV or computer). But, I would add, we must not ignore the places where these perspectives overlap, influence each other, and presuppose one another. For example, Seigel (2002) argues that the large-screen video displays found in sporting arenas, at concerts, and other places brings about this sort of double vision of the immediate and the mediated. Giant screens display the same space as the space of the audience, and so the geography of the technology and the phenomenological space is different from what Virilio is talking about, but the relation between the mediated and the immediate is similar: 'The mediated view subsumes the immediate view, even as the immediate consumes the mediated, resulting in an entirely new view characterized by neither one not the other but by the dynamism of their mutual interrelation' (Seigel 2001, p. 51; original emphasis deleted).

The notion of stereo-reality allows us to begin to talk about the virtual nature of the webcam experience in an embodied way. As Grosz has argued, the space of the screen 'can't be your only space. This computerized or virtual space is always housed inside another space – the space of bodily dwelling' (2001, p. 24). 'There can be no liberation from the body, or from space, or the real. They all have a nasty habit of recurring with great insistence, however much we may try to fantasize their disappearance' (2001, p. 18).

Even our model of how we look at the screen leads to this idea of separation of body and virtual space because our model of vision appears a disembodied process. Webcams can remind us of the deterritorialization of the eye. Deleuze (1981) distinguishes between three types of optical space: digital space, which is purely optical space (what we assume the internet to be); tactile/manual visual space, which subordinates the eye to the hand (in painting, the eye follows the hand); and, finally, haptic space where there is no longer strict subordination in either direction. Vision involves the hand. Webcams are not pure digital, optic spaces; they are haptic. Viewing webcams involves looking and clicking.

The awareness of embodiment (both of oneself and of the object of one's gaze via the webcam) brings a corporeal dimension to the otherwise attenuated version of everyday life we had been discussing before. The problem with discourses of the body and technology is that much of the discussion turns to the limits of the body, the line where the body and the technology become radically distinct (subject/object, self/other). We can avoid this through the idea of assemblage–of seeing the question of the relation of the body and technology not as a disjunction (either/or) but of a conjunction (and). This is not the conjunction of the hybrid, the cyborg (part this, part that), but a series of conjunctive syntheses (and . . . and . . . and . . . body and chair and keyboard and mouse and electricity and computer and . . .; see Wise 1998). Grosz writes that 'there is a boundary beyond which the body ceases to be a body. This point is the limit of the viability of technology' (Grosz 2001, p. 17). The boundary is 'a point beyond which things start to function differently – not necessarily worse, but differently. We would then have different kinds of bodies and different kinds of body functioning, and perhaps even the possibility of different becomings' (2001, p. 17). Assemblages of corporeality become articulated to assemblages of incorporeality.

So by prodding us to an awareness of everyday life, webcams make us aware of our assemblages as well, and the living and functioning of ones assemblages in everyday life. I would hesitate to draw a firm distinction between assemblage and everyday life. Webcams are an entry into this revealing of everyday life, but they are only one small part of the assemblage. Webcams lead us to the questions of surveillance, digital enclosures and societies of control, but those too are only just parts of the new assemblages of everyday life. These assemblages (just appearing in a few places today) rely on information and communication to an unprecedented extent. They are also increasingly mobile.

Steve Mann has been studying how this new assemblage is embedded in everyday life through his work on wearable computers (Mann with Niedzviecki 2001). Mann engages in much of his daily life wearing several small computers that act to mediate his experience with the world. A camera captures images of the world around him, eyewear projects those images and other information onto his eye (sometimes filtering out aspects of the environment, like advertising), and a transmitter uploads everything to the internet. Mann builds his systems on the principle of individual autonomy; the system allows users to control the symbolic environment through which they move. He recognizes that the environment created by *other* wearable computers and technologies – the ones produced by the military and corporations – create a world in which we are more easily tracked. Mann's work is to produce viable alternative assemblages to resist the encroachment of control and enhance autonomy. He recognizes that the very technologies he creates can be appropriated for other uses, but insists that one must engage with this technological assemblage using technology itself. But, more importantly for our purposes, he insists that we must engage this assemblage on the level of everyday life, as we move through spaces both private and public.

What differentiates Mann's online experiments from Jennicam and other personal webcams is that rather than pointing the camera at himself he uses the camera to show what he sees.[8] As Mann puts it:

[O]n my 'channel', the absence of a central subject or character constantly challenges the viewer. . . .The tables are turned in my experiment: the watcher cannot rely on objectifying the subject of the spectacle, turning the subject into a stand-in for one's own less eventful life. A (subjectless) life on the Web implicitly demands of the viewer: Why are you watching this? In refusing to provide a real subject, the story is left characterless, and viewers are forced to admit that they have been the subject all along, whether they are watching Steve Mann's hand raise a spoonful of cereal to his mouth or watching Jenni hunched over the breakfast table sipping coffee.

                                         (Mann with Niedzviecki 2001, pp. 134–135)

In addition to challenging the webcam viewers to rethink their own subjectivity, one of Mann's projects seeks to confront surveillance cameras directly in everyday life by pointing his own camera at CCTV cameras in stores and challenging employees and customers on the logic of the institution's cameras. From this project, he derives the term *sousveillance*, by which he means inverse surveillance, from below, from the level of the person, that is 'from down under in the hierarchy' (Mann 2002, n.p.). It is a democratization of surveillance, an attempt to 'level the playing field' (Mann with Niedzviecki 2001, p. 146).

The isolation of the individual using such apparatus does not go unnoticed or unnoted by Mann, but he points out how the apparatus can be used to be in constant communication with others, to allow them to see the same things that he is seeing and for him to see what they are seeing, simultaneously – to almost literally walk in someone else's shoes. As these new assemblages of everyday life become more mobile, they are no longer about watching in any simple sense (or even data gathering, in the broader sense of surveillance), but connectivity with others. Let me give you an example. Rheingold (2002) has coined the term 'smart mob' to describe the behaviours of groups that organize by means of text messages sent via cell phones. Through this technology, a message can quickly be disseminated throughout a decentralized network of people. In 2001, opposition groups in the Philippines were able to use the technology to gather quickly crowds of tens of thousands that eventually brought down President Estrada. This sort of decentralized coordination can also be found among groups of youth in Japan and Finland. The youth coordinate group meetings (changing plans and meeting places on the fly) and simply keep in touch throughout the day. These are haptic technologies, combinations of eye and thumb (used to key in messages, even without looking). In Japan, these groups of youth have been referred to as Thumb Tribes.

Rheingold describes these new networks as 'swarming', a term that may evoke the romance of resistance, the tactics of the oppressed, as they (youth, protesters, etc.) move through spaces they do not control. One turns to de Certeau (1984) and the first volume of *The Practice of Everyday Life* (as Toon (2000) does in his discussion of youth and CCTV, discussed earlier). But we should recall that Foucault (1977) noted that disciplinary mechanisms also 'swarm'. Rather than pit one swarm against the other, it is best to situate these practices within another swarm, 'the swarming structures of the street' that de Certeau refers to in the *second* volume of *The Practice of Everyday Life* (1998).[9] These are practices consisting of both contingency and structure, chance and ritual within everyday life. These terms are not in opposition but are grasped in the same movement.

Rheingold writes that it is a mistake to think of mobile connectivity of this sort as similar to the surfing of the Internet done on personal computers; it is a very different network put to very different uses. Therefore, this is a different set of practices and a different assemblage from that of the desktop webcam discussed above. But these networks highlight a dimension that we can then read back through the webcam assemblage. If we are to understand this new assemblage of everyday life we have to consider that studies of these youth indicate that these mobile technologies are not communication and information technologies but *phatic* communication technologies – that is, technologies that maintain relationships.[10] Indeed, this assemblage is one of distributed presence, but not in Turkle's (1995) sense of distributed personality or multiple windows of the self. Rather, following Coyne's (1999) turn to Heidegger, this type of presence is marked by care rather than personal experience per se.

Heidegger writes that part of Dasein (Being) is Being-with, and that this sense of being-with (or nearness) is part of what it means to be in the world.

> There is a collectivity to Dasein that precedes the notion of many selves, society, or intersubjectivity . . . Digital communities are not to be understood primarily as those formed from isolated selves communicating through networks, but there is already a solidarity, a being-with that is the human condition, into which we introduce various technologies, such as meeting rooms, transportation systems, telephones, and computer networks.
>
> (Coyne 1999, p. 147)

Being-with then becomes a starting point for one's analysis and not its end result, the starting point of our encounter with a webcam (to return to that technology), not its result. To clarify this notion of being-with, Coyne draws on Heidegger's concept of 'care'.

> Care is not simply an individual disposition of philanthropy or a concern for people and things, but a disposition of Dasein toward the world as it presents itself to us at any moment. Within our experience of being in the world, there is a pragmatic understanding of proximity or closeness, and this closeness precedes any (ontic) notion of *measurable* distance. Distance is a function of our being concerned, or caring, about aspects of the world. So that which we care about the most at any particular moment is the closest to us. In our walking down the street, the pavement is as near as anything could be (measurably), yet it is remote compared with the nearness of an acquaintance one encounters several paces away. The commuter on her mobile phone is measurably close to her fellow travelers in the railway carriage but nearer ontologically to the person at the end of the phone.
>
> (Coyne 1999, p. 149)

The cell phone users amidst the crowds that Rheingold describes are closer to their friends than those they jostle past as they cross the street. Reading this dimension of smart mobs back across our discussion of webcams, we could say that ontologically we are much nearer to the place and person in the webcam image than to those physically nearby. Care, however, is not an ontological necessity in this instance. Just because someone appears on my screen does not mean that I feel closer to them. Care is, however, one of the territorializing forces shaping these assemblages. It does allow another dimension of everyday life to be added to the repertoire revealed by the study of webcams: thisness, the *longue durée*, an awareness of everyday life, embodiment and assemblage, and care. Though we have not reproduced the sensoria of that place does not mean that one cannot be close to it or that it cannot clue us in to the processes and dimensions of everyday life.

The immense and unexpected field of action is not the unfolding of view upon remote view of the world, but a revealing of intertwined networks of care and control that constitute a particular formation of contemporary everyday life.[11] The assemblages of everyday life are territorialized by networks of control and regimes of truth, but they also contain within them networks of care, at least as a possibility. These are not distinct networks but inhabit the same technologies and practices, as we saw in our discussion of the digital enclosure. What the notion of networks of care and networks of control gets us is the beginning of a map of articulations of the assemblages of everyday life that takes seriously the technological stratification of everyday life without solely remaining on the plane of technology. To return to Benjamin's commentary on photography from which we began, we cannot exclude the apparatus itself. The field of action is not simply a visualization of the subject or even a regime of subjectivity but also the revealing of assemblages that include subject, subjectivity, camera, photographer and so forth, and that articulate the moment of image capture to the moment of visualization in complex ways. Immense and unexpected, indeed.

Notes

1   Like most of the Internet, counting webcams is a difficult process. Cameras go on and offline at different times; some transmit constantly, and some only once. Webcam portals (such as Earthcam.com and webcamworld.com) typically provide links to 3000 to 5000 cameras at a time, but the number of potential live webcams is easily in the millions worldwide.

2   Despite their potential for this *longue durée*, webcams can be particularly transitory as well, continually going on and offline.

3   www.sudftw.com/paintcam.htm – the site also has a feature where one can view a timelapse of the last 30 days; and even at this accelerated speed it is difficult to see paint actually peeling. The point is made whether this is a 'real' image or not.

4   Baudrillard addressed this conceit in his discussion of *An American Family*, the TV verité programme of the life of the Loud family in 1973.

> More interesting is the phantasm of filming the Louds *as if TV wasn't there*. The producer's trump card was to say: 'They lived as if we weren't there'. An absurd, paradoxical formula – neither true, nor false, but utopian. The 'as if *we* weren't there' is equivalent to 'as if *you* were there'. . . In this 'truth' experiment, it is neither a question of secrecy nor of perversion, but of a kind of thrill of the real, or of an aesthetics of the hyperreal, a thrill of vertiginous and phony exactitude, a thrill of alienation and of magnification, of distortion in scale, of excessive transparency all at the same time.
>
> (Baudrillard 1983, p. 50)

5   See, for example, Snyder's discussion of Ana Voog's webcam (Anacam.com) as 'pushing the boundaries of what people think a woman is and isn't' (Voog, quoted in Snyder 2000, p. 70).

6   Senft's forthcoming book *Camgirls: Gender, Micro-celebrity and Ethics on the World Wide Web* (Peter Lang) should make a contribution in this regard.

7   Studies of CCTV in Britain have shown that when women were surveilled, 10 percent of the time it was for purely voyeuristic reasons (Norris and Armstrong 1999).

8   We should note that the particular comparison that Mann makes of his project and Ringley's tends to reproduce the gendered relations of surveillance: men look, women are looked at. The gendering of the gaze is not a question that Mann addresses.

9   See Felski (2002) for a brief discussion contrasting the character of the two volumes of *The Practice of Everyday Life*.

10   The term *phatic* is used by Jakobson (1960), who borrows it from Malinowski (1953).

11   It is worth noting that Lyon writes that surveillance has two faces: care and control: 'The same process, surveillance – watching over – both enables and constrains, involves care and control' (2001, p. 3). Although he is not using 'care' in Heidegger's sense, but in an ethical sense, this adds an important dimension to the argument presented here.

Acknowledgements

This paper has had a long period of percolation and I wish to acknowledge those who have helped to form my thinking on these matters, including the students in my visual communication class at Arizona State University West who worked through the semiotics of webcams with me. A version of these ideas was presented at the National Communication Association conference in Washington, DC (and my thanks to Ananda Mitra for giving me the opportunity to do so), and a later version at Conjunctures, Montreal. My thanks to those who have allowed me to bounce ideas off of them, provided input in various ways and/or who have read versions of this and provided their critique; I am especially grateful to Mark Andrejevic, Michael Gardiner, Ron Greene, Steve Jones, Richard Morris, Daniel Palmer, Greg Seigworth and a host of others.

References

Andrejevic, M. (2004) 'The webcam subculture and the digital enclosure', in *Media/Space: Place, Scale, and Culture in a Media Age*, eds A. McCarthy & N. Couldry, Routledge, New York.

Baudrillard, J. (1983) *Simulations*, trans. P. Foss, P. Patton & Philip Beitchman, Semiotext(e), New York.

Baudrillard, J. (1988) *The Ecstasy of Communication*, trans. B. Schutze & C. Schutze, ed. Sylvère Lotringer, Semiotext(e), New York.

Benjamin, W. (1969) 'The work of art in the age of mechanical reproduction', in *Illuminations*, ed. H. Arendt, trans. H. Zohn, Schocken, New York.

Benjamin, W. (1979) 'A small history of photography', in *One-Way Street and Other Writings*, trans. E. Jephcott & K. Shorter, New Left Books, London, pp. 240–257.

Bolter, J. & Grusin, R. (1999) *Remediation: Understanding New Media*, MIT Press, Cambridge, MA.

Burgin, V. (2000) 'Jenni's room: exhibitionism and solitude', *Critical Inquiry*, vol. 27, pp. 77–89.

Calvert, C. (2000) *Voyeur Nation: Media, Privacy, and Peering in Modern Culture*, Westview, Boulder, CO.

Campanella, T. J. (2000) 'Eden by wire: webcameras and the telepresent landscape', in *The Robot in the Garden: Telerobotics and Telepistemology in the Age of the Internet*, ed. K. Goldberg, MIT Press, Cambridge, MA, pp. 22–46.

Carey, J., with Game, J. A. (1998) 'Communication, culture, and technology: an Internet interview with James W. Carey', *Journal of Communication Inquiry*, vol. 22, no. 2, pp. 117–130.

Coyne, R. (1999) *Technoromanticism: Digital Narrative, Holism, and the Romance of the Real*, MIT Press, Cambridge, MA.

Crary, J. (1999) *Suspensions of Perception: Attention, Spectacle, and Modern Culture*, MIT Press, Cambridge, MA.

de Certeau, M. (1984) *The Practice of Everyday Life*, trans. S. Rendall, The University of California Press, Berkeley, CA.

de Certeau, M. (1998) 'Entrée', in *The Practice of Everyday Life, Volume Two: Living and Cooking*, eds M. de Certeau, L. Giard, P. Mayol & L. Giard, trans. T. J. Tomasik, University of Minnesota Press, Minneapolis, pp. 1–4.

Deleuze, G. (1981) *Francis Bacon: Logique de la Sensation*, Editions De La Difference, Paris.

Deleuze, G. (1988) *Foucault*, trans. Seán Hand, University of Minnesota Press, Minneapolis.

Deleuze, G. (1995) *Negotiations, 1972–1990*, trans. M. Joughin, Columbia University Press, New York.

Dovey, J. (2000) *Freakshow: First Person Media and Factual Television*, Pluto Press, London.

Felski, R. (2002) 'Introduction', *New Literary History*, vol. 33, pp. 607–622.

Foucault, M. (1977) *Discipline and Punish: The Birth of the Prison*, Peregrine, Harmondsworth.

Gardiner, M. (2000) *Critiques of Everyday Life*, Routledge, London and New York.

Goldhaber, M. H. (1997) 'The attention economy and the Net', *First Monday*, vol. 2, no. 4, available at http://www.firstmonday.dk/issues/issue2_4/goldhaber

Grosz, E. (2001) *Architecture from the Outside: Essays on Virtual and Real Space*, MIT Press, Cambridge, MA.

Highmore, B. (2002) *Everyday Life and Cultural Theory: An Introduction*, Routledge, New York.

Jakobson, R. (1960) 'Closing statement: linguistics and poetics', in *Style in Language*, ed. T. A. Sebeok, MIT Press, Cambridge, MA, pp. 350–377.

Kellner, D. (1999) 'Globalisation from below? Toward a radical democratic technopolitics', *Angelaki*, vol. 4, no. 2, pp. 101–113.

Lefebvre, H. (1971) *Everyday Life in the Modern World*, trans. S. Rabinovitch, Transaction Publishers, New Brunswick.

Lefebvre, H. (1991) *Critique of Everyday Life, Volume One*, trans. J. Moore, Verso, New York.

Lefebvre, H. (1996) *Writings on Cities*, trans. E. Kofman and E. Lebas, Blackwell, Cambridge, MA.

Lyon, D. (2001) *Surveillance Society: Monitoring Everyday Life*, Open University Press, Buckingham.

Malinowski, B. (1953) 'The problem of meaning in primitive languages', in *The Meaning of Meaning*, 9th edn, eds C. K. Ogden & I. A. Richards, Harcourt, Brace and Co., New York, pp. 296–336.

Mann, S. (2002) 'Sousveillance, not just surveillance, in response to terrorism', *Chair et Métal / Metal and Flesh*, vol. 6, available at http://www.chairetmetal.com/cm06/mann-complet.htm

Mann, S., with Niedzviecki, H. (2001) *Cyborg: Digital Destiny and Human Possibility in the Age of the Wearable Computer*, Anchor Canada, Toronto.

McLemee, S. (2001) 'I am a camera'. *Lingua Franca*, February, pp. 6–8.

Michaels, E. (1994) *Bad Aboriginal Art: Tradition, Media, and Technological Horizons*, University of Minnesota Press, Minneapolis.

Mieszkowski, K. (2001) 'Candy from strangers', *Salon.com*, 13 August, available at http://dir.salon.com/tech/feature/2001/08/13/cam_girls/index.html

Norris, C. & Armstrong, G. (1999) *The Maximum Surveillance Society: The Rise of CCTV*, Berg, New York.

Palmer, D. (2000) 'Webcams: the aesthetics of liveness', *Like, Art Magazine*, vol. 12, pp. 16–22, available at http://users.bigpond.net.au/danielpalmer/webcams.html

Rheingold, H. (2002) *Smart Mobs: The Next Social Revolution*, Perseus, Cambridge, MA.

Rose, N. (1999) *Powers of Freedom: Reframing Political Thought*, Cambridge University Press, New York.

Siegel, G. (2002) 'Double vision: large-screen video display and live sports spectacle', *Television and New Media*, vol. 3, no. 1, pp. 49–73.

Snyder, Donald (2000) 'Webcam women: life on your screen', in *Web.studies: Rewiring Media Studies for the Digital Age*, ed. D. Gauntlett, Oxford University Press, New York & Arnold, London, pp. 68–73.

Stafford-Fraser, Q. (1995) 'The trojan room coffee pot: a (non-technical) biography', available at http://www.cl.cam.ac.uk/coffee/qsf/coffee.html

Tomas, D. (1996) 'From the photograph to postphotographic practice: toward a postoptical ecology of the eye', in *Electronic Culture: Technology and Visual Representation*, ed. T. Druckery, Aperture, New York, pp. 145–153.

Toon, I. (2000) '"Finding a place on the street": CCTV surveillance and young people's use of urban public space', in *City Visions*, eds D. Bell & A. Haddour, Prentice-Hall, New York, pp. 141–165.

Turkle, S. (1995) *Life on the Screen: Identity in the Age of the Internet*, Simon and Schuster, New York.

Virilio, P. (2000) *The Information Bomb*, trans. Chris Turner, Verso, New York.

Wise, J. (1998) 'Intelligent Agency', *Cultural Studies*, vol. 12, no. 3, pp. 410–428.

John Shotter

RESPONSIVE EXPRESSION IN LIVING BODIES

The power of invisible 'real presences' within our everyday lives together

In the past, in our talk of meanings, we have been used to thinking of them as working in terms of inner mental representations, and to thinking of such representations as passive objects of thought requiring interpretation in terms of shared rules, conventions or principles if their meaning is to be understood. This view of communication and understanding as 'information processing' has been hegemonic in social theory now for quite some time. Here, however, this paper will explore an alternative to it: the realm of expressive-responsive bodily activities occurring spontaneously between people in their meetings with each other. The spontaneous understandings occurring in this sphere 'pre-date', so to speak, the more self-conscious understandings we have as autonomous individuals. In this realm, in such meetings, direct and immediate, non-interpretational physiognomic or gestural forms of understanding can occur. Indeed, central to activities occurring between us in this sphere, is the emergence of dynamically unfolding structures of activity – 'real presences' in Steiner's terms – in which all involved participate in 'shaping', and to all involved must be responsive in giving shape to their own actions. It is the agentic influence of these invisible but nonetheless felt presences that is explored in the paper. Their influence can be felt as acting upon us in a way similar to the expressions of more visible, and authoritative beings – in that they can directly 'call' us into action, issue us with 'action guiding advisories' and judge our subsequent actions accordingly with their 'facial' expressions or 'tones' of voice. This paper will explore how this form of participatory thought and understanding can help us to understand the 'inner' nature of our social lives together and the part played by our expressive-responsive activities in their creation.

Keywords   real presences; responsiveness; dialogical; chiasmic; expression; physiognomic; corporeal

The purely corporeal can be uncanny.

(Wittgenstein 1980a, p. 50)

Cultural Studies Vol. 18, No. 2/3 March/May 2004, pp. 443–460
ISSN 0950-2386 print/ISSN 1466-4348 online   © 2004 Taylor & Francis Ltd
http://www.tandf.co.uk/journals   DOI: 10.1080/0950238042000201608

Routledge
Taylor & Francis Group

A 'corporeal or postural schema' gives us at every moment a global, practical, and implicit notion of the relation between our body and things, of our hold on them . . . For us the body is much more than an instrument or a means; it is our expression in the world, the visible form of our intentions.

(Merleau-Ponty 1964, p. 5)

There is something very wrong, it seems to me, with our current 'official' academic and intellectual forms of inquiry into our own nature and the nature of the others and othernesses in our surroundings – especially in those spheres of the social and behaviour sciences and social theory, which affect social policy making and the implementation of actual social programmes. While many of the themes I want to explore in this essay are not new – for every Plato there was a Heraclitus, for every Descartes a Montaigne, for every simplifier a complexifier – it is still the case that currently, in the practical affairs of everyday life, simplistic, quantitative modes of reasoning prevail. Thus, our task is to understand not only *why* this is so, but also to understand why attempts to *argue*, rationally, against such forms of policy making and implementation must always fail.[1] For, in being oriented ultimately only toward claims that can be formulated in quantitative terms, in terms that necessitate our thinking of things as constituted of 'separate elements of reality' that can be independently counted, measured or weighed, the *relational* dimensions of our world are in fact rationally excluded. But if life and the livingness of things is *in* the *internal* relations existing, not only spatially – between the constituent or participant parts of a living, organic whole at any one moment – but also in the internal relations existing between its earlier forms and their later developments, then such quantitative forms of reasoning eliminate both life, and with it, true temporality, the irreversibility of time, and the uniqueness of living events. Dynamic understandings occurring over time, in the course of ongoing, unfinished, incomplete, everyday life activities, are eliminated also. Time becomes merely a fourth dimension of space, and life is considered only in its dead forms. What crucially is also eliminated, is our living, bodily embeddedness in a ceaseless, pulsating flow of spontaneously unfolding, reciprocally responsive inter-corporeal, inter-activity, between us and our surroundings – a whole background flow of activity that *happens* to us, and in the context of which, what we *choose* to do takes place and has its significance.

My project, then, in what follows below, is to explore what alternative forms of social inquiry – if current forms of evaluation or assessment in terms of cost-benefit analysis, empirical and statistical evidence, 'proof' in terms of laboratory tests or public questionnaires, work to eliminate such dynamic, embodied understandings – might make their emergence into the general consciousness of the public possible? If we begin to re-think everyday life by taking corporeal forms of reciprocally responsive expression as central, instead of thought (supposedly occurring somewhere inside the heads of individuals), how might our forms of social inquiry change?

Williams (1977), in a chapter entitled 'Structures of feeling', long ago outlined many in adequacies in our attempts to understand the dynamic, un-finished character of social structures in terms of static, finished concepts. He began by noting that: 'In most description and analysis, culture and society are expressed in an habitual past tense . . . institutions and formations in which we are still actively involved are converted, by this procedural mode, into formed wholes rather than forming and formative processes' (1977, p. 128). If we are to deal with social experiences still in process, with changes of meanings and values that are actively lived and felt, with changes which are experienced as '*changes of presence*', then such changes can be defined, Williams claimed, as 'changes in *structures of feeling*' (1977, p. 132). Where by this term, he wanted to refer to 'social experiences *in solution*, as distinct from other social semantic formations which have been *precipitated* and are more evidently and more im-mediately available' (1977, pp. 133–134). To rethink our inquiries into the nature of everyday *life*, we must first, I think, bring the livingness of 'life' back into our considerations. This, I feel, was Williams' project, and I would like to think of my project in this paper – that of assembling 'a body of thinking still in motion' (1977, p. 1) for the re-thinking of our lives from within the midst of our living them – as a continuation of his.

From a grounding in measurement to a grounding in living responsiveness

If I had to choose just two founding statements of our current, 'official', empiri-cally-based, quantitative ways of knowing, I would choose the following. The first would be Socrates's claim, in book ten of *The Republic* (Plato 1987), that in the face of the ease with which we can be deceived or misled by appearances, 'measuring, counting and weighing have happily been discovered to help us out of these difficulties, and to ensure that we should not be guided by apparent differences of size, quantity and heaviness, but by calculations of number, meas-urement, and weight . . . and these calculations are performed by the element of reason in the mind' (Plato 1987, p. 432). The other would be Descartes's (1968) foundational resolve 'to speak only of what would happen in a new world, if God were to create, somewhere in imaginary space, enough matter to compose it, and if he were to agitate diversely and confusedly the different parts of this matter, so that he created a chaos as disordered as the poets could ever imagine, and afterwards did no more than to lend his usual preserving action to nature, and to let her act according to his established laws' (1968, p. 62). For such claims as these express the essential features of the world-picture that has informed our more self-conscious thought, talk, and action for many centuries here in the West. Only occasionally in the past have objections been raised to it – although much more so recently, as we shall see.

It is a picture of reality as made up of separate, self-contained, localized *parts or elements* (i.e. atoms or particles), that are connected to other such elements only through various 'dynamical' effects (movements considered as changes of configuration), occurring in both space and time, thought of as 'containers' for such effects, which in the first instance are thought of as God's responsibility. It is this picture that has unconsciously informed almost all our academic and intellectual enterprises until very recently. However, clearly and crucially, what is missing from such a picture, is life, the activities of living, embodied beings, and the fact that for us here on earth, life does not come from a mysterious god on high, but only from other life, in an unbroken chain of creativity that occurs whenever two or more living forms meet, and actively 'rub up against' each other, so to speak.

Thus, if I had to adopt a single foundational statement to mark the new approach to our intellectual inquiries that I would like to adopt below, it would be this remark of Wittgenstein's: 'Our attitude to what is alive and to what is dead, is not the same. All our reactions are different' (1953, no. 284). Indeed, if we move from considering ourselves and the world around us as constituted by dead, mechanically-structured processes to living, organically-structured ones, everything changes.

Even the most complex of 'man-made' systems, machines for instance, are constructed piece by piece from objective parts, i.e. from parts which retain their character unchanged irrespective of whether they are parts of the system or not. Living processes, however, are certainly not constructed piece by piece; on the contrary, in an unbroken process of reproduction, while older forms die, new embryonic forms are created which *grow* into more mature forms. In their growth, they develop from simple individuals into richly structured ones in such a way that their 'parts' at any one moment in time owe not just their character but their very existence both to one another *and* to their relations with the 'parts' of the system at some earlier point in time – their history is just as important as their logic in their growth, and because of this it is impossible to picture natural systems in spatial diagrams. As Capek remarks, 'any spatial symbol contemplated at a given moment is *complete*, i.e. all its parts are given *at once*, simultaneously, in contrast with the temporal reality which by its very nature is *incomplete* and whose "parts" – if we are justified in using such a thoroughly inadequate term – are by definition successive, i.e. non-simultaneous' (1965, p. 162).

Thus, in focusing here on the dynamics of temporally unfolding, living processes – on the shape or contours of their unfolding – our focus is not at all on simple changes of rearrangement, on the reconfiguration of a set of elements each remaining in themselves unchanged. For such changes as these, in being reversible (undoable), lack temporality, the irreversible unfolding of events temporally dependent on one another. The kinds of changes of interest to us, are irreversible changes, changes of growth and development, further inner articulations, differentiations, or 'differencings', within individual living beings which otherwise retain their identity as the individuals they are. There is something very special, then, in the organization, in the inter-structural properties of living processes, that have still not yet, I feel, been properly acknowledged in our current approaches to social theory.

Following Wittgenstein (1953) and Merleau-Ponty (1962), we can call such changes within an indivisible living whole, *physiognomic* changes in that like facial expressions, they are dispersed throughout or within the whole, in its total aspect, not centred in any particular part. But, I feel, we need to go further, we need to characterize the nature of the responsive intertwining of living, physiognomic events with events occurring in their surroundings – for they are events *sui generis*, of a kind utterly different from any so far familiar to us and taken by us to be basic in our intellectual inquiries. I shall call them *chiasmically*-structured events. In adopting the term chiasmic, I am following the lead of Merleau-Ponty (1968) who entitles chapter 4 of his book *The Visible and the Invisible* – 'The Intertwining – The Chiasm' – and in the rest of this article, I will attempt as best I can their characterization.[2]

As such, dynamical relations of this kind are radically different from those we think of as the causal relations occurring between *externally* related 'separate elements of reality'. Indeed, if we are to talk of such changes as involving 'parts' at all, we must begin to think of them as *internally* related 'participant parts' of a larger, dynamically unfolding whole, parts of a unique unity. Thus in no sense can such parts be simply objective, generalized, self-contained parts. They come, so to speak, with certain specific 'strings attached', with 'intrinsic affinities or valences', with an embeddedness within an already existing 'grammar' (Wittgenstein, 1953) – indeed, as we shall see, unlike inert objects, they can have living, agentic functions.[3] Like a 'thou', they can 'call out' various responses from us. Hence Wittgenstein's claim that a word has 'familiar face' for us, that it is 'as it were a picture of its meaning' (1980b, p. vol. I, no. 6), and that as such, a word not only 'looks at us' (1953, p. 181) as a face does, but in doing so, it can 'move' us like a smile or a frown can move us – not to *cause* a movement of reconfiguration, but expressively to 'call out' a similar expressive response in us. It is in this way, in their meetings with the othernesses in their surroundings that, to different degrees in different circumstances, they can become chiasmatically intertwined in with them also.

It is this power of living beings, as indivisible living unities, to affect each other in this *expressive* way through their physiognomic movements, and the special characteristics of the momentary and transient unities they create between them when they meet and become chiasmatically *involved* with each other in this *expressive-responsive* fashion, that I want to explore further in the next section. Here, I want to ponder why it is, when this form of mutual influence is so prominent to us in our lives – and occupies us almost totally in our leisure times: not just in our everyday lives together, but also in our arts, in literature, drama, music, cinema and so on – that we can still, nonetheless, ignore it in our so-called 'rational' inquires with the fervor devoted to the observance of a religious sacrament.

As I see it, it is our double commitment both to the value of pure theory, and to our belief that major new intellectual developments occur first in the heads of special individuals. Both these commitments are manifested in what a colleague and I have called 'the ritual of theory-criticism-and-debate' implicit in our institutionalized forms of inquiry in academe (Shotter & Lannamann 2002). Central to the Ritual is a form of talk and writing all but devoid of any contact with its surrounding circumstances. As Dreyfus and Rabinow comment:

> By passing the appropriate tests statements can be understood by an *informed* hearer to be true in a way that need make no reference to the everyday context in which the statement was uttered. This exotic species of speech act flourished in especially pure form in Greece around 300 B.C., when Plato became explicitly interested in the rules that enabled speakers to be taken seriously, and, by extrapolating the relative context independence of such speech acts to total independence, invented pure theory.
>
> (1982, p. 48, emphasis added)

Thus it was that certain special individuals *informed* in their special training – i.e. scientists and philosophers – became licensed to speak with authority beyond the range of their merely personal experience and power: 'It's not me, it's science that says it's true!'

This, of course, is not to be regretted in itself. The power of reflective thought to pick out (abstract) a crucial feature from a global whole and to highlight its crucial influence in the functioning of the whole is truly amazing. However, what is to be regretted is the hubris, the conceit of scholars, who will have it that without their having formulated 'proper' modes and methods of thought, ordinary folk would be incapable of conducting their daily lives aright.[4] It is Wittgenstein's (1953) achievement, despite its difficulty, to have overcome the refinements that our civilized minds are prone to, and to have provided us with some methods 'to bring words back from their metaphysical to their everyday use' (1953, no. 116). In so doing, to bring to our attention how many of our capacities and abilities reside in our prior training as everyday users of language in our practical, everyday dealings with each other. Thus, even our seeing of objects *as* objects of *this* kind rather than *as* of *that* kind, is not prior to our learning of language, but a consequence of it. 'Now he's seeing it *like* this', 'now like *that*' would only be said of someone *capable* of making certain applications of the figure quite freely. The substratum of this experience is the mastery of a technique' (Wittgenstein 1953, p. 208) – not only the technique of giving names to things, but also (see the quote from Merleau-Ponty 1964, p. 69 below) the technique of sustaining our visual attention, of being able to *gaze* at something. 'One forgets that a great deal of stage-setting in the language is presupposed if the mere act of naming is to make sense,' notes Wittgenstein (1953, no. 257).

What *is* our everyday use of language like? Why is it so difficult to grasp its nature? Indeed, why it so difficult to grasp what it is that Wittgenstein is after in his philosophy, written as it is in disconnected fragments? Why is it so difficult to move from what we do deliberately, as self-contained, self-conscious agents, acting in accord (we say) with a prior plan or theory, to what we do spontaneously, unthinkingly, in response to events occurring around us? Because, as we shall find below, in almost all the problems we set ourselves as to how we come to an understanding of things – problems such as, how is it that we can see and name objects in the world around us? – there is no problem. For, paradoxically, we would not be able to formulate such a 'problem' without our having already 'solved' it, so to speak, i.e. solved it in the history of our own cultural development.[5] Thus, instead of facing ourselves with *problems* requiring solutions or explanations and the formulation of theories, we must undertake another form of inquiry altogether. Merleau-Ponty justifies it thus:

> If it is true that as soon as philosophy declares itself to be reflection or coincidence it prejudges what it will find, then once again it must recommence everything, reject the instruments reflection and intuition had provided themselves, and install itself in a locus where they have not yet been distinguished, in experiences that have not yet been 'worked over', that offer us all at once, pell-mell, both subject and object, both existence and essence, and hence give philosophy resources to redefine them. Seeing, speaking, even thinking (with certain reservations, for as soon as we distinguish thought from speaking absolutely we are already in the order of reflection), are experiences of this kind, ... they are the repeated index, the insistent reminder of a mystery as familiar as it is unexplained, of a light which, illuminating the rest, remains at its source in obscurity.
>
> (1968, p. 130)

However, an aspect of that mystery is, we shall find, that 'all perception, all action which presupposes it, and in short every human use of the body is already *primordial expression*' (Merleau-Ponty 1964, p. 67). Before we turn to an exploration of the world of expressive responsive, living activities, we must first explore our 'bewitchment' (Wittgenstein 1953, no. 109) by certain unquestioned propositions in terms of which we currently conduct our intellectual inquiries.

'The world conceived and grasped as a picture' (Heidegger)

So many constitutive features of our current intellectual inquiries are informed by the Platonic-Cartesian world picture alluded to above, that it is impossible in the short space allowed here to list them all. Clearly central to it is our thinking that all the material changes, the dynamical effects, taking place, both in ourselves and in the world around us, are changes of a 'causal' kind, i.e. changes in which a number of *unchanging* elementary particles of matter move through *unchanging* space to give rise to a new 'state of affairs', to a new 'configuration' of the still externally related particles. We can call this a movement of rearrangement, or simply, a reconfiguration. Is this the character of change in living beings? Could we ever create life on the basis this kind of knowledge in the laboratory?[6]

A classical formulation of our purely symbolic, detached relations to our surroundings is the one given by Hertz back in 1894: 'We form for ourselves', he said, 'images or symbols of external objects; and the form we give them is such that the necessary consequents of the images in thought are always the images of the necessary consequents in nature of the things pictured' (Hertz 1894/1954, p. 1) – i.e. so that our representations work mechanically as effective predictors of future outcomes. This is an important formulation because, as Hertz sees it, it is not just a matter of a momentary, static conformity between our symbolic pictures and our surroundings, but, to an extent, of a dynamic one too: as our surroundings change so should our symbolic picture. But, as Hertz goes on to say, 'We do not know, nor have we any means of knowing, whether our conceptions of things are in conformity with them in any other than this *one* fundamental respect' (1894/1954, p. 2). Indeed, in a famous statement of Quine's, 'the totality of our so-called knowledge or beliefs, . . . is a man-made fabric which impinges on reality only along the edges' (1953, p. 42).

Yet, there is something lacking in the above formulations (see note 5). For, although movement and change are of central concern within them, the changes involved consist in a sequence of self-contained, discontinuous configurations, as in the frames of a movie. An intellectual conjuring trick has been executed. Instead of an indivisible flow of unfolding movement, a sequence of separate static pictures juxtaposed in external relations to each other has been substituted, and the intervals between them left unbridged. Just as in the well known visual illusion, in which a light going off at one point and another coming on at a point not too distant from it is seen as the movement of a single light between the two points, so we – subjectively, in our minds, we might say? – contribute the supposed movement. We then puzzle over how, in such a sequence of static representations, we can ever represent, picture or characterize living movement, living activities. For what we fail to capture here is how, in our everyday dealings with things, even when we catch only the briefest glimpse of them, for us, as beings almost always already in movement ourselves, those things are not so easy to fix as such, as the actual things they are for us. Many of them seem, not only to have come from somewhere, but also to be on the way to somewhere else, i.e. to be in a state of change themselves.

More is missed here in this intellectual sleight of hand – in which a sequence of juxtaposed dead representations are substituted for the indivisible temporal unfolding of living movement – than a supposed subjective or cognitive component. What is missing is what our bodies 'do for us spontaneously', so to speak, without us having mentally to 'work it out', as Merleau-Ponty makes clear:

> It is not the object which obtains movements of accommodation and convergence from my eyes. It has been shown that on the contrary I would never see anything clearly, and there would be no object for me, if I did not use my eyes in such a way as to make a view of a single object possible. And it is not the mind which takes the place of the body and anticipates what we are going to see. No; it is my glances themselves – their synergy, their exploration, and their prospecting – which bring the imminent object into focus; and our corrections would never be rapid and precise enough if they had to be based on an actual calculation of effects.
>
> (1964, p. 66–67)

In other words, words reminiscent of those from Wittgenstein that I took as my foundational statement above, Todes remarks: 'My knowledge of what it is, is largely fixed by my response to it, which is first possible only after some anticipation of it' (2001, p. 63). It is this 'colouring', this 'infecting', this 'chiasmatic intertwining' of the present moment with accumulated influences from the past and directional influences toward the future, which is ignored in Hertz and Quine's formulations. Heidegger, in his essay 'The Age of the World Picture', captures our present intellectual commitments nicely, when he writes: 'world picture, when understood essentially, does not mean a picture of the world but the world conceived and grasped as a picture' (1977, p. 129).

I quote these claims here to highlight the hidden contrast that is being drawn here: Knowledge that is deemed within the Platonic-Cartesian world view to be 'proper' knowledge, is objective knowledge, knowledge which, even though it 'impinges on reality' in terms of only a few isolated experiments, can nonetheless be *said to be certain* because it has empirical support by reference to what can be counted, measured, or weighed. This is to be contrasted – not just with the intimate knowledge we have, say, of our friends or relations, of their face, of the *style* of their speaking, their voice, the 'order of possibilities' implicit in their style or character – but that kind of knowledge we have, due only to our training into being the appropriate kind of *informed* individuals, which enables us *to judge* whether the theories being proposed, and the evidence being offered in their support, are such as to warrant being accounted true. Truth does not in and of itself announce itself to us. To repeat, as Wittgenstein reminds us, the prior mastery of a technique is involved (1953, p. 208). Those unable to make such judgments as these would be unable to tell in their experiments, which results were due to their manipulations and which not.

To sum up then, the whole Platonic-Cartesian scheme rests squarely on the unquestioned presumption, that we ourselves and the world around us can be completely understood in terms that can be captured in a static picture or sequence of static pictures, i.e. in visible terms. Here, then, in being pictured, time is spatialized simply as a fourth spatial dimension. Thus time, in this view, like space, becomes simply an empty 'container' of spatially arrayed states of affairs, with the successive moments of a movement being thought of as all already co-existing simply as places within it, with some of the possible places it contains not as yet occupied. Time is thus not qualitatively distinct from space. Indeed, to the extent that we seek eternal truths, claims true for all time, the Platonic-Cartesian world is essentially a timeless place, in which the temporal 'directionality' of a momentary event – from a particular past toward a limited range of possible futures – cannot be represented as a real aspect of its nature. Indeed, it is in the very nature of living beings that there is, so to speak, always 'more of them to come', or differently put, they are at any one moment always 'on the way to becoming other than they are'. They can act in utterly unique and novel ways that can surprise us. It is this that makes us say that, besides their outer lives that are visible to us, they have an 'inner' life that is invisible – or so it seems – to us. Can we in fact capture the nature of living processes within the idea of such an external reality in which time is spatialized, as it is in the eternalized Platonic-Cartesian world picture? If not, what is involved in taking the qualitatively distinct nature of unfolding temporal processes seriously?

Involved, I shall claim, following Wittgenstein and Merleau-Ponty, is first the acknowledgment of our body's spontaneous, responsive-'feelingful'-expressiveness. Thus, in returning to our task of understanding our conduct of our everyday activities, we will find ourselves concerned with meanings and values as they are actively lived and felt, and with thought, feeling, and action existing, not as separately existing, externally related parts of a picturable whole, but as internally related participant parts of an indivisible living whole: not feeling set over against thought and action, nor action set over against thought and feeling, but thoughtful action as felt, and responsive feeling as thought, and all as aspects of a living whole with specific internal relations with each other that are at once both inter-animating and in tension with each other. It is to the spontaneous expressive responsiveness of our body's living activities that we now must turn, and especially, to the strange outcomes of *meetings* between a living body and the others and othernesses in its surroundings.

The centrality of living meetings: chiasmatic interweavings

There is something very special at work in the spontaneous, expressive responsiveness of our bodies to events in our surroundings. In the active relations between us, in the unfolding, contingent or paired interplay, between our outgoing responsiveness toward an other or otherness and its incoming, complementary responsiveness toward us, a third (at least partially) living unity is created in our meetings with these others – an invisible unity which is nonetheless felt as a 'real presence' (Levy-Bruhl 1926, Merleau-Ponty 1964, Steiner 1989). In a moment, I will connect this notion with Wittgenstein's (1953) idea of grammars as being at work in shaping our utterances in a context, with Steiner's (1989) remarks on our experience in reading texts, and with Levy-Bruhl's (1926) comments of participatory thought in so-called primitive peoples, but here let me introduce the notion of 'real presences' with a remark of Merleau-Ponty's: 'Perception does not give me truths like geometry but presences. I grasp the unseen side [of an object] as present, and I do not affirm that the back of the lamp exists in the same sense that I say the solution of a problem exists. The hidden side is present in its own way. It is in my vicinity [the vicinity of my body]' (1964, p. 14) – and as such, my sense of the other side as really present to me, plays a real part in my reaching out confidently to touch, say, the lamp's switch that happens to be on its other, hidden side.

In general then, we can say about the dynamic unities giving rise to such invisible, but felt real presences, that, to the extent that they are 'outside' of our individual agency to control, they are external to us, but, to the extent that we are participant parts in them, we have our being 'within' of them (or, they have their being 'within' us). Indeed, it is just this 'ambiguous fullness', the as-yet-undifferentiated wholeness of the momentary living unities formed in our meetings that is hinted at by Merleau-Ponty in his comment quoted above – that we need to turn to 'experiences that have not yet been *worked over*, that offer us all at once, pell-mell, both *subject* and *object*, both existence and essence, and hence give philosophy resources to redefine them' (1968, p. 315). Hence his feeling that to return to this realm, is to return to the *primordial knowledge* (see note 5) upon which our everyday dealings with things is based. And, as we shall see, this *partially-this-and-partially-that* character of such momentary unities, is a major feature of our everyday realities as we encounter them in our daily dealings with each other.

What is produced in such dialogically- or chiasmatically-structured exchanges is a very complex mixture of not wholly reconcilable influences – as Bakhtin (1981) remarks, both 'centripetal' tendencies *inward* toward order and unity at the centre, as well as 'centrifugal' ones *outward* toward diversity and difference on the borders or margins. They are a complex mixture of many different kinds of influences. This makes it very difficult for us to characterize their nature: they have neither a fully orderly nor a fully disorderly structure, neither a completely stable nor an easily changed organization, neither a fully subjective nor fully objective character; nor need they be wholly made up of living processes, dead entities may come to play a participatory role within them as well. They are also non-locatable: they are 'spread out' among all the entities participating in them. They are neither 'inside' people, but nor are they 'outside' them; they are located in that space where inside and outside are one. Nor is there a separate before and after (Bergson), neither an agent nor an effect, but only a meaningful whole which cannot divide itself into separable parts. Indeed, it is precisely their lack of any pre-determined order, and thus their openness to being specified or determined *by those involved in them*, in practice – while usually remaining quite unaware of having done so – that is their central defining feature. Hence the impossibility of any outsiders imposing on them a single, logical or systematic order of connectedness that can capture the character of their dynamic, multi-dimensional openness to further growth and development ex-perienced by those involved as participants within them.

Perhaps the most obvious sphere in which real but invisible presences make themselves felt to us, intermingled in with our objective perceptions of a circumstance before us – besides, perhaps, our sense of 'openings' as well as of 'spaces to avoid' while driving on interstates or motorways – is in our reading of texts. Steiner (1984, 1989) has discussed this issue extensively. He begins by noting the difference between a critic's and a reader's approach to a text. A critic 'is an epistemologist' (1984, p. 67), one who 'steps back' from an object 'in order to perceive it better' (1984, p. 68). For a reader, however, texts 'are not "objects" even in a special "aesthetic" category, but "presences," "presentments" whose existential "thereness" (Heidegger's word) relates less to the organic, as it does in Aristotelian and Romantic poets and theories of art, than it does to the transubstantial' (1984, p. 85). In other words, what Steiner wants to suggest in his use of the term 'real presence', is that 'the reader proceeds *as if* the text was the housing of forces and meanings, of meanings of meaning, whose lodging within the executive verbal form was one of "incarnation". He reads *as if* – a conditionality that defines the "provisional" temper of his pursuit – the singular presence of the life of meaning in the text and work of art was "a real presence" irreducible to analytic summation and resistant to judgment in the sense in which the critic can and must judge' (1984, p. 85).

Indeed, just like Levy-Bruhl's (1926) so-called primitives, we read as if the circumstances, events and people participating in them, are all really 'there' present to us, not because of an imaginative effort on our part to conjure them up in all their detail, but because *they all* express their lives in some way, if not actually within the textual forms, at least in our reading of them. Levy-Bruhl calls this 'participatory thinking', because in this form of thought, certain entities – names, pictures, totems, etc. – which we would simply think of as a neutral image or representation, as having only an arbitrary or conventional relation to what it is they happen to stand for, were taken as themselves in fact '*participat[ing]* in the nature, properties, life of that of which it is the image' (1926, p. 79). 'Primitive man', he says, 'lives and acts in an environment of beings and objects, all of which, in addition to the properties that we recognize them to possess, are imbued with mystic attributes. He perceives their objective reality mingled with another reality. He feels himself surrounded by an infinity of imperceptible entities, nearly always invisible to sight, and always redoubtable' (1926, p. 65). But so do we, as we have seen above, in our everyday worlds of walking along the street or driving on our highways or when reading our texts.

To see this, let us return to Merleau-Ponty's discussion above of the deceptively simple-seeming task of looking over the visual scene before us. There, he notes that it is our 'glances themselves – their synergy, their exploration, and their prospecting – which bring the imminent object into focus' (1964, p. 67). As I look over my room now, as my eyes 'flick' from one fixation point to the next, looking first at a distant point to the right, next at a near point to the left, I nonetheless get a sense of a seamless whole, an indivisible 'something' that is not just 'there' before me as a picture, but as a set of 'invitations' and 'resistances', a set of openings and barriers exerting an agentic influence on my possible actions – given my present 'position' within 'it'. But then, we can add, even with something as simple as looking over a visual scene, a picture, a painting, a sculpture, an art object of any kind, there are different *styles* of looking, different bodily ways of using your eyes, and 'orchestrating' into those movements, other basic bodily capacities – we can move up closer to the painting or further away, adopt a new angle, pause for a moment to make a comparison (in fact or from memory), we can stop to ask a friend's opinion or to recall a text's account, and so on, and so on. If in these movements we open ourselves out to the 'calls' coming to us from the object as look over it, we find ourselves not so much looking *at* it – as in our instrumental looking *at* our neighbour – as looking *according* to it. Then, over time, as I 'dwell with' the work of art, between it and myself, a *real presence* emerges with 'its' own requirements, with 'its' own calls to which I must answer – if I am to do the work 'justice', to 'dwell with it' responsibly.

Yet, for all the variations in *styles* of looking available to us, there is a sense in which in such involvements as these, we all – more or less – see the same whole, the same landscape, the same face, etc. So that, although I might look from the door to the left of the chair on which I am seated to see the window on the right, and you might look from the window to see the door to the left of it, from within the overall time-space we share, everything is similarly ordered. Thus, if there are some disagreements over exactly what it is before us, we can make use of what we do agree on to discuss the features we see differently. In other words, in many temporally unfolding circumstances (but not in all), there is something special in the sequencing of our activities – not so much in how *we* order them, as in how the 'somethings' out there require us to order them. It is as if the separate elements we encounter seem to unfold in a special way, not just haphazardly but according to their own unique character, their *there-ness* as what they are. They give rise in all who encounter them, *spontaneously*, i.e., prior to any thought or deliberation on their part, a *shared* (or at least *shareable)* sense of the *shared surrounding circumstances* in which all our individual actions can be seen as playing a part, as each making 'a difference that makes a difference' (Bateson 1973, p. 286).

This claim, that *the sequencing* of our human activities is not just formless, that not just anything can follow or be connected with anything, is clearly connected with Wittgenstein's (1953, 1974) claim, that most of our activities on investigation seem to have a 'grammar' to them. As he sees it, it is their *shared* grammar that we *must* observe if our expressions and utterances are to be intelligible to those around us. It is this — not the constraints imposed on us externally by a physical reality — that makes it impossible for us just to talk as we please: 'Grammar is not accountable to any reality', he claims, 'it is grammatical rules that determine meaning (constitute it) and so they are not answerable to any meaning and to that extent are arbitrary' (Wittgenstein 1974, no. 133). 'Grammar tells us what kind of object anything is' (Wittgenstein 1953, no. 373).

Now to many, this may seem as outrageous a claim as the claim that there is no prior, already fixed and categorized physical reality to which to appeal in adjudicating the worth of our claims to truth. However, it has at least the implication that, prior to any of the claims as to the nature of things and events in our surrounding that we might as individuals address to those around us, all such claims must be couched in terms of certain *shared* circumstantial require-ments. If they are not, then they will not be properly understood by those to whom they are addressed; they will be confusing or misleading. In other words, although there may be no prior criteria to which to appeal in judging *the truth* of a person's claims — for their truth must be investigated in terms of their entailments — there are criteria immediately available as to *their intelligibility* in the context of their utterance. These criteria arise out of the fact that all the elements involved are mutually determining, interwoven, or inter-related with each other in a certain way, according to a certain style or grammar.

Summary and conclusions

Above, then, I have been severely critical of the Platonic-Cartesian world picture informing almost all our social inquiries and the formulation and implementation of social policy. Central to it is a concern with the inner workings of individual people's supposed subjectivities or mentalities, and in general, a search for supposedly fixed realities 'hidden behind appearances'. Having begun with scene-setting references to Raymond Williams' early work, I would like to end here with his critique of this approach:

The mistake, as so often, is in taking terms of analysis as terms of substance. Thus we speak of a world-view or of a prevailing ideology or of a class outlook, often with adequate evidence, but in this regular slide towards a past tense and a fixed form we suppose, or even do not know that we have to suppose, that these exist and are lived specifically and definitively, in singular and developing forms. Perhaps the dead can be reduced to fixed forms, though their surviving records are against it. But the living will not be reduced ... All the known complexities, the experienced tensions, shifts, and uncertainties, the intricate forms of unevenness and confusion, are against the terms of the reduction and soon, by extension, against social analysis itself.

(Williams 1977, pp. 129–130)

Instead, we have turned to a direct focus on the unique concrete details of our daily living, bodily involvements – or *participations* – in the world around us. In so doing, we have become concerned both with what goes on within the different 'inner worlds of meaning' we *create* in our different *meetings* with the others and othernesses around us, along with noticing the ever present *background* flow of spontaneously unfolding, reciprocally responsive inter-activity between us and our surroundings. It is as embodied 'participant parts' within this flow, considered as a dynamically developing complex whole, that we all have our being as members of a common culture, as members of a social group with a shared history of development between us. It is the recent discovery of this previous unnoticed background of spontaneously responsive, living bodily activity that is one of the most important features of the new approach that I have tried, at least partially, to articulate.

In the past, we have been used to thinking of mental representations – especially in their guise as theories – as central to our intellectual and cognitive lives, and when doing so, thinking of them as passive objects of thought, as logical structures requiring *interpretation* if their meaning is to be understood. In the approach I have set out above, their central place has been taken by 'real presences', presences that can act as agencies within us, as *powerful others* embodied within us that can 'call' us to action, issue 'action guiding advisories', and judge our subsequent actions accordingly in terms of the *grammatical* pressures they exert on us. As we have seen, Levy-Bruhl's (1926) account of the 'participatory thought' of so-called primitive peoples, come closest to capturing the nature of the living realities in which real presences are operative, but many, many other writers also express subtle aspects of their character brilliantly as well. To end this article – which is clearly merely a beginning for an entirely new approach to our inquiries into our living of our everyday lives together, an approach that tries to take their livingness seriously – I would like to return Merleau-Ponty (1962) and Wittgenstein's (1953) suggestion, that 'meaning' in everyday life is a *physiognomy*. For the mark of a physiognomic kind of understanding at work in our daily activities is the smooth, unhesitating, unthinking way in which in which we spontaneously respond to our current circumstances as if they were 'gesturing' toward us, as if we could see their 'facial' expression or hear the intoning of their 'voices' (thus to go way beyond any rule-governed form of understanding).

Although this 'magical' (Levy-Bruhl) form of understanding, in which our surroundings become inhabited by 'little-gods', can create major problems for us in our inquiries into human affairs, it can also provide us that sense of social experiences *still in process* that we need if we are to satisfy Williams' concerns. We need an account of, 'not feeling against thought, but thought as felt and feeling as thought: practical consciousness of a present kind, in a living, inter-relating continuity' (Williams 1977, p. 132). In other words, this is just the kind of understanding we need if we are ever – as practitioners out in the world, not as theorists talking in seminar rooms – to understand the part our expressive bodily activities (including our talk) plays in the creation of our 'inner realities' together, and which we need to draw on between us, if we are to refine, correct, and elaborate our everyday practices together.

Notes

1   Taylor notes that: 'In certain circles it would seem that an almost boundless confidence is placed in the defining of formal relations as a way of achieving clarity and certainty about our thinking, be it in the (mis)application of rational choice theory to ethical problems or in the great popularity of computer models of the mind' (1995, p. 6). What would it take to shake this seemingly unshakeable confidence?

2   Recently, Evans and Lawlor (2000) have edited a collection of essays on Merleau-Ponty's (1968) notion of 'flesh'. Although of tremendous impor-tance, none of the essays in the collection quite orients in the same way toward the issues treated here.

3   Thus, not only our thoughts, but everything *we talk of* and *gesture* toward is 'surrounded by a halo. – Its essence, its logic, presents an order, in fact, the a priori order of the world: that is, the order of possibilities, which must be common to both world and thought . . . It is *prior* to all experience, must run through all experience; no empirical cloudiness or uncertainty can be allowed to affect it – It must rather be of the purest crystal' (Wittgenstein, 1953, no. 97). Indeed, 'grammar tells us what kind of object anything is' (Wittgenstein, 1953, no. 373).

4   'Can only logical analysis explain what we mean by the propositions of ordinary language? Moore is inclined to think so. Are people therefore ignorant of what they mean when they say "Today the sky is clearer than yesterday"? Do we have to wait for logical analysis here? What a hellish idea!' (Waismann 1979, pp. 129–130).

5   'For if I am able . . . to bother my head about the distinction between imaginary and real, and cast doubt upon the "real", it is because this distinction is already made by me before any analysis . . . the problem then becomes one of not asking how critical thought can provide for itself secondary equivalents of this distinction, but of making explicit our primordial knowledge of the "real", of describing our perception of the world as that upon which our idea of truth is for ever based' (Merleau-Ponty 1962, p. xvi).

6   In this connection, see Doyle (1997), who examines closely Schrödinger's (1943) rhetorical 'code-script' model of the gene that influenced Crick and Watson in their discovery of the now famous helical model of DNA. As Doyle points out, unlike Crick and Watson, Schrödinger at least in part aware of the duplicitous significations hidden in the term, in that it requires both code and decoder to be folded into a single entity. 'The term code-script is', he says, 'of course, too narrow. The chromosome structures are at the same time instrumental in bringing about the development they foreshadow. They are law code and executive power – or to use another simile, they are architect's plan and builder's craft in one' (1997, p. 23). I write this quotation out in full here, as this issue – the unrepresented agentic power of an entity represented within a theory as merely an inert, self-contained object – is central to our whole discussion here.

References

Bakhtin, M. M. (1986) *Speech Genres and Other Late Essays*, trans. V. W. McGee, University of Texas Press, Austin, TX.

Bakhtin, M. (1981) *The Dialogical Imagination*, ed. M. Holquist, trans. C. Emerson & M. Holquist, University of Texas Press, Austin, TX.

Bakhtin, M. (1984) *Problems of Dostoevsky's Poetics*, trans. & ed. C. Emerson, University of Minnesota Press, Minneapolis.

Bateson, G. (1973) *Steps to an Ecology of Mind*, Paladin Books, London.

Capek, M. (1961) *The Philosophical Impact of Contemporary Physics*, Van Nostrand, New York.

Descartes, R. (1968) *Discourse on Method and Other Writings*, trans. with intro. F. E. Sutcliffe, Penguin Books, Harmondsworth.

Doyle, R. (1997) *On Beyond Living: Rhetorical Transformations of the Life Sciences*, Stanford University Press, Stanford, CA.

Evans, F. & Lawlor, L. (2000) *Chiasms: Merleau-Ponty's Notion of the Flesh*, SUNY Press, Albany, NY.

Heidegger, M. (1977) 'The age of the world picture', in *The Question Concerning Technology and Other Essays*, ed. M. Heidegger, trans. W. Lovitt, Garland Publishing, Inc., New York and London.

Hertz, H. H. (1956 [orig. German pub. 1894]) *The Principles of Mechanics*, Dover, New York.

Levy-Bruhl, L. (1926) *How Natives Think*, trans. L. A. Clare, George Allen and Unwin, London.

Merleau-Ponty, M. (1962) *Phenomenology of Perception*, trans. C. Smith, Routledge and Kegan Paul, London.

Merleau-Ponty, M. (1964) *Signs*, trans. R. M. McCleary, Northwestern University Press, Evanston, IL.

Merleau-Ponty, M. (1968) *The Visible and the Invisible*, Northwestern University Press, Evanston, IL.

Peat, F. D. (1990) *Einstein's Moon: Bell's Theorem and the Curious Quest for Quantum Reality*, Contemporary Books, Chicago.

Plato (1974) *The Republic*, trans. with intro. D. Lee, second edn, revised, Penguin Books, Harmondsworth.

Quine, W. V. (1953) 'Two dogmas of empiricism', in *From a Logical Point of View*, ed. W. V. Quine, Cambridge University Press, Cambridge.

Schrödinger, E. (1967) *What is Life?*, Cambridge University Press, Cambridge.

Shotter, J. (1980) 'Action, joint action, and intentionality', in *The Structure of Action*, ed. M. Brenner, Blackwell, Oxford, pp. 28–65.

Shotter, J. (1984) *Social Accountability and Selfhood*, Blackwell, Oxford.

Shotter, J. (1993) *Conversational Realities: Constructing Life through Language*, Sage, London.

Shotter, J. (1993) *Cultural Politics of Everyday Life: Social Constructionism, Rhetoric and Knowing of the Third Kind*, Open University Press, Milton Keynes.

Shotter, J. & Lannamann, J. W. (2002) 'Resituating social constructionism: its "imprisonment" with the ritual of theory-criticism-and-debate', *Theory & Psychology*, vol. 12, pp. 577–609.

Steiner, G. (1984) 'Critic'/'Reader', in *George Steiner: a Reader*, Penguin Books, Harmondsworth.

Steiner, G. (1989) *Real Presences*, University of Chicago Press, Chicago, IL.

Taylor, C. (1995) 'Overcoming epistemology', in *After Philosophy: End or Transformation?*, eds K. Baynes, J. Bohman & T. McCarthy, MIT Press, Cambridge, MA, pp. 464–488.

Todes, S. (2001) *Body and World*, introductions H. L. Dreyfus & P. Hoffman, MIT Press, Cambridge, MA.

Waismann, F. (1979) *Wittgenstein and the Vienna Circle*, trans. J. Schulte & B. McGuinness, ed B. McGuinness, Blackwell, Oxford.

Williams, R. (1977) *Marxism and Literature*, Oxford University Press, Oxford.

Wittgenstein, L. (1978) *Philosophical Grammar*, Blackwell, Oxford.

Wittgenstein, L. (1980a) *Culture and Value*, trans. P. Winch, introduction G. Von Wright, Blackwell, Oxford.

Wittgenstein, L. (1980b) *Remarks on the Philosophy of Psychology*, vols 1 and 2, Blackwell, Oxford.

Wittgenstein, L. (1981) *Zettel*, 2nd edn, eds G. E. M. Anscombe & G. H. V. Wright, Blackwell, Oxford.

Nigel Thrift

ELECTRIC ANIMALS
New models of everyday life?

The literature on everyday life has only imperfectly taken to itself the influence of modern information and communications technology, generally through the work of authors like Benjamin and the lettristes like de Certeau and Virilio. Part of the reason for this relative absence seems to be a concern that these technologies are, in some way, inauthentic. But such a reaction is no longer adequate. As software plasters the everyday world with a new and active surface, so the character of the everyday world is being changed. This change is based on theoretical models of the world that are written into software and which have as one of their key roots particular notions of biology. How can one understand this new kind of everyday life in which theoretical models of biology come back to haunt the surfaces that define us as they are incorporated in all manner of increasingly 'lively' devices? Obviously, a series of characterizations could be made but this paper proposes that one of the best of these may turn out to be that of the companion animal. Everyday life is chock full of these animals yet they too are hardly ever remarked upon in the literature: their strange familiarity is so obvious that they are deemed to be unworthy of notice. However, as software makes the world increasingly lively, perhaps we should start to think of its agency, especially as it is incarnated in various increasingly mobile objects, as calling forth similar kinds of relationship of dominance and affection – and a pressing ethical task.

Keywords animality; biological metaphors; companion animals; everyday life; robotics; software

. . . most of our engineering achievements to date are quite simple, at least in comparison to Nature's.

(Sipper 2002, p. 186)

Nature (the Art whereby God hath made and governes the World) is by the *Art* of man, as in many other things, so in this also imitated, that it can make an Artificial Animal.

(Hobbes 1651, p. 1)

Routledge
Taylor & Francis Group

Cultural Studies Vol. 18, No. 2/3 March/May 2004, pp. 461–482
ISSN 0950-2386 print/ISSN 1466-4348 online   © 2004 Taylor & Francis Ltd
http://www.tandf.co.uk/journals   DOI: 10.1080/0950238042000201617

Malebranche used to kick his dog in the name of animal-machines. Madame de Sevigné put Descartes and his theory in their place: 'machines that love, machines that make a choice for someone, machines that are jealous, machines that are fearful'. And she added, in a moment of indulgence, 'Never would Descartes have meant us to believe it'.

(Grenier 2000, p. 65)

Introduction

Biological metaphors have circulated in society for so long now that they have gradually sunk into the undertow of conscious thought. In this paper, I want to think about how these metaphors have taken root in the everyday life of an increasingly informational society and how that process is currently producing new artificial ethologies in which the biological and informational feed off each other and create new hybrids which demonstrate a certain kind of 'animality'.[1]

My interest in this area has been stimulated by three different but related impulses. One of these impulses is a general dissatisfaction with the literature on everyday life. My concern is that it does not take in recent technological developments in any meaningful way and indeed in some senses actively resists them by concentrating on conventional structures and sites of communication. In particular, its emphasis on a kind of proto-authenticity – as found, for example, in the stress on 'evasive everydayness' (Morris 1998) or the renewed emphasis on rhythm as a practice of feeling right with world, taken from the historically specific accounts of authors like Bachelard, de Certeau and Lefebvre – seems to me to express a yearning for a romantic holism that it has taken a long time to unlearn.[2] The second impulse has been born out of a general interest in the effectivities of software (Thrift 2003, Thrift & French 2002). I believe that software constitutes a new actor in the world: as a kind of mechanical writing, it is gradually producing a whole new informational ecology that is forming a dense undergrowth of muted but potent cause and effect that is present in the background of most events and which, because of its increasing extent and almost baroque complexity, is producing all kinds of large emergences and small hauntings, different densities and queer intensities, whose exact origins we can no longer trace. The third impulse is practical. I have been taken by the degree to which since the 1970s the writers of software have increasingly drawn on biological models more or less exactly based on biological metaphors – genetic algorithms, artificial ethologies and other forms of biomimicry – which express solutions to problems only faintly perceived. In particular, I have been taken by the desire to build electric animals for reasons that do not seem clear to either their inventors or users. In other words, biological metaphors, having become firmly entangled with computer programmes and lines of code, are producing an afterlife of 'artificial' 'organisms' that seem set fair to become companions to everyday practice in much the same way as pets now do.

This paper is a first exploration of this terrain and it can therefore hardly claim to be definitive. However, I hope that by its end I will have been able to achieve the following. First, I hope to have begun to show how software produces an intensely theoretical underlay to the practices of everyday life. Miller (1998) has called the process whereby in contemporary Euro-American societies theories have gradually changed the world to fit to their image 'virtualism' and I agree with this prognosis. Second, I hope to show that the desire to build software-driven entities like electric animals is more than just a bit of fun but reflects the working out in practice of these essentially theoretical dilemmas about what it means to be human and nonhuman, living and nonliving, cultural and natural which have been a constant of writings on both animals and machines. Third, I hope to briefly demonstrate that such projects are at least an indication of new disciplinary models and the kind of everyday life that is therefore likely to arise in the future.

The layout of the paper is in three main parts, which correspond to these three hopes. Thus, the first part of the paper considers the way in which software is producing a new layer of causality in the world which by its very nature is modest in scale but adds up to something more. The second part of the paper is concerned with how software has allowed new kinds of artificial nature to be built, especially electric 'animals'. The final part of the paper considers some of the dilemmas that have arisen or will arise by reference to the world of pets. Some brief conclusions round the paper off. Here, I begin to discuss how new kinds of disciplinarity are becoming possible.

A new underlay to everyday life

As a term in general use, 'software' dates only from the 1950s. Its genesis, of course, was bound up with the invention of the first electronic computers and, more particularly, the first use of these computers for business applications in the late 1950s, a development that, in turn, led to the growth of companies specializing in the supply of software (Hayles 2000). At the time, it referred to just a few lines of code that acted as a bridge between input and output. However, over the last 20 years in particular, software has grown from a small thicket of mechanical writing to a forest covering much of the globe in a profusion of over 200 different languages that now run all manner of everyday devices, from electric toothbrushes to cars (Thrift & French 2002).

Almost since its inception, the biological and the informational have been intertwined in software. Right at the birth of the modern computer, the new machines were framed in biological terms. For example, from the 1940s John von Neumann had been interested in the connections between computational logic and biology. The classic *First Report on the EDVAC* (1945) likened electronic circuits to neurons and the input and output part of the design to organs (Ward 1999). Since those early days, biological metaphors have become, if anything, more prevalent in the world of software and computation. In some senses, this prevalence should not be thought of as surprising. After all, many early cybernetic and systems theory metaphors were in part drawn from reductive notions of the workings of the biological domain and one might argue, as Sedgwick (2003, p. 105) has, that the problem was that the 'actual computational muscle' was not as yet available to operationalize them. Biology itself has seen a long drawn out war between those who believe that the biological domain can be reduced to a set of computations and those for whom the organism cannot be reduced to the sum of its parts. For the former group of biologists at least, cybernetic models were simply a natural extension of machinic thinking that had clear and obvious antecedents in the nineteenth century (but might even be traced further back to the Cartesian separation of man from machine-like animals). This kind of thinking finds its latest incarnation in a 'predictive biology' that hopes to model the behaviour of individual cells (and then tissues, organs and even organisms) in computers.[3]

Thus, software writers' initial flirtations with the biological may be seen as nothing more than business as usual but with a slightly more exotic tinge. However, at the same time, these flirtations were also expressing a need for something more. As software became more complex, reductive models became increasingly inappropriate. Software increasingly resembled a kind of ecosystem in which thickets of new code surrounded stands of legacy code that often stayed unchanged through many versions of a package. As the sheer length of code became a problem in its own right, so all kinds of unexpected interactions and hidden errors came into play. The constant tinkering of numerous programmers started to produce programs large enough and complex enough to make it possible to regard programs as forming their own ecologies, complete with various niches and evolutionary tendencies. The result was that programs have increasingly come to be framed as environments in their own right, motivated by quasi-biological principles. Interestingly, such descriptions are used both by those only interested in programs as manifestations of narrow technique and by those who argue that programs occupy the realm of something more. For example, in the latter camp, Nardi and O'Day (1999) want to argue for the creation of healthy 'information ecologies', which will exhibit several biological principles: systemic interrelation, diversity, co-evolution, keystone species and the importance of local habitation.

Added to this, new algorithms were introduced which were clearly modelled on biological lines. The longest-running tradition of this kind of work is to be found in the so-called genetic algorithm and the more general phenomenon of evolutionary computing (Mitchell 1996). Though there were antecedents, it is generally agreed that genetic algorithms were invented by John

Holland in the 1960s as a way of mixing natural and artificial systems (Holland 1975). Holland introduced a population-based algorithm that ran on evolutionary lines and could therefore produce programs that were able to do massively parallel searches (in which many different possibilities are explored simultaneously), that were adaptive, and that sought out complex solutions. In evolutionary computation, the rules are typically based on an idea of natural selection with variations induced by crossover and/or mutation: 'The hoped-for emergent behaviour is the design of high-quality solutions to difficult problems and the ability to adapt these solutions in the face of a changing environment' (Mitchell 1996, p. 4). However, evolution has not been the only biological metaphor used to motivate computer programs. Another metaphor has come from neuroscience. Connectionism, which includes such models as neural networks, consists of the writing of computer programs inspired by neural systems. In connectionism, 'the rules are typically simple "neural" thresholding, activation spreading, and strengthening or weakening of connections. The hoped-for emergent behaviour is sophisticated pattern recognition and learning' (Mitchell 1996, p. 4). It would be possible to go on but, hopefully, the point is made: in amongst the continual rustle of many computer programs, biological analogy now holds sway.

To summarize, on a whole series of levels, one of the most prevalent descriptions of programming environments is now a biological one. This description operates at a number of levels: as a means of framing programs, as a means of framing wider technological systems and as a means of making assumptions about how the world turns up. Perhaps it is no surprise, then, that the next step should be made: to try to produce 'artificial' 'life' and, in particular, artificial animality.

Electric animals

Lippitt (2000) points out that the first known usage of the term 'anthropomorphism' is dated by the *Oxford English Dictionary* to the second half of the nineteenth century.[4] It is probably no coincidence that at much the same time the history of technology and animals begins to intertwine ever more intimately.

> As they disappeared, animals became increasingly the subjects of a nostalgic curiosity. When horse-drawn carriages gave way to steam engines, plaster horses were mounted on tramcar fronts in an effort to simulate continuity with the older animal-driven vehicles. Once considered a metonymy of nature, animals came to be seen as emblems of the new industrial environment. Animals appeared to merge with the new technological bodies replacing them. The idioms and histories of numerous technological innovations from the steam engine to quantum mechanics bear the traces of

an incorporated animality. James Watt and later Henry Ford, Thomas Edison, Alexander Graham Bell, Walt Disney and Erwin Schrodinger, among other key figures in the industrial and aesthetic shifts of the late nineteenth and early twentieth centuries, found uses for animal spirits in developing their respective machines, creating in the process a series of fantastic hybrids. Cinema, communication, transportation and electricity drew from the actual and fantastic resources of dead animals. In this manner, technology and ultimately the cinema came to determine a vast mausoleum for animal being.

(Lippitt 2000, p. 187)

One might argue that Lippitt exaggerates in her desire to present a kind of techno-animal crypt – after all, early twenty-first-century cities are still chock full of animals that are very much alive (Amin & Thrift 2002) – but the point is still made: the cultural intersection between technology and animals has grown and continues to grow (Simondon 1958/1989). However, just as the materiality of technology has become an insistent force in the world of animals so the materiality of animals has become an insistent force in the world of technology. There is constant traffic between the two realms to the point where technology and animality have become suspect terms, perhaps better replaced by a standard actor-network theoretic depiction of a number of hybrid networks and other forms of flow that are perennially involved in diplomatic experiments which as one outcome perenially re-define prevailing cultural definitions of 'technology' and 'animal' (Whatmore 2002).[5] Whatever the case, it is clear that a notion of animality is a motivating force in current information technology, as various teams of scientists and programmers vie to produce something closer to bio-logical life than heretofore has been possible.

Perhaps the best way to attempt to begin to show this work of shuttle diplomacy is by attending to the numerous attempts to produce simulations of organic life in computers. The point I want to make here is that these programs are being used to work through what organic life might consist of. They are experiments in action that are unfortunately accompanied by a good deal of hyperbole about 'life', 'virtual organisms' and 'living, breeding software' (Ward 1999, p. 279), which conceals their essentially primitive nature. Attempts to produce artificial life in the form of computer programs date from the 1980s when a series of biologists and programmers like Larry Ray began to produce artificial computer worlds like *Tierra*.[6] These worlds, in part, were born out of a dissatisfaction with the pre-defined and therefore closed system nature of genetic algorithms which meant that they had no independent ability to reproduce – what lives and what dies is decided externally; 'self-replication is critical to synthetic life because without it, the mechanisms of selection must also be pre-determined by the simulator. Such artificial selection can never be as creative as natural selection' (Ray 1991, p. 372). Such worlds have undoubtedly been successful in that they exhibit certain evolutionary characteristics but they have also proved to have flaws, most notably that the organisms produced are all made up of fewer instructions than the original ancestor; the simple Tierran organisms have not been able to make themselves into larger creatures. Though there is still considerable optimism that such constraints can be overcome, other tacks seem just as productive.

Of these alternatives, the most obvious is to build artificial organisms that have genuine physical extension: artificial creatures, in other words. Currently, there are a number of inter-related approaches to this conundrum. The first of these is bio-mimetics. Bio-mimetics is a young discipline that studies models from nature and then imitates or takes inspiration from these designs and processes to solve various problems. It therefore potentially spans a vast range of different scientific areas and processes, only a few of which I will point to here; those that are most relevant to my argument. Though in the past, bio-mimetics has tended to concentrate on areas like materials, more recently considerable effort has been invested in animal mechanics. Many animal organs would display obvious utility if they could be imitated, such as the sticking power of mussels' feet or the ability of spiders to spin immensely strong silk (Benyus 1997). However, interest has also been shown in trying to produce programs that approximate animal brains and are therefore equipped to analyse patterns in ways which conventional programs find difficult or impossible, such as through the use of redundancy to handle or even generate side-effects, to ride unforeseeable as well as foreseeable forces. These programs may use 'tacti-lizing' processors, which are effectively large biosensors or optical protein processors that detect light absorption at any site and recognize a pattern from that pattern, amongst a host of similar technologies (Benyus 1997). Biomimetic robots range widely, from robots containing sensors that mimic a particular animal body part (for example, an electric analogue of the fly's motion-sensitive compound eye or the ant's polarized light sun compass) to attempts to construct a series of rapid prototypes that allow some degree of co-evolution (Holland & McFarland 2001).

The second approach focuses on imitation. Over the last ten years or so imitation has emerged as a topic of interest in disciplines as different as psychology, ethology, philosophy, linguistics, cognitive science, computer science, biology, anthroplogy and robotics (cf. Zentall & Galef 1988, Cypher 1993, Heyes & Galef 1996, Nadel & Butterworth 1999, Zentall 2001, Dautenhahn & Nehaniv 2002). It is no surprise that a series of attempts have therefore been made to program animal characteristics by imitation, both as a functional approach and as a topic that is interesting and valuable in its own right.[7] Imitation has been found to be one of the principal means of social learning by animals (including human beings) and aspects of its study are clearly able to be transferred to the artificial domain, especially when this domain is thought of as more than just a simple mapping between perception and action, sending and

receiving. In particular, much work now revolves around understanding imitation as a property of situated and embodied agents operating in a particular
environment that includes other agents as well as other sources of dynamic
change (Dourish 2001). So far as the building of artificial animals is concerned,
the impetus behind this work is clear: to be able to develop complex affective
skills like facial expression.

The third approach is perhaps the most obvious: the construction of actual
artificial creatures. Of course, the construction of artificial creatures is hardly a
new ambition. It dates from at least the automata of the early eighteenth century,
and electronic automata date from the 1940s. For example, in the 1940s and
1950s Walter (1951, 1952, 1953) built a series of artificial creatures ('simple
animals') that were intended to display spontaneity, autonomy and self-
regulation. Based on a combination of vacuum tubes, actuators and two sensors
(light and bump) these creatures exhibited conditioned reflex learning and a
wide variety of behaviours.[8] Since that time, large numbers of attempts have
been made to build such creatures by roboticists and others culminating in the
current vogue for creating artificial ethologies.

> Mobile robots have now existed for some 50 years. During that time, most
> robots were developed within the technical and conceptual horizons of
> contemporary engineering, computer science, and artificial intelligence and
> only a small number, for a variety of reasons, were specifically designed to
> resemble animals in one way or another. Now it happens to be the case that
> animals and mobile robots, whether animal-like or conventional, necessarily
> share so many features that, in many ways, all mobile robots resemble
> animals to some extent. On the other hand, all robots, whether animal-like
> or conventional, have things in common that set them apart from animals.
> (Holland & McFarland 2001, p. 15)

Most particularly, animals grow and evolve and as a result have to be, to
some degree, functionally adaptable. Thus, though simple mimicry may produce
animal-like behaviour, behaviour which may well be impressive in its apparent
faithfulness, this may simply be because the robot and animal have converged on
solutions dictated by the same restricted domain. Whatever the case, it is fair to
say that perhaps the largest breakthrough in building artificial creatures has been
the result of taking the environment more seriously in recognition of the fact
that many animal cognitive tasks are off-loaded onto the environment. The
environment provides a host of peripheral devices that store, enhance, stream-
line and generally re-represent meaning (Dennett 1997). This is the 'subsumption' approach favoured by Brooks (1999, 2002; Thrift 2003b, Arkin 1998). In
that approach, an intelligent system is composed of a series of behaviour-
producing subsystems, each of which independently connects sensing with
action to achieve some particular behavioural competence such as 'avoid',

'wander' or 'explore'.[9] This series of very basic affects could be linked in various ways but were, above all, able to respond to many domains precisely and economically because they did not rely on internal representations but instead used the environment to do much of the 'thinking': in the by-now famous phrase 'the world is its own best model'.[10] This behaviour-based approach has been extended in various directions, and chiefly by making each affect and the entire system subject to evolutionary selection (as represented by genetic algorithms, neural networks and the like), thus introducing a definite learning trajectory. This adaptive approach, usually known as 'evolutionary robotics', is becoming increasingly popular as a means of selecting out and reinforcing particular competencies over time and as a means of co-evolving different kinds of robots (cf. Nolfi and Floreano 2000). In turn, such developments are leading to an interest in 'collective robotics' in which populations of robots are co-evolved and exhibit a distributed intelligence, rather like insect colonies (cf. Bonabeau *et al.* 1999).[11]

The fourth approach is simply to graft a living part of an animal into a robot, thereby producing an organic-artificial hybrid or 'hybrot'. Given the profound difficulties of preserving function in an isolated animal body part, such hybrids remain rare.[12] For example, the antennae from silkworm moths have been dissected out and mounted on a small robot as a means of tracking pheromones. Similarly, the nervous system of a sea lamprey has been dissected out and used to drive motors and register light sensitivity in a small robot (Holland & McFarland 2001, Geary 2002). More recently, a part mechanical, part biological robot has been created that operates on the basis of the neural activity of rat brain cells grown in a dish. This robot has actually gone on the market (through the Swiss robotics maker, K-Team) (Eisenberg 2003). Such experiments, and others like them, might be seen as part of a more general tendency to mix the organic and the digital in ways which take advantage of animal senses that cannot as yet be engineered or as a means of framing new 'bionic' senses or as simply part of further enquiries into animality.[13]

The ambition that underlies each of these kinds of approach is clear enough. Though it is always dangerous to take the writings of ideologues as typical, still their very extremity has its uses in pointing to the dreams and ambitions of those currently attempting to design electric animals. This is, I think, to design a machine nature driven by a 'bio-logic'. This machine nature would display at least the following characteristics: an open-ended evolution or at least emergence, a capacity for learning, very large amounts of problem-solving power arising from large populations of agents. Why? Because 'technology keeps getting more and more complex, which means that our traditional methodologies run up against a wall much sooner than they did before: more and more often they are overstretched . . . That's when we start considering the biological, which often permits us to make do with but a partial design – to be completed through evolution, learning, and other biologically-inspired techniques' (Sipper 2002,

p. 187). Some authors want to go further, of course. For example, Brooks envisages a world not far from now in which there is a burgeoning artificial ecology of machines. These 'machines to live with' will have a hodgepodge of capabilities and will continually scurry about, tending to human needs in all manner of ways.

> There are going to be more and more robots in our homes. Pretty soon we will stop bothering to count them. They will be a new class of entity, moving about under their own free will, doing their tasks as they decide they need to be done. The ecology of our homes will be visibly more complex than it is today. Just as our houses with their refrigerators, washing machines, dishwashers, stereos, televisions and computers would look sort of like a house but with a whole lot of weird stuff littered about, so too will the houses a century from now look a little strange to us.
>
> (Brooks 2002, p. 126)

This may seem to be a perfect example of the kind of rampant technological hyperbole that typified the late 1990s. Except for these facts: primitive robot vacuum cleaners and lawnmowers are now on general sale in North America and Western Europe; in Japan new generations of consumer robots are becoming generally (if usually very expensively) available; a number of companies have viable plans for combining wireless sensor networks and mobile robots so that the robots will need less brain power because they will be able to share it (Butler 2003); environmental activists are already trying to produce 'feral' packs of AIBOs and other robotic dogs that can participate in staged media events – or just play soccer (Feral Robotics 2003).[14,15] In other words, wherever we look in modern Euro-American cultures, we can see new surfaces and objects appearing powered by the motivating force of software and more and more of these surfaces and objects will be quite literally animated by software. Further, this kind of animality is becoming more and more prevalent (Lupton 2002). It is no longer far-fetched to think that in twenty years or so small machines will scuttle about largely unremarked upon in Euro-American households and workplaces carrying out mundane, specialized tasks or offering all manner of solace. The question that occupies the next section of the paper is what kind of cultural model will be drawn on to describe these new 'wild things'.

Pets and power

So how will the new machines sink into the background of everyday life? Nearly every writer seems to fall back on a quasi-biological analogy in that they agree that the sheer density of informational devices is beginning to create something like a digital ecology. But, thereafter, the accounts diverge, apparently radically.

One account is dystopian: consumers are drawn into a seamless world of electronic interconnectivity and speed that constitutes a kind of 'connective dementia'. Following on from the millenarian accounts of writers like Virilio and Harvey – who foresee a further round of time–space compression in which the real-time instant rules, in which here-and-now becomes all the there that there is – a new generation of dystopians have forecast the end of reflexivity, since time to ponder the alternatives to what presents itself will become increasingly scarce.

> This top-to-bottom, inside-and-out connectivity, uniquely in the history of technological development, has created its own ecology – an ecology based on interconnectivity that is becoming more pervasive. To live in the digital ecology is to live within a chronoscopic temporality of the constant present. This is creating its own form of tyranny, 'the tyranny of real time' (Purser 2000, p. 5). Linear, narrative times, through which we gain a sense of past, present and possible futures are becoming compressed into instantaneity. Those 'multitude[s] of times which interpenetrate and permeate our daily lives' (Adam 1995, p. 12) are themselves interpenetrated and permeated by ICT interconnectivity, digitizing them onto a single, temporal plane. Psychological research into human-computer interaction suggests that we are only able to perceive what we concentrate upon, and when we do not have time to concentrate on a particular thing we suffer from 'inattentional blindness' (Nardi & O'Day 1999, p. 14). In an information ecology based upon real-time chronoscopic temporality, this poses serious problems. If we are effectively 'blind' to that which we cannot devote a durational time-span, in 'the buzz of the flickering present' (Purser 2000, p. 5), then major problems loom as interconnectivity spreads deeper and wider.
>
> (Hassan 2003, p. 102)

The other account is utopian. A favourite of 1990s commentators, it sees the emerging digital ecology as a kind of playground for a new and calmer generation of technologies in which everyday life becomes everyday life plus, a playground of augmented association and incidental learning taking place through a new set of cohabitees (Dertouzos 2001). Thus,

> the science of digital ecologies is just beginning. More than just simulations running in the mind of a computer, artificial life has worked its way into the real world, in a variety of robotic forms. From robotic 'insects' to intelligences with faux human bodies, these robots learn from their continuous interaction with the environment, defining goals and changing strategies as they encounter with world. Theses machines have crossed an imaginary line from procedural to unpredictable, which delights their creators. . . . Encountering a quirky, nonhuman, but thoroughly real intelligence is

thrilling to both children and adults. In some way, it is life, and we instinc-
tively recognize it.

(Pesce 2000, pp. 8–9)

Somewhere in these utopian accounts' future, the artificial and the biological
usually become as one. Digital implants will augment the body while computers
will increasingly depend on biological substrates. There will be a 'marriage of
silicon and steel with biological matter' and, as we move 'beyond cyborgs', the
'distinction between us and robots is going to disappear' (Brooks 2002, p. 233,
p. 232, p. 236).

However, both of these accounts are actually rather similar to each other. In
particular, they both rely on technological determinism (whether that technology is silicon or cellular) to see them through. Everyday life is a mirror of the
qualities of the machines (whether silicon or cellular) that are present. The
heterogeneous and often historically accidental archive of practices that take
these machines in, rather than vice versa, are ignored or minimized.

Perhaps there is another way of framing the relationships between people
and the new generation of biologically-inclined machines, one that draws
precisely on our relationship with a particular subset of animals, namely
companion animals or *pets*. Certainly, it seems a crucial political move at this
juncture to think about ways of inhabiting everyday life which can think beyond
these two impoverished ways of proceeding towards ways of conceiving the
biological and the artificial as not just us but more than just other. Further,
companion animals are a key part of Euro-American everyday life that have been
widely and oddly ignored. For all the raft of writings about the powers of
mundane objects and even of 'wild things' (Attfield 2000), here is a set of entities
that have been comprehensively overlooked, even though it would be relatively
easy to make a case that companion animals provide a good part of the practical
and affective life of many, many households (Wolfe 2003a, 2003b).

Certainly, the sensory worlds of animals, whether wild or domesticated, are
very different from those that humans inhabit, a claim made by von Uexküll in
the late nineteenth century and since substantiated by numerous scientific studies
(cf. Budiansky 1998). There is no reason why his umwelten approach cannot be
applied equally to machines, in that machines also consist of a set of particular
affects bound to the world and offering a particular sensing of it. However, it is
clear that electric animals are meant to turn up helpfully in a human world, able
to at least partially sense its needs and priorities. Given this, perhaps they are
best thought of as like domesticated animals and most particularly as something
akin to pets. Insofar as these animals are meant to be pet-like rather than simply
commensal (that is symbiotic with their hosts), then their chief function seems
to be to produce some of the same affective relationships and satisfactions that
are best summarized by the now standard term 'companion animals'.

Of course, animals have a very long history of being companions to the everyday lives of humans. For example, cats are thought to have been domesti-cated for about six thousand years and though it might be that to begin with they were primarily used to keep down rats and mice in grain stores, it is also clear that from an early period they also formed affective relationships with human beings (Sunquist & Sunquist 2002). For example, from early in the Egyptian period, cats were given special respect and by 1000 BC, cats were commonly owned purely as pets, with their own appropriate rites of mourning – including the placing of the embalmed body in one of many vast cat cemeteries. Similarly, dogs can be found from a comparatively early period in human history. It is possible that dogs lived in villages some 12000 years BC.[16] By Neolithic times there starts to be good evidence for the presence of dogs but evidence for dogs as pets dates from rather later: 'By four thousand years ago, there were dogs in abundance, but little evidence of identifiable breeds. By Roman times, two thousand-plus years ago, writers are describing both sheepdogs and hunting dogs, and what sound like village curs are described in the Bible and other works written less than a thousand years before Roman times' (Coppinger & Coppinger 2001, p. 286).[17] In other words, for most of recorded historical time, human beings have had pet-like relations with animals and one of the key components of everyday life has been the rhythms and requirements of these animals. They have become a key element of human inhabiting, something more than passive context, with their own demands and needs adding a vital affective gloss to many people's everyday lives. So, for example, it has been estimated that there are over 50 million household dogs in the USA and a further 35 million in Europe (Coppinger & Coppinger 2001), most of which are pets.[18] In the USA, it has been reckoned that half of all households have a dog or cat, or both (Tuan 1984). So what are the reasons why pets have come into existence?

In recent years, the pleasures and rewards of pet ownership have been the subject of considerable research from a mixed collection of anthropologists, sociologists, biologists and veterinarians with the result that it has become possible to state with some degree of certainty the exact motivations behind pet ownership.[19] First, it is clear that many people gain substantive emotional benefits from pets, benefits that can be shown to exist physiologically (in, for example, lowered blood pressure, better sleep patterns and increased longevity). Second, pets can provide enhanced means of social association, all the way from simply meeting fellow dog walkers to participating in clubs for enthusiasts. Third, pets can give people more confidence, for example, by providing a sense of emotional or physical protection. Fourth, pets can act as style accessories or other indexes of social worth in that how they look can be important for bolstering a person's self-esteem. Finally, pets provide companionship: in societies where single person households are on the increase and many therefore live alone, this motivation is probably growing.

Pets, therefore, can clearly give a positive gloss to being human. However, they are also the subjects of great cruelty. Not only are they regularly shown affection but they are also the object of various forms of domination. They are regularly culled: on one estimate, the majority of North Americans keep their dogs for two years or less and then tire of them (Tuan 1984). Breeding involves selection, which may be quite ruthless. Again, making a pet may require harsh treatment. Dogs are often trained simply 'because power over another being is demonstrably firm when it is exercised for no particular purpose and when submission to it goes against the victim's own strong desires and nature' (Tuan 1984, p. 107). There may even be what Garber (1996) calls an 'erotics of dominance' in which the human portrays herself as falling under the spell of a pet because it is deserving of the human's love, thus valorizing her own actions and giving the pet no space to make difference.

However, all this said, pets clearly can and do inspire affection in and for themselves. Whilst this reaction is clearly part of a developing discourse of sentimentality towards animals whose origins date from the seventeenth century, it cannot be entirely reduced to just this story (Ritvo 1987). For example, writers like Grenier (2000) have taken up the threads of the sensual history of dogs and shown how it intersects with the history of humans, spinning out of that intersection a kind of respectful rapport that recognizes the full range of affective responses to dogs: sincerity, love, disdain, indifference and so on. Most particularly, a certain kind of faithfulness tends to be celebrated. Yet, even here, at the apparent apotheosis of the human-dog relationship, we see an instrumental attitude of sorts, rather well expressed by Lorenz (1964, pp. 194–195):

> The place which the human friend filled in your life remains forever empty; that of your dog can be filled with a substitute. Dogs are indeed individuals, personalities in the truest sense of the word and I should be the last to deny this fact, but they are much more like each other than are human beings. In those deep instinctive feelings that are responsible for their special relationship with man, dogs resemble each other closely, and if on the death of one's dog, one immediately adopts a puppy of the same breed, one will generally find that he refills those spaces in one's heart and one's life, which the departure of an old friend has left desolate.

Finally, there is, of course, the pet's point of view, a view which tends to be placed to one side because that would mean acknowledging that pets have their own umwelts that may still be very far from those of humans.

> The French, perhaps even more than others, talk to their dogs and cats as if they were human. They are totally surprised whenever their pet exhibits a sudden return to animality. When, for example, rediscovering its ancient instinct to camouflage itself for hunting, a dog rolls in shit. How could our favourite conversation partner – one whose wit, wisdom and even (why not?) philosophy we so admire – go so far astray? Baudelaire takes up this

theme in his prose poem 'The Dog and the Flask'. The creature described as the unworthy companion of Baudelaire's sorry existence resembles the reading public. Exasperated by delicate perfumes, it sniffs with delight at carefully selected garbage. Henri Michaux, in *Passages*, remarks that you never see a dog stopping to smell a rose or a violet: 'They carry a goddam dossier around in their heads, constantly updated. Who understands the menu of stink better?'

(Grenier 2000, pp. 11–12)

Even so, given the rather jolly tone of these kinds of contributions, it might be thought that, for all their differences, the population of pets has been able to arrive at the best kind of commensalism, a generally well-serviced ecological niche. For example, 'ecologically speaking . . . the domestic dog is an incredibly successful species' (Coppinger & Coppinger 2001, p. 231), having reached an equilibrium environment that sustains the canine ability to find food, avoid hazards and reproduce. But, equally, pets can be seen as suffering from the worst kind of amensalism (a living together in which one species hurts another, sometimes unknowingly). They are captured animals: animals that we adopt, rather than vice versa. Their lives are manipulated for the human host's benefit with generally malign results. Take the example of the dog again: 'When I look at the benefits for the dog [of a] symbiotic relationship with humans, it looks well-nigh hopeless. . . . I believe the modern household dog is bred to satisfy human psychological needs, with little or no consideration for the consequences for the dog. . . . These dogs fill the court-jester model of pet ownership' (Coppinger & Coppinger 2001, pp. 251–252).

What the literature on pets shows us, therefore, is the wide variety of responses to companion animals that exist in everyday life: domination and cruelty combined with sugary sentiment, a matter-of-fact instrumentalism combined with an awareness of a lurking otherness, and general uncertainty about the costs and benefits of the relationship for either party. As machines are loaded up with software and gain more and more independent mobility, so the same kinds of ethical dilemmas are likely to occur. These dilemmas may become more severe as some machines are invested with a capacity for emotional response, conversational capability, and so on.[20] They will surely begin to demand some of the same kinds of ethical responses as are found in the case of companion animals. But the case of companion animals should also give us pause: indeed, as we have seen, it would be possible to argue that the world of companion animals too often lacks any concerted ethical response. Surely, this underlines once again the case for an everyday ethics of the kind favoured by Varela (2000), but one that does not stop at the 'human' world but rather acknowledges other intelligibilities as well.

Conclusions

Deleuze and Guattari's disdain for a culture that is locked into individualistic, possessive concerns is clear, not least in their comments on pets: 'individuated animals, family pets, sentimental, Oedipal animals each with its own petty history, "my" cat, "my" dog. These animals invite us to regress and they are the only kind of animal psychoanalysis understands' (Deleuze & Guattari 1988, p. 240). In their rush to conjure up what is essentially a Spinozan world of prepersonal natural forces, they clearly throw down a challenge to make the comfortable world of everyday life uncomfortable by stripping it of some of its most reassuring denizens. They want to head out in the direction of a wilder animality that is both frightening – and creative. It is possible to have considerable sympathy with this approach whilst at the same time having considerable doubts about it, ranging from the empirical (being scratched by a cat on fairly regular basis) through the anthropological (many cultures through history seem to have kept pets in circumstances that are difficult to equate with Western possessive individualism) through to the ethical (is it necessarily so awful for people with very little in the way of companionship to seek it out in animal form?).

These same tensions are to be found in the construction of electric animals. What kind of culture is to be assumed? A wild electric panorama bereft of human figures but traversed by various lines of affect? A scurrying ecology full to bursting with all manner of informational life? A consumer mall of companions waiting to be sold and played with and as easily discarded? Or a welfare system gently caring for the emotional needs of its charges?

What I have tried to show in this paper is that the advent of software-driven entities modelled on biological assumptions is a significant event that has the potential to decisively change everyday life by adding in a new range of cohabit-ees. In particular, it offers a new set of ethical dilemmas that have clearly not been solved in the case of companion animals (Gaita 2003).

One might argue that, in certain senses, the issue of electric animals is more pressing because these entities have the potential to discipline conduct in more explicit and rigid ways (Lecourt 2003).[21] They are being socially engineered but, in turn, they can become a part of a new means of social engineering, half way between the disciplinary and the pastoral and combining elements of each. For it is quite clear that these animals can be made more or less lively and more or less threatening by the lines of code that animate them – not just in their capacity for surveillance (which is substantial) but also in their capacity to pass on and inculcate behaviours that may be inimical (for example, all manner of corporate dictates). There is, therefore, a lively politics of interspecies ethics to be pursued that can ensure that new hybrid relationships that will be brought into existence are not malign, or simply vapid (Plumwood 2002), and are able to produce resolution through alliance and mutual assistance rather than domination. For example, there is nothing to stop surfaces and entities being designed that can inculcate values and practices of critical responsiveness by retaining ambiguity, ambivalence and respect of the kind that is sometimes seen in human dealings with companion animals.

Such scenarios have been the bread and butter of science fiction for many years now, of course, but that does not necessarily make them invalid. Rather, because the future has a tendency to turn up not as some kind of gleaming and polished modernity but as overused and battered pieces of equipment our critical senses are dulled and we do not recognize that there are any similarities. However, at this time, that might be a dangerous assumption to make.

Notes

1   Everyday life is often framed as a kind of subterranean force, an intense conglomeration of the countless contingent situations that line the present that has come to be driven by the repetitive demands of capitalism that have gradually come to overlay all other cycles. Though everyday life is often envisaged to be controlled by the routines of capitalism, it is also regarded as somehow oblique to it. Thus, according to Lefebvre (1994, p. 18), it is 'the most universal and the most unique condition, the most social and the most individuated, the most obvious and the most hidden'. In the interstices of everyday life, then, should be expected to be found not just the alienations, reifications and fetishisms pushed by all the agents of a commodified capitalism but also something more; spaces, times and situations that arise from other traditions that are not yet fully attenuated, from the unexpected and eventful nature of the present, and from the highly variable exigencies of particular times and places (Crang & Thrift 2001). I do not wish to dispute this kind of depiction/diagnostic, which is now commonly accepted in large parts of academe and elsewhere. But I do dispute some of the commonly accepted consequences: an inevitable erosion of all relations except those of the commodity, a gradual gridding of space and time so that they follow the contours of capitalist production, distribution and consumption, and an increasingly quietist politics, whose silence is broken every now and then by periodic doomed outbreaks from the dominant ideology. As I hope to show in this paper, all kinds of possibilities are still open, though they will have to be fought for. I therefore lean towards a vision of everyday life that adopts something closer to a Certeauian emphasis.

2   I am convinced that the accounts of authors like these are rooted in the assumptions and practices of another time and have only a limited purchase on the current period (see Thrift 2004).

3   Recently, social scientists have spent considerable time considering the writings of biologists who believe that organisms cannot be reduced to the sum of their parts but it needs to be stressed that, in the context of modern bioscience, these writings are very much in the minority.

4   Until this time, it was used to refer to mistaken attributions of human traits to deities.

5   One good example of this traffic is the increasing prevalence of chips in pets, which will allow them to be easily identified if they get lost. Such chips are now being mooted for children and even adults.

6   *Tierra* is only one of many of these artificial worlds. Others include variations on *Tierra* like *Avida*, *Evita* and *Bugs* as well as rather different worlds like Holland's *Echo* and Taylor's *Cosmos*.

7   The programs produced are usually connectionist.

8   Expanded accounts of Walter's work at the Burden Neurological Institute in Bristol can be found in Ward (1999), Holland and McFarland (2002) and Brooks (2002). In time-honoured fashion, Walter is now being claimed as a founding father of robotics.

9   The use of a Deleuzian terminological universe might be highly appropriate at this point since in a number of ways this kind of work is an engineered conception very similar to certain aspects of Deleuze's thought.

10   That said, the issue of internal state does not disappear and still causes certain problems for this kind of approach (cf. Holland & McFarland 2001).

11   Note that the vocabulary of life is absolutely crucial to the claims made for these creatures as both standard and justification (see Doyle 1997).

12   Never mind the ethical implications!

13   I do not here go into the attempts to produce biological computers, though there are now a number of these.

14   Robot vacuum cleaners include the Roomba produced by iRobot, Rodney Brooks's company and the Electrolux Trilobite. Other major vacuum cleaner manufacturers like Hoover, Matsushita and Dyson are working on similar projects. Husqvarna, a subsidiary of Electrolux, sells two different models of robot lawnmower.

15   I am not concerned here with demonstrators like the four feet high Honda Asimo but rather with genuine mass market products like the new Sony humanoid SDR-4X II, which at 7 kg has all the features that might now be expected (such as bipedal movement, conversational capabilities based on speech recognition of about 20,000 words, and so on), the Toshiba ApriAlpha (which also has face and speech recognition and looks like R2D2) and, of course, the by now familiar Sony Aibo dog in its various incarnations (Thrift 2003, Wray 2003). Whereas the SDR-4X II is the price of a luxury car, the Aibo is coming down rapidly in price. Another development is the growth of relatively cheap do-it-yourself robotics kits like the Evolution ER-1, which work with laptops to allow the performance of a large number of tasks and can be built as one of several standard variants or customized.

16   The evidence is difficult to interpret: 'one can't tell whether a woman was buried with a choice lunch to take her to the happy hunting grounds or whether she was taking her pet puppy to heaven with her' (Coppinger & Coppinger 2001, p. 277).

17   Indeed, genetic evidence suggests that dogs may first have appeared about 50,000 to 15,000 years ago (Haraway 2003).

18   One should not, of course, over-sentimentalize the relationship. In the USA, for example, about five percent of dogs are culled ('put to sleep') each year (Coppinger & Coppinger 2001).

19   This account would be deemed hopelessly human-centric by some since there is good evidence to suggest that in the recent evolutionary record animals in certain senses chose to become pets, filling a new and more secure niche without having to make significant compromises. However, since the emphasis of this paper is on the derivation of electric animals I do not think that this is a besetting sin, although at some point future informational versions of bio-ethicists may start to invest these animals with rights.

20   I have considered this issue in more detail by reference to toys. See Thrift (2003b).

21   The issue has become much more pressing since the recent announcement of injectable radio frequency identifier chips that can be used as human bar codes (Murray 2002, Thrift 2004).

References

Adam, B. (1995) *Timewatch. The Social Analysis of Time*, Polity Press, Cambridge.

Arkin, R. (1998) *Behavior-Based Robotics*, MIT Press, Cambridge, MA.

Attfield, J. (2000) *Wild Things. The Material Culture of Everyday Life*, Berg, Oxford.

Baker, S. (2000) *The Postmodern Animal*, Reaktion, London.

Beck, A. & Katcher, A. (1996) *Between Pets and People: The Importance of Animal Companionship*, Purdue University Press, West Lafayette, IN.

Bentley, P. (2002) *Digital Life: A New Kind of Nature*, Headline, London.

Benyus, J. M. (1997) *Biomimicry: Imitation Inspired by Nature*, William Morrow, New York.

Bonabeau, E., Dorigo, M. & Theraulez, G. (1999) *Swarm Intelligence: From Natural to Artificial Systems*, Oxford University Press, Oxford.

Brooks, R. (1999) *Cambrian Intelligence: The Early History of the New AI*, MIT Press, Cambridge, MA.

Brooks, R. (2002) *Robot: The Future of Flesh and Machines*, Allen Lane, London.

Budiansky, S. (1998) *If a Lion Could Talk: Animal Intelligence and the Evolution of Consciousness*, Free Press, New York.

Butler, J. (2003) 'Mobile robots as gateways into wireless sensor networks', [online] Available at http://www.linuxdevices.com/articles/AT2705574735.html

Coppinger, R. & Coppinger, L. (2001) *Dogs: A New Understanding of Canine Origin, Behaviour and Evolution*, University of Chicago Press, Chicago.

Crang, M. & Thrift, N. (eds) (2001) *TimeSpace*, Routledge, London.

Cypher, A. (ed.) (1993) *Watch What I Do: Programming by Demonstration*, MIT Press, Cambridge, MA.

Dautenhahn, K. & Nehaniv, C. (eds) (2002) *Imitation in Animals and Artifacts*, MIT Press, Cambridge, MA.

De Waal, F. & Tyack, P. (eds) (2003) *Animal Social Complexity: Intelligence, Culture, and Individualized Societies*, Harvard University Press, Cambridge, MA.

Dennett, D. (1997) *Kinds of Minds: Towards an Understanding of Consciousness*, Phoenix, London.

Dertouzos, M. (2001) *The Unfinished Revolution: Human-Centred Computers and What They Can Do For Us*, Harper Collins, New York.

Dourish, P. (2001) *Where the Action Is: Embodied Interaction*, MIT Press, Cambridge, MA.

Doyle, R. (1997) *On Beyond Living: Rhetorical Transformations of the Life Sciences*, Stanford University Press, Stanford.

Dyson, G. (1997) *Darwin Among the Machines*, Allen Lane, London.

Eisenberg, A. (2003) 'Wired to the brain of a rat, a robot takes on the world', *New York Times*, 15 May, pp. 13–26.

Feral Robots (2003) 'Feral Robotics: Dog Report', [online] Available at http://xdesign.eng.yale.edu/feralrobots/

Gaita, R. (2003) *The Philosopher's Dog*, Routledge, London.

Garber, M. (1996) *Dog Love*, Simon and Schuster, New York.

Geary, J. (2002) *The Body Electric: An Anatomy of the New Bionic Senses*, Weidenfeld and Nicolson, London.

Grenier, R. (2002) *The Difficulty of Being a Dog*, University of Chicago Press, Chicago.

Haraway, D. (2003) *The Companion Species Manifesto: Dogs, People, and Significant Otherness*, Prickly Paradigm Press, Chicago.

Harootunian, H. (2000) *History's Disquiet: Modernity, Cultural Practice and the Question of Everyday Life*, Columbia University Press, New York.

Hassan, R. (2003) 'The MIT media lab: techno dream factory or alienation as a way of life', *Media, Culture and Society*, vol. 25, pp. 87–106.

Hayles, N. K. (2002) *Writing Machines*, MIT Press, Cambridge, MA.

Heyes, C. & Galef, B. (1996) *Social Learning in Animals: The Roots of Culture*, Academic Press, San Diego.

Hobbes, T. (1651) *Leviathan; or, The Matter, Forme, and Power of a Commonwealth Ecclesiasticall and Civill*, Andrew Crooke, London.

Holland, J. (1975) *Adaptation in Natural and Artificial Systems*, University of Michigan Press, Ann Arbor, MI.

Holland, O. & McFarland, D. (2001) *Artificial Ethology*, Oxford University Press, Oxford.

Lecourt, D. (2003) *Humain, Posthumain. La Technique et la Vie*, Presses Universitaires de France, Paris.

Lippitt, A. (2000) *Electric Animal: Toward a Rhetoric of Wildlife*, University of Minnesota Press, Minneapolis.

Lorenz, K. (1964) *Man Meets Dog*, Penguin, Harmondsworth.

Lupton, E. (2002) *Skin: Surface, Substance, Design*, Princeton Architectural Press, Princeton, NJ.

Mackintosh, J. (2003) 'Robots lose out to human touch', *Financial Times*, May 1, p. 11.

Mitchell, M. (1996) *An Introduction to Genetic Algorithms*, MIT Press, Cambridge, MA.

Murray, C. (2002) 'Injectable chip opens door to human bar code', *EETimes*, 7 January, [online] Available at http://www.eetimes.com/story/OEG20020104S0044

Nadel, J. & Butterworth, G. (eds) (1999) *Imitation in Infancy*, Cambridge University Press, Cambridge.

Nardi, B. & O'Day, V. (1999) *Information Ecologies: Using Technology with Heart*, MIT Press, Cambridge, MA.

Nolfi, S. & Floreano, D. (2000) *Evolutionary Robotics: The Biology, Intelligence and Technology of Self-Organizing Machines*, MIT Press, Cambridge, MA.

Pesce, M. (2000) *The Playful World: How Technology is Transforming Our Imagination*, Ballantine Books, New York.

Plumwood, V. (2002) *Environmental Culture: The Ecological Crisis of Reason*, Routledge, London.

Podberscek, A., Paul, E. & Serpell, J. (eds) (2000) *Companion Animals and Us: Exploring the Relationships between People and Pets*, Cambridge University Press, Cambridge.

Purser, R. (2000) 'The coming crisis in real-time environments: a dromological analysis' [online] Available at online.sfsu.edu/~rpurser/revised/pages/DROMOLOGY. htm

Ray, T. (1991) 'An approach to the synthesis of life', in *Artificial Life II: Santa Fe Studies in the Sciences of Complexity*, Volume XI, eds C. Langton, C. Taylor, J. D. Farmer & S. Rasmussen, Addison Wesley, Redwood City, CA, pp. 371–408.

Ritvo, H. (1987) *The Animal Estate: The English and Other Creatures in the Victorian Age*, Harvard University Press, Cambridge, MA.

Rothfels, N. (ed.) (2002) *Representing Animals*, Indiana University Press, Bloomington, IN.

Schwarz, M. (1997) *A History of Dogs in the Early Americas*, Yale University Press, New Haven.

Scott, C. (2002) *The Lives of Things*, Indiana University Press, Bloomington, IN.

Sedgwick, E. K. (2003) *Touching Feeling: Affect, Pedagogy, Performativity*, Duke University Press, Durham, NC.

Serpell, J. (1986) *In the Company of Animals*, Cambridge University Press, Cambridge.

Simondon, G. (1958/1989) *Du Mode d'Existence des Objets Techniques*, Aubier, Paris.

Sipper, M. (2002) *Machine Nature: The Coming Age of Bio-Inspired Computing*, McGraw Hill, New York.

Stafford, B. M. and Terpak, F. (2001) *Devices of Wonder: From the World in a Box to Images on a Screen*, Getty Research Institute, Los Angeles.

Sunquist, M. & Sunquist, F. (2002) *Wild Cats of the World*, University of Chicago Press, Chicago.

Thrift, N. (2003a) 'Driving in the city', *Theory, Culture & Society*, forthcoming.

Thrift, N. (2003b) 'Closer to the machine? Intelligent environments, new forms of possession and the rise of the supertoy', *Cultural Geographies*, forthcoming.

Thrift, N. (2004) 'Remembering the technological unconscious by foregrounding knowledges of position', *Environment and Planning D: Society and Space*, forthcoming.

Thrift, N. & French, S. (2002) 'The automatic production of space', *Transactions of the Institute of British Geographers*, vol. 27, pp. 309–335.

Tuan, Y.-F. (1984) *Dominance and Affection: The Making of Pets*, Yale University Press, New Haven, CT.

Varela, F. (2000) *Ethical Know-How*, Stanford University Press, Stanford.

Walter, W. (1950) 'An imitation of artificial life', *Scientific American*, vol. 96, pp. 123–137.

Walter, W. (1953) *The Living Brain*, Penguin, London.

Ward, M. (1999) *Virtual Organisms: The Startling World of Artificial Life*, Pan, London.

Whatmore, S. (2002) *Hybrid Geographies*, Sage, London.

Wolfe, C. (2003a) *Animal Rites: American Culture, the Discourse of Species and Post-humanism*, Chicago University Press, Chicago.

Wolfe, C. (2003b) *Zoontologies: The Question of the Animal*, University of Minnesota Press, Minneapolis.

Wray, R. (2003) 'Our new best friend', *Guardian*, 4 April, p. 23.

Zentall, T. (2001) 'Imitation in animals: evidence, function and mechanisms', *Cybernetics and Systems*, vol. 32, pp. 53–96.

Zentall, T. & Bennett G. (eds) (1988) *Social Learning: Psychological and Biological Perspectives*, Lawrence Erlbaum Associates, Hillsdale, NJ.

Barry Sandywell

BEYOND METAPHYSICS AND NIHILISM
In Memoriam: Steve Crook, sociologist and teacher (1950–2002)

This special issue of *Cultural Studies* is dedicated to the memory of Professor Stephen Crook (1950–2002). He had been involved with this project in its earliest stages, but, sadly, was not in the end able to contribute. Steve, as he was always known to his friends and colleagues, died in 2002 after a lengthy and brave struggle with cancer. Steve is survived by his wife, Rosemary, and daughter, Felicity.

Steve was well respected in the sociological communities of the UK and Australia. He had longstanding interests in social theory, the sociology of culture and political sociology. His books include *Modernist Radicalism and Its Aftermath: Foundationalism and Anti-Foundationalism in Radical Social Theory* (1991), *Post-modernization: Change in Advanced Society* (co-authored with Jan Pakulski and Malcolm Waters, 1992), *Adorno: The Stars Look Down to Earth and Other Essays on the Irrational in Culture* (ed., 1994), *Environmentalism, Public Opinion and the Media in Australia* (edited with Jan Pakulski, 1998). In addition to his scholarly work, Steve served as the President of The Australian Sociological Association from 1999 to 2002 and the joint-editor of its journal from 1993–1997. In his role as President, he played a key role in the initial organization of the 15th World Sociological Congress held in 2002 in Brisbane. Sadly, however, illness prevented Steve from attending.

In the following brief space I would like to celebrate aspects of Steve's life and work from the point of view of my changing involvement with him over several decades as, chronologically speaking, his doctoral supervisor, his friend, and, occasionally, colleague in the common pursuit of a shared conception of sociological inquiry that is fully aware of the contingent facts of its historical origins, its public and ethical responsibilities and, above all, its enormous reflexive potential for our understanding and transformation of modern society. Immediately one should enter a caveat that Steve would have undoubtedly endorsed. Namely, that a life as full and complex as his cannot be compressed into a biographical 'unity' and that what follows should not be seen as a summary of the force fields and contingencies that marks such a singular exist-ence. I do not wish to condense the substance and attributes of a life, but simply

![Routledge logo] **Routledge**
Taylor & Francis Group

Cultural Studies Vol. 18, No. 2/3 March/May 2004, pp. 483–493
ISSN 0950-2386 print/ISSN 1466-4348 online   © 2004 Taylor & Francis Ltd
http://www.tandf.co.uk/journals   DOI: 10.1080/0950238042000201626

to re-collect moments from a complex sociological itinerary. I believe that this more truly reflects the whole thrust of Steve's conception of the place of theorizing, sociological analysis and education in the wake of the grand narratives of modernity. In remembering Steve, I wish to commend his life as itself an instance of the kind of reflexivity made available in his work – leaving it to those who knew and respected him to provide other stories, other accounts and reflections that will help to reconfigure the person and his work. In the concluding words of his doctoral thesis: 'It would work against the thrust of the entire essay to urge a "unity" of these moments, or a "synthesis" of the projects associated with them. But it would be quite in keeping with that thrust to argue that it is only within those moments and projects that the precarious hope of a radicalism which is neither metaphysical nor nihilistic can be preserved' (1984, p. 382).

Steve came from a middle-class family and *milieu*; he was brought up and educated in the small manufacturing city of Leicester. He followed a not untypical early education that led to the study of philosophy as an undergraduate at the University of York in the early 1970s and to sociology as a postgraduate student. His disappointment with the aridity of the then dominant tradition of analytical philosophy led him away from philosophy as a career and he came to register as a doctoral student in the Department of Sociology at the University of York in the late 1970s. Knowing my own interests in reflexive sociology and in exploring the genealogy of philosophy and social theory, I recall a youthful and somewhat diffident figure, enveloped in an old ex-Army and Navy trench coat appearing unannounced at my office door. An individual with a beaming face graced with an infectious smile introduced himself as a prospective research student. Was I willing to supervise material he had been thinking about for a year or more on the nature and origins of sociological thought? I was both surprised and a little suspicious of his ambitious project to isolate and uncover the origins and assumptions of radical social theory. To trace the presuppositions of the idea of a securely founded social science in the writings of Marx, Durkheim, Weber, Althusser and Habermas? To deconstruct the genealogy of social thought in three years? I remained sceptical. However, I listened and Steve talked. Perhaps three hours passed and many cups of coffee later, my doubts about his intellectual credentials had receded and I was more or less persuaded that he could indeed fulfil the programme of research he had set out for himself, or at least, contribute significantly to the history of social thought. We arranged a further meeting and he promised to write out some of his ideas. In the light of these rough drafts, Steve became one of my research students. We both shared an interest in what was then referred to in a deprecatory manner as 'continental philosophy' and, more specifically, a profound respect for the German tradition of critique and critical social theory. Thus began a steady stream of discussions and programmatic texts; texts, it should be said, initially pervaded by the then-dominant influences of continental structuralism – in the form of the Althusserian revision of Marxism – and debates current within British Marxism influenced by Althusser, along with contributions from Gramsci, Poulantzas, Balibar and others. I still recall the animation in Steve's face when debating the relevant merits of the Hindess-and-Hirst line on some esoteric problem of structural determination that then exercised the left academic community. Steve had already seen that the pseudo-scientificity of Althusser's epistemology, even when 'purified', by the hyper-structuralism of Hindess and Hirst, could not avoid metaphysical postulates and, as we would learn in later works, the threat of nihilism disguised as an imperative of sociological reasoning. Despite the variety and heterogeneity of his early drafts, however, his intellectual potential and analytical flair were no longer in doubt.

In hindsight, it is clear that Steve was one of a remarkable generation of postgraduate students that converged in the Department of Sociology at York in the 1970s. Many of these have produced important works in sociology and gone on to become important figures in the sociological world in their own right. Although the list is incomplete, I would like to single out Andrew Webster, Steve Yearley, Pete Cressey, John Hill, Shule Pojon and Pete McGavin in this context. Like many of his contemporaries, Steve's basic orientation toward social thought and the unity of theory and critical research was forged in the aftermath of the 'theory wars' that then characterized academic sociology, especially by the heated debates between different forms of Neomarxism, semiotics and structuralism, phenomenology and interpretive philosophy. 'Radicalism' was both a central theme and a *desideratum* of responsible intellectual work. Theory was no ivory tower option but the very lifeblood of a politically engaged sociology. However, theory without a sense of its own limits and accountability was equally arid. Not surprisingly, Steve's many-sided interests settled upon the question of the epistemological status of the 'foundationalist' discourses within the classical human sciences, in particular represented by the foundational claims made by Durkheim and Durkheimian sociology, Althusserian Marxism and the Frankfurt School tradition of critical theory represented by the work of Jurgen Habermas. In hindsight, the idea behind his thesis can be understood as an early attempt to evaluate the debates on modernity and postmodernity that were looming on the horizon of the sociological fraternity. Steve had the insight and prescience to identify the coming epistemological storm. Steve successfully graduated in 1984. His thesis, 'Beyond foundationalism: a critical analysis of three foundational projects in radical social theory' was revised and published in 1991 with the more emphatic title, *Modernist Radicalism and Its Aftermath*. In retrospect, the intersection of these three radical projects in social thought – classical normative sociology, influenced ultimately by Durkheimian functionalism, structuralist Marxism and critical theory – can be said to have formed the creative matrix out of which all of the later themes in Steve's work would emerge and find their intellectual rationale.

Steve remained a lifelong sceptic about the claims of what he called 'foundationalism' in social theory and of any attempt to initiate programmes of research that failed to take into account the complex mediations of existing critical discourses and the complex entanglement of social research, ideology and ethical questions. The threat of scorched earth 'radicalisms' that ignored the resources of the past, the cynicism of 'atheoreticism' in social research, and the general nihilism of mainstream sociological research would remain guiding concerns throughout Steve's productive career. This is where our ideas converged: an authentically reflexive sociology could still maintain its radical edge unencumbered by the illusory promises of both first philosophy or nihilism (it is relevant to note that the concluding chapter of Steve's doctoral thesis has the title, 'Conclusions: radicalism, metaphysics and nihilism'). Reflexive sociology uniquely questions the traditional images of certainty and foundational groundedness – ultimately derived from positivist and transcendentalist discourses – but with a commitment to transcend the limited solutions of both modernist revisionism and postmodernist fatalism. This, *in nuce*, is the task of what Steve called post-foundational theorizing.

After graduating from York, Steve taught sociology for six years at the College of St Mark and St John in Plymouth (now affiliated with the University of Exeter). During this period, he had met and married Rosemary – known to all their friends as Rosie. Steve left the UK to take up a position as lecturer in the University of Tasmania in Hobart where, within a short period, he was appointed Head of Department. It is here that Steve began an intense and fruitful dialogue with Jan Pakulski and Malcolm Waters (who would later collaborate and publish an important work on the global processes and dynamics of structural postmodernization). After leaving Tasmania in 1997, Steve accepted a position in the Department of Sociology at the James Cook University in Australia. He was appointed to the foundation chair in Sociology in 1998 and shortly thereafter to the Headship of the then School of Psychology and Sociology. In 2000, Sociology merged with Anthropology and Archaeology and Steve became the most senior academic in the School. His colleagues have spoken of his effectiveness as a course organizer and administrator in the School of Anthropology, Archaeology and Sociology. To honour his contributions to Australian Sociology, the Australian Sociological Association has instituted a bi-annual prize – the Stephen Crook Memorial Prize – for the best-authored monograph within the discipline of sociology published over the previous three years.

In many respects, it is possible to see that Steve's metacritique of sociological fundamentalism (what he earlier called 'foundationalism') anticipated the later postmodern turn against metaphysical identities and unities of every description. Steve had already grasped the idea that foundationalism within social theory was both logically and historically tied to the fate of modern philosophy. His encounter with the German tradition of critical thought here proved decisive in exploring the problem of how to integrate a critical concept of reasoning with a political engaged sociology. Indeed, the issue of how to 'do' creative theorizing, how to engage in reflection and responsible social criticism, after the 'end of philosophy' was already an explicit theme in his early writings. It was Steve's firmly held conviction that a form or a tradition of radical sociology – the tradition of post-foundational radicalism – could survive the necessary purge of metaphysical categories and concerns. Critical work could proceed without the self-certainties of philosophy – whether positivist, transcendental or dialectical. Indeed, once rid of both its pretensions to scientific certainty or interpretive self-righteousness, a radically reflexive sociology could proceed unencumbered toward a more open and reflexive analysis of important problems and issues – among these the growing hegemony of transnational capitalism, the entanglement of the mass media in that hegemony, acute social problems of self-identification and social control, chronic inequalities of globalization and the significance of the rise of postmodern culture – or what Steve along with his Australian colleagues Pakulski and Waters more accurately grouped together under the generic title of the 'postmodernization of society', in their important and influential text *Postmodernization: Change in Advanced Society* (1992). This collaborative work gave new directions to his post-foundational critical perspective, linking issues of global power and control with the study of transnational institutions, technologies and cultures and their impact upon the texture of everyday life. Indeed, the theme of everyday life and its difficult history and controversial conceptualization form the central theme of his paper 'Minotaurs and other monsters: "everyday life" in recent social theory' (1998). Here again we find a paradigm case of Steve's erudition and critical acumen focused upon one of the central concepts of contemporary sociology. The essay remains a brilliant example of both Steve's acerbic wit and sociological imagination and will undoubtedly serve to generate an agenda of issues and themes that will need to be explored in greater depth in the years to come.

In the last decade of his life, Steve's work took new directions. These were, as I have intimated, influenced by a more urgent sense of understanding the transformation of the world system under the compound configurations of global capitalism, economic and cultural globalism and the cultural turn in all spheres of social thought. Social theory was not merely beset by foundational *aporiae*, but now contested by what has come to be called the postmodern condition (the term 'postmodernism' marking a complex and diverse set of critical responses and reflections on the limits of modernity and modernist ideology).

It is an important testimony to Steve's creative insight and intuitions that the nexus of problems associated with 'post-philosophical' reflexivity – what becomes of radicalism in social theory after the deconstruction of its metaphysical frameworks – and the question of the impact of the globalization of all societal and cultural relationships remain major themes on the contemporary agenda of critical social thought (Sandywell 2004, in this volume; Robertson 1992, 2001, Waters 1995, Urry 2000).

Three problematics should be cited in this context. First, Steve's increasing concern with the analysis of popular culture and the mass media, particularly national and international television as a powerful global monopoly in which reality is shaped and manufactured (for example, Crook 1989). Second, theories of (post)modernization and the impact of social and technological change in advanced industrialized societies. Where the earlier 'crisis of western sociology' had questioned the ideological presuppositions of the dominant paradigms, now key postmodern thinkers were speaking of the recession of the object of social theory, the imminent 'end of the social' in Baudrillard's apocalyptic idiom. It is not merely that radical sociology has no secure foundations; but rather that it no longer has an identifiable topic, and that what passes for social theory is the recycled ruins of one or more discredited 'grand narratives' (Lyotard 1984). One of Steve's last essays, 'Social Theory and the Postmodern' (2001), is a careful analytic deconstruction of the claims and arguments of postmodern theory with respect to the globalization of power and society (in Ritzer & Smart 2001). It also contains the outlines of a more complex theory of social 'ordering' as we move into an increasingly heterogeneous and disorganized phase of global capitalism. Finally, the numerous problems associated with the understanding and analysis of contemporary forms of everyday life and cultural experience (which Steve was particularly concerned with under the headings of popular culture, global tourism, environmentalism and biotechnology). It is again one example of Steve's own contemporaneity that questions of language, culture and communication were placed at the centre of all three of these problematics. The referents of the term 'language', of course, could not be taken at face value and required careful respecification and redefinition. Here the unique experience of Australian social life and politics undoubtedly played a seminal role. The transformation of Australian society under the combined impact of global tourism, the new technologies, and the spread of more powerful state institutions provided Steve with an image of what was occurring in other advanced industrial societies. I would also argue that the singular innovations made in the field of radical social theory by Australian theorists — with their interweaving of thought from Nietzsche, Foucault and contemporary feminism — was also decisive in expanding Steve's sociological imagination in the 1990s.

These transformations in theory and empirical research would have resonated with insights established in Steve's postgraduate days. I recall a line from his doctoral thesis where he observes, thought-provokingly, that any form of post-foundational radicalism 'must take from Foucault (and from Nietzsche) the lesson that the history of the proliferation of discourse is not a coming to self-consciousness. It has no "goal" but it is deployed in the pursuit of goals' (1984, p. 376). Steve understood that the breakdown of foundationalist accounts of theory and practice, the rejection of representationalist conceptions of language, and the demotion of value questions to questions of personal choice and idiosyncratic subjectivity had momentous consequences not just for social theory, but for the wider social and political world. Once these points are fully understood, we see that they are certainly 'obvious', but also that they run against the grain of entire traditions of social thought and praxis (1984, p. 376). In some respects, the fate of radical social thought is an icon or allegory of the fate of radical social reform and political engagement in the twentieth century.

As sociologists, we now live in the aftermath of the decline of empiricism, the ruins of Derridean deconstruction and the new problematics of poststructural anti-theory – whether of Foucauldian genealogy, Baudrillardian postmodernism or radically immanent discourse (de Certeau, Virilio, Serres, Deleuze, Latour and others). If there is no going back to the illusory certainties of the past and no creative mileage in reinventing the grand narratives of agency and structure in revamped terminologies, where should theory be heading? Where is the path beyond the impasse of both modernism and postmodernism? Steve saw lines of possible advance prefigured in the writings of Simmel, Benjamin and Adorno. All three had struggled with the grand narratives of their day and all had a fundamentally ethical conception of the reciprocal relations between theory (writing) and the ordinary textures of social praxis. He also saw the importance of concrete empirical research problems – whether in understanding environmental risk, the social consequences of the new technologies or the ethical issues raised by, for example, xenotransplanation – in disabusing high-altitude theorizing of its pretensions to knowledge. What modernist radicalism and postmodernist anti-radicalism both elide is the pregiven constellations of the ordinary that sustains all projects of thinking and writing. The 'end of philosophy' might well be the name for a process that leads inquiry back to a radical reappraisal of the sustaining powers of the ordinary. Had Steve lived he would have no doubt seen the theme of a renewed interest in ordinary life and everyday cultural formations as the storm-centre for a more empirically sensitive theory of postmodernization processes. The return to the ordinary is also perhaps another fruitful way in which questions of value and judgement can again enter critical discourse and find their point of articulation (Crook 1991, ch. 7, Sandywell 2004). If the 'unity' between theory and practice is no longer intelligible, if we are now more pragmatically inclined toward a fallible, post-empiricist conception of scientific research, if ethical issues cannot be cleanly separated from substantive and empirical questions, then the future of robust ventures in radical critique is *more*, not *less* important. We cannot dispense with 'theory' as though this was a realizable strategy (indeed all such attempts are themselves exercises in 'first philosophy'). Against this know-nothing stance, theorizing has to be redefined and respecified as a mundane accomplishment grounded in particular historical relations and generated by specific communities and their ongoing and unfinished work of 'ordering'. The ordering work of the ordinary must be redefined to include the diverse activities of theorizing as a range of embodied, practical regimes. As an accomplished practice, each of the discourses of radical social theory is necessarily a mundane cultural form, established and consolidated by diverse forms of practical sociological reasoning. In *this* respect, theory is no different from any other form of sense-making activity or 'world work'. In this respect, many of the radical sociological insights of ethnomethodology and conversation analysis had already pointed the way to something like a radical perspective of empirically informed studies of social organization.

But unlike mundane world-making, theory has a systemic and programmatic side. Theorizing is also explicitly oriented to others, to the implicit or explicit intersubjectivity of its own projected audience and community. It follows that we must, as responsible social theorists, be able to engage with and work through the discourses of theory, we must rediscover a more existential understanding of the value of theorizing and the endemic risks of cynicism and nihilism to which the life of theory is subject. There is no privileged ground or site for theorizing. We begin, inevitably in *media res*. However, we do not begin with nothing. As social thinkers and researchers, we begin with a singular responsibility for the subjects of research, the audience of our work and the hoped-for impact upon a transformed society. Rather, on the other side of metaphysics and nihilism we need to return to the richness and complexity of the ordinary.

If rhetoric – like language and the density of past social relations and institutions – is a boundary and limit of our thinking, we can imagine new rhetorics. We can even imagine rhetorics whose goal is the critique and analysis of rhetorical formations (including the complacencies of 'everyday language' and 'ordinary practices'). Again, to cite Steve's doctoral work, the 'moment of reflexion' has 'no access to discursive resources which grant a "privileged" self-knowledge . . . reflexion must be constituted out of the ordinary stuff of discourse. The elements of rhetoric and simulation are inescapable' (1984, p. 381). Once again, the urgency of rethinking the mundane as the horizon of thought remains one of Steve's most pressing legacies:

> 'Radicalism' is not defined in a new unity of theory and practice. From a mundane perspective, radicalism lies in the production of new insights into processes that are pragmatically defined as problematic. In orthogonal enquiry, radicalism lies in problematizing the boundaries of the mundane idiom itself. 'Theory', considered as speculative and programmatic synthesis, yields its privilege in both strategies to specific programmes of substantive enquiry, whether into mundane problems and processes or into the production of mundanity itself.
>
> (1991, p. 22)

This sensitivity toward the rhetoricality and reflexivity of all theory was Steve's life-long commitment and the source of his analytical rigour. He found the life of critique in many thinkers and traditions – most seminally in the work of Adorno and Derrida, but also in Foucault, Habermas, Heidegger and Gadamer. However, critique – or theorizing – is not a possession that can be 'owned' or commandeered by individuals, no matter how gifted or skilled in the arts of reading and appropriation. Rather, it remains the task and the passion of those who are still committed to the future of genuinely reflexive social inquiry. Above all else, theory must be accountable and open itself to the ethical horizon of its relation to the Other (indeed, Steve's working definition of nihilism is a failure in the accountability of social theory; 1991, p. 18). The interlocking themes of the mundanity of theoretical strategies and the ethics of reflexivity may, perhaps, be the thread that links all of Steve's later work. But neither mundanity nor reflexivity on their own can provide a 'solution' to unreflexive inquiry. Steve imagined this path beyond foundationalism by citing the literature of analytical sociology (Blum 1974, McHug et al. 1974, Sandywell et al. 1975). Reflection here takes the form of an explicit requirement that the constitutive practices of reading and writing sociology should be made thematic topics within the projects of social inquiry. Even more radically, both ordinariness and reflexivity have to be historically specified and critically explicated (Sandywell 1996). In this vein, he speaks of a continuum of reflection:

> Projects of enquiry vary according to the type of reflexivity, or self-reference, they engender. Some may have only a minimal reflexivity centred on 'relation to method', while others may explicitly aim for a high degree of reflexivity about all their auspices. It would not be appropriate to insist on a uniform type and intensity of reflexivity for post-foundational radicalism. A minimal demand might be that any project be able to account for the particular balance of reflexivity and non-reflexivity it entails. Such accounts can lay projects open to an always corrigible judgement about the costs and benefits of a particular balance.
>
> (1991, p. 21)

Analytical sociology and the 'textual' turn in literary theory are viewed as parallel forms of mundane reflexivity upon their respective 'objects' and 'practices':

> At a different level, the Heideggerian turn in reflexive sociology offers the most highly developed exploration of the possibilities of reflexivity as a form of intellectual community. The reflexive dimension of textuality itself might be developed in experiments with the textual forms of social theory. The point on which these diverse projects converge is simply the rejection of foundationalist formulae for reflexivity which must appear, from the standpoint of a post-foundationalism, as formulae for its postponement and evasion.
>
> (1991, p. 206)

Theorizing, as Steve knew, is the joy and burden of thinkers, a precarious and fragile achievement negotiating the temptations of both nihilistic complacency and metaphysical certainty. Steve managed to avoid both of these temptations and in his person embodied an exemplary resolution of the difficulties facing the radical intellectual in modern society. Above all Steve was committed to dialogue and thoughtful reason. In the words spoken by one of his friends, Andrew Webster, at his memorial service, Steve 'was a good man, honest, companionable and highly intelligent. He was also good fun. He will be sorely missed by his colleagues and friends here in the UK and elsewhere'. It is in this spirit of our common commitment to critical reason that the preceding essays are dedicated to the memory of Steve Crook.

References

Blum, A. (1970) *Theorizing*, Heinemann, London.

Crook, S. (1984) 'Beyond foundationalism: a critical analysis of three foundational projects in radical social theory', unpublished DPhil thesis, submitted to the University of York, February.

Crook, S. (1989) 'Television and audience activity: the problem of the television/ viewer nexus in audience research', *Australian and New Zealand Journal of Sociology*, vol. 25, pp. 356–380.

Crook, S. (1991) *Modernist Radicalism and Its Aftermath: Foundationalism and Anti-Foundationalism in Radical Social Theory*, Routledge, London.

Crook, S. (ed.) (1994) *Adorno: The Stars Look Down to Earth and Other Essays on the Irrational in Culture*, Routledge, London.

Crook, S. (1998) 'Minotaurs and other monsters: "everyday life" in recent social theory', *Sociology*, vol. 32, no. 3, pp. 523–540.

Crook, S. (2001) 'Social theory and the postmodern', in *Handbook of Social Theory*, eds G. Ritzer and B. Smart, Sage, London, pp. 308–23.

Crook, S., Pakulski, J. & Waters, M. (1992) *Postmodernization: Change in Advanced Society*, Sage, London.

Lyotard, J.-F. (1984) *The Postmodern Condition*, Manchester University Press, Manchester.

McHugh, P., Raffel, S., Foss, B. & Blum, A. (1974) *On the Beginning of Social Enquiry*, Routledge and Kegan Paul, London.

Ritzer, G. & Smart, B. (eds) (2001) *Handbook of Social Theory*, Sage, London.

Robertson, R. (1992) *Globalization: Social Theory and Global Culture*, Sage, London.

Robertson, R. (2001) 'Globalization theory 2000+: major problematics', in *Handbook of Social Theory*, eds G. Ritzer and B. Smart, Sage, London, pp. 458–471.

Sandywell, B. (1996) *Logological Investigations, vol. 1 Reflexivity and the Crisis of Western Reason*, Routledge, London.

Sandywell, B. (2004) 'The myth of everyday life: toward a heterology of the ordinary', *Cultural Studies*, vol. 18, nos 2 & 3, pp. 160–180.

Sandywell, B., Silverman, D., Roche, M., Filmer, P. & Phillipson, M. (1975) *Problems of Reflexivity and Dialectics in Sociological Enquiry*, Routledge and Kegan Paul, London.

Urry, J. (2000) *Sociology Beyond Societies: Mobilities for the Twenty-First Century*, Routledge, London.

Waters, M. (1995) *Globalization*, Routledge, London.

Webster, A. (2002) 'Memorial service address for Professor Steve Crook', unpublished, 2 November.

Notes on contributors

Ian Burkitt is a Reader in Social Sciences at the University of Bradford, UK. His main research interests are in social and social psychological theory, the social construction of the self, and the relation between culture and forms of human embodiment. He is the author of *Social Selves: Theories of the Social Formation of Personality* (Sage, 1991) and *Bodies of Thought: Embodiment, Identity and Modernity* (Sage, 1999).

Patrick ffrench is Reader in French at King's College London. He is the author of *The Time of Theory: A History of Tel Quel* (Oxford University Press, 1996) and of *The Cut: Reading Bataille's Histoire de l'oeil* (The British Academy / OUP, 2000), and co-editor (with Roland-Francois Lack) of *The Tel Quel Reader* (Routledge, 1998). He is currently working on a book on the poetics of sacrifice, and a book on legacies of French theory since 1968.

Keya Ganguly is an Associate Professor in the Department of Cultural Studies and Comparative Literature at the University of Minnesota, Twin Cities. She is the author of *States of Exception: Everyday Life and Postcolonial Identity* (University of Minnesota Press, 2001), and is currently finishing a book-length study on avant-garde Indian film titled *Threshold Goddesses: Women and Modernity in the Films of Satyajit Ray*. She is co-editor of *Cultural Critique* and has published essays on postcolonialism, popular culture, cinema, modernity and the Frankfurt School. She teaches courses in cultural studies, film, postcolonial theory, Marxism and critical theory.

Anne Galloway is a PhD candidate in the Sociology of Virtual Spaces program at Carleton University, Ottawa, Canada. Her dissertation research focuses on ubiquitous computing, sociality and design. She maintains a research weblog at www.purselipsquarejaw.org.

Michael E. Gardiner is an Associate Professor in Sociology at the University of Western Ontario. His books include the edited four-volume collection *Mikhail Bakhtin* (Sage, 2003) in the Sage 'Masters of Modern Social Thought' series, *Critiques of Everyday Life* (Routledge, 2000), *Bakhtin and the Human Sciences: No Last Words* (Sage, 1998, co-edited with Michael M. Bell), and *The Dialogics of Critique: M. M. Bakhtin and the Theory of Ideology* (Routledge, 1992), as well as numerous articles dedicated to dialogical theory, ethics, everyday life and utopianism published in such journals as *History of the Human Sciences*, *Theory, Culture and Society*, *Theory and Society*, and *Utopian Studies*.

Melissa Gregg is a Research Fellow at the Centre for Critical and Cultural Studies, University of Queensland, Australia. 'Remnants of Humanism'

Cultural Studies Vol. 18, No. 2/3 March/May 2004, pp. 494–497

Routledge
Taylor & Francis Group

ISSN 0950-2386 print/ISSN 1466-4348 online   © 2004 Taylor & Francis Ltd
http://www.tandf.co.uk/journals   DOI: 10.1080/0950238042000201635

(*Continuum*, vol. 16, no.3, 2002) and ' A Neglected History: Richard Hoggart's Discourse of Empathy' (*Rethinking History: The Journal of Theory and Practice*, vol. 7, no. 3, 2003) explore her interest in cultural studies' political potential.

Harry D. Harootunian is Professor of History and Director of East Asian Studies at New York University. He is the author of *Toward Restoration: The Growth of Political Consciousness in Tokugawa Japan* (University of California Press, 1991), *Things Seen and Unseen: Discourse and Ideology in Tokugawa Nativism* (University of Chicago Press, 1996), *History's Disquiet: Modernity, Cultural Practice, and the Question of Everyday Life* (Columbia University Press, 2000) and *Overcome by Modernity: History, Culture and Community in Interwar Japan* (Princeton University Press, 2000), and has co-edited (with Masao Miyoshi) *Postmodernism and Japan (Post-Contemporary Innovations)* (Duke University Press, 1989), *Japan in the World* (Duke University Press, 1993) and *Learning Places: The Afterlife of Area Studies* (Duke University Press, 2003).

Ben Highmore is Senior Lecturer in Cultural Studies at the University of the West of England, Bristol, UK. He is the author of *Everyday Life and Cultural Theory* and editor of *The Everyday Life Reader*, both published by Routledge.

Michel Maffesoli is Professor at the Sorbonne and Director of the Centre for the Study of the Actual and Everyday. He is the author (in English translation) of *The Shadow of Dionysus: A Contribution to the Sociology of the Orgy* (SUNY Press, 1993), *The Contemplation of the World: Figures of Community Style* (University of Minnesota Press, 1996), *The Time of the Tribes: The Decline of Individualism in Mass Society* (Sage, 1996) and *Ordinary Knowledge: An Introduction to Interpretive Sociology* (Polity, 1996).

Andrew Metcalfe and Ann Game have collaborated as teachers and writers for twelve years. Their books include *The Mystery of Everyday Life* (Federation Press, Sydney, 2002) and *Passionate Sociology* (Sage, London, 1996). The present article signals the shift from the desire-based post-structuralism of the earlier book to a more inclusive love-based understanding of sociality in the later one. Both writers are Associate Professors in the School of Sociology at the University of New South Wales. Their new book, *A Student's Guide to University* (Federation Press, Sydney), will be published in 2003.

Michael Pickering is Reader in Culture and Communications in the Department of Social Sciences at Loughborough University, UK. He taught at the University of Sunderland, and Massey University in New Zealand, before moving to Loughborough in 1992. His most recent books are *History, Experience and Cultural Studies* (Palgrave, 1997), *Researching Communications* (Arnold, 1999) (with David Deacon, Peter Golding and Graham Murdock), and *Stereotyping: The Politics of Representation* (Palgrave, 2001).

Mark Poster is Director of the Film Studies Program at UCI and a member of the History Department. He has a courtesy appointment in the Department of Information and Computer Science, and is a member of the Critical Theory Institute. His books include: *The Mode of Information* (Blackwell and University of Chicago Press, 1990), *The Second Media Age* (Blackwell, 1995), *Cultural History and Postmodernity* (Columbia University Press, 1997), *What's the Matter with the Internet: A Critical Theory of Cyberspace* (University of Minnesota Press, 2001) and *The Information Subject* (Gordon and Breach Arts International, 2001).

Elspeth Probyn is Professor of Gender & Cultural Studies at the University of Sydney. Her most recent book is *Blush: Faces of Shame* (Minnesota, forthcoming), and she has co-edited with Catharine Lumby, *Remote Control: New Media, Changing Ethics* (Cambridge, 2003). Her previous publications include *Sexing the Self: Gendered Positions in Cultural Studies* (Routledge, 1993), *Outside Belongings* (Routledge, 1996) and *Carnal Appetites: Food, Sex, Identities* (Routledge, 2000), and is co-editor (with Elizabeth Grosz) of *Sexy Bodies: The Strange Carnalities of Feminism* (Routledge, 2001).

Barry Sandywell is Senior Lecturer in Sociology in the Department of Sociology at York, UK. He is the author of *Logological Investigations* (Routledge, 1996), a multi-volume work on the history of reflexivity, alterity and ethics in philosophy and the human sciences: *Reflexivity and the Crisis of Western Reason* (vol. 1), *The Beginnings of European Theorizing: Reflexivity in the Archaic Age* (vol. 2), and *Presocratic Reflexivity: The Construction of Philosophical Discourse* (vol. 3). He is also the co-editor of *Interpreting Visual Culture: Explorations in the Hermeneutics of the Visual* (Routledge, 1999) and essays on Baudrillard, Bakhtin and Benjamin and others published in various journals and collections. His most recent publications include: 'E-topia as Cosmopolis or Citadel: On the Democratizing and De-democratizing Logics of the Internet, or, Toward a Critique of the New Technological Fetishism' (with Martin Hand), in *Theory, Culture and Society*, Special Issue on Cosmopolis, 2002, and 'Metacritique of Information', in *Theory, Culture and Society*, vol. 20, no. 1, 2003.

Gregory J. Seigworth is an Associate Professor in the Communication and Theatre Department at Millersville University, and, most recently, has co-edited (with J. Macgregor Wise) an issue of the journal *Cultural Studies* (2000) on the work of Deleuze and Guattari. He has published essays previously in *Antithesis*, *Architectural Design*, *Cultural Studies* and *Studies in Symbolic Interactionism*.

John Shotter is a Professor of Interpersonal Relations and Chair in the Department of Communication, University of New Hampshire. His long-term interest is in the social conditions conducive to people having a voice in the development of participatory democracies and civil societies. He is the author of *Images of Man in Psychological Research* (Methuen, 1975), *Human Action and its Psychological Investigation* (with Alan Gauld) (Routledge, 1977), *Social Accountability and Selfhood* (Blackwell, 1984), *Cultural Politics of Everyday Life: Social Constructionism, Rhetoric, and Knowing of the Third Kind* (Open University, 1993) and *Conversational Realities: The Construction of Life through Language* (Sage, 1993).

Nigel Thrift is a geographer known for his work on international finance, on financial exclusion, and on the new economy. He has been Head of the School of Geographical Sciences at The University of Bristol, UK, and is currently Chair of the University's Research Assessment Panel, which is concerned with maximizing the outcome of the RAE. His most recent work has been concerned with the likely social and cultural effects of mobile telecommunications. In particular, he is interested in new kinds of content that will produce new geographies.

J. Macgregor Wise is Associate Professor and Chair of the Department of Communication Studies at Arizona State University West, USA. His work is situated at the intersection of cultural studies, media studies, and the sociology and philosophy of technology. He is the author of *Exploring Technology and Social Space* (Sage Publications, 1997) and co-author (with Jennifer Daryl Slack) of the forthcoming *Culture and Technology: A Primer* (Peter Lang).

Notes for contributors

Submission

Authors should submit three complete copies of their paper, including any original illustrations to:

Prof Lawrence Grossberg and Della Pollock, Editors of *Cultural Studies*, Department of Communication Studies, CB#3285, 115 Bingham Hall, University of North Carolina at Chapel Hill, Chapel Hill, NC 27599–3285, USA; e-mail: cs-journ@email.unc.edu

It will be assumed that the author has retained a copy of his or her paper. Submission of a paper to *Cultural Studies* will be taken to imply that it presents original, unpublished work not under consideration for publication elsewhere. In submitting a manuscript the authors agree that the exclusive rights to reproduce and distribute the article have been given to the publishers. This includes reprints, photographic reproductions, microfilm, or any other reproduction of similar nature and translations, though copyright is retained by the author.

Manuscript format

All submissions should be in English, typed or computer printed in double spacing on one side of the paper only. Please include an abstract of up to 300 words (including 6 keywords) for purposes of review. The authors name should not appear anywhere on the manuscript except for on a detachable cover page along with an address, short biographical note and the title. Please supply an e-mail address if you have one and a contact number.

Photographs, tables and figures

Photographs should be high contrast black and white glossy prints. Tables and figures need not be rendered professionally but should be neatly drawn in black ink.

Copyright-protected material

Written permission to reproduce photographs, tables, figures, song lyrics or any other copyright protected material must be obtained by authors from the copyright-holders before submission.

Cultural Studies Vol. 18, No. 2/3 March/May 2004, pp. 498–502

R Routledge
Taylor & Francis Group

ISSN 0950-2386 print/ISSN 1466-4348 online © 2004 Taylor & Francis Ltd
http://www.tandf.co.uk/journals

Citation style

Manuscripts must conform to the Havard reference style. When an author's name is mentioned in the text, the date alone is inserted in parentheses immediately after the name: Smith (1970). When a less direct reference is made the name and date are given together in parentheses. Several authors are separated by a comma: (Smith 1970, Mbene 1984).

When the reference is to dual or multiple authorship use: Smith and Jones (1971) for two authors and; Smith *et al.* for more than two. Only use initials if two authors have the same surname: (Smith, A. 1970; Smith, B. 1971).

If two or more works by the same author are cited for the same year, add lower case letters after the date to distinguish them: (Smith 1970a, 1970b).

When using a republished book, a translation or a modern edition of an older book, give the date of the original publication as well: Smith (1970/1999). When using a reprinted article, cite the date of the original publication only.

When referring to mass media materials, include relevant information within parentheses: (Women's weekly, 16 July 1983, p. 32).

Treat recorded music as a book: the musician or group is the author, the title is underlined and the distributor is listed as the publisher; treat television series and films similarly. Treat television episodes, poems, songs and short stories (i.e. works that are not usually published separately) as articles, placing the title in single quotation marks.

Reference List

Submissions should include a reference list conforming to the style shown in the following examples:

Book
Leach, E. (1976) *Culture and Communication*, Cambridge University Press, Cambridge.
Two or more references to the same author
Leach, E. (1976) *Culture and Communication*, Cambridge University Press, Cambridge.
Leach, E. (1974) *Levi-Strauss*, Fontana, London.
Multiple authors
Ogden, C. G. & Richards, I. A. (1949) *The Meaning of Meaning*, 2nd edn, Routledge and Kegan Paul, London.
Two references published in the same year; translated text; two places of publication
Lacan, J. (1977a) *Ecrits: A Selection*, trans. Alan Sheridan, Norton, New York and London. (Originally published 1966).
Article in reader not already cited; multi volume work; article in book by same author
Leavis, F. R. (1945) '"Thought" and Emotional Quality', in *A Selection from Scrutiny*, ed. F. R. Leavis, vol. 1, Cambridge University Press, Cambridge, pp. 211–230.

Article in journal

Macherey, P. & Balibar, E. (1978) 'Literature as an ideological form: some Marxist propositions', *Oxford Literary Review*, vol. 3, no. 1, pp. 4–12.

Article in magazine or newspaper

Burstall, T. (1977) 'Triumph and disaster for Australian films', *The Bulletin*, 24 September, pp. 45–54.

Film or TV programme

The War Game (1966) Dir. Peter Watkins, BBC.

Proofs

Page proofs will be sent for correction to the author whose name appears first on the title page of the article unless otherwise requested. The difficulty and expense involved in making amendments at this stage make it essential for authors to prepare their typescripts carefully: any alteration to the original text is strongly discouraged. The proofs should be returned as quickly as possible.

Offprints

An 'eprint' of the finished article and a copy of the issue in which the article appears will be supplied free of charge to the author; offprints are available on request, further information will be supplied with page proofs. There is no remuneration for publication in *Cultural Studies*.

Guidelines for Book Reviews

Cultural Studies publishes reviews of current books that are of potential interest to the journal's main audience: i.e., an international readership of scholars, students, activists, and cultural workers interested in cultural studies (broadly defined). Given the cross/multi-disciplinary nature of the journal's focus, reviews should focus specifically on the relevance of the book(s) in question to cultural studies (rather than to either the author's or the reviewer's 'home' discipline).

Completed reviews should be concise – i.e., 1000 words or less – and carefully proofread. External citations and endnotes do count against your word limit, so use them sparingly (if at all). Your review should include:

Heading information:
• Your name
• Title of the book review (short, preferably 5–6 words)
• Publication information: book author(s)/editor(s), book title, city/cities, publisher, date, page count, ISBN number and price for cloth/hardback, ISBN number and price for paperback.

Body of review:
- Brief description or explanation of the book's contents
- Discussion of the book's relevance to cultural studies
- Critical engagement with and assessment of the book's contents

Other information (on separate page):
- Word count of your review (excluding the heading information)
- Brief biographical note for the reviewer (2–3 lines)
- Your address/contact information (including phone number(s) and e-mail address)

General formatting guidelines:
- Reviews should be written in English and adhere to the journal's usual style guidelines (i.e., Harvard style).
- Reviews should be submitted in one of the following formats: WordPerfect (version 9.0 or earlier), Microsoft Word (2000 or earlier), or RTF (Rich Text Format).
- Reviews should be submitted either as an e-mail file attachment or on an IBM-compatible 3.5' floppy disk to one of the book review editors:

Stuart Price
School of Arts
de Montfort University
The Gateway
Leicester LE1 9BH
UK
poumista@hotmail.com

Gil Rodman
Department of Communication
University of South Florida
4202 East Fowler Avenue, CIS1040
Tampa, FL 33620 7800
USA
grodman@chuma.cas.usf.edu

Alvaro Pina
Rua Jose P. Chaves
6-3 Dto
1500-377 Lisboa
Portugal
alvaro.pina@mail.telepac.pt

Ien Ang
Institute for Cultural Research
University of Western Sydney
Parramatta Campus
BCRI Building L2
Locked Bag 1797
Penrith South DC NSW 1797
Australia
I.Ang@uws.edu.au

New in the Transformations series

Edited by **Maureen McNeil**, and **Lynne Pearce**, both at Lancaster University, UK, and **Beverley Skeggs**, Manchester University, UK.

Transformations is a series that not only displays the continuing innovations through feminist scholarship itself, but also registers the impact of feminist thought on intellectual enquiry and debate more generally.

Class, Self, Culture

Beverley Skeggs, University of Manchester, UK

Class, Self, Culture puts class back on the map in a novel way. The book shows how class has not disappeared, but is known and spoken in a myriad of different ways, always working through other categorisations of nation, race, gender and sexuality and across different sites: through popular culture, political rhetoric and academic theory.

> Oct 2003: 234x156: 240pp   Hb: 0-415-30085-1: **£70.00**   Pb: 0-415-30086-X: **£19.99**

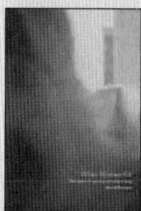

When Women Kill

Questions of Agency and Subjectivity

Belinda Morrissey, Charles Sturt University, Australia

This book looks at the ways in which female killers are constructed in the media, in law and in feminist discourse almost invariably as victims rather than as actors in the crimes they commit. Morrissey argues that by denying the possibility of female agency in violent crimes, feminist theorists are actually denying women the full freedom to be human.

> March 2003: 234x156: 256pp   Hb: 0-415-26005-1: **£65.00**   Pb: 0-415-26006-X: **£19.99**

Haunted Nations

The Colonial Dimensions of Multiculturalisms

Sneja Gunew, University of British Columbia, Canada

Haunted Nations sets out to interrogate the ways in which the transnational discourse of multiculturalism may be related to the politics of race and indigeneity. Gunew analyses the political ambiguities and the pitfalls involved in a discourse of multiculturalism haunted by the opposing spectres of anarchy and assimilation.

> Sept 2003: 234x156: 192pp   Hb: 0-415-28482-1: **£65.00**   Pb: 0-415-28483-X: **£18.99**

The Rhetorics of Feminism

Readings in Contemporary Cultural Theory and the Popular Press

Lynne Pearce, University of Lancaster, UK

By a close stylistic and rhetorical analysis across contemporary feminist writing - from the cultural theory of Judith Butler to the newspaper journalism of Naomi Wolf - Lynne Pearce demonstrates how feminist thought is created as well as communicated by the frameworks in which it is presented.

> Sept 2003: 234x156: 256pp   Hb: 0-415-28182-2: **£70.00**   Pb: 0-415-28183-0: **£19.99**

For credit card orders: call **+44 (0)1264 343071** or email book.orders@routledge.co.uk
To find out more about titles in this series, or for a free Sociology catalogue, please contact Caroline Breakwell on 0207 842 2078 or email caroline.breakwell@routledge.co.uk

Routledge
Taylor & Francis Group

www.routledge.com   available from all good bookshops

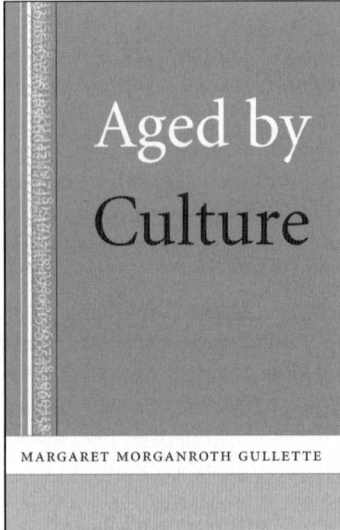

Angelaki: journal of the theoretical humanities

GENERAL EDITOR: *Pelagia Goulimari, Oxford, UK*
MANAGING EDITOR: *Gerard Greenway, Oxford, UK*

Angelaki: journal of the theoretical humanities was established in September 1993 to provide an international forum for vanguard work in the theoretical humanities. In itself a contentious category, 'theoretical humanities' represents the productive nexus of work in the disciplinary fields of literary criticism and theory, philosophy, and cultural studies. The journal is dedicated to the refreshing of intellectual coordinates, and to the challenging and vivifying process of re-thinking.

Angelaki: journal of the theoretical humanities encourages a critical engagement with theory in terms of disciplinary development and intellectual and political usefulness, the inquiry into and articulation of culture, and the complex determination of change and its relation to history. The journal is committed to fostering the theory of minor movements, disciplines, and emphasizing their formative power rather than their oppositional entrenchment. The journal promotes the inquiry into questions of existential and political definition and agency, on the personal, collective and institutional levels, and encourages the work of spirited and experimental theoretical writing in all areas of value production.

Angelaki: journal of the theoretical humanities publishes chiefly in the areas of philosophy, literary theory and cultural studies.

This journal is also available online. Please connect to www.tandf.co.uk/online.html for further information.

To request a sample copy please visit: **www.tandf.co.uk/journals**

SUBSCRIPTION RATES
2004 – Volume 9 (3 issues)
Print ISSN 0969-725X
Online ISSN 1469-2899
Institutional rate: US$295; £180
(includes free online access)
Personal rate: US$69; £43 (print only)

Routledge
Taylor & Francis Group

For further information, please contact Customer Services at either:
Taylor & Francis Ltd, Rankine Road, Basingstoke, Hants RG24 8PR, UK
Tel: +44 (0)1256 813002   Fax: +44 (0)1256 330245 Email: enquiry@tandf.co.uk
Website: www.tandf.co.uk

Taylor & Francis Inc, 325 Chestnut Street, 8th Floor, Philadelphia, PA 19106, USA
Tel: +1 215 6258900 Fax: +1 215 6258914 Email: info@taylorandfrancis.com
Website: www.taylorandfrancis.com

cang

Cultural Trends

Now published by Routledge from 2004

EDITOR
Sara Selwood, *University of Westminister, UK*

Cultural Trends has been providing in-depth analysis of cultural sector statistics since 1989. It focuses on key trends within the fields of material culture, media, performing arts and the historic environment, and it includes coverage of issues which impact on the sector as a whole, such as the internet, poverty and access to the arts, and funding.

Cultural Trends is based on the assumption that cultural policy should be based on empirical evidence and it champions the need for better statistical information on the cultural sector. It aims to:

- stimulate analysis and understanding of the arts and wider cultural sector based on relevant and reliable statistical data;
- provide a critique of the empirical evidence upon which arts and wider cultural policy may be formed, implemented, evaluated and developed;
- examine the soundness of measures of the performance of government and public sector bodies in the arts and wider cultural sector; and
- encourage improvements in the coverage, timeliness and accessibility of statistical information on the arts and wider cultural sector.

Cultural Trends is not asociated with any political party or pressure group

This journal is also available online.
Please connect to www.tandf.co.uk/online.html for further information.

To request an online sample copy please visit: **www.tandf.co.uk/journals**

SUBSCRIPTION RATES
2004 – Volume 13 (4 issues)
Print ISSN 0954-8963
Online ISSN 1469-3690
Institutional rate: US$300; £191
(includes free online access)
Personal rate: US$213; £126 (print only)

Routledge
Taylor & Francis Group

ORDER FORM   ccut
PLEASE COMPLETE IN BLOCK CAPITALS AND RETURN TO THE ADDRESS BELOW
Please invoice me at the ☐ **institutional rate** ☐ **personal rate**

Name _____

Address _____

_____

_____

Email _____

Please contact Customer Services at either:
Taylor & Francis Ltd, Rankine Road, Basingstoke, Hants RG24 8PR, UK
Tel: +44 (0)1256 813002 **Fax:** +44 (0)1256 330245 **Email:** enquiry@tandf.co.uk **Website:** www.tandf.co.uk

Taylor & Francis Inc, 325 Chestnut Street, 8th Floor, Philadelphia, PA 19106, USA
Tel: +1 215 6258900 **Fax:** +1 215 6258914 **Email:** info@taylorandfrancis.com **Website:** www.taylorandfrancis.com

South Asian Popular Culture

EDITORS
Rajinder Kumar Dudrah, *University of Manchester, UK*; **K Moti Gokulsing**, *University of East London, UK;* **Gita Rajan,** *Fairfield University, USA*

South Asian Popular Culture is an interdisciplinary journal designed to respond to the growing interest in South Asian popular culture within the different subject disciplines in the social sciences and humanities. 'South Asian popular culture' is defined in a broad and inclusive way to incorporate lived and textual cultures, the mass media, ways of life, and discursive modes of representation.

South Asian Popular Culture seeks to serve as an innovative and informative venue to discuss and debate the emergence and vibrancy of new forms of social, cultural and political strategies and representations in film, music, radio, television, visual cultures, the internet, fashion and sexuality. These forms, in fact, pose a challenge that need to be understood within a context of culture that allows a transnational focus and open attitude towards difference and diversity.

South Asian Popular Culture also features a regular section entitled 'Working Notes' that includes contributions from cultural practitioners within South Asian popular culture (film-, radio- and television-makers, musicians, artists, personnel cultural activists, fashion designers, and sexuality campaigners). It offers original insights into their work and current debates by way of interviews, diary notes, short essays, visual images and discussions.

This journal is also available online.
Please connect to www.tandf.co.uk/online.html for further information.

To request a sample copy please visit: **www.tandf.co.uk/journals**

SUBSCRIPTION RATES
2004 – Volume 2 (2 issues)
Print ISSN 1474-6689 Online ISSN 1474-6697
Institutional rate: US$220; £134
(includes free online access)
Personal rate: US$39; £24

Routledge
Taylor & Francis Group

- -

ORDER FORM   rsap

PLEASE COMPLETE IN BLOCK CAPITALS AND RETURN TO THE ADDRESS BELOW

Please invoice me at the ❑ **institutional rate** ❑ **personal rate**

Name _____

Address _____

_____

_____

Email _____

Please contact Customer Services at either:
Taylor & Francis Ltd, Rankine Road, Basingstoke, Hants RG24 8PR, UK
Tel: +44 (0)1256 813002 **Fax:** +44 (0)1256 330245 **Email:** enquiry@tandf.co.uk **Website:** www.tandf.co.uk

Taylor & Francis Inc, 325 Chestnut Street, 8th Floor, Philadelphia, PA 19106, USA
Tel: +1 215 6258900 **Fax:** +1 215 6258914 **Email:** info@taylorandfrancis.com **Website:** www.taylorandfrancis.com